STUDIES IN LABOUR
AND SOCIAL LAW

GENERAL EDITORS

The Making of Labour Law in Europe

The Making of Labour Law in Europe

A Comparative Study of Nine Countries up to 1945

Edited by Bob Hepple

MANSELL PUBLISHING LIMITED

LONDON AND NEW YORK

First published 1986 by Mansell Publishing Limited
(A subsidiary of The H. W. Wilson Company)
6 All Saints Street, London N1 9RL, England
950 University Avenue, Bronx, New York 10452, U.S.A.

British Library Cataloguing in Publication Data

The Making of labour law in Europe: a
comparative study of nine countries up
to 1945.—(Studies in labour and social
law)
1. Labor laws and legislation—Europe—
History
I. Hepple, Bob. II. Series
342.4′1125′094 [LAW]

ISBN 0–7201–1697–X

Library of Congress Cataloging-in-Publication Data

The Making of labour law in Europe.
(Studies in labour and social law)
Bibliography: p.
Includes index.
1. Labor laws and legislation—Europe.
I. Hepple, Bob. II. Series.
KJC2855.5.M35 1986 344.4′01 86–5426
ISBN 0–7201–1697–X 344.041

Printed in Great Britain

CONTENTS

APPENDICES

THE AUTHORS

BOB HEPPLE	Professor of English Law in the University of London, at University College
ANTOINE JACOBS	Formerly Lecturer in Social Law and Social Policy at the University of Tilburg
THILO RAMM	Professor of Civil Law and Labour Law at the Distance University, Hagen
BRUNO VENEZIANI	Professor of Labour Law and Comparative Trade Union Law in the University of Bari
ELIANE VOGEL-POLSKY	Professor of Labour Law and Comparative Labour Law at the University of Brussels

With the assistance of:

OLE HASSELBALCH	Professor of Private and Commercial Law at Århus School of Economics
JEAN-CLAUDE JAVILLIER	Professor of Labour Law and Director of the Centre for Comparative Labour Law and Social Security at the University of Bordeaux-I

PREFACE

This comparative study has been a long time in the making. In 1978 Thilo Ramm prepared an outline and recruited a group of legal scholars who each prepared a national report in response to an agreed questionnaire. The reports covered the then Member States of the EEC: Belgium (Eliane Vogel-Polsky), Britain and Ireland (Bob Hepple), Denmark (Ole Hasselbalch), France (Jean-Claude Javillier), Germany (Thilo Ramm), Italy (Bruno Veneziani) and the Netherlands (Antoine Jacobs), and account was also taken of Luxembourg. These reports were discussed at a meeting in Bad Schlangenbad in December 1979, and individuals were then assigned to draft the separate chapters. Drafts were discussed at a series of further meetings in Canterbury (September 1980), Bari (December 1980), Bordeaux (September 1981), Vught (May 1982) and Bari (May 1985). The drafts were rewritten in English by Bob Hepple, who also edited the book as a whole and prepared the various appendices. The book is thus a co-operative effort, although individuals have accepted ultimate responsibility for particular chapters.

Our purpose, more fully explained in the Introduction, has been to explain the origins of, and the relationships between, the labour laws of nine European countries in their formative period from the beginning of the industrial revolution until 1945, from the viewpoint of comparative law. This is not a 'history' in the traditional sense, but it will be obvious that we have drawn extensively on the writings of historians, sociologists and other social scientists as well as many now forgotten law books. We run the risk of being criticised by the historians for inadequate narrative, by the sociologists for a preoccupation with rules and institutions and by the lawyers for too little technical detail. But the subject has been sadly neglected, and we shall be satisfied if we stimulate a broader perspective in comparative law and in the study of comparative labour relations. We hope that our colleagues in Member States which joined the EEC after this study was begun, and elsewhere, will match their national experiences against the trends discussed in this book. The study could also now be carried forward into the period since 1945.

The book is likely to be used by students who have relatively little knowledge of the development of the constitutions, legal systems, political parties and trade unions of all the countries covered by this study. For their benefit we have included a short guide on these matters (Appendix I), a chronology of labour law from 1789 to 1945 (Appendix II) and comparative statistics (Appendix III). The selection of documents (Appendix IV), which has had to be limited for reasons of space, makes available in English a few examples of the diversity of labour laws in this period. The Bibliography (Appendix V) includes not only works from which direct quotations will be found in the text, but also a wide range of other publications on which the authors have relied.

London
September 1985

B.H.

ACKNOWLEDGMENTS

The authors wish to thank Ole Hasselbalch for providing information on Denmark, for participating in all the meetings and commenting on the various drafts. We also thank Jean-Claude Javillier for preparing a report on France and participating in four of the meetings, including one at Bordeaux which he arranged. We gratefully acknowledge the help of the following: Friedrich Mehrhoff and Carole Bailey for research assistance; Professor B. S. Frenkel, Professor Vic George, Dr David Nelken, Professor Paul O'Higgins, Dr Gerry Rubin, Ms Sandra Fredman and Mr J. Zeÿen for comments and advice; Dr Brian Napier for permission to draw on his unpublished thesis on the contract of service; Sarah Gale, Robert Leurs, Josephine Shaw and Christopher Williams[1] for translations; Ann Lewis for typing three chapters and Bernadette Hurd for typing the rest of the manuscript (presented to her in numerous illegible drafts) and in generally helping to prepare it for publication.

We acknowledge the permission of Macmillan, London and Basingstoke, to draw on statistics from *European Historical Statistics 1750–1970* by B. R. Mitchell, and from *European Political Facts 1848–1919* and *European Political Facts 1918–1973* by Chris Cook and John Paxton.

We received financial assistance from a number of sources to cover travel and some other research expenses. We express our gratitude to the British Academy; the Commission of the European Communities (grant for the development of joint programmes of study between higher institutions in the Member States); Ministero della Pubblica Istruzione (Italy); Ministerium für Wissenschaft und Forschung des Landes Nordrhein-Westfalen (Germany); the Social Science Research Council (Britain)/Deutsche Forschungsgemeinschaft research exchange scheme for social scientists; and the Danish Employers' Confederation research fund.

1. Attention is drawn to the article by Christopher Williams based on his experiences in this translation, 'Towards an Italian–English Glossary of Labour Law Terminology' in *The Incorporated Linguist*, vol. 22 (1983), pp. 70–7, and the comment by Martin Weston, ibid., pp. 207–11.

We had the advice of the late Sir Otto Kahn-Freund in planning this project. With the permission of his widow, this book is dedicated to his memory.

INTRODUCTION

Bob Hepple

AIMS, METHODS AND SCOPE

The title of this book uses the word 'making' in order to underline the theme that labour law is part of a *process*. This theme stands in opposition to conceptions of labour law as a relatively static and neutral set of rules and institutions which regulate employment. The authors share the view that the rules and institutions are shaped by the historically given possibilities within which various sectional groups pursue their often conflicting objectives. Labour law is made by men and women in a society not of their own making.

This idea is far from being a new one. In recent years it has influenced, either explicitly or implicitly, a number of studies of national labour laws. However, save in the hands of a few masters of the craft, such as Kahn-Freund, comparative studies have tended to concentrate on narrow topics within a very limited time-frame. Sometimes there is a brief 'historical introduction', but then all ideas of process are forgotten as the author becomes immersed in the ephemeral details of the present. Much of comparative labour law remains in the age of still photographs and is only beginning to discover motion pictures.

What this book seeks to contribute to the understanding of labour law as part of a process, is an explanation of the relationships between the development of labour laws in a number of European countries, in the formative stages of those laws from the start of the Industrial Revolution until the end of the Second World War. Those relationships are of two main kinds. The first is the direct historical relationship of legal transplants. The second is the 'inner' social, economic and political relationship of parallel developments in different countries.

The adaptation of the model of nineteenth-century British factory legislation by other countries was described by Stephan Bauer (1924, p. 401) as being at least as important for humanity as the reception of the Roman law of property and obligations. Bauer (1865–1934) was Secretary of the International Association for Statutory Workers' Protection, founded in 1901, and Director of the International Labour Office (ILO), which became an organ of the League of Nations in 1919. His claim was extravagant, not least because the British Acts cannot be compared with the Romanistic legal techniques which promoted national civil laws (see Ch. 2, below). But his analogy serves to emphasise the historical relationship between the labour laws of different countries.

Many other examples will be found in the pages of this book. These include the extraordinary influence of the *Code Napoléon* in the development of contractual ideas of the employment relationship in Belgium, the Netherlands, Luxembourg, Italy and the German territories west of the Rhine, long after the withdrawal of French occupation (see Ch. 1, below); the spread of Bismarckian-style schemes of compulsory insurance to the Netherlands, Luxembourg, Britain and later to most other European countries (see Ch. 3, below); the emulation in Britain of the German system of labour exchanges; the popularity of the Belgian (Ghent) system of publicly subsidised voluntary unemployment insurance in the Netherlands, Germany, Italy and France; and the inspiration given by Article 84 of the Weimar Republic's Works Councils Act of 1920 to the concept of unjustified dismissal throughout Europe (see Ch. 4, below). The internationalisation of labour law, especially since the foundation of the ILO, has accelerated this process of 'harmonisation upwards'. The ILO's conventions and recommendations are based on the practice of leading countries and have had an important influence on national developments (see Ch. 7, below).

The point is that many rules of national systems of labour law are either derived from or have been strongly influenced by other systems. The generalisation that 'borrowing (with adaptation) has been the usual way of legal development' (Watson, 1974, p. 7) is at least as true for labour law as it is for other branches of law. These borrowings prompt the question: Do transplantations survive, and if so, under what circumstances and with what adaptations? In considering this question, two theoretical insights are useful. The first belongs to Renner (1949): the same rule can have different functions at different times dependent upon changes in material society. To this Watson adds a comparatist's rider, that 'a rule transplanted from one country to another . . . may equally operate to different effect in the two societies, even though it is expressed in apparently similar terms in the two countries' (1974, p. 20). An example from the present study (see Ch. 1, below) is the material change in function of the Romanistic concept of *locatio conductio* (letting and hire) in the civil law countries to support the employer's power of subordination and control of dependent workers in large-scale capitalist enterprises.

A second insight belongs to Kahn-Freund (1974): while the transplantation of rules directly regulating the individual employment relationship may be relatively straightforward, rules and institutions relating to collective labour relations are usually too closely connected with the structure and organisation of political and social power in a particular environment to be successfully imported elsewhere. The emergence of trade unions from illegality was a series of parallel developments rather than the adoption of 'models'; the timing and extent of the repeal of the bans on combinations and strikes was heavily influenced by national features such as the ideology and strength of the workers' movements, the stage at which the working-class was enfranchised and the power enjoyed by the judiciary within the different legal traditions of the common law and civil law systems. Moreover, there were different routes to trade union recognition, through positive legal rights in some countries such as Germany (1918–23) and France (1936–39), but by negative immunities and voluntary methods in Britain and Denmark (see Ch. 5, below). This did not, however, preclude foreign influences on specific matters. For example, German and French ideas moulded the law of collective agreements in the Netherlands (see Ch. 5, below), and Luxembourg copied the German law on works councils (see Ch. 6, below).

Historical relationships of the kind described are the most obvious form of connection between legal systems, including labour law. A second, far more complex object of comparative study is what has been described as the 'inner relationship' between systems (Watson, 1974, p. 8). At times the search for such a relationship has rested upon the belief 'now regarded as invalid . . . that mankind, with its common psyche, follows the same path of development in everything regardless of location or race' (Zweigert and Kötz, 1977, p. 8). The idea that a natural relationship exists between all early legal systems and that each system follows the same process of development until special national characteristics are imprinted upon it, was influential in the nineteenth century, through the writings of legal anthropologists such as Sir Henry Maine (1861). As recently as 1933 Edouard Lambert could write that the comparative history of law endeavoured to 'bring out . . . the rhythms or natural laws of the succession of social phenomena which directs the evolution of legal institutions' (1933, p. 127). This approach still dominates some contemporary theories of labour law, such as the claim that there is a universal trend in democratic industrial societies towards 'juridification' (Simitis, 1984), and the much-criticised convergency thesis that the 'logic of industrialism' (i.e. the structural requirements for industrialisation) *necessarily* involves the expansion of government and the development of a complex 'web of rules' (Kerr *et al.*, 1960).

An alternative view, which we espouse, is that the development of a legal system, and in particular of labour law, is the product of a variety of historical factors, which are neither 'necessary' nor 'natural'. The capitalist industrialisation of Western Europe opened up a number of options, some more compelling than others. The choices made were not inevitable solutions to the social problems created by the workings of the market. If social structure was regarded as the sole determinant of labour law, it would be impossible to explain why Germany, which industrialised relatively late, was the first country to recognise the 'need' for compulsory social insurance (see Ch. 3, below), or why Britain, for long the most 'advanced' capitalist nation, instead of leading its Continental neighbours in granting positive legal rights to trade unions, in fact did not even emulate those countries when they did so (see Ch. 5 below). The comparative labour lawyer has to examine the specific features of historical change: to explain why in the Continental countries the work-book and police supervision were a significant feature of the so-called 'free' labour market, while in Britain they were not (see Ch. 1, below); why in some countries, in particular industries, the 8-hour day was achieved by collective bargaining and in other countries, either generally or in particular industries, as a part of statutory protection of the individual worker (see Ch. 2, below); why 'protection' is treated as a gift from the state in some periods and as a 'right' in others (see Chs. 2 and 3, below); and why 'workers' participation' took the form of shop stewards in Britain and Denmark but of works councils in Germany and Luxembourg (see Ch. 6, below).

In seeking answers to questions such as these we have had to examine how particular measures came to be introduced in each country. Labour legislation is seen as the outcome of a process of struggle between different social groups—monarchy, bureaucracy and middle-class; bourgeoisie and aristocracy; bourgeoisie and working class; townspeople and countryfolk—and of competing ideologies of conservatives, liberals and socialists, and of religious and secular groups. But 'what any particular group of people get is not just a matter of what they choose or want but what they can force or persuade other groups to let them have' (Abrams, 1982, p. 15). The crucial element in the making of labour law is *power*. Many of the demands made by labour movements and social reformers were unsuccessful because they were unacceptable to those with greater economic and political power. From this perspective labour law as it developed in Europe can be seen as an alternative both to *laissez-faire* capitalism and to the abolition of wage-labour and the creation of some form of socialism. The powerfulness of the opponents of reform was the decisive factor in the making of labour law. It is in power relationships, which are rooted in social structure, that we may find a key to understanding both the common tendencies and the divergences in the labour laws of societies which have shared the experience of capitalist industrialisation.

It will be seen that we reject a purely functional approach which treats the development of labour law as a series of evolutionary stages in response to the demands of industrialisation. However, deductive models are a useful tool of comparative analysis and the authors have utilised theoretical 'ideal types', such as those of 'status' and 'contract' to understand changes in the employment relationship (see Ch. 1, below), and 'repression', 'toleration', 'recognition' and 'integration' to explain the nature of collective self-regulation and workers' participation (see Chs. 5, 6 and 7, below). Models of this kind, freed of specific national features, help to illuminate the common tendencies and the divergences in various countries, but they are not intended as a substitute for empirical evidence of actual events. Another method which the authors have used has been to treat a particular country as a 'model'. Specific rules and institutions—such as protective legislation in Britain (see Ch. 2, below) and social insurance in Germany (see Ch. 3, below)—are explained in their national context. These are then compared with 'functionally equivalent' rules and institutions (Zweigert and Kötz, 1977, p. 25) in their own milieu in other countries.

The comparison is limited in geographical scope to Belgium, Britain, Denmark, France, Germany, Ireland, Italy, Luxembourg and the Netherlands.[1] The grandiose description in the title of these nine territories as 'Europe' must be excused as a form of shorthand. 'Western Europe' would have been no more accurate because the frontiers of the territories, during the period with which we are concerned, stretched into Central and Eastern Europe. In 1945, when this study ends, not one of the countries had the same boundaries or system of government as in 1789. They represent a sample of European countries which underwent capitalist industrialisation at different times and under different political conditions. But they are not a random sample. They have been chosen for a pragmatic reason. These countries are at present Member States of the EEC. Within the EEC there are strong pressures for the harmonisation and approximation of

1. Appendix I, p. 301, below, contains an historical profile of each country in respect of territory, constitutional development, legal system, political parties and trade unions. Appendix II, p. 330, below, is a comparative chronology of labour law from 1789–1945. Appendix III, p. 360, below, has comparative statistics of population, emigration, economic activity.

labour laws; indeed, several articles of the Treaty of Rome expressly envisage this. But the number of measures has been limited and these have had a mixed reception. This suggests that there are underlying structural constraints which limit the practical possibilities of a uniform labour law within a common market. Why has labour law proved to be far more resistant to harmonisation than, say, company or commercial law? One impetus for this study, which helps to explain its geographical scope, is the desire to understand those obstacles to a common labour law which are submerged in the 'organic' relationship between labour law and the social structure of particular countries.

A comparative study of this kind rests upon two further premises. One is that a common definition can be found of what is meant by 'labour law', which is the focus of our study. The other is that it is possible to identify those factors which stand in a significant cause-and-effect relationship to the phenomenon of labour law. Both premises conflict with Maitland's truism that all history is a 'seamless web'. To tear the strand of labour law from other branches of law and to separate legal from economic, political and ideological factors is to distort and even to destroy an intricate pattern. But some kind of analytical framework is necessary if the comparatist is to make sense of the place of labour law in a changing society.

It is first necessary to consider the idea of an autonomous labour law, and then four of the factors which may provide the basis for hypotheses about the relationship between labour law and social structure. These are (1) industrialisation and economic development; (2) the modernisation of the state; (3) the character of employers' and labour movements; and (4) ideology and the growth of legal rationality in labour relations.

THE 'SOCIAL QUESTION' AND THE EMERGENCE OF LABOUR LAW

The subject which is now generally called 'labour law' is of recent origin. In most countries it became recognised as a distinct division of law only after the Second World War. Before then, with the notable exceptions of Germany and Denmark, labour law was preoccupied with the contract of employment and less frequently with protective legislation. Collective bargaining and collective agreements were rarely studied. Wedderburn comments that in Britain:

> The Webbs had published a short section on law and collective

> bargaining in 1902 [in the 2nd edn of *Industrial Democracy*, App. I] but even . . . the 1962 edition of [a leading textbook on industrial law] . . . contained just two pages on collective agreements; a major book on 'Master and Servant Law' devoted not one of its six hundred pages to the subject. And all this is the very motherland of collective bargaining. [1983, p. 31]

Britain was behind the Continental countries, but even there collective labour problems tended to be neglected by legal specialists. For example, in Italy, Barassi (1901) wrote the first work on the individual contract of employment at the turn of the century, but the issues he raised were put aside during the fascist period when labour law was absorbed in corporative law. Even after the Second World War, Italian labour law was characterised by a formalistic and technical approach, until the mid-1960s, when the sociology and politics of labour law became a new focus of interest.

The exceptions were Germany and Denmark. In the latter, Carl Ussing, a Supreme Court judge who presided over the 'August Committee' of 1908–10, combined academic and practical expertise to produce a sharp analysis which helped to lay the foundations of Denmark's collectivist system. There were also important studies by Elmquist (1918), Kruse (1920) and Illum (1938), but mainly for reasons of language the impact of the Danish innovations was limited to Scandinavia.

The German scholars, however, had a profound influence throughout Europe and can be regarded as the founding fathers of the modern subject. A series of studies from 1874 had begun to turn away from the narrow traditional concerns with *locatio conductio operarum* or *Dienstmiete* (contract for the hiring of services) and the *Gesinderecht* (law on domestic servants) towards a general approach which included industrial workers. The 'law of the workers' (e.g. Bornhak, 1892) brought together workers' insurance and workers' protection. There was also scholarly interest in the important topic of the works rule (*Arbeitsordnung*) (see Ch. 6, below). The most important development was the discussion of legal policy. The Vereinigung für Sozialpolitik (the *Kathedersozialisten*, or academic socialists, as they were called by their adversaries), most of whose members were economists who had been trained as lawyers, the Gesellschaft für Soziale Reform, and the Deutscher Juristentag (Association of German Lawyers) all took an interest in the 'social question'. This expression denoted a set of 'problems' resulting from industrialisation, including the degradation of children and women, poverty, unemployment and strikes as well as the legal treatment of trade unions and collective agreements. The members of these groups, some liberal and some conservative, had friends among the bureaucracy and shared the ideology, so powerful in Germany, that these problems required *state* action. At the same time they tended to the view that pure police measures were counter-productive, and they wanted to promote the development of trade unions and the legal recognition of collective agreements.

As we shall see later, the 'social question' became, in Poggi's words:

> progressively locked into the political process largely by (1) the enfranchisement of social groups that expected the state to attend to such issues, (2) the resulting notion of 'social' rights of citizenship, and (3) the assumption of some responsibility for ameliorating the phenomenon in question. But the decisions involved in this protracted development were contested bitterly and widely. Within the complex story of the relations between liberalism, democracy and socialism in the nineteenth century, much revolved around these decisions. [1978, p. 114]

It was into this context that several remarkable lawyers immersed themselves. One of these was Philipp Lotmar. In an essay (1900) and book (1907/8) he produced a theory of the collective agreement by combining precise legal analysis with the sociological method, and gave broad and deep empirical descriptions. Another was Hugo Sinzheimer (1875–1945), who himself acknowledged Lotmar as the founder of the discipline of labour law, and then proceeded to give 'form and content to German collective bargaining law in particular and German labour law in general' (Kahn-Freund, 1981, p. 73). The legal recognition of the collective agreement, and many of the social rights in the Weimar Constitution, especially Article 165,[2] owed their inspiration and their drafting to him. To him belongs 'the conception of labour law as a unified, independent legal discipline' (Kahn-Freund, 1981, p. 75). In an article entitled 'The development of labour law and the task of legal theory' (1910–11, p. 1237) he put forward the following justification for regarding labour law as a separate legal discipline and for studying it as such:

1. The importance of the subject matter. The number of persons who are dependent on a contract of service grows ever greater, and for these people Labour law forms the very basis of their lives. Labour law is the heart of their social existence.
2. The special nature of the subject matter. There is no other area

2. The text of Articles 157, 159 and 165 of the Weimar Constitution are translated in Appendix IV, p. 385, below.

of law in which public and private law are as closely intertwined as Labour law. In general, legal theory separates public and private law. Labour law can only be perceived as the unity of public and private law.

3. The special treatment which Labour law demands. This must adhere to social principles which permit one to discover the present state of the law and to shape its future. Prevailing legal theory is dogmatic and concerned only with positive statements. The theory behind Labour law must also be concerned with sociology and matters of legal policy.
4. The necessity of specific auxiliary sciences. These include sociology, social policy and the theory of business organisation. Legal theory must cover all these subjects. A theory of Labour law which tied the study of Labour law to the study of other areas of the law could not do this.
5. Finally, the unity of the goal! This is based on the prevailing principle of the unity of human labour as the embodiment of the human personality and on the special function of the law which governs it as the guardian of human beings in an age of almost unrestrained materialism. In our time this is uniform Labour law, based purely on the needs of the employment relationship, rather than on the law of property or commerce.

In this passage, and later works, Sinzheimer pushed aside 'the fetish of the division between public and private law' and the 'untenable distinctions between different categories of employees' (Kahn-Freund, 1981, pp. 75–6) which had held back the development of labour law. Another writer, Potthoff (who with Sinzheimer edited a journal titled *Labour Law* from 1914) introduced the idea of an *Organisationsverhältnis* (organisation relationship) which deviated from the traditional individualistic understanding of this relationship, and he tried to develop the employment contract on the basis of the social 'rights' guaranteed by the Weimar Constitution of 1919. It was this constitution, with its promise of a labour code, and the promulgation of many Acts (e.g. on collective agreements, works councils, labour courts and social insurance) which brought labour law to a point not reached anywhere else before the Second World War. Even in France, where there was a tradition of *conseils de prud'hommes* (labour courts) since Napoleonic times, where work had begun on the codification of existing legislation in a *Code du Travail* from 1910, where the Matignon Agreement of 1936[3] laid the basis for the legal promotion of collective

3. The text of this agreement will be found in Appendix IV, p. 380, below.

bargaining, and where several scholars developed new ideas about the collective agreement, there was no parallel with the Germans' comprehensive conception of labour law as an integral part of a political and economic democracy.

The Nazis brought a dramatic end to Weimar labour law, which had already been undermined by the judiciary, against the background of Germany's economic and political crisis (see Ch. 7, below). Sinzheimer and his school emigrated. Although removed from their native land, their influence continued to be felt throughout Europe. In Leyden, where Sinzheimer had taken refuge, the first Dutch Chair of Labour Law was established in 1936 (M. G. Levenbach was Senior Lecturer in Labour Law at Amsterdam from 1926, but only later had a Chair), and in 1937 the Dutch law of collective agreements was amended to follow both German and French conceptions. Sinzheimer's pupil, Kahn-Freund, came to the London School of Economics and from that base transformed the study of British labour law utilising his teacher's theories as well as his own brilliant observations and analysis. Sinzheimer's ideas about labour law in general and, in particular, the different functions of collective agreements—normative, obligatory, organisational (see Ch. 5, below)—became 'a part of the common property of lawyers in Europe' (Kahn-Freund, 1981, p. 82).

What then are the specific features of this conception of labour law? The first is that labour law is created not only by the state (executive, legislature and judiciary) but also by autonomous groups, in particular employers and trade unions. The employer's works rules, trade union 'custom and practice', mutual aid societies and collective agreements are as much part of the ordering, control and organisation of labour relations as are legislation, executive orders and judicial decisions. The interaction between the autonomous norms (self-help) and state law (state intervention or, in the German usage, state 'help') is a central theme of the study of labour law (see in particular Chs. 5 and 7, below). When analysing state labour law it is especially important to distinguish between direct coercion (of which the criminal law is the prime example) and so-called 'facilitative or power-conferring laws', which afford 'the parties concerned the opportunity to make their own law (private law-making) and even, the opportunity, on occasions, to bypass or attenuate state law' (Sugarman and Rubin, 1984, p. 10). Facilitative laws—such as those in support of collective bargaining—have played a particularly important part in promoting and legitimating autonomous realms for the making of labour law. To these we need to add the international legal order which has been significant in promoting both direct state regulation and facilitative law in the twentieth century (see Ch. 7, below).

A second feature of the modern conception of labour law is the separation of the contract of employment from ordinary contracts. This is a process which is examined in detail in Chapter 1. It was of central importance in the civil law systems in 'the emancipation of human work as a legal concept from the nexus of property law' (Kahn-Freund, 1981, p. 78). One indicator of the development of labour law is the extent to which a particular system sees the contract of employment as an appendage of the law of contracts and of property. It will be seen that in the civil law systems this stage was reached by the early twentieth century.

However, this form of autonomous contract rested upon a third feature of labour law as it developed in Europe. This is the subordination of the individual worker to the capitalist enterprise. This perspective owes much to Otto Gierke of the German historical school (Lotmar himself was a scholar of Roman law), and to Anton Menger, a sharp critic of the German Civil Code. Sinzheimer's elaboration of the notion of 'dependency' was also influenced 'by Marx's and (following him) Renner's insight that capitalist property is domination over human beings' (Kahn-Freund, 1981, p. 79). Once labour law is seen as the law of 'dependent' labour, two consequences follow. The first is that the scope of the subject excludes independent workers (peasant proprietors and the self-employed generally) and is limited to those who, broadly speaking, fall within the notion of 'dependent' labour. So an indicator of the development of labour law is the extent to which all classes of dependent workers—manual, white-collar, domestic servants, agricultural labourers, state officials—are brought within its ambit (see Chs. 1 and 2, below).

A second consequence of this idea of dependency is that all forms of regulation which seek to order or control the worker's subordination to the employer's commands form the essential subject-matter of labour law. Among the main indicators of the development of this subject-matter are the following:

1. The protection of children and young persons in factories, mines and so on.
2. The protection of women.
3. The protection of all workers from abuses in the payment of wages.
4. The protection of all workers from industrial hazards.
5. The limitation of the working day and provision of paid holidays.
6. Minimum wages legislation (on items 1–6, see Ch. 2, below).
7. Provision of compensation for accidents, sickness payments,

invalidity and old-age pensions and family allowances (see Ch. 3, below).

8. Measures to provide relief from unemployment, such as public works schemes, labour colonies, labour exchanges and unemployment insurance.
9. Protection against termination of employment (on items 8 and 9 see Ch. 4, below).
10. Measures to facilitate self-regulation by tolerating freedom to organise and freedom to take industrial action.
11. Measures actively promoting self-regulation through employers' organisations and trade unions, either by voluntary means or positive rights (on items 10 and 11, see Ch. 5, below).
12. Measures facilitating workers' participation in the making of managerial decisions at the plant or company level.
13. Measures actively promoting such participation.
14. Measures integrating workers' representatives in the administration of the economy (i.e. regional and national councils, etc.) or of the state (e.g. special labour courts) (on items 12–14, see Ch. 6, below).

The list is by no means exhaustive, but it provides a set of indicators which together constitute an autonomous phenomenon. Various hypotheses about their significance may be applied to these indicators. The first of these hypotheses concerns the relationship between labour law and economic development.

ECONOMIC DEVELOPMENT AND INDUSTRIALISATION[4]

According to Landes, 'the timing of changes in legal institutions can and does materially affect the pace and character of economic development' (1969, p. 199). To what extent can this generalisation be applied specifically to labour law?

Labour law is the product of the Industrial Revolution, of the shift from an agrarian handicraft economy to one in which machine manufacture in mills and factories dominated. Landes explains:

> the factory was more than just a larger work unit. It was a system of production, resting on a characteristic definition of the functions

4. The changes in population and economic activity in the period of this book are to be found in Appendix III, p. 360, below.

> and responsibilities of the different participants in the productive process. On the one side was the employer, who not only hired the labour and marketed the finished product, but supplied the capital equipment and oversaw its use. On the other side there stood the worker, no longer capable of owning and furnishing the means of production and reduced to the status of a hand (the word is significant and symbolizes well this transformation from producer to pure labourer). Binding them were the economic relationship—the 'wage nexus'—and the functional one of supervision and discipline. [1969, p. 2]

The economic relationship rested on a concept of private property (now transformed into capital); the functional one could be secured by a system of labour law which left uncontrolled the employer's power of supervision and discipline, which was an integral aspect of the power of property. A glance at the chronology of labour law[5] shows an extremely varied time-lag between the 'take-off' of economic growth (in Rostow's famous phrase) in each country and the enactment of specific controls over the employer's power. One problem in attempting to examine such time-lags is that industrialisation is generally confined to particular regions within and across national boundaries, while labour law is linked to national states. Another problem is that economists are by no means in agreement about the concept of 'take-off' nor on how to date the phenomenon in particular countries.

The so-called 'first industrial revolution' (signified, above all, by steam power, machines, factories and railways) began in Britain around 1780 and then spread over a long period to the Continent. In Belgium, the peak of industrial revolution is often placed during the French period (1794–1814). Although this is largely true for Ghent cotton and Verviers wool, it was the years between 1820 and 1830 which were of decisive importance for the coal and iron industries. In France there was an importation of British technology up to 1790, then a slowing-down during the French Revolution and Napoleonic period, with a gradual resumption of industrialisation from 1815 to 1850, and a spread after 1850. It is a matter for debate whether the German industrial revolution began around 1833, with the formation of the *Zollverein* (customs union) or between 1842 and 1843, a period of heavy growth, or only after 1850. Undoubtedly, by the mid-1870s Germany had emerged from relative backwardness as a strong industrial nation. But the pace was uneven; some regions like Saxony had been industrialised before 1850, while others like East Prussia continued to

5. Appendix II, p. 330, below.

be dominated by the agricultural estates of the *Junkers* (landowners). The Netherlands remained largely outside the first industrial revolution until about 1870 when economic growth was spurred by the industrial boom in the German Ruhr. Northern Italy (1896–1915) and Denmark (1901–40) were later still, taking off in effect during the so-called 'second industrial revolution', which is characterised by electrical power, petroleum fuel, the internal combustion engine, motor cars and science-based chemical (synthetic) manufacture.

When one compares these 'take-off' dates with each of the main indicators of labour law (above) the only generalisation that seems possible is that the time-lags are longer in the case of the early industrialising countries than for those which industrialised later. In all cases, however, the main indications of labour law are found some time after the process of industrialisation had begun. This suggests that labour law is not directly constitutive of relations of production but rather that it tends to lag behind and, ultimately, to reflect the economic structure, sometimes after a considerable lapse of time. The most striking example of early industrialisation and the late emergence of labour law is Belgium. It was only in 1884 that the first protective legislation was enacted (and then only for boys under 12 years and girls under 14 in mines), and abuses in the payment of wages were controlled only from 1887. There are many explanations for this late development, including the strength of liberal contractual ideas and the grip of religion on the workers. Pirenne (1920) gives the example of workers from Ghent who in 1846 believed that the celebration of mass was the only effective protection against work accidents. It was only from 1903, after the franchise had been extended following major political strikes, and the Belgian Workers' Party had entered Parliament, that labour law grew on a significant scale. At the other extreme, in the late industrialising countries—Italy and Denmark—a number of the indicators of labour law emerged within a relatively short period after 'take-off'. Somewhere in between lie France, Germany and the Netherlands, while Britain, as the first country of the Industrial Revolution, stands in a unique position. In all these countries it is remarkable how long it took for the concept of the contract of employment to emerge (see Ch. 1, below).

If it is impossible to make any mechanical connection between an economic 'base' and a 'superstructure' of labour law, then we have to look for the relationship in very specific contexts where law and economic development may be said to be 'imbricated'[6] (Sugarman, 1983, p. 223). For example, did legislation cause the end of child labour

6. 'Imbricate': 'to place so as to overlap like roof-tiles' (*Shorter OED*).

or had technological developments already rendered the use of children obsolete when these laws were enacted, so making them of symbolic importance only (see Ch. 2, below)? Did the truck system decline as a result of economic prosperity and the growth of large-scale enterprise or because of legislation (see Ch. 2, below)? Was the social welfare system a reflection of economic growth or rather an attempt to increase labour productivity and redistribute income so as to stimulate a home market, or was it to meet the needs of imperialist expansion for healthy soldiers (see Ch. 3, below)? Was the relatively late introduction of a welfare system in France (1928–30) due to the slow pace of industrialisation in that country (see Ch. 3, below)? Did the social acceptance of the 'inevitability' of unemployment under capitalism make it necessary to invent relief measures and, if so, why was this problem 'discovered' only some time after cyclical crises had begun to appear (see Ch. 4, below)? Why did the toleration of freedom of association in Britain occur in an economic upsurge, while in Germany the Anti-Socialist Act was in force during a period of rapid economic growth and in France the Waldeck-Rousseau law legalising trade unions was passed soon after a financial crisis (see Ch. 5, below)? Were the works councils and other forms of labour representation a response to the general economic crisis after the First World War (see Ch. 6, below)?

No simple answers are possible to questions like these. The most liberal laws could be frustrated by economic factors. The classic example is France where the *Loi Le Chapelier* of 1791 suppressed coalitions and the *Code Napoléon* appeared to create the most favourable conditions for property and the accumulation of capital, but at the same time France's loss of markets and colonies following the downfall of Napoleon, as well as the entrenchment by the Revolution of a substantial rural population in possession of the land, created an irremediable backwardness. It is only by seeing the interaction of law and economic growth that we can get the whole picture. In particular, it is essential to grasp the nature of the state and its role in the process of industrialisation.

THE MODERNISATION OF THE STATE

The form of state under which industrialisation took place was liberal constitutionalism. The rights of the rising middle class to participate in political power with the upper classes were guaranteed by law and the constitutional system.[7]

7. The constitutional developments in each country are outlined in Appendix I, p. 301, below.

This form of state first emerged in the Republic of the United Provinces (the Netherlands), where it paved the way for the 'Golden Age' of Dutch commercial capitalism in the seventeenth century. In Britain, the outcome of the Civil War of the seventeenth century and the 'Glorious Revolution' of 1688 was the achievement of a fairly stable political compromise. The landed gentry increased their political power in Parliament; the big landowners dominated the House of Lords (of importance well into the nineteenth century because cabinets were dominated by members of this House) and also the army, the Church and the public service. The merchant and financial classes enjoyed freedom to trade and, under the patronage of the gentry and merchants, there was a spirit of liberty and dissent for the professional classes. 'From 1688', says Christopher Hill, 'England was, for the propertied class, an exceptionally free society by contemporary European standards' (1969, p. 29). In substance, though not in form, the monarchy was replaced by the gentry as the dominant power in the state. The transformation of Britain from an agricultural country, ruled by wealthy landowners, country squires and parsons, into an industrial nation dominated by industrial and financial capitalists was achieved within the constitutional framework of parliamentary supremacy, without a written constitution but supported by the common lawyers.

The changing character of Parliament is most dramatically illustrated by the enactment of the first labour laws of the period of the Industrial Revolution, the Combination Acts of 1799 and 1800. The story cannot be fully told here (see Ch. 5, below), but the point worth noting is that until the mid-eighteenth century, Parliament, then consisting almost entirely of landowners, with little sympathy for the emerging industrial employers, tended to support artisans who petitioned Parliament against low piece-rates or the introduction of the new processes which had reduced their living standards or put them out of work. But after 1750 the changing class structure resulting from the investment in industry by landowners and the purchase of land by wealthy merchants, brought about a change in the protective attitude to the artisans. As the old system of wage regulation broke down, there was increasing repression of trade unions and strikes, including the passing of the Acts of 1799 and 1800. J. L. and Barbara Hammond (1919, p. 113) commented that these Acts marked an entirely new principle of labour legislation. Previously, combinations of workers had been illegal in certain trades because they challenged the state's monopoly of industry. After 1800 the law sought to protect the monopoly of the employers and not of the state. Labour law upheld, for the first time, the unilateral power of the *individual* employer (combinations of employers were nominally unlawful but not prosecuted in practice) to fix wages and conditions of employment. The liberal state had emerged.

In the Continental countries, unlike Britain, there were written constitutions. The Belgian Revolution of 1830 was the signal and the beginning of these changes for most of these countries. The constitution of 1831 was the most liberal in Europe at the time, but the electorate was so limited by property qualifications that political power was in the hands of wealthy landowners, industrialists and the professional classes. In France the restored monarchy of 1815–30 was constitutionalist and parliamentary in form (without an Opposition on British lines), but, as in Britain at the time, the vote was restricted to the wealthy classes and its policies were conservative. It was the July 1830 Revolution which produced Louis Philippe, who in Thomson's words was 'everything that a liberal King in 1830 could be expected to be: middle class, respectable and unspectacular' (1966, p. 168). Liberal constitutionalism spread in the wake of the 1848 revolutions to the Netherlands (1848, and finally confirmed in 1866–68), Denmark (1849) and Piedmont-Savoy (1848), whose liberal constitution formed the model for that of the Kingdom of Italy in 1861.

Germany stands in a special position. The 'late nation', which had missed unification in the sixteenth century, established a form of 'enlightened absolutism' which prevented a confrontation between the relatively undeveloped middle class and the monarch. Frederick the Great of Prussia, who spoke of himself as the 'first servant of the state', became the model for other German princes. The army was the source of inspiration for the modern system of administration which he introduced. After the devastating defeat of Prussia by Napoleon (1806), the reform policy—which included the emancipation of the serfs (1807) and the development of independent courts—was the work of an intellectual élite of aristocrats and recently ennobled members of the middle class. After 1815 Frederick William III of Prussia lost interest in reform and relied on the support of the conservative *Junkers* of East Prussia, whose power increased. The promise of a representative liberal constitution for Prussia was not fulfilled. In the southern states Saxe-Weimar, Bavaria, Württemburg, Baden and Hesse-Darmstadt, new liberal constitutions, modelled on the French Constitutional Charter of 1814, were granted, but even in the most liberal of these only the wealthy classes of men could vote, and the assemblies had relatively little power over the governments. German liberalism was weak and divided, particularly in the North.

The liberal revolutions of 1830 left the political structure intact, apart from the smaller states—in particular, Brunswick, Saxony and Hanover—where liberal constitutions were granted. The social pressures for reform were limited because more than two-thirds of the population remained in agriculture and the middle class was small and relatively scattered. Prussia was granted a liberal constitution only in 1850. Even under the constitutional monarchy the traditional power of the monarch remained important: legislation had to be agreed between the monarch and Parliament, and the monarch retained executive power and supreme command of the army. Even more crucial, was the fact that the monarch acted as arbitrator between the nobility and the middle class and between the middle class and the rising class of workers. The nobility retained economic power as landowners because the peasants had to compensate them for emancipation. The middle classes were helped by the liberalisation of trade (first in Prussia in 1807–10 and 1845) and the legislation for a customs union. The North German Confederation, formed in 1866, gave them what they had long demanded by introducing a uniform trade law (1869) which included a unified industrial law.

The Constitution of the Empire (1871) made the Chancellor dependent upon the confidence of the Kaiser and not of the Parliament. The real centre of state power was in the army and in the large number of *Beamte* (state officials), dominated by the Prussian bureaucracy and loyal to the monarch and the state. This ensured the continuation, despite liberalisation, of the tradition of the paternalist 'enlightened' state. The 'socialism of the throne' helps to explain the history of German protective legislation (see Ch. 2, below) and also the welfare legislation of Bismarck (see Ch. 3, below). In Germany labour law was part of the attempt by a paternalist state to solve the social question.

Leaving aside the special features in Germany, what were the main characteristics of liberal constitutional states and how did these influence the development of labour law? First, these states actively promoted liberal doctrines, purporting to leave the economy alone (*laissez-faire*) to be regulated by market forces operating through the legal mechanism of voluntary contracts. This was, of course, a form of 'intervention' in the sense that it gave uncontrolled support to the power of property (in the form of capital). But this was an 'intervention' different in kind from mercantilism, the main economic policy of the absolutist states, which had directed economic and labour relations. The liberal states swept aside the guild regulations and other obstacles to free labour markets (see Ch. 1, below), used the Poor Laws to promote the development of those labour markets (see Chs. 3 and 4, below), and maintained 'order' and the disciplinary power of the employer through the work-book system, on the Continent, and penal sanctions on deserting workers in Britain and most other countries until the last quarter of the nineteenth century (see Ch. 1, below). Until freedom of association was tolerated (see below) the workers were thus exposed to the domination of the employer in the 'private' sphere of the factory and the surveilance of the police and Poor Law authorities in the 'public' sphere.

A second feature of liberal societies lay in the somewhat artificial distinction between this 'private' sphere of economic life—what Adam Smith called 'civil society'—and the 'public' sphere of all that was directly controlled or administered by the state. This was conceptualised in the Continental countries in the distinction between 'public' and 'private' law. The state did not rule over 'society'. It left economic interests to take care of themselves, except by preventing fraud, facilitating the enforcement of contracts and the like. State intervention to protect children and women could be reconciled with this concept of society, on the grounds that these groups lacked capacity to contract as legal 'equals', and protection against such matters as abuses in wage payment could be seen as a means to aid the working of the 'free' market (see Ch. 2, below).

The challenge to *laissez-faire* and to the line drawn between 'state' and 'society' came from those who were subjected to the domination of state and 'society'. This challenge was manifested in a variety of forms, such as the silk weavers' riots in Lyons in 1831, the Chartist movement in Britain (1836–54) and the revolutions of 1848.

Poggi points out that the safest way to uphold the domination of the capital-owning class was 'to exclude from the constitutional political process the claims and demands of groups in whose interest it may lie to abolish capital ownership, to modify its distribution or to interfere with its chances of profit or its control over accumulation' (1978, p. 122). In the nineteenth and early twentieth centuries the chief means of doing this was by the restriction of suffrage. The liberal states limited the right to vote to men with property, tax and/or educational qualifications; that is, those with a stake in the established order. The lengthy struggles for the franchise did not alter the basic features of the liberal state, but they modified it to create the liberal-democratic state.

In Germany the lower house (Reichstag) of the North German Confederation was elected by equal male suffrage and the Reichstag of the Empire (1871) was similarly elected. This was seen by the bureaucracy as a means of welding the working class to the state. Although the Reichstag could vote on the budget, Bismarck was able to divide and rule, splitting the Liberal Party into two factions, persisting in his *Kulturkampf* against the Catholic Church and outlawing the Social Democratic Party and the trade unions by his Anti-Socialist Act from 1878 to 1890. France had universal male suffrage from 1871 onwards (reviving the laws of 1848), giving the vote to some 10 million

Frenchmen. In Britain the Reform Act of 1867 extended the franchise to working men in the towns, doubling the electorate to about 2 million, and the Reform Act of 1884 extended this to many agricultural workers, so increasing the electorate to 5 million. But nearly a quarter of the adult male population remained without the vote until 1918. In Belgium universal male suffrage, with plural voting for men with special qualifications, was achieved in 1893. In the Netherlands reforms of 1887 and 1897 meant that the electorate increased from 2 per cent to 14 per cent of the population, but universal suffrage was granted only in 1917. In Italy reforms in 1882 gave the vote to about 7 per cent of the population, with universal male suffrage only in 1912.

Denmark was the first of the countries studied to extend the franchise to women (1915), following in the wake of Norway and Finland; then Britain in 1918 (until 1928 restricted on grounds of age and marital status), the Netherlands, Germany and Luxembourg in 1919 and Ireland in 1921, but not in Italy, France and Belgium until after the Second World War.

How did liberal democracy influence labour law? The new electorates made demands upon the state to attend to the host of social questions produced by capitalist industrialisation. This occurred at a time when the state was already under pressure to improve administration in order to deal with the immense growth of population,[8] and the problems of urbanisation, such as public health and housing. The political parties had to compete for working-class votes, and working-class and socialist parties emerged.[9] The British movements for factory legislation in the early nineteenth century had been too weak politically to secure general legislation applying to all workers, so they had to secure minimum standards by collective action. The workers in the Continental countries, on the other hand, were able to use their votes to secure the amelioration of their conditions (see Ch. 2, below). The case of Belgium has already been mentioned. In Britain the new-found political power was mainly of importance in the removal of penal sanctions for breach of contract and securing the freedom of association (1871) and the freedom to strike (1875 and 1906) against renewed judicial attack (see Ch. 5, below) and to prevent 'sweating' in certain trades where this threatened to undermine the collective bargaining system (see Ch. 2, below). In Germany Bismarck sought to wean the workers from socialism by his successful welfare legislation (1883–89; see Ch. 3, below) and this was emulated, with some modifications, by the Liberal government in Britain (1906–11). In France the relatively

8. See Appendix III, p. 360, below.
9. See Appendix I, p. 301, below.

slow pace of industrialisation and of population growth, the presence of a large number of *petits patrons*, some self-employed and some owning small workshops, and the absence of a homogeneous proletariat, as well as the fragmentation of the ruling-class parties, delayed any major response to the social question. Thomson comments that 'the most effective French labour regulations derived not from politics at all but from the activities of the bureaucracy' (1966, p. 357). This legislation included the laws ending the work-book system (1890), establishing workers' representatives in mines (1890), creating a labour inspectorate (1892), setting up a workmen's compensation system (1898), and limiting the working day to 10 hours (1900) and the working week to 6 days (1906). In the Netherlands and Italy the main output of labour legislation came immediately after the First World War, also as a response to the social demands of the new electorates.

This participation by workers in the 'public' sphere in order to improve their situation in the 'private' realm of the economy had two consequences which eroded the division between public and private law. The first was the development of social 'rights' of citizenship, which included labour law. Protective labour legislation changed its character from the gift of the 'bourgeois' liberal state or of the 'enlightened' bureaucracy into a 'right' of the workers (see Ch. 2, below). These new 'rights' were different from the 'rights and liberties' of the individual proclaimed by the French Revolution and written into most of the liberal constitutions (but not that of Germany). The constitutions were based on the theory that individuals entered into a 'social contract' with the state in exchange for the defence of those rights and liberties, which were regarded as 'natural', such as the 'freedom' to trade and to work. The 1848 Revolution had raised the vision of new rights such as the 'right to work' in the sense of committing the state to provide work (see Chs. 1 and 4, below). In the liberal-democratic states the capitalist mode of production remained dominant and dictated the range of solutions to the social question and so no right to work could be guaranteed. But the state could concede new 'rights' for the protection of collective interests such as the rights to organise and to strike.

A second consequence was that collective groups were now able to organise pressure on the state, even to bargain with it, in order to further their interests. Liberal doctrine had come, first in Britain, to espouse freedom of association for workers. In the 'private' sphere, this entailed modifying the classical liberal ideas of the 'free' market. In the 'public' sphere it meant labour legislation to tolerate and later actively to promote collective bargaining (see Ch. 5, below). The state itself came in the twentieth century to integrate the collective groups of employers and workers into its own activities, consulting with them on economic and social policies, and bringing them into the organs of government (see Ch. 6, below).

The modernisation of the state can thus be seen as one of the key determinants of the emergence of labour law. This modernisation was accelerated by the First World War, during which states assumed direction of the economy and of labour. The totalitarian states were another 'solution' to the social question (see Ch. 7, below). The 'welfare state', although originating in the reforms of the early twentieth century and the inter-war years, reached its high point, with a new wave of labour legislation, only after 1945.

THE CHARACTER OF THE EMPLOYERS' AND LABOUR MOVEMENTS[10]

In liberal democracies the organisations of employers and workers had the power to influence the character of labour law. This influence could be direct when parties they supported held or shared power or indirect when those in power sought to pre-empt their opponents' policies in order to gain votes. We have seen that even in the paternalist German state the indirect influence of the socialists was crucial to the emergence of social legislation (see Ch. 3, below).

On the employers' side, technological change and the drive to limit competition had led to the growing concentration of capital. By the 1890s over half the labour force of Belgium, Britain and Germany was working in enterprises with more than twenty workers. An extreme example was the German electrical industry in which two firms, AEG (Allgemeine Elektizitäts Gesellschaft) and Siemens, controlled over 90 per cent of national production and had multinational links. New techniques of management of labour were acquired by these firms, and the growing use of the corporate form changed the nature of ownership, reducing personal control by the shareholders and giving the managers new status and power. The reduction of competition by monopolised cartels gave many managers the opportunity to improve the wages and benefits of their workers, and to bind them to the corporation. These paternalistic welfare measures influenced later state provision (e.g. family allowances; see Ch. 3, below). At the same time large-scale organisation meant the compulsory association of large groups of

10. For details of political parties and trade unions in each country, see Appendix I, p. 301; see also Ch. 5.

workers on production lines. The workers were disciplined by the production process to accept rules and to act as part of a collective entity. Increasingly separated from personal contact with the owners of capital, they developed independent organisations which struggled for the improvement of their working and social conditions. But the power of the new business giants was such that the gains by collective action were often short-lived. When the workers turned to political action, the employers brought to bear not only the traditional levers of power through their political parties, but also formed lobbying associations, such as the Comité des Forges in France, to co-ordinate relations between employers and government. The growth of employers' associations (see Ch. 5, below) affected not only collective self-regulation but also the relations between employers and the state.

On the workers' side, the first reaction was radical rejection of the liberal order and demands for a new society, based on several varieties of 'utopian' and 'scientific' socialism, anarchism and syndicalism. Utopian socialists such as Robert Owen, Henri Comte de Saint-Simon and Charles Fourier promoted the ideas of co-operation, harmony and fraternity and influenced the small but active groups of working men demanding social and political rights. In Britain there was some socialist influence on British Chartism in the 1830s. In France, Louis Blanc's *L'Organisation du travail*, published in 1839, argued that the state was an essential instrument to achieve the 'right to work' and this idea was prominent in the revolution of 1848 in France (see Ch. 4, below). The *Communist Manifesto*, written by Marx and Engels and published in London in February 1848, played no part in the revolutions of that year, but within twenty years it had become the inspiration of movements throughout Europe dedicated to establishing a proletarian state and ultimately a classless society. The International Working Men's Association (the First International) formed in 1864 spread Marxist ideas until its demise in 1873, following the suppression, two years earlier, of the Paris Commune, described by Marx as 'the glorious harbinger of a new society'.

As industrialisation spread in Continental Europe in the following decades, there was a growth of socialist parties, some revolutionary and some following reformist tendencies.[11] The strength and character of these parties was important to the timing and content of labour laws. The conquest of effective political power by these parties proved to be elusive. In Germany, where the Social Democratic Party (SPD) was the largest party in the Weimar Republic from 1919 to 1932; in Denmark, where the Social Democratic Party dominated governments

11. See Appendix I, p. 301, below.

from 1924; in Luxembourg, where Christian socialists led governments from 1914; and in France, where the socialists, communists and radical socialists formed a Popular Front government from 1936 to 1939 and were pushed from below by a major wave of strikes and occupations—in these countries there was major legal support for a collectivist system of labour relations. These gains proved to be short-lived in Germany and France, being eclipsed by the Nazis and the Vichy régime, respectively, but they were revived and extended after the Second World War.

In Belgium the Workers' Party (POB) had won over one-third of the seats in Parliament by 1919, but was never able to acquire power on its own to effect major social changes and served in coalition governments on three occasions between 1919 and 1939. In the Netherlands the Social Democratic Workers' Party (SDAP) remained in opposition until it entered the government under the threat of war in 1939. In Britain there were minority Labour Party governments in 1924 and between 1929 and 1931, but without producing any significant labour legislation. Indeed, they were unable to muster sufficient parliamentary support even to repeal the hated Trade Disputes and Trade Unions Act which the Conservative government had introduced in 1927 to restrict the unions after the unsuccessful General Strike of 1926. That repeal was delayed until 1946, after a majority Labour government had been elected. In Italy the Socialist Party (PSI) secured 32 per cent of the popular vote in 1919 (156 deputies), but never shared power and was suppressed, with the rest of the labour movement, when the Fascists took power.

The fluctuating fortunes of the socialists can be ascribed to a number of factors. Most important of all was their inability to alter the basic economic and social structure of capitalism, which, despite the economic crisis after the First World War, proved to be resilient and was revitalised by public investment and rearmament in the 1930s. The Weimar labour laws, like those elsewhere, struck against the rock of unemployment. 'What meaning does labour law have', asked Sinzheimer in 1933, 'if it is at most a law for an élite of workers, who have the good fortune to remain in work, if alongside the existence of labour law an economic graveyard of "structural unemployment" opens up?' (1933, p. 1). The separation of labour law from economic policy left the reformist socialist governments in the position of having to implement cuts in living standards dictated by the great depression.

A second problem was, in Kendall's words that 'the socialists had a reform programme for capitalism and a revolution programme for socialism, but there was no adequate bridge between the two' (1975, pp. 20–1). The German SPD, the first mass socialist party and the model for many others on the Continent, had in its Erfurt programme of 1891 combined the long-term aim of a proletarian state with immediate demands, including the 8-hour day and the extension of social insurance. The First World War proved to be a turning point. Socialists and trade union leaders entered the governments and rallied around the patriotic cause and helped to develop the state machine of 'war socialism' which directed labour relations. They achieved an accommodation with the ruling classes, who were now willing to accept some of the socialists' immediate demands, in particular those in the field of labour law. This is reflected in Part VIII of the Treaty of Versailles (see Ch. 7, below) and the great wave of labour legislation in 1919, the *annus mirabilis* of labour law. For those who remained revolutionaries, the inspiration came from the Bolshevik Revolution of 1917. The socialist parties split everywhere, and communist parties were founded, but these remained relatively small. The fears of Bolshevism were a major influence on governments in the inter-war years and formed the backcloth of developments such as the works councils in Germany and the Whitley reforms in Britain. The mood of labour relations became one of collaboration and economic peace between the trade union leaders, the employers and governments.

A third aspect of the socialist movement was the way in which the political parties interacted with the trade unions,[12] particularly in the formulation of labour law. In Germany, Belgium, the Netherlands and Italy trade unions grew as appendages to the socialist parties being mobilised to achieve political reforms and labour legislation. In Britain and Ireland, on the other hand, the Labour Party was the creation of the trade unions in alliance with the socialists. From about 1850 the energies of the working class had been devoted to building trade unions. These unions were usually willing to use the law to the full extent if it would benefit their members; when the law was used against the unions by employers the unions supported candidates of any party who would press for reforming legislation. The *Taff Vale* case of 1901 (see Ch. 5, below) led the Trades Union Congress (TUC) to participate in founding the Labour Representation Committee (later the Labour Party). Once the unions had obtained as much as they thought possible in the Trade Disputes Act 1906, they returned to industrial activity. It is significant that even in the years of minority Labour Party governments, the unions deliberately preferred the method of collective bargaining to legislation.

In France, where the unions were weak and divided, the Confédération Générale du Travail (CGT) adopted a revolutionary anarcho-

12. For details, see Appendix I, p. 301.

syndicalist policy, stood apart from the political parties and rejected parliamentarianism until 1914 when CGT leaders entered the state institutions. The split in 1921, when the anarchists and communists seceded to form a rival to the CGT, the Confédération Générale du Travail Unitaire (CGTU), created a new type of union led (after 1924) by the communists and aimed towards organising a disciplined revolutionary force. However, the wave of strikes and occupations in 1936, which sparked the Matignon Agreement, was not dictated by the communists and socialists. 'The workers', says Zeldin, 'saw their action as signifying that it was no use relying on unions, or even on governments; they were taking matters into their own hands' (1979, p. 281). They negotiated with their own employers; almost none of the occupations 'seemed to have envisaged any destruction of the capitalist system' (Zeldin, 1979, p. 281). The Matignon Agreement sought to bring this spontaneous movement under control.

There is a well-known hypothesis that labour legislation tends to be made when the political power of workers exceeds their industrial power. If one applies this hypothesis to the various indicators of labour law (above), at least two qualifications have to be made. The first is that the 'political power of the workers' has to be understood very broadly. Labour legislation is not exclusively or even mainly the outcome of avowedly working-class parties. Indeed, some of the most important pieces of legislation were enacted under Liberal and Conservative governments, and even under strongly anti-socialist régimes like that of Bismarck. Labour legislation was a reponse to the indirect as well as the direct pressure of those who felt the adverse effects of industrialisation.

The second qualification is that the hypothesis gives insufficient weight to the role of law as ideology.

IDEOLOGY AND THE GROWTH OF LEGAL RATIONALITY IN LABOUR RELATIONS

In every system of domination the rulers have to persuade the ruled not only that compliance with authority is necessary in order to avoid unpleasant consequences but also that compliance is right. In absolutist systems this sense of moral obligation rested upon what Weber called 'traditional power'. The influence of this ideology survived in the paternalist German Empire, and in its social legislation. However, the typical form of legitimation in liberal constitutional states is legal rationality. Obedience to rules is demanded because they are issued in accordance with just procedures and they are based on valid general norms applicable to all citizens and even to the state itself. The law thus appears as a neutral and rational body of rules , discovered by objective principles, which therefore commands universal respect.

This kind of rationality in the legitimation of the power of the dominant interests in the state, is paralleled in the (much slower) growth of rationality in the sphere of labour relations. The domination of capital was asserted through the instrumentality of the absolute rule of the employer in 'his' factory, as reflected in the works rule and the system of fines and other punishments which constituted the criminal law of the workshops. But as Carson (1974) has shown in relation to the British factory legislation, many of the larger employers were anxious to remove the stigma attached to their profit-making activities, which endangered life and limb and degraded children and women, so they supported the movement for protective legislation. The discipline of the factory system was secured not only by penal measures but also by the education of the factory children and the growth of belief in the 'natural' authority of the master based on his humanitarian concerns.

Labour law is not the outcome of a single ideology of the dominant classes but is the product of conflicting ideologies. Among the most important of these have been the ideology of the market, the ideology of self-help, the ideology of state help, the ideology of patriarchy, the ideology of social Christianity, and the ideology of socialism.

The ideology of the market was in the ascendant in the early stages of capitalist industrialisation. It is expressed in the ideas of *laissez-faire*, of French individualism and of classical English liberalism and utilitarianism. It finds concrete expression in the doctrines of freedom of contract (see Ch. 1, below), in the opposition to direct regulation of labour markets (e.g., the aversion to minimum wages laws; see Ch. 2, below) and in the use of the contract of employment as the basis of the social insurance systems (see Ch. 3, below). The failures of the market were to be blamed not on the market but on the idle and 'undeserving' poor (see Ch. 4, below), on trade unions and other combinations which obstructed the working of the free market. When the followers of Jeremy Bentham promoted freedom of association it was on utilitarian calculations (which proved unfounded) that legalisation would make these combinations less attractive to the workers (see Ch. 5, below).

The ideology of self-help was closely related to the idea of the market. This ideology reached its high point in the period which Kahn-Freund dubbed 'collective *laissez-faire*' (1959, p. 224). It is seen in the Danish September Agreement of 1899,[13] in the so-called 'abstention' of

13. The text is set out in Appendix IV, p. 383, below.

the law (something of a misnomer because the law is a framework of rules even in the absence of direct legislation) from British and Danish labour relations, and the widespread use of facilitative law to promote conciliation, arbitration and collective bargaining (see Ch. 5, below). Self-help was also the dominant ideology in the formation of mutual aid societies. This was a necessary response by workers to the destruction of traditional means of support by the early industrial system, and it was legitimated by the legal recognition of friendly societies and 'state help for self-help' in the development of social insurance (see Ch. 3, below).

The ideology of state help also rested on notions of traditional power (above) and was particularly influential in Germany, where Hegelian ideas of the primacy of the state held sway. It was reflected not only in the paternalist social legislation but also in the statist ideas of the Lassallean socialists. In France, despite Louis Blanc's espousal of state instrumentality, in Britain and in the other liberal democracies, these ideas were far less popular. There were, however, survivals in all these countries of pre-industrial ideas such as the allegiance owed by state officials to the state, the status of domestic servants within the family and of agricultural workers within the rural economy (see Ch. 1, below). Sometimes feudal notions were actually revived (e.g. the 'estates' principle in the Netherlands to justify the representation of labour; see Ch. 6, below).

The ideology of patriarchy played a crucial role in the shaping of protective legislation not only in the period of industrialisation (see Ch. 2, below) but also in some of the twentieth-century international labour standards; for example, on night-work by women (see Ch. 7, below). In the early period of industrialisation the working-class family tended to work as a unit. Children assisted their parents in the factories or went to work independently in order to help support the family. Women were a large percentage of the workforce in textiles and contributed to the family's earnings. The authority of the factory owner over women and children was seen as an extension of the authority of the father and husband over the family, in which children and women played a subordinate role. But this was also subversive of the family and of male domination within the family unit. As technological changes threatened the semi-skilled work of men, they sought to protect their position by excluding the competition of women from the labour market by supporting a variety of restrictions on female labour. This could be justified by the rising middle-class ideas of the woman as home-maker, mother and servant of the family. The First World War was a turning point, opening up job opportunities for women in armaments and other manufacturing industries. Although there was a decline in these opportunities during the Depression years, women were increasingly asserting their claims to equal pay and equal treatment with men. The challenge to patriarchy had begun.

The ideology of social Christianity became extremely important after the Papal Encyclical *Rerum Novarum* (1891) and strengthened the growth of Christian trade unions, and a policy of social reform by Christian parties. The ideology of socialism, too, had been reflected in labour laws. The struggles for particular laws have been great focal points of working-class and socialist activity. The Ten Hours Act in Britain was hailed by Marx and Engels as 'a legislative recognition of particular interests of the workers, by taking advantage of the divisions among the bourgeoisie itself' (1848, reprinted in 1973, p. 76). The 'right to work', although castigated by Marx as 'in the bourgeois sense, nonsense, a wretched, pious wish' (1850 reprinted in 1973, p. 69), was one for which many socialists died in the barricades of June 1848 in France. These and many other examples to be found in this book indicate that the labour laws, as well as having instrumental effects, are seen by the participants as a crucial part of the struggles for socialism, even if these laws do not abolish wage-labour itself.

The process of labour law does not end with the enactment of specific legislation. The instrumental aspect of the law requires enforcement and the adjudication of disputes. At this stage ideology continues to be of importance. This can be seen in the way in which state inspectors came to emphasise not the penal but the 'conciliatory' role of legislation as a means of industrial harmony (see Ch. 2, below). It is also a key to understanding the role of the judiciary in labour relations.

The judiciary has been far more important in the common law than in the civil law systems in influencing labour law. The 'rule of law', according to Dicey (1914), was synonymous in Britain with the rule of the ordinary courts. The common law recognised the inherent power of the judiciary to adjudicate, a notion which by and large the Continental countries rejected. This is reflected in the personal and informal style of judgments, and in the clear statements in those judgments of the ideas of classical liberalism (e.g. in the case of *Priestley* v. *Fowler*, 1837; see Ch. 3, below).

In general, in all the countries surveyed, positivist theories of law emphasised the neutral role of legal rules in maintaining the interests of all groups within the defined 'rules of the game'. The judges were umpires of these rules. Where industrial arbitration was established, the aim was generally to find a compromise which would win the widest consensus. The incorporation of representatives of employers and workers into special labour courts (see Ch. 7, below) sustained the belief of liberal democracy that there are independent values over and above those of conflicting social groups. The courts, especially the special labour courts, were seen as the guardian of the interests of the community as a whole.

In assessing the role of law in legitimating the social order it is important to ask how far employers and workers were actually affected by the ideas of labour law. Did the workers regard themselves as free and equal contracting parties? Did they see individual legal rights as a substitute for collective strength? Were workers deterred from using the law by their relative lack of access to the courts and their lack of education? Even the most extensive legal regulation may fail to change social attitudes and social practice, where the ideology the law represents fails to take hold of the people for whom it is intended.

The systems of labour law which emerged from the industrialisation of Europe were, above all, an attempt to order the conflicts between employers and workers and to bring these conflicts within a system of legal rationality. On the one hand, the state recognised the inevitability of these conflicts; on the other hand, it sought to avoid taking sides. In 1932 the young Kahn-Freund asked:

> Is it possible to legalise the class system in a class-divided society and to make it a component of the legal system? Can the state recognise the idea of class and yet remain 'neutral'? Must not the conflict eventually break up the legal system or the legal system suppress the conflict? [1981, pp. 190–1]

Those questions were soon answered by the dramatic suppression of the Weimar labour laws by the Nazis, but this, as he showed, had been preceded by the development of corporatist philosophies by the unions, employers and judiciary. In the liberal democracies it was the ideological consensus of collaboration and industrial harmony which sustained labour law until the Second World War.

The outcome of the Second World War brought hope of a new beginning, of universal social justice. Forty years later, as the countries of this study enter a new phase of deregulation and neo-*laissez-faire*, we may benefit from studying the defeats, as well as the successes, of those who built labour law as an answer to social questions which we have yet to resolve.

1

The Evolution of the Contract of Employment

Bruno Veneziani

INTRODUCTION

The main aim of this chapter is to outline the process by which the notion of the contract of employment evolved during the period from the fall of the guild system to the beginning of the twentieth century.

This concept had by the beginning of the twentieth century reached maturity and throughout Western Europe the employer–worker relationship was no longer tied to the ideology of servile hiring but was classified under the heading of the contract of employment. Although regulated to a great extent by the same general priniciples of law as other contracts, the contract of employment became distinct and autonomous. From the juridical viewpoint, this concept grew in strength in almost all countries. By the beginning of the twentieth century, at least the basic outlines of the contractual model had been enshrined in the legislation of the civil law countries, and in the judicial precedents of the common law systems.

The relationships between individuals as producers and, theoretically, as equals before the law, entered the world of contract. In the civil law countries this was integrated within the framework of *locatio conductio* (letting and hire)—for example, the Napoleonic Code of 1804 (Arts. 1710, 1779, 1780 and 1781), the Italian Code of 1865 (Arts. 1625, 1627 and 1628) as well as the codes of the preunification period in Italy; the Belgian Code of 1804 (Art. 1710); the Danish Act of 1878 (Art. 65); the Dutch Code of 1838 (Arts. 1583, 1585, 1637–9); and in the German Code of 1896 (BGB) (Arts. 611–30), although with some peculiarities (see p. 59, below). These codes did not, however, create an autonomous model for the contract of employment but defined the employment relationship as one of *locatio conductio operis faciendi* (an agreement to make something or to do a job for a person in relation to materials belonging to another), thus likening it to *locatio conductio rerum* (letting the use of things) but only in the sense that doing a job of work and letting land or chattels are two species of the wider genus of 'lease'.

The influence of Roman law can also be seen in the way this notion was put into practice, although the concept encapsulated a phenomenon different from that of Roman times. It indicated a different type of function. In fact, in Roman legal philosophy, *locatio conductio operarum* (an agreement by which one party let out his services to another) was an extension of *locatio servi* (letting the use of a slave) and thus expressed a value judgment that the post-revolutionary European states found repugnant. The Roman idea was that mercenary work lessened the state of a free man by degrading him to the condition of a slave hired out by his master: 'a free man hires out himself just as the master hires out the slave' (Mengoni, 1971, p. 10). It is interesting to note the legal fiction to which the codes resorted in applying this model, which is the same as the old *locatio conductio* in name only. In fact, in Roman law it was an elementary juridical form, a unitary category that defined a simple economic transaction on the basis of which someone temporarily assigned a thing to someone else, who in turn promised to pay him money.

The first significant modification of the Roman model came about during the period of reception in the Middle Ages when the commentators, such as Cuiacius, Carocius and Azo, added another element, that of *uti frui* (use and enjoyment), which for the Roman jurists had been outside the sphere of *negotium* (commercial transactions). Nevertheless, this was also related to persons and not as yet to objectivised *operae* (jobs of work). Moreover, the notion was still a unitary one and no attempt was made to distinguish between the various types of *locatio*, which in the usage of the Pandectists meant *dare aliquid utendum* (to give something to be used).

This is certainly not the model that found its way into the post-revolutionary codes. However, the element of *uti frui* and the increased objectivisation of the employment relationship made themselves felt through the creation of submodels or types. A distinction was drawn between the *locatio* of things as opposed to services, the worker being said to let his working power. The old Roman model of *locatio conductio* was replaced by a definition which was only nominally like the Roman one, while the underlying economic relationship was completely different. In other words, it had undergone a 'radical substitution of content', since it now indicated a free exchange between 'equal' individuals who were exerting their own free will over the letting and hiring of the worker's services (Mengoni, 1965, p. 675).

In the common law countries, where the Roman law conceptions had no influence, freedom of contract and the equality of the contracting parties was achieved by a different route. Until the eighteenth century the scope of labour law was determined not by the kind of contract under which a person was employed but by the nature of his work. Legislation regulating wages and other matters applied to specific categories such as agricultural labourers, artificers, colliers and so on. As late as 1827, when the Industrial Revolution was already well advanced, there was no clear description of a contract of service between 'master and servant'. It was only when the penal legislation against deserting servants, and the Poor Law, had to be applied to new employments in the mid-nineteenth century, that the courts evolved a general concept of a contract of service. When in 1875 Parliament finally repealed the Master and Servant laws, with their penal sanctions, the law seemed to promise a freely bargained exchange between equal contracting parties.

By the beginning of the twentieth century, this new conception of labour law, reached by different techniques in the civil law and common law systems, embodied the ideology of freedom of contract, seen as the freedom of the employer and worker from the interference of the state in the labour market, the freedom of choice of the contracting parties and the freedom of private will to determine the content of the contract. However, we shall discover the 'curious fact' (Atiyah, 1979, p. 523) that despite the apparent universality of freedom of contract, the movement from status to contract was never completed. The contractual model, instead of bringing about genuine equality, simply underlined the property rights of the employer and his greater economic power to dictate the terms. Collective bargaining and protective legislation developed in spite of, and largely outside the framework of, the civil law *locatio conductio* and the common law contract of service.

THE REMOVAL OF RESTRICTIONS ON FREEDOM OF CONTRACT

Freedom of Movement, the Right to Work and the Right to Assistance

There is no doubt that the continuation in various countries of rigid state control over the labour market was an obstacle to the formation of a system of contractual relationships in the labour field, and this delayed the recognition of a 'right to work'. The existence of a free labour market is the economic prerequisite of freedom of exchange between the party demanding labour and the party supplying his working power. The legal or *de facto* recognition of free movement of labour (*liberté du travail*) and, later, of a 'right to work' is the prerequisite of the realisation, in practical terms, of this freedom of contract.

But these conditions did not come into being simultaneously. The creation of a mobile labour market did not coincide with the effective recognition of the right to work. The idea of a 'right to work' was widespread in England during the sixteenth century, stimulated by Protestant social philosophy. This was also to inspire the French physiocrat Turgot and the German Fichte in upholding the principle that man must work in order to live. But 'right to work' in this sense has a specific meaning quite different from modern usage. In practice it referred to the idea of state intervention aimed at maintaining an inflexible labour market by assigning compulsory work to the needy. A factor which reinforced this notion was the unemployment crisis which hit Europe, especially England, in the period of transition from feudalism to mercantilism. This led to a desire to put a stop to vagrancy and internal migration, and to ensure that the agricultural sector was not short of labourers. The system of regulating the poor which was to inspire the Poor Laws was born in England and was also widespread in the Netherlands and in the reformed parishes of the Rhineland. The Danish *Danske Lov* of 1683, although it used different operative techniques, was also motivated by the same desire to control the mobility of labour and to ensure the existence of a workforce that was sufficient to meet agricultural needs.

In the mercantilist economy of England labour relationships were regulated by legislation which essentially denied the idea of freedom of contract. It was the antithesis of the modern ideas of the free movement of labour and the right to work. The principle behind the legislation was, in fact, that of the 'duty to work'. The English Statute of Artificers of 1563 and the entire Poor Law system were based upon a universal obligation to work on the part of all those able to work, and upon the direction of labour into appropriate jobs. The fact that the fundamental principle behind them was identical can be explained by the absence of a mobile labour market and by the desire to create close ties between employment and the development of agriculture.

This was the era of expansion of the philosophy of aid and assistance, inspired by Turgot's Calvinist and Lutheran principles as well as by the egalitarian spirit of the French revolutionaries with their *ateliers de charité*, where work was still seen in terms of a means of helping the poor and needy and not as an ideal value worthy of a place in positive law. Work was a value contained within the community's obligation towards the needy rather than a positive guarantee of the right to a job or a worker's freedom to offer his own energies on the labour market as a free man. This was precisely the philosophy behind the 'right to work' proclaimed by the Prussian *Allgemeines Landrecht* (General Code) in 1794 and the constitution of the (Dutch) Batavian Republic in 1798.

Other obstacles also prevented the worker from being considered a person capable of producing wealth through his own abilities. Alongside state policy, essentially based on the principle of assistance and protection for the needy, we should also consider the influence of an inflexible closed mercantile economy and of a guild organisation of professions and trades based on the principle of jealous protection of its own interests by each trade.

These factors were major impediments to the birth and evolution of the legal model of the contract of employment which, under the name of *lacatio conductio*, was to develop after the Industrial Revolution in those countries whose legal systems were based on Roman law. In England the Ordinance and Statute of Labourers of 1349 and 1351 and the Statute of Artificers of 1563 with their penal restrictions on labour mobility, as well as the Poor Law system, explains why 'the law of master and servant was largely . . . the law of status' (Kahn-Freund, 1977b, p. 513) rather than that of the contract of employment.

The legal recognition of the contract of employment presupposed the idea of a society composed of 'equals' before the law. It also presupposed the affirmation of a general principle of the 'right to work' seen as the freedom to work, an idea that was only to become prevalent after the French Revolution. The most significant legislative precursor of such concepts was expressed in Turgot's edict of 1776 in France which abolished the guilds and was based on the idea of a 'guaranteeist' state ('we must ensure that our subjects may have full and entire enjoyment of their rights') which protected those who had only 'the possession of their labour and their industry' (Fohlen and Bedarida, 1962, p. 47).

The state which emerged out of the French Revolution reacted against the *ancien régime* and aimed to remove from the guild system the duty of controlling the supply of labour and aid for the needy. The new freedom to work was seen as being independent of all corporative and associative ties, but this did not in practice mean the provision of concrete opportunities to work, through the regulation of the supply and demand of labour. Although the basic right to work was defined in France in the 1793 Constitution as being 'natural', no planned opportunities for work were provided but rather each individual was left free to offer his services or labour on the labour market in a relationship that never implied a contractual link capable of 'alienating the person'.

However, the authors of the French Constitution around the middle of the nineteenth century came close to granting constitutional recognition to the right to work: the National Assembly of 1848 discussed the subject at length, after the revolutionary uprising of February. But the June 1849 version of the Constitution contained no reference to the concept of the right to work, and it was instead transformed into the right to public assistance. Nevertheless, France in 1848 represents the country most committed, at least on the constitutional level, to transforming the labour market. This was one of the bases of the Republic (preamble to the Constitution, Art. 4). The freedom of work and industry for its citizens was guaranteed (Art. 13) and positive legislation favoured the development of opportunities to work by providing for free primary education, job training and public works for those without jobs in the *départements* and the *communes* (Art. 13).

The constitutional monarchies of Europe never went this far. Either they ignored the principle completely (the Albertine Statute in Italy in 1848, the Belgian Constitution of 1831, the Constitution of the German Empire of 1871, the Prussian Constitution of 1850, that of Bavaria in 1818 and of Baden in 1818), or else they recognised the principle of the right to charity (the Dutch Constitution of 1887, Art. 92) or of the freedom to choose and practise a trade or profession (Art. 28 of the 1831 Constitution of Saxony; Art. 29 of the Constitution of Wurtemburg of 1819), or at most the right to aid (Art. 84 of the Danish Constitution of 1849). In Britain the right to work proposed by the labour movement in the Unemployment Bill of 1907 was rejected and 'the gap caused by its disappearance was filled by the new principle of compulsory social insurance in the National Insurance Act of 1911' (Hepple, 1981, p. 65). Despite the strictures of Dicey, a vigorous critic, that this Act recalled 'the *droit au travail* for the sake of which socialists died behind the barricades of June 1848' (1914, p. xxxviii), in fact it represented a shift in ideas from the right to work to the right to maintenance on the basis of mutual insurance.

The truth is that the creed of the French revolutionary constitutions, as well as that of the constitutions of the European monarchies, despite their different rhetoric, was still a fundamentally individualistic one, based on the myth of freedom and equality in a society in fact characterised by the inequalities of power and capitalist property. The right to work was to become a constitutional guarantee in Continental régimes only after the Second World War (France, 1946, preamble; Italy, 1948, Art. 4; Germany, 1949, Arts. 14–18; Denmark, 1953, Art.

75; the Netherlands, 1983, Art. 1.18), although it had appeared earlier in the Weimar Constitution (Art. 163).

The Guild System

The guild system which existed in Europe during the eighteenth century constituted, as has already mentioned, a major obstacle to the establishment of freedom to contract. But its disappearance did not automatically lead to the growth of a network of contractual relationships, nor even to the creation of an embryonic system of contracts of employment. To discover why the concept of the contract of employment was unable to develop during the era of the guilds requires a comparative analysis of the economic, political and social as well as the juridical aspects of the guild régime in the period prior to and during the French Revolution.

The guild régime produced a set of norms regulating the relations between employers and workers which, on the one hand, maintained strict control over the numbers in the trade or profession, including rules governing entry, and, on the other hand, kept a close check on the skill and capability of each newcomer, prescribing the tools and methods of work, requiring a lengthy period of training and the passing of an examination or the production of a 'masterpiece'. This was often followed by a period in which he worked for wages as a journeyman (from the French *journée*). Regulations also governed members' behaviour. The rules were established by internal statutes of individual guilds which were often dominated by the wealthiest masters, who abused their privileges and monopolised their trades in each town, limiting apprenticeships to the sons of members. This process is particularly apparent in Italy, France and Britain.

Another obstacle hindering the creation of a free labour market was the close link between the political system and the guilds. This enabled governments to have control over the labour market and to ensure 'social peace' by directing workers towards those sectors where there was a low concentration of labour in order to meet the productive needs of the home economy. For instance, in Italy the 'Universities' of Piedmont had long since abandoned any degree of autonomy from the political powers, and far from wielding local power and acting as a counterbalance, by the eighteenth century they operated as an efficient means of controlling and regulating labour. Similarly in France, statutes had to *emaner de la royauté* in order to be fully recognised, and in Germany the guilds were part of the city government. The guild statutes were in fact under the direct control of the city magistrates, and ultimately therefore of the monarchy which, with the compliance of the most powerful guilds—the French Corps Marchands, the Italian Arti Maggiori and the English livery companies—helped to ensure social peace in their respective countries. In England the Statute of Artificers of 1563 extended and supported guild regulation. The seven years' apprenticeship already enforced by many guilds was made universal and statutory.

Under the guild system of the *ancien régime* in France the origin of the relationship may be found in the manifest free will of both *compagnon* (journeyman) and *maître* (master) and therefore in contract, but such contracts were governed by the rules dictated by the guilds and by the public authorities, whose aims were strict control over the supply and mobility of labour. For example, in France, penal sanctions such as fines and imprisonment were enforced against the *compagnon* for breach of contract if the terms of the contract had not yet expired, while 'maximum wages and, more rarely, minimum wages were fixed by police order' (Durand and Jaussaud, 1947, p. 45).

Apprenticeship in the Guild System

The monopolistic logic behind the guild system thus dictated the type of vocational training which was provided in the form of a strictly disciplined apprenticeship. 'The organisation of apprenticeship is conceived above all in the interest of the guild' (Durand and Jussaud, p. 50), and thus was essentially a status relationship. This is one of the reasons for the failure of the notion of the contract of employment to develop. Under the guild system the identification of a contractually binding relationship would have meant recognising freedom of contract and with it social mobility. The resultant creation of a class of wage-earners could have undermined the foundations of the guild system and political institutions.

In late-eighteenth-century Germany, Italy and France, the guild statutes laid down rigid rules: the written contract that was drawn up was deposited in the guild archives, while the master's obligations included not only giving professional training but also the wider duty of protection. Apart from swearing obedience and allegiance and agreeing to receive no income for his services, the apprentice had to pay his master a fee. This kind of contract cannot be classified as a hiring of services, and even less as a form of subordinate employment. It was closer to the relationship of family subordination based on status found in the predominantly feudal type of cottage industries, with a low level of investment. When the economic structure began to change, so did the structure of the relationship.

Apprenticeship was one of the first problems which had to be faced by countries undergoing an industrial revolution. The new machines required unskilled labour, particularly the supple hands of young persons. Formal training was unnecessary. At the same time craftsmen were needed to build and repair machines, so apprenticeship continued, but in a new form in which the employer was a factory owner and the apprentice, after his training, a skilled (craft) factory worker. In Britain, to an extent not matched in the Continental countries, the craft trade unions inherited the legacy of the guilds, by controlling recruitment and standards of apprentices so as to protect skilled workers. The attempts made by groups of workers to enforce the apprenticeship clauses of the Elizabethan Statute of Artificers, which had largely fallen into disuse, were generally unsuccessful. In 1814 these clauses were repealed by Parliament despite the strong opposition of trade unions and some of the masters of small craft shops. The Apprentices Act of 1814 swept away the old compulsory system. Instead of living without wages under the strict control of the master, the apprentice could live at home, was sometimes paid in lieu of board and lodging, and had his obligations defined by contract. The *laissez-faire* principle was not so successful in Continental Europe. In France the legislation under which the guilds administered their trades was abolished by the National Assembly in 1791, but the reaction to free admission to trades was unfavourable and legislation regulating apprenticeship was reintroduced in 1803 and greatly strengthened by the law of 4 March 1851, which was modified before the end of the century. Similar tendencies can be found in Denmark (1881–89), Germany (1897) and Italy (law on the *probiviri* of 1893; but above all in the 1902 parliamentary bill on the contract of employment). In Germany the law of 1897 provided that the contract be deposited with the guild under the restored neo-corporative system. This underlined the renewed control of the labour market by the monarchy in support of small industry and their common interest in having competent workers.

Despite this reassertion of state regulation, however, a common characteristic of legislation was the relaxation of rules created by the guild system in order to control the workforce. The first obstacle to fall was the temporal tie of the master–apprentice relationship. Its maximum duration was either established by law (three or four years in Germany, five in Denmark) or else entrusted to local customs and practices. The French law of 1803 provided for dissolution of the contract and the payment of damages to apprentices who had been kept for periods longer than those stipulated. The written form prevailed almost everywhere.

Thus there was a change in contractual obligations which revealed the new protective rationale behind the laws. We see this in France, where legislation on the causes of termination of the contract was more comprehensive than that of the civil code. If the apprentice became ill, his employer was held responsible for payment of medical expenses (e.g. Denmark), while, according to French law, an apprentice could not be used to carry out family duties. The apprentice was seen as distinct from a domestic servant and closer to an industrial worker. At the same time, the apprentice was regarded as a feature of small industries. Under the re-created neo-corporative system in Germany in 1897 (see Ch. 6, below) apprenticeship was not compulsory for large-scale industry, while its position was consolidated in small-scale industry. In Italy the 1902 parliamentary bill on the contract of employment considered the apprentice as a worker operating within the industrial sector—which was predominantly small and medium scale—with the right to receive training in exchange for a fee, while French legislation described the type of contract in relation to small-scale industry. In the Netherlands, the Apprenticeship Act of 1919 laid down basic requirements for apprenticeship contracts and promoted their conclusion by subsidising them.

Legislation provided detailed regulation, but it did not specify the actual form the contract of apprenticeship should take. The fact that such legislation applied only to the industrial sector was the result of decisions made by the legislators in order to support the development of the manufacturing industries, but there was no reference to the type or category of contract under which such a relationship was to be classified. This example denotes an institutional unwillingness to define the relationship since it cannot be compared to any other type of contract. If the apprentice was obliged to pay a fee in exchange for his training, then it was an example of *locatio*; if the master was obliged to give him lodgings, then it was *bail à loyer*; if he had to feed him, it was a contract of sale. But if we approach the question from the point of view of size of industry, then it would appear to be easier to give a definition. It was in this way that the situation was clarified at the beginning of the twentieth century: it was a contract of employment if it occurred in large-scale industry, and *locatio* in small-scale industry. In Italy (in view of the fact that the law on the *probiviri* of 1893 and the law on industrial accidents of 1898 defined the apprentice as a worker) the dilemma was simply resolved by deciding on the *causa negotii* (basis of the transaction): Was it a mixed contract or *locatio*? In the English common law, however, the contract of apprenticeship remained distinct from the contract of service, with special obligations on the master to train and maintain the apprentice, but the apprentice could not enforce these obligations unless the contract was in written form. The distinction between large and small industries was not adopted in Britain.

PENAL LAW AND THE NEW SOCIAL ORDER

The Work-Book[1] and Penal Sanctions

After the fall of the guild régime the survival of old institutions can be explained if we take a look at the characteristics of labour law within the post-revolutionary framework during the initial industrialisation process. Alongside the growth of labour relationships regulated by the will of the contracting parties, public law (predominantly penal law) continued to play an important role.

The extension of freedom of contract is a process that was not infrequently interrupted by the desire of new political régimes to ensure a sufficient degree of stability in order to protect their own interests. Restrictions on the mobility of labour by public authorities, penal sanctions for breach of contract and prohibitions on the right to combine are some of the features of a policy that is characteristic of societies in the process of industrialisation. This is to be explained not so much by 'changes in ideas' but more by the 'great growth of the factory system' (Atiyah, 1979, p. 523). It became necessary to include in the 'social contract' between the state and the rising middle classes of industry and commerce, legislation that regulated the supply and demand for labour, vocational training and apprenticeships. One expression of this policy was the legislation which appeared in all European states—with the exception of Britain—regarding the *livret d'ouvrier* (work-book). This was an excellent way of defending the aims of political self-protection of the liberal régimes and giving indirect legislative support to free trade.

Some traces of this form of control over the labour market can be found as far back as the mid-eighteenth century: in 1764 in Italy there were rulings which made it compulsory for a worker to possess a *benservito* (reference or testimonial). In France, by 1749, legislation 'tended, by various means, to tie the worker to his *atelier*' (Levasseur, 1903, p. 509). Workers were obliged to stay with their masters until they had received 'written leave or permission' showing that they 'had fulfilled all obligations' (Pic, 1903, p. 842). Similarly, in the case of

1. An example of a work-book will be found in Appendix IV p. 367, below.

maltreatment a worker's mobility was conditioned by the need to have written permission authorised by the *juge de police* of the city. But the *livret*, in the proper sense of the word, did not come into being in France until the *Lettres Patentes* of 1781, which fulfilled two functions: external control of the relationship by the police and internal control as a kind of guarantee of a worker's loyalty.

Significantly, the French law of 12 April 1803 and the decree of 9 April 1803, promulgated under the Napoleonic Consulship, opened the new era with the reinforcement rather than the rejection of the work-book as a means of controlling the labour market and preventing conflicts; it also tightened the continued veto of the right to associate and in general responded to the needs of a consolidated industrial bourgeoisie. These provisions constituted a model for at least three countries: Belgium and the Netherlands—annexed to France in 1795 and 1810, respectively—and Italy. But we should also not forget the Prussian legislation of 1810, 1846 and 1854, which, together with the Danish *Tyendeloven* of 1854, all followed the same pattern. In the latter case the law was confined to domestic servants and agricultural labourers, reflecting Denmark's late industrialisation.

The work-book meant restrictions on the worker's freedom of contract, especially on termination of the contract since, in some cases, the worker was obliged to continue working until he had paid back all the advance wages paid to him by his employer. The same logic lay behind the Belgian imperial decrees of 3 October 1810 and 6 November 1813, which required enrolment in special registers for hired domestic servants, including their change of masters, and imposed the use of the *livret*, so placing servants of this class completely under the will of their masters. The master could refuse to release the domestic servant until he had finished his work or paid back his debts. But the police-like nature of the *livret* comes out clearly in the rules (law of 1803, Art. 3) which prevented a worker from finding a job unless his *livret* had previously been authorised by the mayor and the place where he intended to find employment had been indicated.

The overall importance of the *livret* did not diminish as Europe entered the second half of the nineteenth century, because the penal characteristics of the laws remained, giving a unique and exceptional character to the general principles of law as they affected contractual relationships in the field of employment. Thus the French laws of 14 May 1851 and 22 June 1854—the expression of the Napoleonic monarchy and of the first phase of the authoritarian Empire—on the one hand, did away with the right of the master to keep a worker's *livret* until the latter had fulfilled his obligations of work, but, on the other hand, there was no change in the nature of this instrument of police investigation (decree of 30 April 1865 following the 1854 law) or in the continued existence of elements of public law, with its provision of penalties such as fines and imprisonment for both worker and employer for failure to comply with this legislation.

In Prussian law, the work-book constituted 'the only case in which the public authorities took note of the fulfilment of contracts of private law' (Menger, 1894, p. 125). The basic principle behind it was one of 'manifest lack of trust' in the subordinate worker (Pic, 1903, p. 88), to the extent that legislation tended in some cases to evaluate the work-book as certification of credits owed by the worker. The work-book was never completely abolished, but its social function was transformed; for example, in the French law of 1890 it became a means of protecting minors under eighteen years of age and, in German legislation, it became a means of defining the concept of worker.

But this new type of legislation was part of a change in the legal framework resulting from the technique of codification in all European countries, with the exception of Britain, where, in any case, the work-book in its Continental form was unknown. The codes set out general principles of law, and the new legislation on work-books was a specific derogation from those principles.

However, the work-book system remained intact for most of the nineteenth century. It was abrogated in Germany by the Reich Trade Act of 1869 and under the law of 17 July 1878 it was required only for minors under 21 years; in Italy it was revised in a consolidation Act on police legislation (Art. 130); in Belgium it was no longer compulsory under the law of 10 July 1883; in France compulsion was removed by the law of 2 July 1890, while in the northern provinces of the Netherlands the work-book system fell into disuse soon after 1815 and was never reintroduced. The work-book was transformed in these countries into something more specifically relevant to the internal workings of the contractual relationship, as mere certification of activities previously carried out, indicating the period and the type of work. In France, the worker even had the right to claim compensation for damages if the master refused to comply.

Britain did not experience the work-book régime (although British colonial administrators used and expanded similar pass laws in possessions such as the Cape Colony, ceded by Continental powers). However, in Britain, as in the Continental countries apart from the Netherlands, penal sanctions against servants were a feature of the law until the late nineteenth century. A British statute of 1823 provided the basis for most of the mid-nineteenth-century prosecutions of manual workers for offences such as desertion, neglect of duties or 'any other misconduct or misdemeanour'. If convicted, the servant could be imprisoned with hard labour for up to three months, his wages abated and his services discharged. On the other hand, an employer who broke a contract of service was liable only to be sued for damages or payment of the agreed sum. The employer sued for breach of contract could give evidence on his own behalf, while the servant, prosecuted in a criminal court (before Justices of the Peace, many of whom were employers or landowners), could not testify in his own defence. The sentence of imprisonment was no discharge of the debt, so the servant could be imprisoned over and again for the same breach of contract. The Master and Servant laws were an important weapon against strikes: 'it was a recognised tactic of the employers, particularly in dealing with smaller strikes, to cause all the strikers to be arrested for breach of contract and then to confront them with the alternatives of returning to work on the employer's terms or suffering up to three months' imprisonment' (Bagwell, 1974, p. 30, and see Ch. 5, below). Between 1858 and 1875 an average of 10,000 prosecutions of workmen for breach of contract took place in England and Wales (Simon, 1954, p. 160). The agitation against these laws came from the trade unions and led for the first time to a national meeting of trade unions to deal with the reform of labour legislation. A bill, sponsored by the unions, failed to become law, but in 1866 a parliamentary select committee was appointed to investigate the matter, and in 1867 an Act was passed which removed the worst features of the old law. The sanction of imprisonment for 'aggravated misconduct' remained, and there was a spate of prosecutions against increasingly militant trade unionists. In 1875, however, Disraeli's Conservative government, anxious to maintain the support of the newly enfranchised urban male working class, repealed the penal sanctions in respect of breach of contract. All that remained, in the Conspiracy and Protection of Property Act 1875, was a criminal sanction for wilfully and maliciously breaking a contract of service knowing or having reasonable cause to believe the consequences would be to cause injury to person or property—a provision never used in practice.

Breach of Contract and Private Law

By the end of the nineteenth century the system of penal sanctions for breach of employment contracts had disappeared in all European countries. It was replaced by a system of compensation or damages so bringing breach of employment contracts within the general framework of law governing private contracting parties.

The Dutch Civil Code of 1838, the Employers and Workmen Act

1875 in Britain, the Italian Civil Code of 1865, the German law of 17 July 1878, the French law of 27 December 1890 and the Belgian law of 10 March 1900 exemplify the new sphere in which the employment relationship now operated. Penal sanctions were removed and what was left was the private law remedy of compensation or damages, in some cases accompanied by detailed indications where termination was permitted without prior notice (German law of 1878; Belgian law of 1900). The change was determined by political factors and by economic choices; thus the repeal of the penal Master and Servant laws in Britain by the Conspiracy and Protection of Property Act of 1875 was a product of the extension of the parliamentary franchise to a significant section of urban working-class men by the Representation of the People Act of 1867. Behind the French law of 1890 we see the spirit of the Third Republic, with the rise to power of the Radical Party and the Socialist Party's entry into Parliament, while the Belgian law of 10 March 1900 followed a period of acute social conflict concerning the extension of the parliamentary franchise and which ended with the foundation of the Belgian Labour Party. The German law of 17 July 1878 was the product of similar circumstances, as was the Danish *Tyendeloven*, which as early as 1854 abolished penal sanctions with regard to the master–servant relationship, restricting itself to pecuniary sanctions for breach of contract. This was only shortly after the new constitution of 1849 which extended the parliamentary franchise, albeit with certain exceptions, to the male population. The exceptions to this general picture—in Germany, for instance, corporal punishment for domestic servants was not abolished until 1896—can be explained by the continued existence of pre-capitalist remnants in the master–servant relationship. These remnants were of particular importance in three specific relationships—domestic service, agricultural labour and public employment—which we must now examine.

SOME PRE-INDUSTRIAL REMNANTS

Domestic Servants

The domestic servant was not defined in the French Code, nor in those of the Netherlands, Belgium and Italy, but the principles of *locatio* were applied to them. The need for legislative norms for domestic workers arose because of the specific characteristics of their employment relationships: direct dependency on the head of the house, paternalism, subordination (even on a personal level) and requirements of loyalty and trustworthiness. This explains why the employment relationship was initially governed by family law, in both civil law and common law systems. The *de facto* recognition of the supremacy of the head of the household over the person of the domestic servant had for a long time identified his servile status, and Art. 18 of the Declaration of the Rights of Man of 24 June 1793 aimed at overcoming this.

The Italian Code of 1865, silent on this matter, was criticised because the relationship appeared to be left to local customs and the conscience of the head of the household. Legal and social inequality remained until the end of the nineteenth century in Germany. The *Gesindeordnungen* of German states (8 November 1810 in Prussia and 10 January 1835 in Saxony) reflected the medieval principle that domestic servants, although classified as workers integrated within the family of their employer, were still menial retainers or attendants. Germany was a society fettered by the remnants of feudalism longer than anywhere else. The Reich Trade Act of the North German Confederation, adopted in May 1869, had allowed freedom of association but excluded domestic servants, sailors and public servants from this freedom (see Ch. 5, below).

The inclusion of domestic workers in the category of *locatio* of *domestiques et ouvriers* in the French Civil Code and the fixing of a temporal limit on their obligations to work meant that a domestic servant could leave the master without the latter's consent, and without being subject to the laws against vagrancy. However, the equality apparently established by this Code was only formal. In France and in Italy, a domestic servant was not allowed to make use of testimonials nor was he allowed to swear an oath in legal proceedings. Even after these exceptions to the general law were removed, in France by the law of 2 July 1868 and in Italy by the 1865 Civil Code, the burden of proof upon the domestic servant was higher than that on the master. As already noted, similar inequality of treatment in legal proceedings existed in Britain for many classes of servant until at least 1867.

There were few references to domestic servants in the codes, apart from Germany and Denmark (Art. 1628 of the Italian Civil Code; Art. 1789 of the French Civil Code; Arts. 1637–9 of the Dutch Civil Code). This was because the Napoleonic Codes were concerned with principles rather than specific contractual models. Such models as did exist reinforced the ideology of freedom of the commodity goods market. A labour market in which the domestic servant was deprived of the opportunity to determine his own working conditions did not fit well with those models.

Moreover, any developments in social legislation almost completely ignored the category of domestic servants. In those countries where industrialisation was growing apace, domestic servants were of secondary importance. In Britain the Employers and Workmen Act of 1875, which formally recognised the equality of the contracting parties, applied to manual workers but, like other protective legislation (e.g. the Truck Acts), excluded domestic and menial servants. The Factories Acts were concerned only with industry, at first cotton textiles, and there was never general protective legislation for domestic servants in Britain. Similarly, in France they were not included in the law on the limitation of working hours and on weekly rest days; in Belgium the law of 1900 on the contract of employment excluded them from its range of application; in the Netherlands they were excluded from the laws on working hours and on the protection of women and minors (but not from the law on the contract of employment of 1907). Moreover, in Italy neither the law on the *probiviri* of 1893, nor the one on industrial accidents of 17 March 1898, nor subsequent legislation of 26 September 1903 and 31 January 1904 referred to domestic servants who were thus excluded from their application.

The truth is that the attention of legislators was concentrated on the factory system, which had generated a new social stratification among workers. In the domestic sphere in the civil law countries the old *locatio conductio* had to be applied, although it was meaningful only in the case of higher servants who, linked by a tie of subordination, could 'render services to the person employing them, but were not at their service' (Vita Levi, 1876, p. xliv). In Britain the judges were reluctant, even under the guise of contract, to interfere with the patriarchal authority of the master within his own household. Only one piece of legislation—the Apprentices and Servants Act 1851—protected domestic servants from the worst forms of ill-treatment.

Agricultural Labourers

In the agricultural sector in Europe protective legislation for subordinate agricultural workers was very late in developing. It first appeared around the beginning of the twentieth century, and even later in some countries. One obstacle was the survival of customs and practices rooted in the *ancien régime* and handed down in the form of archaic contractual relationships typical of countries whose economies were predominantly agricultural, such as Italy, France, Belgium, the Netherlands and Denmark. Even in the mid-ninteenth century, in France and Belgium, the status of the agricultural labourer as a free man had been only partially realised.

Progress was hindered by the continued existence of the system of payments in kind and the exclusion of agricultural workers from protective legislation, such as the Belgian law of 1887 and the Italian parliamentary bill of 1893.

Economic circumstances conditioned the form of legislation, which tended towards the protection of the national economy rather than improving the position of the subordinate agricultural worker. In almost all cases legislation took the form of control over the labour market by measures setting up forms of compulsory labour. The oldest example is the English Ordinance and Statute of Labourers of 1349 and 1351 which, in order to cope with the problems of acute labour shortage following the Black Death, set up a system for establishing maximum wage rates enforced under heavy penalties and also restricted the movement of labour. Other legislation followed, and by the time of the Statute of Artificers of 1563 there was in effect a national system of direction of labour, with priority being given to agriculture, based upon a legal obligation to work. The minimum period of employment was one year.

The landowning classes hoped to preserve the social order from change by using penal sanctions. This was the logic that led to the provisions in the *Danske Lov* of 1683 with penal sanctions for vagrancy, and its attempt to retain sufficient labour for agriculture by fixing a legal minimum (not less than six months) for the duration of the employment relationship, by instituting compulsory labour and by imposing severe punishments for failure to comply. Another example is the Italian law of Tuscany of 2 August 1785, which determined the period and terms of notice in contracts for share-croppers and regulated the relations between outgoing and incoming share-croppers. The public authorities were concerned with the stability of the labour force and its numbers. The police-state régime in agriculture was mostly in the hands of big landowners in Germany until as late as 1925. Revolutionary France did not undergo the English experience of the enclosure system. In place of the clergy or the nobility the bourgeoisie took over the position of *rentier* while the rent system and management of farm land remained generally unchanged. So legal relationships were untouched by the new ideology of freedom of contract, or by protective legislation.

Changes in the social scene were much more rapid than they were in the field of legislation. The growth in population as a result of the Industrial Revolution led to a significant increase in the number of persons on the labour market. The number of agricultural jobs did not increase by the same proportion, and non-agricultural jobs did not grow at a sufficient rate in the agricultural countries to absorb the excess workforce. Alongside those workers who owned enough land to ensure their livelihood and who were bound by so-called associative ties to their landlord, a labour market had now been created made up of workers with holdings too small for them to be able to make a living and who were employed directly by a landowner. Social subordination considerably limited their freedom of contract. These special employer–worker relationships were given a place in European codification: we find *agistment* or *bail à cheptel* (lease of livestock) in its various forms in Article 1800 of the French Civil Code and Article 1665 of the Italian Civil Code; *metayage*, a share-cropping system under which the farmer pays rent in kind (from Art. 1647 onwards of the Italian Civil Code); and the leasing of farm land (Art. 1614 of the Italian Civil Code). These categories did not come under the specific heading of *locatio conductio operarum* but under the generic heading of *locatio*, even though the Italian Code of 1865, in order to emphasise the economic nature of the exchange, placed *metayage* under the heading of *locatio*, but on its own, distinct from both *locatio conductio rerum* and *locatio conductio operarum*. Meanwhile, in France the law of 1889 left it unclear as to whether *metayage* was considered a variety of *locatio* or a contract of partnership.

These embryonic employment relations in agriculture did not receive sufficient stimuli to be able to add another piece to the mosaic of the autonomous contract of employment. Legislation merely restricted itself to an attempt to give stability to the relationship by regulating certain essential features such as working hours and wages. The German law of 1919 was concerned with working hours, wages and dismissals, while the Belgian law of 1900 on the contract of employment applied also to agricultural workers. In France the *Code Rural* of 1889 (Art. 15) provided that the duration of agricultural employment was to be based on custom, while the law of 18 January 1929 protected apprenticeship, wages and accidents at the place of work. The Italian law of 1907 on rice-field workers prohibited minors of 14 years or under from working and limited working to 9 or 10 hours a day, as well as prohibiting the employer from making any deductions from a worker's wages.

However, most of this legislation came late, at a time when the process of the creation of an agricultural proletariat was already well under way, and reflects the sluggishness of legislators in dealing with the problems of agricultural labour. These attitudes were probably an outcome of the conception that the employment relationship in agriculture was of a special nature, based on residual elements of trust and subordination between master and worker, and in any case it was considered to be of secondary importance compared with the contractual model being developed in industry. The reintegration of these workers into unified legislation only occurred at a late stage in the industrialisation process. The Dutch law of 1907, the Belgian law of 1900 on the contract of employment and the Italian parliamentary bills of 1902 and 1908 all included them within their sphere of application. But this was also due to the fact that by then agricultural workers were becoming unionised. In this respect careful distinctions must be made. With the exception of Italy, where this developed at the end of the nineteenth century, collective bargaining in agriculture in the period before the First World War occurred only in a few cases, and even then agricultural workers lacked sufficient strength to be able to exert a permanent influence on conditions of employment. This was the case in Britain, where despite the early growth of agricultural workers' unions, the lack of effective bargaining prompted the establishment of a system of minimum wage-fixing by tripartite committees from 1924. Some collective bargaining on a local level existed in the Netherlands by 1908 and in Germany by 1912.

Public Servants

In many respects the public service in all countries is regulated by a type of labour law that is distinct from that operating in the private sector. The legal development of the German *Beamte*, the French *fonctionnaire* or the British Crown servant, lies largely outside the sphere of the contract of employment.

The reasons which prevented, at least until the beginning of the twentieth century, the identification of the relationship between public employee and state with that of the private sector are to be found in the political and institutional history of the European states and in their respective forms of government before and after the French Revolution. The effect of the Revolution was to end aristocratic society, but without abolishing the aristocratic social hierarchy; indeed, in France the *noblesse de charge*, created by Napoleon, was joined to the old aristocracy in order to form the class of most highly trusted officials. The same happened in Italy.

We may take as our dividing line the beginning of the twentieth century, since it was only then that many European states started to consider seriously the problem of public employment by comparison with contracts of employment in the private sector.

Depersonalisation and Neutrality

In the absolutist monarchical states it was the Crown that conferred title upon state officials who were not paid a salary but received benefits of a personal and hereditary nature, a relationship which may be characterised by the Weberian 'ideal type' of 'traditional power' (Weber, 1950, pp. 256, 338). This finds its expression in the Prussian *Beamte* of 1794 and the much earlier holder of an office granted by the English Crown. The office was in the nature of a freehold, which the holder had the right to sell. Another example was in feudal Italy where a personal tie bound the official as *fidelis* to his overlord.

The second phase in this historical process could be described as an attempt at the depersonalisation of the duty of loyalty which coincided with changes in the institutional form of the state. In the constitutional monarchies the nomination of a state official started to be considered in terms of a particular career. This change in relationship was the result of two factors. One was the need to have a class of officials linked to the state, rather than the monarch, by a secure and stable relationship. The other factor was the supremacy of the new constitutional charters. The French Constitution of 1795 had already begun to dismantle feudal privileges. The constitutions that emerged out of the revolutionary uprisings of the mid-nineteenth century abolished the rights of the nobility in relation to the presentation or nomination of persons to public office. These constitutions also established certain key principles; for example, while the head of state (on constitutional advice) was recognised as having the power of nomination for all state offices, all citizens could be admitted to civil or military offices.

The third phase was that of the complete depersonalisation of public office and the political neutralisation of the bureaucratic machine. This was the point of transition, as Weber pointed out, from 'traditional power' to 'legal power'. This is the 'ideal type' that we can identify in the neutral *Beamte* in the German Weimar Republic (1919), and in the Danish *embedsmaend* of the same period, in the French *fonctionnaire* of 1909, in the Belgian and Dutch *ambtenaar* of 1900 and in the Italian public servant of 1908.

This process occurred earlier in Britain. Public officials in medieval times were simply members of the King's household. The Crown could grant an office in the same way as it could grant land. The grant conferred an estate in the office and its profits, protected by the King's courts. Public offices were included in the class of freeholds that could be bought and sold, and might be for a person and his heirs, or for life, or for a term of years, or during the King's pleasure only. This power to create offices was singled out by the revolutionaries of the seventeenth century as one of the 'intolerable grievances' of the people (Hepple and O'Higgins, 1971, p. 88). As part of the constitutional settlement of 1689, which secured the supremacy of Parliament, those holding any office of profit under the Crown were excluded from membership of Parliament. Although the feudal link with the Crown was retained in form, ultimate power over public officials now rested with Parliament. In the seventeenth and eighteenth centuries public offices could still be bought and sold and these offices were often granted as a reward for political services. The expansion of the British Empire, particularly in India, made it necessary to replace the corrupt old system with a meritocratic civil service, and after 1870 a competitive examination was introduced for entry into the civil service. However, the historical origins of the relationship of the Crown and its servants meant that this relationship could never be fully integrated within the framework of the emergent contract of service.

In Germany Nazism, and in Italy Fascism, put a halt to the trend of depersonalisation. To use Weberian terms, 'legal power' once again became, or tried to become, 'traditional power', founded on the 'free will of the overlord'. The bureaucratic machine took on new recruits in an 'extrapatrimonial' way among individuals linked on the basis of 'personal relations of trust' (Weber, 1954, p. 256), even though the process was formalised by legislation. Both these historical experiences coincided with the period in which public bureaucratic power and the bureaucracy of the leader-party were closely intertwined. In Germany the infiltration of the Nazi Party into the public administration was realised by the law of 1933, which expelled all non-Aryans, by the indoctrination of staff and by the Party's monopolisation over the appointment of all new staff. This was the idea of the party-state which bound the public employee by an 'ethical relationship'. The principles contained in the Italian decrees of 17 December 1932 and 3 June 1938 (no. 827), making membership of the Fascist Party a prerequisite for public employment are to be found in the German law on *Beamte* of 26 January 1937, which stated that 'the entire conduct of the *Beamte* has to be determined by the fact that the Nazi Party as the bearer of the German idea of state is indissolubly connected with the people' (para. 3).

The Legal Definition of Public Service

As far as the legal framework regulating the relationship between public employee and the state is concerned, we should perhaps speak of two separate phases. In the first we see a 'depersonalisation' of the relationship as a result of the separation of executive and legislative power. In this phase the existence of a career as a reflection of the bureaucratic organisation of the services of the state, the growing number of administrative bodies, the manning of such bodies and the existence of a staff which did not directly participate in acts in which the powers of the state were manifest, characterise a relationship of special private law based on the old model of *locatio conductio operarum*. This was the situation in Belgium up to 1932 and, similarly, in Italy in the post-unification period, where careers were divided into various groupings or grades. The norms on equal pay and the limitations regarding the creation of new posts were dictated by the need to control the workings of the administration. But behind this pattern in the public employment relationship there was an element which, in some cases, made the contractual category of *locatio* a legal fiction. This was the presence of ethical and juridical considerations—'the special relationship of power', as it was called in Germany. Thus we cannot speak of a contract of employment when termination of employment could be brought about in accordance with special legal rules; for example, Crown servants in Britain were said to be liable to dismissal at will and, according to one school of thought, could not claim arrears of wages or pensions. Similarly, in Denmark violation of the duties of office on the part of a public servant was treated not as a case of breach of contract but as making one liable to disciplinary prosecution.

In the second phase the nature of the relationship was debated in detail in legal theory and case law. This was the result of a combination of factors that were partly intellectual: in Italy an office was considered as a juridical good (thus allowing the holder to resort to the protection of the courts), partly the result of trade union action (as public employment became unionised) and partly of a normative nature (comprehensive legislation on the contract of private sector employment influenced the situation of public employment). The debate in France was a reflection of the uncertain situation created by the exclusion from protective legislation of those public officers working in similar conditions to those employed in the private sector. In Britain the Crown was not bound by most statutes protecting employees, and the position of Crown servants under common law was a matter for debate. However, the Italian judges of the Council of State created the jurisprudential precedents necessary in order to establish the basis of the law of 1908, the first unitary source of legislation regarding the public employment relationship, recognising that *locatio conductio operarum* could not explain or justify the public employment relationship. In 1909 the French Conseil d'Etat accepted the idea of the contract of public duty for state officials, different from *locatio*. During the decade 1920–30 the Dutch High Court affirmed the principle that the relationship was based not on a contract but was regulated by public law, and thus, according to the law of 1929, the norms regarding the contract of private employment were no longer applicable. German case law and theory oscillated between those who considered public employment as coming under labour law, since the latter applied to 'human activity', and those who rejected the idea and saw the relationship as appertaining to public law and as being characterised in any case by the ethical duty of loyalty.

However, a new factor emerged which was to help close the factual gap between private and public labour law. This was the process of trade unionisation, which through social pressure and collective bargaining achieved comparability between public employees and those in the private sector. For example, in Britain the existence of negotiated disciplinary procedures generally made it unnecessary to decide whether or not Crown servants could be dismissed at will. However, this did not clear up the underlying problem of the nature of the public employment relationship.

LOCATIO CONDUCTIO AND THE CONTRACT OF SERVICE

From Status to Contract

Thus far we have examined the removal of obstacles to the development of a 'free' labour market: the guild system, state direction of labour, and police or penal laws. We have also noted the continued importance of pre-capitalist legal forms in certain traditional relationships: domestic service, agricultural labour and public service. We can now turn to the development of the central legal concept to emerge from the process of industrialisation, the contract of employment. It was this concept which by the beginning of the twentieth century had been applied to the vast majority of employer–worker relationships.

No branch of legal discipline could demonstrate better the truth of Maine's statement (1861, Ch. 9) that the movement of progressive societies has been one from status to contract. But at the same time this did not mean that the individual worker had control over deciding the content of the contract. The individual worker, released from the spider's web of police regulation on the Continent and the Master and Servant laws in Britain, was now subject to the employer's power to regulate his working life under the guise of contract.

The idea of the contract of employment did not fit easily with a social system based on the concept of status. In this situation the employment relationship was regulated by the law of things. This did not mean that some 'free' contracts of employment could not be found alongside forced employment relationships, but they were not a 'typical expression of the system of employment' (Sinzheimer, 1928, p. 218). At best they were governed by family law, as in the case of employment relationships in Germany for journeymen, domestic servants and miners. But these alone were insufficient to form the basis of a complete system of employment relationships out of which a fully fledged labour law could be built. Similarly, in England Blackstone's conception of the contract of service was, at the end of the eighteenth century, still rooted in the law of persons and family relationships, well behind the economic and social development of a wage-earning proletariat all around him.

It is to the codifications of the early nineteenth century, in particular the French Code of 1804, that we must turn for an expression of a new form of society. The idea of the employer–worker relationship as one of an exchange between free and equal contracting parties was linked to the political and economic phenomena of the previous decades, in particular the French Revolution. The previous legislation of the *ancien régime* had been characterised by differentiations on the basis of social class. The new type of society was based on the formal equality of citizens of a community founded on the 'social contract' or common will, not regulated by intermediary bodies but capable of the widest possible expression of freedom of choice. In terms of legal relations, these principles were translated into the freedom of economic initiative (freedom of trade) and freedom of contract, which became articles of faith. The freedom of the parties was affirmed in the *Loi le Chapelier*[2] (Arts. 2 and 4; see Ch. 5, below), while in the civil codes the principle of a contract between the parties ruled supreme (Art. 1134 of the French Civil Code and Art. 1123 of the Italian Civil Code). Contract was the only legal device that could give effect to the formal freedom and equality of the parties ('qui dit contractuel dit juste') and at the same time make it possible for the liberal bourgeoisie to plan and oversee the accumulation of capital.

But what is the nature of the employment relationship within the framework of the contract? Above all, what is the relation between *locatio*, as laid down in all the nineteenth-century codes and in the contract of service developed by the judges in Britain, and the real employer–worker relationship existing in industrial society?

2. The text will be found in Appendix IV, p. 376, below.

The Evolution of the *Locatio Conductio* Model in the Civil Law Systems

Essentially, three factors brought about the evolution of the category of *locatio*, the importance of which was noted in the Introduction. Primarily, there was the desire of the legislators to abolish all traces of the feudal system and prevent the possible rebirth of the guilds. Secondly, there was the wish to affirm the supremacy of individual free will seen as freedom from all ties. Finally, there was the aim of emphasising the value of freedom of contract seen as the freedom of choice of the contracting party in contrast to the system of status. This was reflected in the provisions which precluded the creation of legal relations in perpetuity. Article 1780 of the French Civil Code in fact laid down that an employee could be engaged only for a limited period or to perform a specific task ('on ne peut engager ses services qu'a terme ou pour une entreprise determinée'). Similar wording is contained in Article 1628 of the Italian Civil Code of 1865 and in Article 1637 of the Dutch Civil Code. Paragraph 624 of the German BGB stated that 'If the service relationship is stipulated for the life of a person or for more than five years it can, after the five years have expired, be terminated by the person under obligation. The term of notice required is six months'. Earlier references are to be found in Paragraph 40 of the *Gesindeordnung* of 8 November 1810 and in Paragraph 7 of the edict of 14 September 1811, which forbade *locatio* of agricultural work for a period exceeding twelve years. The value of this principle lay in its force as a deterrent against the *usages anciennes* that were typical of the burdensome servile conditions of the worker. By establishing a time limit to the use that could be made of a worker the principle of duration became an important characteristic of the contractual tie. This type of legislation was useful in an economy that needed a more mobile labour force, and at the same time it reflected the liberal belief that wages should be protected from increases in the cost of living by preventing the situation in which a worker was bound to a certain wage for an excessive length of time.

By way of contrast, although in Britain forms of compulsory labour had persisted until as late as the end of the eighteenth century (e.g. in the coal mines in Scotland), there was never a prohibition on life-long or indefinite duration contracts. In agriculture there was a legal presumption of an annual hiring, but by the mid-nineteenth century it had become the practice of the judges to allow contracts in the newer industries to be terminated upon 'reasonable' notice, and what was reasonable depended on the usages of the trade, which could be as short as one hour; in several trades the hirings were casual, sometimes from day to day, so that no question of notice arose.

The definition of the employment relationship as *locatio conductio operarum* in the civil law countries implied the depersonalisation of the relationship since the content of the contract lay not in the person but in the working power of the worker who places his labour on the labour market, just like the owner of a commodity, having a price that varies in accordance with its exchange value. This is possible because the 'equality' of the parties is a reflection of the equality between the commodities exchanged. This process ran parallel with the liberalisation and mobilisation of land and was all part of the logic behind the Napoleonic Code which favoured the landowning middle classes. A similar ideology lay behind the Italian Codes prior to unification, the Danish *Tyendeloven* and the Dutch and Belgian Codes. Labour power was thus regarded as a commodity that could be exchanged just like money and land, while the wages given in exchange were regulated by the law of supply and demand which governed the prices of all commercial transactions.

As regards a general definition within the framework of the codes, it is clear why the codes attached little importance to the type of services rendered by the worker. Everything was in fact absorbed within the model of *locatio*, which was considered as one of the special contracts of civil law, along with sale and *locatio conductio rerum*, and any difficulties in interpretation were resolved by applying the norms of Book 3 Title 3, 'On Contracts and Conventional Obligations in General'. The decisive importance given to the category of *locatio* resulted from theoretical ideals, such as the interpretations provided by Pothier and Domat. There were also economic reasons, such as the flexibility which allowed the stronger party to determine the use to which he put the worker's services. This becomes evident if we look at the structure of the contract of *locatio conductio operarum* in the law of obligations. This category was linked by Pothier and Domat to *locatio conductio rerum*, the only difference concerning the obligation of the *conductor operis* (the worker). These two types of *locatio* were considered as being on the same level, their similarity lying in the fact that both have a *res* (thing) as the central feature of the contract. *Insula aedifacanda* (building contracts) or *operae* (jobs of work) are not considered as separate categories; indeed, they are objectivised by the fact that labour power can be distinguished from the person who actually lends his services. But there is a terminological difference: the *locator* (worker) is always the person who gives something to be used while the *conductor* (purchaser) is the one who makes payment in exchange. Work is the subject matter of the obligation of the *locator operarum* since, within the framework of social and economic relations, it is a commodity which the owner can freely decide to hire out in exchange for a money payment. He is the absolute owner, just as he is the owner of a commodity. The identification of labour power as a commodity that can be exchanged—which came about under the influence of the doctrines of the French physiocrats and Adam Smith—was such that Pothier himself affirmed that this type of contract 'has several analogies with that of sale'.

The French Code, like those of Italy, Belgium, Luxembourg and the Netherlands created three main kinds of *locatio* of services (*operae*) and jobs of work: the *locatio* of *gens de travail* (servants), who commit themselves to the services of someone else; the *locatio* of *voituriers* (carriers); and the *locatio* of *entrepreneurs* of services *par suite de devis ou marches* (Art. 1779 of the French Civil Code; Art. 1627 of the Italian Civil Code of 1865; and Art. 1779 of the Belgian and Luxembourg Civil Codes). The first of these groups, according to the logic of the Code, refers to those domestic servants and industrial workers included in the heading of Section 1 of Chapter 3, Articles 1780–1, of the French Code, while the second refers to all those not included in the first because they are involved in transport (*voiturier*) and the third refers to those who must carry out a definite task (*entrepreneur*) and who are paid for so doing.

It was therefore impossible to distinguish between different types of self-employed and employed labour as was done in England between the contract for services and the contract of service. The civil law codes handed down the unitary framework of *locatio conductio operarum* that Pothier and Domat had made their own. According to them, three basic elements were necessary: a piece of work to be done, a price and the consent of the parties to the contract (French Civil Code, Art. 1710). One distinction did emerge, however, between *locatio conductio operis* and *locatio conductio operarum* over the question of liability for failure to fulfil obligations and the imputation of risk. To this extent there is a parallel with the English distinction between a 'servant' and an 'independent contractor'.

The feature which distinguished the English common law from Continental civil law was the absence in the former of a sharp difference between an obligation of means and one of result, a conceptual device on which the difference between *locatio conductio operis* and *locatio conductio operarum* took shape. It would appear, in fact, that in the Napoleonic Codes, as well as the German BGB of 1900, a distinction emerged according to whether the good promised was considered as an activity in itself and productive of something useful or as the result produced by work. We find this both in the French and Italian Civil Codes (Arts. 1779 and 1627, respectively) and in Paragraphs 611 and 631 of the

German BGB, which did away with the framework of *locatio* by destroying its unitary nature and regulating, according to *jus dispositivum, dienstvertrag* (*locatio conductio operarum*) and *werkvertrag* (*locatio conductio operis*). The contract of service present in the Prussian *Allgemeines Landrecht* of 1794 was an attempt to make a distinction with respect to *locatio*, but while it was one of the first forms of an autonomous legal definition of the employment relationship as a contract of service to be contained within a code of law, it nevertheless came under the more general heading of obligations. It was subject to the rules of contracts with mutual obligations and was grouped along with commission contracts and contracts of guarantee. It attempted to release the contract of employment from the tradition of Roman law (from Para. 869 onwards, Part 1, Heading 2) but brought it back within the field of customary law.

The German Code of 1896, which came near to providing a unitary notion of the contract of employment (Paras. 611–30), once again defined contract of exchange under the heading of 'single obligatory relations' but, again, along with sale, *locatio* and rent. Germany accepted the *locatio conductio* model, like the other codes, but it added, under the influence of the leader of the German historical law school, von Gierke, the idea of social protection, especially in case of illness and incapacity. It was the revival of the principle of the domestic relationship that the master was obliged to care about the servant whose work was not to be considered as a commodity. The employment relationship was thus considered as an authoritative relationship of civil law, a category which included the relationship of parents *vis-à-vis* their children.

The persistent undervaluation of the employment relationship which was a common denominator of the French, Belgian, Dutch, Luxembourg, Italian and German Codes, as well as the Danish *Tyendeloven*, was probably dictated by the same reasoning. The social world that formed the background to such codes was that of an economy still predominantly based on cottage industries and on family-run businesses. But if the sluggishness in creating a suitable legislative framework in which to define the employment relationship was caused on the Continent by the relative slowness in the industrialisation process, we are forced to ask why the notion was so slow in evolving in England, the most industrially advanced country.

The Contract of Service in England

Although Pothier's *Traité des obligations* was translated into English in 1806, his unitary theory of contract had no direct influence on the common law. Instead the English writers, notably Blackstone, and judges continued to regard the master–servant relationship as falling within the sphere of the law of persons.

One reason for this was the historical legacy of the Ordinance and Statute of Labourers of 1349 and 1351, and the Statute of Artificers of 1563. The former had regulated the wages and mobility of labourers in specific employments, namely 'agricultural labourers, servants and artisans'. The courts interpreted these statutes as not applying to those who were under no obligation to 'serve' such as chaplains, knights and 'gentlemen'. The 1563 Statute was limited to 'servants in husbandry'. Later statutes regulating employment also adopted this categorised approach of dealing with specific types of status, rather than a general category of a contract of service. As pointed out in the introduction to this chapter, it was only when the Master and Servant laws had to be applied to the new industrial employments in the mid-nineteenth century that a general concept evolved by judicial interpretation.

The criterion laid down by the courts was that in order to be under such a contract the servant had to render 'exclusive service' to his master, with the result that a servant who rendered services to a number of persons was not the servant of any of them! However, the interpretations were inconsistent because some servants were held to be within the scope of the penal Master and Servant laws, but outside the protection of the Truck Acts. It was, in fact, in connection with problems of poor relief (whether a worker had acquired a 'settlement' so as to make a local authority responsible for his upkeep) that the new conception of a contract of service emerged. The courts held that the essential criterion was that the servant should be under the power and coercion of the master during the whole time and that the master had a 'residual right to demand service at any time of the day or night' (Napier, 1975, p. 120). Although this was later modified and the notion of exclusive service disappeared, the criterion of control or subordination became the legal basis of the contract of service. The concept developed without distinction between manual and non-manual employees. It was only after 1950 that the emphasis on control came to be severely criticised because of its inadequacy in dealing with modern relationships between professional workers and the managers of corporations.

Another explanation for the lack of a unitary theory of contract in Britain is the absence of the technique of codification found in Napoleonic Europe. Codes create a kind of dictionary of juridical concepts, a definition of legal terms. English common law, as well as the uncodified Scots law, developed on a case-by-case basis. The social figures of pre-industrial society inhabited the judicial mind until long after the Industrial Revolution.

This casuistic approach was compounded by the selective technique of the British Parliament when enacting protective legislation (see Ch. 2, below). Not only did legislation tend to be confined to particular industries or sectors of industry (e.g. cotton textiles) and particular premises (notably factories) but also the coverage *ratione personae* was limited to specific classes of worker. In other words, status rather than any general concept of service dominated legislation. Moreover, the very inadequacy of the contractual model meant that the courts preferred to regard the duties 'not as operating on a contract but as imposing extra-contractual obligations enforceable through criminal prosecution and through actions in tort' (Kahn-Freund, 1967, p. 641). The Truck Acts from 1831 to 1940, and the Factory Acts from 1802 to 1961 are examples of this.

Thus we are a long way from the distinction made on the Continent between *jus cogens* and *jus dispositivum*. In Britain legislation operated largely outside the sphere of contract. It is also worth noting the tension inherent in the English common law between the contract of service and the emergent freedom of workers to combine. The Master and Servant laws continued to be used to impose penal sanctions on strikers who broke their contracts of service, despite the lifting of the laws against combinations in 1824 (see Ch. 5, below). Even when the penal laws were repealed and the collective freedom to strike was recognised after 1875, employees who went on strike were not protected from dismissal or other sanctions imposed by the employer for breach of contract. The gap between the contract of service and legislation and between individual and collective labour law in Britain reflects the excessive importance which Blackstone and others attributed to status and to pre-industrial concepts of obligation in the employment relationship. The absence in Britain of any specialised judicial institution concerned with the employment relationship, such as the *conseils de prud'hommes* created in France by Napoleon in 1806 (developed into joint commissions after 1848) and copied in Belgium in 1859, or the industrial *probiviri* in Italy after 1893, probably contributed to the relatively slow evolution of the concept of the contract of service.

FREEDOM OF CONTRACT AND THE NEW CONCEPTION OF LABOUR LAW

Inequality of the Contracting Parties

The freedom of contract proclaimed by the French Revolution and projected into subsequent codifications was soon revealed as a myth. The French Civil Code was impregnated with the dogmatic individualism of late-eighteenth-century jurists and is an example of class inequality. The legislators who drew up the French Code more or less ignored the emergence of industry. Their main concern was with landed property. The social function of freedom of contract in employment relationships was to strengthen the power of property (now in the form of capital) and the circulation of goods. In other words, property became 'individualised' (Solari, 1980, p. 9) and revealed its intrinsic nature as a source of social power. The new 'freedom' did not liberate the worker from an oppressive system of employment relations.

Moreover, the internal contradictions of the codes were self-evident: while, on the one hand, *locatio conductio operarum* for life was prohibited in order to prevent a possible return to the feudal system of serfdom, on the other the codifications based on the French Civil Code reproduced the norm of Article 1781 which established that the master was to be believed on his word as regards the *quotité des gages* (amount of wages) as well as whether wages had been paid for the previous year. It was precisely this norm which showed how the legislators in France, Belgium, the Netherlands and Italy (in the Albertine Code) still adhered to the idea of work as being part of a domestic community. It was referred to in the French Code under the heading of '*Locatio* of Domestic Workers'. The contradiction lay in the legal system itself; the employment relationship came under the *locatio* model and was therefore subject to the general principles of civil law. But the only kind of derogation justified by the special nature of the relationship was not in favour of the worker but the employer (Art. 1781 of the French Civil Code; Art. 1638 of the Dutch Civil Code; Art. 1781 of the Belgian Civil Code provided that 'the master is believed on his word in matters of the amount and payment of wages'). The fact that the Italian Code which appeared some decades later was silent on this point, while elsewhere it virtually reproduced the French Code to the letter, can be explained by the influence of discussions in France, which had already begun in 1851, in favour of the abrogation of Article 1781. In fact, the law was abrogated in France in 1868 and in Belgium in 1883, but only in 1907 in the Netherlands. The reason it survived for so long was because of middle-class fears following the civil disturbances of 1848.

Not even the subsequent and more detailed codification in Germany (in force, 1 January 1900) did away with the disparities between employer and worker when it placed the employment relationship in an autonomous contractual model different from *locatio*. The change in legal definition did not redress the uneven balance of social power which existed between the parties to the contract. The employment relationship was either placed under the contract of service (Arts. 611–30, Heading 6) or under the contract for works (Arts. 631–51, Heading 7) and referred to a wide range of categories founded on the archetypal classification of debtor–creditor relations within a *Gesellschaft* (society). The idea of *Gesellschaft* disguised the factual inequality which existed between the parties and was to contribute towards the reification of the principle of authority and to 'destroying the rationality' of the contract of employment (Neumann, 1942, p. 378).

The new element characterising the nineteenth-century developments was the creation of large enterprises. The effects of the increase in scale and concentration are to be seen in the spread of joint stock companies as a legal mechanism for the employment of capital. At the same time large-scale enterprises absorbed home industries and other forms of independent work and thus spurred on the development of employment relationships based on economic dependency or subordination. The 'socialisation' of capital did not mean the socialisation of economic power but, on the contrary, the domination of management over the enterprise and its means of organisation, including labour. In this new economic and social context, freedom of contract was respected in commercial trade but existed only on a formal level so far as the employment relationship was concerned.

The Notion of Subordination

The theorists of the early nineteenth century regarded *locatio* as a relationship of equality between commodity and price. Subordination was treated as a characteristic only of the relationship of domestic servants to their masters. Pothier wrote:

> Now it can rightly be said that the domestic servants that we possess in our household are at our service even when they are ill; because during their illness they continue to be, or may continue to be defined as our servants. But this does not apply to the contract of *locatio*; because when a man hires out services to me for a year in

exchange for an agreed sum this is in the intentions of the parties to the contract, the price for the actual services that he shall carry out and not the price for the title or definition of his being my servant. [1820, p. 121]

Subordination thus referred to only a limited sphere of persons. The free professions as well as shop assistants were excluded, the latter being considered as coming under the heading of *locatio conductio operis*, and in any case subject to the regulations of the Commercial Code (e.g. Italy, Art. 579 of the 1882 Commercial Code). As we have seen in Britain in Blackstone's *Commentaries*, superior servants were distinguished from menial servants in that the latter 'are liable to serve at any time of the day or night at the master's request' (Kahn-Freund, 1977b, p. 521). This obligation 'to serve at any time' appears to have been the English version of the continuous availability of the person found in France, Belgium, the Netherlands and Italy, where it applied only to domestic servants.

But the type of subordination of the domestic servant found in the French Code was different from the one described by Pothier. In the Code it was no longer seen in terms of the availability of the person (except in the norm laid down in Art. 1781); instead it merged into the category of the contract of *locatio*. While subordination appeared as subjection to orders in the German *Gesindeordnung* of 1810 (No. 895), thus giving the impression of being ahead of its time, the law in fact referred only to a closed economy based on agriculture and the home industries run on a family basis.

The notion of subordination changed because of the expansion of large-scale industry. The characteristic feature of the contract of employment within the factory was not the type of remuneration which the employee agreed to exchange for his services (either proportional to time if the work was of a time-based nature or proportional to results in the case of piece-work). The essential criterion was dependency and control. Both the piece-worker (a 'result-based' worker, i.e. the *locator operis* or self-employed worker under the old régime) and the 'time-based' worker are dependent because they are subject to the orders, control and instructions of their employer.

The feature that stands out in this new context is the fact that they are 'employed' and bound by a contract of employment. This was the focal point of labour law around the end of the nineteenth century. The contract of employment defined in terms of dependency and control was used in order to define the sphere of influence of the French laws of 9 April 1908 on industrial accidents, of 27 March 1907 on the *conseils de prud'hommes* and of 5 April 1910 on the *retraites ouvrières et paisanes*, and of the 1904 Italian law on industrial accidents and the earlier law on the *probiviri* of 1893.

The term 'employment' indicates dependency on the orders of someone and helps to identify a class of persons linked by exactly the same interest. This is reflected in British legislation restricted to 'servants' until 1875, then to manual 'workmen' but by 1906 embracing 'all persons employed in trade or industry' at least as far as the law on strikes was concerned.

Around the end of the nineteenth century, subordination was given different shades of meaning. At times it manifested itself as subjection to 'direction, authority and control' (as in the Dutch law of 1907, Art. 1637a, and in the Belgian law of 10 March 1900 and in Art. 1 of the Italian parliamentary bill of 1902), or to orders, as in the German Code of 1896. In Germany the real point was seen as social dependence, not only because the employer had capital and was more powerful but also because in his person the many contracts with employees met. In some cases it was referred to as the 'power of alien will' or, as in Britain, the command power or the 'power of control' of the employer over the employee. Basically what was meant was the exercise of power in which there is control not only over what but also over how and when work must be done. In Britain the measure of control exercised by the employer was the chief criterion of the distinction between autonomy and subordination (see p. 60, above). In the case law of the Italian *probiviri*, on the other hand, the continuous availability of the worker over a period of time (i.e. the continuity of the juridical obligation to work) was regarded as the hallmark of subordination. The *probiviri* affirmed the principle that 'the *locator operarum* has the right to a wage for as long as he remains available to his employer, even if he does not actually work' (Bugni, 1907, p. 160). The provisional nature of the relationship, on the other hand, did not give rise to any guarantees: in a series of decisions from 1899 to 1905 the judges ruled that the newly appointed worker had no right to receive notice in the case of dismissal, nor could he claim damages for instant dismissal (see Ch. 4, below). The criterion of subordination was thus seen in the commitment to work for a relatively long period of time, thus presuming a certain stability in the contractual relationship. But the *probiviri* did not confine a definition of subordination to the principle of continuity but also included the worker's obligation to follow out instructions and the employer's power to see that they were carried out.

In practice these two conceptions of subordination—the Continental one, as reflected in Italian case law, and the English one—were simply two sides of the same coin, namely the acceptance of the power exercised by the employer. In Britain the lack of an explicit legislative definition meant that the contractual model could be constructed on the basis of the judicial technique of 'implied terms', a genuine 'disguise for the exercise of their own law-making power', by the judges (Kahn-Freund in Renner, 1949, p. 162). In fact, it was precisely the technique of implying terms that made it possible for the judges to establish the principle that 'wrongful termination of the contract of employment gives rise to an action for breach of an implied undertaking by the employer to maintain the employment relationship' (Freedland, 1976, p. 23). They recognised that the simple relationship 'is typically transformed into a continuing contract of employment by virtue of the mutual obligation of the parties to maintain the employment relationship' (p. 23). Around the mid-nineteenth century the courts began to consider the relationship as implying, within the contract of employment, the principle of 'co-operation' structured on the basis of bilateral promises.

The history of the idea of subordination does not end here. It was to evolve, as an idea linked to the corporate enterprise. This institutional approach was corrupted when it came into contact with a different cultural and political régime: the connection between 'work' and 'enterprise' was used by the Fascist dictatorships in order to strengthen the principle of authority (Art. 2086 of the Italian Civil Code) and the German *Führer prinzip*. In these régimes the employment relationship was to become permeated by the idea of trust, and work was seen as being essential in order to create a 'community of interests'. Fundamentally, there was an organically inspired vision of the relationship deriving from the romantic and medieval conception based on the loyalty of the worker and on the protection of the employer.

The Third Reich's Act on the Order of National Labour of 20 January 1934 was similar in inspiration to the Italian Charter of Labour. Both were founded on the idea of the 'interest of the firm', and the 'higher interest of national production', which was the guiding principle behind the Italian Civil Code of 1942 and the Vichy French Charter of Labour of 4 October 1941. Subordination to the authority of the enterprise was to the contract of employment what general interest, hierarchy, responsibility and social collaboration were to the new social order.

The New Conception of the Contract of Employment

The notion of equality and freedom of the parties to the relationship of subordinate employment was rejected by doctrines of various tendencies, including social Catholicism and Marxist socialism. They criticised the idea of labour as a commodity; on the contrary, they underlined the involvement of the worker as a person in the employment relationship. Labour is not a commodity to be exchanged since a person's working power cannot be separated from the person himself. This view is reflected in the Dutch law of 1907, which treated the contract of employment not as a means of placing the commodity of labour under the dependency of the enterprise but, on the contrary, as 'an agreement that is constantly and totally concerned with the person who works' (Levenbach, 1965, p. 571).

When social legislation appeared upon the scene it developed in two directions, both tending to restrict the sphere of contractual will but without compelling the parties to incorporate certain terms in the individual contract of employment. Just as the liberation of the employment relationship from the law of persons and of things came about in the civil law countries under the liberal régime through the construction of the *locatio* model, the transition from the liberal period to that of expanding industrialisation led to a rejection of *locatio* and to the creation of an autonomous model of the contract of employment. But on the Continent social legislation evolved outside and beyond the category of the contract of employment, which, when it finally received the attention of the legislator, had already been preceded by a relatively large amount of social legislation, thus reducing its importance as a source of the employment relationship. The dominant legal opinion of the Bismarckian period was that this type of legislation which also included the law on safety, was public law and therefore not directly enforceable through the contract of employment, which belonged to private law. When after the First World War the new discipline of labour law was recognised, and when the legal scene was altered by the establishment of works councils, Nipperdey categorised the law on safety (see Ch. 2, below) as part of private law, while social insurance remained outside as a separate branch of public law. Thus over a lengthy period social legislation on the Continent, like that of Britain, was considered as protection for the weaker party to the contract. However, in Britain no distinction was made between *jus cogens* and *jus dispositivum*. The notion of free will, or the 'intention of the parties', continued to be used by the courts in Britain as the 'principal conceptual instrument' for the resolution of concrete cases (Kahn-Freund, 1967, p. 641).

By the early twentieth century, the Continental countries had witnessed the establishment of the contract of employment as an autonomous legal category distinct from other types of contract, such as subcontracting, self-employment and mandate. Even the German Civil Code of 1896 'broke the conceptual unity of *locatio* handed down from Roman law . . . and created separate categories . . . which were quite distinct from each other' (Stolfi, 1934, p. 268). *Dienstvertrag* (exchange of services) came under a different heading (Book 4, Heading 4, Paras. 611–30) from *Werkvertrag* (subcontracting, Heading 7, Paras 631–51), and a similar distinction was made by the Italian and French laws on obligations and contracts (Arts. 507–16). The new idea which pervaded the codes was the understanding of employment as a broader social phenomenon which included persons economically dependent on others, such as workers from home and the self-employed.

Once the employment relationship had freed itself from *locatio*, it also tended to free itself from the dominion of the general principles of law and constituted an original branch of law regulating this social phenomenon. The various laws on the contract of employment that appeared over roughly the same period of time are evidence of this: the Italian parliamentary bill of 1902, the law regulating rice-workers of 1907 and the law on the contract of private employment of 1924; the German Code of 1896 (with attempts at renewal in 1913, 1919 and 1938), the Belgian law of 10 March 1900 and the law of 7 August 1922 on the contract of private employment; the Luxembourg laws of 31 October 1919 and 7 June 1937 on the contract of private employment; the Dutch law of 13 July 1907, which was integrated into the Civil Code (amended by the law of 17 December 1953); the French *Code du Travail* of 1910 (Book 1, Heading 2); the report of the Danish commission of 1910 and the Danish laws of 6 May 1921 and 13 April 1938.

In some countries the attempt to confer autonomy on the employment relationship was pursued by trying to include the whole of labour law within the framework of a specialised codification, thus removing the worker from the clutches of the general principles of private law. In France it led to the creation in 1901 of the Commission for the Codification of Working-Class Legislation, while in Italy exponents of juridical or academic socialism spoke in favour of the creation of codes of 'social private law'. But comprehensive codes were not realised.

The sphere of application of protective legislation was generally limited. In some cases it was restricted to industrial workers, or to workers in agriculture, or industrial enterprises, or to manual workers only. In other legislation, however, few distinctions were made between the various types of workers; for example, the Dutch law of 1907, the French parliamentary bill of 2 July 1906 and the German Civil Code. In Britain, too, we find the 'workman' defined in the Trade Disputes Act 1906 (one of the foundations of the freedom to strike) so as to include both manual and non-manual workers, a remarkable reversal from the trend of ninteenth-century legislation (e.g. the Truck Acts) which had been almost exclusively applied to manual workers. In Britain the progressive extension of the sphere of application of legislation can probably be explained by the growing importance of white-collar employment. While this factor was also present in other countries, the coverage there of all employed workers was strongly influenced by the desire to place all categories within the framework of a unified body of special labour legislation. It was also influenced by the consideration that a labour law restricted to industrial workers alone was bound to be seen as class-based. Paradoxically, it was precisely the belief that white-collar workers, as part of the intellectual class, were an *instrumentum regni* of the ruling establishment, that more favourable terms were generally applied to them in law and practice. The continuing distinction between the employment and trade union rights of different categories of employee had a particularly important impact on the development of trade union organisation and social policy in the German Weimar Republic. The promise in the Weimar Constitution of a unified labour law was regarded as a revolutionary commitment.

Legislation was essentially aimed at industry and sometimes agriculture, with the inclusion of the commercial sector but the exclusion of merchant shipping and other seafaring occupations. In some instances the extension of legislation came about by judicial interpretation; for example, in Britain, where the Trade Disputes Act 1906 (protecting the freedom to strike) referred to 'workmen' in 'trade' and 'industry' and this was interpreted so as to include virtually all forms of activity, including local government. (The specialised British law meaning of 'trade' as any activity, must be distinguished from the common expression which refers to commercial or distributive 'trades'.) In the civil law countries, the relationship between shopkeeper and shop assistant came under the norms of the Commercial Code among the 'acts of trade' of an enterprise. However, the laws in Belgium and the Netherlands, and also the Italian parliamentary bill of 1902, referred to work in trade activities as well, thus depriving their respective codes of commerce of the capacity to enforce regulations regarding the employment relationship of workers in trading enterprises. But the fact that this tendency occurred relatively late was due to the awareness of jurists in countries like Italy and France that the role of the worker in the commercial sector 'although constituting a genuine case of *locatio conductio operarum*, is permeated to some extent by the idea of mandate' (Pic, 1903, p. 632). It is certainly no coincidence that the Italian Commercial Code of 1882 regulated the relationship between worker and commercial enterprise under Heading 12 (Commercial Mandate and Commission, Art. 379) in line with a trend that Pic in 1903 already considered to be general in the legislation of that period 'in the sense of the extension of the field of application of the factory laws to include small-scale industry and from small-scale industry to commerce in the true sense of the word' (Pic, 1903, p. 552). This was a trend that was later to gain in strength through *ad hoc* legislation on the contract of employment in Italy (1924) and Belgium (1922). In this way most subordinate employment relationships came to be covered by labour law, especially a little later on in the twentieth century.

CONCLUSIONS

The history of the idea of the 'contract of employment' can be seen as the history of a false aspiration. The promise of freedom of contract in the employment relationship was never fully achieved. The freedom of the worker in the labour market was impeded by his social condition—that is, by his status.

This statement holds true for both civil law and common law countries. The transition from status to contract has been more apparent than real. It would be more accurate to say that in the various phases of the economic, social and political evolution of the employment relationship the worker's status has changed.

This evolution can be divided into three main phases. In the first, which covers the period from the guild era to the French Revolution, the worker's condition was that of a member of a closed society and a closed economy, substantially immobile in a world of economic exchange in which the mobility of money contrasted with the immobility of labour, reflecting the needs of a mainly agricultural economy. The employment relationship was a domestic one which bound the journeyman to his master, mediated by the rules of the guilds which were controlled by public authorities and belonged more to the law of persons than to that of obligations in general and contracts in particular.

The second phase opens with the French Revolution and closes with the end of the nineteenth century; it is an era of major social, political and economic transformations in which the employment relationship developed in the shadow of the formal freedoms proclaimed by the post-revolutionary constitutions but within social structures that were still to some extent tied to the old society. The guilds were formally abolished around the end of the eighteenth century and the start of the nineteenth century. In fact they did not disappear until later. This tardy development prevented the worker from being considered by the state as having the right to work or as being a mature and independent party to a private contract. The position of the worker was that of a party who was weak as an individual but who could be dangerous as part of a collective entity. The employment relationship was regulated, on the one hand, by public and criminal law (see, for example, the penal laws concerning breach of the employment contract and those regulating the workbook), and, on the other, by the directives of the employer.

Moreover, all the social groups taken into consideration by post-revolutionary laws were largely characterised by status. In civil law countries *locatio* for domestic servants was merely a façade hiding social disparity, while the common law countries excluded them from the realm of protective legislation. Agricultural labourers were still conditioned by the hierarchical and patrimonial structure of land-ownership and by the reluctance of the drafters of legal codes to define their relationships as ones of employment. The position of the officials was heavily conditioned by the obligation of loyalty towards the state, the most extreme form of this type of obligation being that of the *Beamte* in Germany.

Thus the contract of *locatio*, which marked the newly reached contractual 'freedom' of those social groups which had emerged from the disorder of the revolutionary period, was the child of classical liberalism. It was the chrysallis out of which no butterfly of equality was to appear but rather, once again, a status. This time the status was that of the worker as an individual in a relatively mobile labour market, governed by police regulations and dominated by the power of the master. The influence of the law of persons, which sometimes absorbed the employment relationship, hindered the development of an autonomous notion of a contract of employment. This reflected the disparity in the social power of the parties.

By the time the third phase began, *locatio* was already an old, outdated notion in industrial society. The employment relationship had evolved more rapidly than the legislative notion to be found in the *Code Napoléon* which was adopted in many countries. By the start of the twentieth century the industrialisation process was well advanced, but it was only then that the contract of employment was generally considered legally as being an autonomous entity. The contract of employment is the legal façade hiding the underlying social relationship; it is, however, a part, though not the most important part, of labour law which developed with social legislation and collective bargaining. It soon became common knowledge that major industrial concentration required a form of employment which had to be subordinate (i.e. completely subject to the power of the employer) in order to favour the accumulation of capital. Subordination was to be the new social model characterising the new status of the worker whose freedom of contract is in effect only a formality. Before stipulating a contract, his status is that of being unemployed. After he has stipulated, his status is that of the weaker party to the contract. Social legislation (see Ch. 2, below) imposes certain obligations on the employer, but such legislation derives from the desire by the state to protect rather than to promote the worker to the position of a contracting party bargaining on equal terms. Collective bargaining (see Ch. 5, below) has been slow in moving forward and is a variable depending on the social strength of the trade unions. It is only with the democratisation of work, the co-operative participation of the individual in control of his job, that the notion of status can disappear and the worker can be considered a contractually mature figure in the true sense of the term. But that is another story.

2

Laissez-faire and State Protection of Workers

Thilo Ramm

LAISSEZ-FAIRE AND STATE PROTECTION

Laissez-faire, laissez-aller, le monde va lui-même. These words can be taken as the programme of economic liberalism. They meant non-intervention of the state in economic relations, and they included the abolition of all regulations set by the guilds. The freedom to work was the freedom of the individual to do as he wished limited only by the will of other individuals who had the same aim to gain the maximum profit. Individual interests were to be balanced by competition, and it was expected that competition would reduce the prices to the lowest level. Competition was self-regulation on the market, but it was even more than this. Where it exists, David Ricardo said, there is no conflict between the interests of individuals and the common interest (Ricardo, 1817, Ch. 7). The German Wilhelm von Humboldt (who, in turn, influenced the British J. S. Mill) stated as the first principle:

> The state shall abstain from all care for the positive welfare of citizens and shall take no step further than is necessary to give them security against themselves and against external enemies. [1792, Ch. 3]

The restriction of state purposes to justice and to defence, or as Jeremy Bentham succinctly put it, 'to protect life and property', was later ironically characterised by Ferdinand Lassalle (1825–64), the founder of the German Social-Democratic Party, as *Nachtwächterstaat* (the night watchman state).

This was not an entirely accurate characterisation of liberal ideology, as developed by Adam Smith. In his famous book, *An Inquiry into the Nature and the Causes of the Wealth of Nations* (1776, Book 4, Ch. 9) he not only listed the costs of transport and foreign trade as falling on the state but also those for education. The lower estates should not be left without elementary instruction because their literacy would be beneficial to the state. Education and liberalism belonged together in the movement of enlightment, but elementary instruction also established a rough-and-ready equality which was the necessary presupposition of competition. Thus equality was more than personal freedom or purely legal equality. It included as well support for education, and if not for all then at least for orphans, as well as care for persons who were chronically sick and therefore unable to earn their livelihood.

Liberalism meant not only freedom of trade and industry, which included freedom to work or the freedom of movement, principally implied freedom of contract, and contract was now seen as a part of the law separated from religion and morally neutral. But freedom of contract at least required the capacity to make a contract, and here the problem was posed of the capacity of the child, the authority of the father and the control of the state. Another question concerned the legal position of women, married or unmarried, and their legal status *vis à vis* that of men. Children and women were the first two subjects of state intervention in the relations between employer and employee.

It should not be overlooked that the protection of children began as an amendment to the Poor Law in Britain. But the Poor Law as a whole had traditionally been concerned with intervention in economic relations in extreme situations, when *laissez-faire* did not function for individuals because they were incapable of earning their livelihood or had become orphans. The Poor Law gained increased importance when the Church lost its property, at first in the Protestant countries, then generally by secularisation introduced by the French Revolution of 1789, and thus was deprived of the means to finance its social functions, especially the relief of the poor. The local communities which had previously been only a secondary pillar of support of the poor had to assume the main burden. This was hard to bear because among the poor there were believed to be many people who preferred idleness to work. So the Poor Law was changed, under the symbol of individual self-responsibility, by the new philosophy of the middle class that labour is the basis of social life. (This aspect of state intervention is discussed in Chs. 3 and 4, below.)

The idea of liberalism and individualism emerged in a society in which traditional social forces still existed, certainly in different degrees of strength in the various countries. There were religious and humanitarian beliefs, and political changes were determined by the struggles between monarchy and middle class, between bourgeoisie and aristocracy, between bourgeoisie and the emerging proletariat, between town and countryside, between conservatives and liberals. These struggles shaped the history of the protection of workers, which was itself only one piece in the political chess game. Although the players were similar in all countries, the game was different because of their different skills and power, and this makes comparisons extremely difficult. One way of simplifying the comparative history of workers' protection is to focus on the ideology and practice of *laissez-faire*, which had to overcome the tradition of state regulation in economic relations as it had been practised nearly everywhere during the eighteenth century and also in many countries during the first half of the nineteenth century.

Liberalism and individualism involved a new understanding of society. They abandoned the ideas of solidarity and mutual help which had led to the suppression of the individual during the Middle Ages and justified the government of the absolute monarch. The liberal society built upon individual egoism, and even selfishness, which was counter-balanced and controlled by other individuals. General competition would maximise social welfare. The history of the realisation of liberalism is the description of the failure of this belief. It belongs to the darkest pages of human history. With it the history of state protection of labour begins, and this is the first chapter of the history of modern labour law. It determined the development of West European labour law during the nineteenth and the early twentieth centuries.

The meaning of state 'protection' of labour has undergone a considerable and significant change. In his survey (more than 300 pages in length) published in 1924, Stephen Bauer defined the purpose of labour protection very widely: 'to ensure the most favourable development of the personality of the worker' (Bauer, 1924, p. 401). 'Protection' included, according to him, the maintenance and reproduction of bodily and mental faculties, a minimum standard of economic security and the creation of a special labour administration giving legal and social guarantees for the execution of labour protection and opening up opportunities for economic and social advancement by the working class. Bauer's definition epitomises the development of labour law during the ninteenth century. It was the phase of the emancipation of labour from repression.

Nevertheless, Bauer's definition is too broad and requires at least two substantial corrections. The first is to acknowledge the separation of labour law and social security as two different legal disciplines, although social security is also based upon the idea of state protection of labour (see Ch. 3, below). The second correction is to exclude collective labour law because it is based upon the idea of self-help. Certainly in a formal sense the suppression of collective organisations and industrial action may be regarded as state intervention. But *laissez-faire* cannot be considered abstractly, as some kind of manifestation of anarchism. It is an historically determined phenomenon which required not only a break from the guilds and mercantilism of the Middle Ages but also the suppression of the powerful organisation of journeymen and the emerging trade unions of the new class of workers. *Laissez-faire* was a social order based upon individual actions in the market. The anti-coalition laws helped to establish this order and to reproduce individualistic liberalism (see Ch. 5, below).

When the law of social security and the law on collective labour relations are removed from Bauer's broad definition there remains the statutory law on working conditions with its special means of supervision.

The subjects of state protection of labour in the narrow sense are nearly the same in all nations: the protection of children, of women, protection against special abuses of the power of the employer like the truck system or dangers from industrial machinery, protection of home workers, and so on, and ultimately the general protection of the adult worker. Theoretically, we may distinguish three different topics: the protection of special workers, the regulation of work in specific industries and the protection of all workers. But in historical reality these were mixed. The protection of certain groups of workers like children and women commenced in certain industries and gradually developed into the idea that these groups must be protected in all industries because of their special need of protection. The protection of all workers also began in specific industries and in respect of what were regarded as special dangers, such as unfenced machinery.

The history of state protection of labour is both national and international. Both aspects have always been mixed together. But during the period up to the First World War national legal developments prevailed. Discussion of the international developments will therefore be postponed to Chapter 7, below, in the context of the internationalisation of labour law. The period of national protective labour legislation stood for about seventy years in the shadow of the British legislation. Britain has served as the model for the other nations. Britain had been the first country of the Industrial Revolution, it had practised free trade on a world scale (based on its colonies) and it was the leading proponent of the economic theory of liberalism.

For this reason British protective labour legislation will be described here as an 'ideal type'. The early defeat (in the seventeenth century) of the power of the absolute king made the struggle between bourgeoisie and workers clearer than in France in the two Empires and in Germany, where the monarch remained powerful in the constitutional system. France had nominally enacted workers' protection in the form of state supervision of unwholesome industries (1790, 1810, 1815, 1825 and 1826) by the introduction of the celebration of Sunday after the return of the Bourbon dynasty (1814) and by the prohibition of the work of children under ten years in the mines in 1813. Prussia exercised a form of control by licensing dangerous industrial establishments. But the aim of protecting workers was most strikingly developed in Britain, and this was achieved despite the principles of the freedom to dispose of one's own capital or labour and despite the rise of the freedom of contract. This was quite different from Germany, where the protection of the workers was part of the attempt by the paternalist state to solve the social problem by the reorganisation of the guild system and of labour protection in the Reich Trade Act of 1869.

After the description of the British model, the developments in the other states will be discussed in respect of two main topics: the protection of specific groups of workers and then the protection of all the workers (as well as the enforcement of the protection). The latter discussions will also mention the developments in Britain after the First World War.

THE MODEL: BRITISH PROTECTIVE LEGISLATION UNTIL THE FIRST WORLD WAR

British protective legislation developed very slowly by a process which was not at all clear or logical but was the product of the struggle by unions and reformers inside and outside Parliament, and the resistance of powerful groups of employers and some intellectual supporters of *laissez-faire*. The legislation began in a relatively unorganised way and concentrated upon the physical and moral health of pauper children. When, in the last third of the eighteenth century, cotton manufacture became mechanised, children were regarded as the best operatives because of their small size and delicacy of touch. They were cheap labour and regular arrangements existed between master spinners and the Poor Law authorities to 'apprentice' orphans and other workhouse children.

The Jonas Hanway Act of 1767 had, as a remedy against the death of thousands of poor children, provided that those under 6 years of age were to be taken to country cottages out of London and cared for at a minimum wage. The local communities became overburdened by this obligation and therefore gave these children as 'apprentices' to the factories of Manchester and its environment. The working day in these factories was up to 15 hours long. Epidemics of fever in 1784 and 1796 led to the intervention of public officials in Manchester. In 1802 the Health and Morals of Apprentices Act, which had been preceded by the Regulation of Chimney Sweepers Act of 1788, attempted to correct the abuses of Poor Law. It covered cotton and textile factories with at least twenty workers and three apprentices, and limited the working day of pauper apprentices to 12 hours, prohibited their employment at night (after 1804) and required the employer to provide them with general and religious education, with separate sleeping rooms for each sex and with suitable clothing. Supervision was entrusted to clergymen and Justices of the Peace. The Act was ineffective because the employers ceased to rely on paupers apprenticed by the Poor Law authorities and began to employ 'free' labour, not protected by the legislation. In 1831 it was reported that these 'free' children were beginning employment at 7, 8 or 9 years of age and working 15 or 16 hours a day with only short meal interruptions. The struggle for the regulation of 'free labour' is linked with the first Factory Act of 1819, which, like the Act of 1802, was introduced into Parliament by the Tory Sir Robert Peel, the elder. But the real inspiration was Robert Owen (1771–1858). As one of the greatest and wealthiest cotton-spinning entrepreneurs of his time, he had ended the employment of children under 10 years, reduced the hours of labour of those above that age, spectacularly improved working conditions and educated the factory children in the New Lanark Mills near Glasgow, where he was partner-manager from 1800. From 1813 onwards Owen had tried to win other industrialists over to voluntary acceptance of the principles which he had practised, but he failed and therefore urged his ideas upon the ruling classes and governments of Europe and America, and even addressed a memorial to the representatives of the Holy Alliance at their meeting at Aix-la-Chapelle in 1818 (see Ch. 7, below).

Owen represents a type of industrialist who is found in all nations: the successful and benevolent entrepreneur (the 'enlightened monarch' at the industrial level) who demonstrates by his example that the present situation is not necessary, that it can be decisively improved and that the improvement is favourable even to employers themselves. He had not only a very strong personality and a belief in humanity but also a conviction in the success of education and the decisive role of environment in the formation of the human character. He was an heir of the eighteenth-century enlightenment and enlisted the help of the great pedagogues of his time, the Swiss Fellenberg, Oberlin and Pestalozzi, to whom he paid visits before he addressed his memorial to the Holy Alliance. The campaign for the protection of the working children thus became a contest between the belief in co-operation and education and the unlimited power of egoism and self-interest. It was a struggle which included an attack upon the separation of the family from society, and against uncontrolled paternal authority and power.

Due to the great international reputation and tremendous energy of Owen, a widespread discussion arose on state intervention in general and on the statutory protection of children in particular. It was a controversy in which familiar arguments were time and again rehearsed, such as whether intervention was really necessary and whether it would damage family life or undermine the authority of parents. It was feared that intervention in favour of children would simply be a first step towards reducing the working time of the adults as well. In fact adult workers in Manchester had petitioned for 12 hours' maximum working time (rests included). The reduction of working time was said to give an advantage to foreign competitors, and it was alleged that it would cause idleness and dipsomania among the children.

With hindsight, the victory of children's protection may ultimately be explained by drawing a distinction between the economic theory of *laissez-faire* and the legal freedom of contract. The child had no freedom of contract. As Mill said in 1848: 'Freedom of contract in the case of children is but another word for freedom of coercion' (Mill, 1965, p. 952). Did the father who contracted the child's services to an employer not violate his duty to educate? Thus seen, children's protection simply meant a step from the control of paternal authority, which had always been practised by the state, to the control of third parties (employers) who were jointly responsible for the abuse of paternal power and derived a benefit from it.

These arguments were not readily accepted, and the fight for the protection of children lasted a long time. The Act passed the Houses of Parliament in 1819, but with severe restrictions. It applied only to cotton-spinning mills; it put the minimum age of employment at 9 instead of 10 as had been demanded; it only limited the work for children between 9 and 16 years to 12 hours, and night-work (permitted for adults only between 9 pm and 5 am) was forbidden; above all, the paid inspectors whom Owen had wanted to enforce the Act were dropped. The employers were extremely hostile to the Act, and its administration was at the mercy of country Justices of the Peace, many of them being employers. There were minor improvements of the legislation in 1825 to 1831. It seems likely that technological changes in manufacturing methods played a far greater role in the decline of children's labour than the legislation.

Before any further major developments in regard to the length of the working day, there was a significant piece of legislation designed to ensure that workers were paid in 'current coin of the realm' (cash rather than in kind) and that they received the whole amount of wages without deductions. This was the Truck Act 1831, passed, with the support of some employers, after a strike of weavers against an employer who had practised the truck system. The Act of 1831 renewed a tradition of legislation, which went back as far as 1465 but was no longer applied by the authorities. 'Truck' comes from the French word *troq* or *troquer* and means that the workers' wages were paid totally or partially in goods, which usually meant a reduction in the amount of payment. Many employers paid by way of coupons or tokens which could be exchanged only in special shops belonging to the enterprise ('tommy shops') where workers were encouraged to buy on credit with usurious rates of interest and at exorbitant prices. The workers were in different ways deprived of the full value of their wages, and the employers who resorted to these practices were able to undercut their competitors. For this reason many of the larger employers sought to outlaw the truck system because of the unfair competition by the smaller, disreputable firms. The coincidence of the economic interests of the larger employers and the social interests of the workers, as well as the background of a legal tradition of regulating the payment of wages, may explain why the opposition against the Act was not too great. Although economists such as Joseph Hume and David Ricardo justified payment in kind on the basis of 'freedom of contract', other liberal economists like Adam Smith accepted this law which, in a sense, 'purified' the wage-labour exchange.

One important feature of the Act was its general application to all 'artificers', a term later defined to mean manual workers of all ages, apart from domestic servants. Unlike most other protective legislation in Britain, it was not confined to women, young persons and children. (There were relatively minor amendments to the Act in 1874, 1877, 1896 and 1940, and it was repealed only in 1986.)

The legislation was, however, relatively ineffective because of the problem of enforcement. The Act denied the employer any action against the worker for goods supplied to him on account of wages. Contracts to pay all or part of the wages otherwise than in current coin of the realm were void and illegal and, on summary conviction, small penalties could be imposed on the employer, and when the worker or his widow or children became the object of poor relief the overseers of the poor could recover any wages earned within the three preceding months and not paid in cash from the employer. But the worker himself who asked for the legal payment of his wage risked dismissal or receipt of a lower wage. Therefore, despite the activities of anti-truck societies, the practice of the truck system was not eliminated, especially in times of depression. Only in 1887 did Parliament confer powers of enforcement of the truck legislation on inspectors of factories and mines.

It was not the legislation but the changed economic situation, the boom years of Britain's mid-Victorian prosperity and the growth of larger-scale enterprises with reduced economic needs to resort to truck, which was mainly responsible for the demise of the truck system. By 1877 the fledgling Trades Union Congress had decided that further legislation to control truck was relatively unimportant. The Truck Amendment Act 1887 made a number of improvements such as clarifying the authorised deductions for items like food, rent and education, and the Truck Act 1896 (which applied to shop assistants as well as manual workers) limited the power to deduct for fines, damaged goods and damaged materials. But the legislation never occupied a critical place in the history of protective legislation.

The centrepiece of the struggle for protection was the movement for the 10-hour day, which received an impetus from the newly legalised trade unions after the repeal of the Combination Acts (1824 and 1825). The name of the 'National Association for the Protection of Labour' set up in 1825 signified the use made by workers of organisations not for self-help, which at that time was considered to be ineffective, but for help by the state.

The organised agitation in Britain began to make headway after 1831 when workers' groups in northern towns formed 'short-time committees'. These committees were composed of organisations of skilled operatives and tradesmen and were patronised and financed by Anglican churchmen, Tory squires (landed gentry) and Radical and Tory industrialists. They were under the leadership of men such as Richard Oastler (a Tory land agent), Michael Sadler (a Tory linen merchant), John Fielder (a cotton manufacturer) and Ashley Cooper, later Earl of Shaftesbury (a Tory inspired by religious ideals). The main aim of the committees was a ten-hour day for *all* workers, regardless of age or sex. They were disappointed with the Factory Act of 1833,[1] which extended the provisions regarding the hours of work for children but did nothing for the rest of the workers.

The 1833 Act introduced the 48-hour week for children in the textile industry. The main importance of the Act was that it established the first salaried independent factories inspectorate to enforce the legislation. This Act of 1833 became the model for European and American factory statutes. Major abuses, however, remained. In particular, industrialists let the children work not continuously during the day but

1. Extracts from the text of this Act will be found in Appendix IV, p. 368, below.

at intervals (the so-called 'relay' system) and thus avoided control, and the legislation was limited to textile factories. A Royal Commission of Inquiry into the Employment of Children and Young Persons (1841–42) revealed the terrible conditions in the mines and collieries. Frederick Engels, who came to England from Germany in 1842, used this material and his own observations to write in his book *The Condition of the Working-Class in England in 1844*:

> Children of four, five and seven years are employed. They are set to transporting the ore or coal loosened by the miner from its place to the horse-patch or the main shaft, and to opening and shutting the doors (which separate the divisions of the mine and regulate its ventilation) for the passage of workers and material. For watching the doors the smallest children are often employed, who thus pass twelve hours daily, in the dark, alone, sitting usually in damp passages without even having work enough to save them from the stupefying, brutalising tedium of doing nothing. [1892, p. 244]

For the more wearying labour of transporting coal, older children and half-grown girls were employed. The Children's Employment Commission had found that the education of these children was widely neglected; as to morality, Engels remarked that this was 'destroyed by their work itself'. Contemporary evidence shows that women were used for work which men refused to do. Women worked in water in the mines and pulled coal wagons for 12 to 14 hours a day, a situation which Lord Shaftesbury compared in the parliamentary debates with the conditions of black slaves who had been emancipated in the British Empire in 1834. The Mines Act of 1842 prohibited the work underground of women and children under 10 years of age, but according to Engels' account the Act was still largely ineffective two years later. There was no effective supervision before an Act of 1860.

So far as the textile factories were concerned, after a brief respite to test the 1833 Act in practice, and a period between 1835 and 1840 when they were overshadowed by the movement of Chartists for reform of the political system, the 'short-time committees' modified their aims to concentrate on the hours of work of adult *women*. There were several reasons for this. First, there was the tactical one that in the political conditions of the time any comprehensive legislation was considered infeasible. But both the manufacturers and the men realised that a limitation on women's hours by legislation would result in practice in a limitation of men's hours by the process of collective bargaining. Second, while there was genuine sympathy for ending exploitation of women, the men were also worried that technological changes, such as the 'self-acting' mule, were putting their own jobs at risk and putting semi-skilled or unskilled women workers into the position of competitors in the labour market. These fears were reflected in resolutions of short-time committees for the withdrawal of female labour from factories or restrictions upon their use. Thirdly, the middle-class began to perceive the plight of women as a 'social problem'. In the new type of family emerging out of the Industrial Revolution, the man was stereotyped as the breadwinner and the woman as domestic servant and childbearer. Evangelists and utilitarian reformers were concerned not only with the physical abuse of women in factories and mines but also sought to uphold the image of the woman as Christian mother and guardian of domestic life. Even the First International (1866) shared this thinking and attributed to women 'the tasks determined by nature' and saw her place as being in the family: 'these are the services which the woman may render the work which she has to perform. It is a bad thing to force others upon her'. The International demanded the prohibition of night and dangerous or unhealthy work for women. But, on the other hand, middle-class feminists and J. S. Mill, the ardent fighter for equal rights for women, opposed further protection because they expected disadvantages to their claims for full equality.

So we see in Britain, with the early growth of collective bargaining, at least four groups agitating for factory reform. There were the 'labour aristocracies' of men, such as the framework knitters and handloom weavers, whose livelihood was being destroyed by the new factory system; the pioneers of social medicine who drew attention to the dangers to the health of the whole community of the conditions in factories and mines; the clergymen and religious men; and last, but by no means least, the Tory landed gentry who were hostile to the new class of industrialists and who, in Marx's words in 1853, 'resolved to resist the middle class by exposing the cause and claims of the working men against their masters and especially rallying around the demands for the limitation of the hours of labour' (Marx and Engels, 1953, p. 368). This last statement needs to be modified to some extent, however, because there were undoubtedly some Whig landowners who opposed the reforms, while some Tory manufacturers supported them, seeing the Acts as a means of legitimating the new factory system and removing unfair competition by those manufacturers who failed to observe minimum standards.

This movement led to a series of Acts which are characterised by their partial and limited application. The first major victory of the short-time committees was the Act of 1844 in which women were equated with young persons between 13 and 18 years for all purposes. Their hours of labour were restricted to 12 hours a day plus meals, these hours to be worked between 5.30 am and 8.30 pm. The 'relay' system was made more difficult to operate by providing that the twelve-hour day began when the first protected person began to work, and protected persons could not remain in the work room during meal times. The minimum age of employment was raised from 8 to 9, and children from 9 to 13 were limited to a $6\frac{1}{2}$-hour day, with night-work prohibited. This Act also included the obligation to attend school under the control of the parents and of the employer, and provisions on health, such as painting and washing of work rooms, and on safety, requiring moving and dangerous parts of machinery to be securely fenced. These provisions show the remarkable influence of the dedicated factory inspectors who brought factory conditions to public notice and who contributed greatly to the legislative reforms. This influence also explains why their enforcement powers were considerably improved. The Act became a model of labour administration, later adopted and developed in other European countries.

After the extension of the prohibition of night-work to the calico printing industry (1845), the Act of 1847 conceded the main demand of the short-time committees by reducing the hours of women and young persons to 10 per day, up to a weekly total of not more than 58 hours. Evasion of the new law was, however, not difficult—the 10 hours could still be worked at any time between 5.30 am and 8.30 pm and the relay system was still in use for women and young persons. An Act of 1850 sought to remedy this by enacting that the hours of protected persons were to be between 6 am and 6 pm or 7 am and 7 pm Mondays to Fridays and not later than 2 pm on Saturdays. There was to be $1\frac{1}{2}$ hours for meals; this meant that for the first time the legal working day was made to coincide with the legal period of employment. Further loopholes in the relay system were closed by an Act of 1853. The lace industry was covered by an Act of 1861, and bakeries by an Act of 1863 which prohibited night-work for young persons and established health standards but left enforcement to local authorities. The Factory Acts Extension Act 1864 extended the application of the earlier legislation to some new industries and also required all factories to be kept in a clean condition and prohibited children, young persons or women from eating meals in the work rooms of textile, pottery and match factories. This was a response to the investigation of a royal commission (1863) which had investigated employment of children in trades and manufactures not already covered by law. Acts of 1867 covered all factories employing at least fifty persons and Acts of 1870 and 1871 added printworks and dyers' and bleachers' premises.

Factory law was thus detailed, complicated and not at all clear. The Act of 1864, for instance, included the pottery factories, exempted the brick and roof tiles industries, but not (as an exception to the exemption!) if the products served for decoration. Interpretation was made even more complicated when the legislature prescribed two or more sets of regulations for one factory; and the labour inspectors did not observe uniform interpretations. This was intolerable for entrepreneurs who were expected to compete on the basis of equality in the market.

It was not until 1878 that there was a general consolidating Act, based on the report of a royal commission (1875–76) which had investigated the possible consolidation, improvement and extension of the legislation. The 1878 Act repealed sixteen earlier statutes and classified factories (places using mechanical power) and workshops into six categories: textile factories, non-textile factories, workshops, workshops without children and young persons, and workshops with only male workers. The degree of protection depended on the classification of the place of work. The Act also reorganised the system of factory inspection, increasing the number of subinspectors and junior inspectors and giving them enhanced powers to enter premises by day or night, to demand records and make investigations.

The remainder of the nineteenth century saw a number of improvements while retaining the basic principles of the earlier legislation. Since 1867 a system of general medical inspection for children in factories had been in operation. The minimum age in factories was raised to 10 years in 1874, 11 in 1891, 12 in 1901, 14 in 1918 and 15 in 1944. The half-time system introduced by the Act of 1844 had made it easier for children to go to school, but the major advancement occurred with the general system of compulsory education for children aged between 5 to 13 by Acts of 1870, 1876 and 1880. The half-time system itself was abolished only in 1920. So far as women were concerned, the only significant changes after the consolidation of 1878 were associated with shift-working and associated exemption procedures. The Factory and Workshop Act 1901 reduced the working day to 10 hours in textile factories and to a 10½-hour day in non-textile factories, with a maximum working week of 55½ and 60 hours, respectively. In mines the minimum age for children was raised from 10 to 12 in 1872, to 13 in 1900 and 14 (for coal-mining) in 1911 and later to 15. One of the most important legislative successes of the miners' unions was the inclusion in the Mines Act of 1860 of a clause providing 'that where persons engaged in mining are paid by weight, the material gotten by them should be duly weighed at the pit bank, and they are empowered to appoint a person at their own charges to take account thereof'. This right to appoint a checkweigher not only met a long-standing grievance, but the person appointed became a source of local leaders for the miners' unions. The mine-owners managed to evade the provisions, for example by dismissal of the checkweigher, despite amendments to the law in 1872 and 1887, and the miners' unions were not satisfied with the requirements until an Act of 1911. Beyond mines, factories and workshops there was relatively little regulation. Shop Hours Acts since 1886 had dealt with trading hours in the retail trade but not the length of the working day. An Act of 1911 was the first to provide for a half-day free weekly, rest periods and a maximum working time of 74 hours per week for persons under 18 years old working in shops. In refreshment and coffee-houses the maximum laid down by an Act of 1913 was 65 hours per week, with 32 rest days and 26 Sundays per year. This legislation had been sponsored jointly by the shopowners and unions. It was only in the twentieth century that an extension to agricultural workers and white-collar workers took place, and then it was not unlimited.

The most striking feature of nearly all the nineteenth-century legislation was that its coverage remained limited to women, young persons and children. One facet of this, already noted, was to encourage the view that a woman's place was at home and thus to increase the industrial segregation of men and women. From a feminist viewpoint the protective legislation reflected the paternalistic attitudes of a male labour 'aristocracy'; from a trade union viewpoint, the legislation was both a means of protecting women from 'double' exploitation as housewife and worker, and a minimum basis on which the method of collective bargaining could be used to improve the conditions of all workers, men and women. The essential feature of British labour legislation (before the mid-twentieth century) was to regulate employment relations only where this could not be effectively done by collective bargaining. Kahn-Freund explained the reason for this phenomenon as being that the manual workers' unions had secured minimum standards, without the aid of legislation, before the franchise was extended to the town artisan in 1867 and to many rural workers in 1884. From the base of legislation protecting children, young persons and women in factories, workshops and mines protective legislation expanded only to those areas 'which negotiation could hardly have reached' (Kahn-Freund, 1959, p. 221). Thus the hours of work of women and young persons in factories and workshops were regulated by statute, but those of adult men (with a few exceptions) came to be regulated entirely by collective bargaining. The exceptions were in industries with special features, such as the railways where an Act of 1893 reduced hours so as to prevent accidents, or where bargaining was ineffective. The most important example was the twenty-year struggle by the Miners' Federation for an Eight-Hour Act. The miners' leaders wavered for some time between the strategy of strike action and parliamentary action to achieve this objective and finally chose the latter because of the resistance of the coal-owners and splits within the Miners' Federation on this issue. It was only in 1908 that the Mines Eight-Hours Act became law; later the working shift was reduced to 7 hours.

Another significant example of general protective legislation was the Trade Boards Act of 1909 which established machinery to set up minimum wages in trades and industries where collective bargaining was ineffective. From 1824, when the power of magistrates to set wages for weavers in Spitalfields (London) was abolished, until 1909 there was no legal control of wages by the state. The Act of 1909 did not establish a legal minimum wage, but it was a radical measure because it used tripartite boards (with union and employer interests represented, as well as a third independent element) to fix wages in a limited number of trades and industries where 'sweating' (the exploitation of the worst-off workers) was prevalent. For twenty years before the Act there had been a combination of the forces of upper class philanthropy and radical action against sweating. In 1890 a House of Lords select committee defined 'sweating' as a combination of three evils:

> a rate of wages inadequate to the necessities of the workers or disproportionate to the work done, excessive hours of labour, and the insanitary state of the houses in which the work is carried on. [cited in Bayliss, 1962, pp. 2–3]

There were three possible remedies. The first, a national minimum wage, was considered unthinkable because of the continuing dominance of *laissez-faire* ideology. Even later, in 1912, when Prime Minister Asquith, an unemotional man, is said to have wept when he was forced by a national coal strike to introduce a miners' minimum-wage bill (which in fact never became operative); wage-fixing by the state was regarded as the certain path to disaster. A second possibility was to extend the Factories Acts to home-workers. The House of Lords select committee saw this as the root of the problem and suggested such an extension. The third possibility was to limit wage-fixing to the 'sweated' trades and to give the state only a limited role. It was this third remedy which was adopted.

The actual form of wage-fixing adopted was influenced by the report of a commissioner, Ernest Aves, appointed by the Home Secretary in 1907 to investigate the Wages Boards and Industrial Conciliation and Arbitration Acts of Australia and New Zealand. Each parliamentary session since 1908, Sir Charles Dilke had introduced private bills modelled on the Boards in the State of Victoria. The essential features of these proposals were included in the Liberal government's Act of 1909. The Act left the determination of a minimum wage to representatives of employers and of trade unions and a third group of independent persons (usually academics or retired civil servants), with the state only using its power to enforce the wage after the Board had made its decision. Winston Churchill, who, as (then) a Liberal minister, introduced the bill, said its primary aim was to encourage collective bargaining. The basic constitution of the Boards remained unaltered after 1909: equal numbers of employers' and workers' representatives and an odd number of independent members. Separate wages Boards were established for each 'sweated' industry, the criterion being that the rate of wages prevailing was exceptionally low and the other circumstances of the trade were such as to render the application of the Act expedient. The Act was a characteristic of the philosophy which Kahn-Freund called 'collective' *laissez-faire* (discussed in Ch. 5, below). This philosophy went even further into the ascendancy when the Trade Boards Act 1918 made the absence of adequate collective bargaining machinery the primary criterion for the establishment of a board. By the end of 1920 about 3 million workers and 300,000 employers were covered by the Trade Boards. Seventy per cent of those whose wages were regulated in this way were women. What is significant, in the present context, is that this protective legislation applied to less than one-fifth of the total workforce.

When we turn from Britain to the other European countries we find that protective legislation there also began with special groups, but the decisive difference was that in those countries state protection was gradually extended to *all* workers, while in Britain regulatory legislation remained confined to the special groups. We now turn to these developments elsewhere in Western Europe.

PROTECTION FOR SPECIAL GROUPS OF WORKERS IN OTHER COUNTRIES

The protected groups of workers may be classified into two classes: the first according to inherent personal qualities like age, sex or disablement, the second according to the nature of the work, in particular, home-work as a special form of exploitation and, later, dangerous and unhealthy work.

Children and Young Persons

The first group to be protected without exception in the different countries was that of children. Their protection was achieved not only by factory legislation but also by the law on apprentices. During the pre-industrial period Prussia and the other German states tried to combine the maintenance of the guild system for special, sometimes narrow, sometimes larger areas of trade, with the recognition of freedom to trade. One of the reasons was to protect skilled labour and vocational training. Even after the recognition of the freedom to trade in Germany in 1869, the guilds were retained as voluntary institutions, which later received official functions in respect of the supervision of training of apprentices.

Children's protection in factories began in 1839 in Prussia, 1841 in France and 1843 in the Austrian part (at that time) of Italy. But most of the legislative work started or was renewed in the 1870s: Denmark and Italy in 1873, the Netherlands in 1874 and 1889 and Germany in 1878, Luxembourg in 1876 and Belgium in 1884 (for the mines) and in 1889. A third wave of legislation followed after the 1890s: France in 1892, Denmark in 1901, Italy in 1902, Germany in 1903 and the Netherlands in 1911.

The history of Prussian legislation on children's protection is interesting because it shows the interplay between bureaucracy and King and the industrialists who were favoured because industrialisation was seen as a solution to the social problem of this time. This history began with an amusing error by, and public exposure of, the District Governor of Dusseldorf and of the Prussian King. On the Governor's report that a Rhineian burgomaster and industrialist had established a factory school, the King expressed his satisfaction with this good example. But shortly after publication of this royal praise in the official gazette the employer was accused of employing children of 6 years of age on shift-work in his spinning mills for 13 hours, interrupted by only one hour's instruction on the day-shift and two hours' after the night-shift. Over a period of more than four years these facts were reported to the Prussian Cabinet. The Minister of Education in consultation with the Minister of Trade demanded investigation of the labour of children (1824). The facts were reported through bureaucratic channels which queried employers, school teachers and priests, but not the children or their parents. The proposals for state intervention, which the Minister of Education also had made, did not go very far.

They mostly concerned medical inspections of the factories, the abolition of evening schools and obligatory minimum instruction. The most advanced proposals were for a minimum working age of 9 years and a certificate of fitness by the local public medical officer. Most of the district governments made no proposals on maximum working time: three of them proposed working days of 6 or 7 hours for the children over 10 years of age. It was not possible to reach a consensus between the Ministers of Education and of Trade on the necessary steps. Accordingly, the Minister of Education explained in a general circular of 1827 the non-intervention of the Cabinet and ordered the regional governments to use 'forcible severity' to ensure that school was attended regularly and uninterruptedly. School attendance was to be compulsory for all children older than 5 until they had acquired the knowledge necessary for their position, according to the judgement of their priests; dispensations required the approval of the priest and the local authority.

The execution of this Order was not very efficient as a police check in Berlin at the end of 1828 displayed. Indeed, as reported, most children were not prevented from attending school by their employment; they attended inefficient Sunday schools. The head of police was censured but he declared that the parents needed the children's wages in order to finance their households: without this income many families would become the subjects of public welfare. One year later General Lieutenant von Horn reported from Silesia that the industrial areas were unable to provide their complete contingents for the *Landwehr* (the Prussian militia) and mentioned in this context that the employers used children for night-work. The King issued an Order to the two Ministers and censured this behaviour 'because it suppressed the physical formation of the tender youth and it must be feared that in industrial areas the future generation will be still weaker and more crippled than the present'. While the Minister of Education reacted promptly to the demand of the King to report and again requested a general legislative act, the Minister of Trade replied with a charge against the 'destruction of health by the overexaggerated demands of school, especially by the required efforts at home to learn old languages'; those complaints would increase daily, and the weaker and more crippled generation created by these scholastic demands would merit the same royal attention!

In 1832 the Minister of Trade asked his colleague to apply for royal permission to introduce a bill, but it took seven more years before the Cabinet issued a 'regulation on the occupation of young workers in factories'. Before this, the *Oberpräsident* (Chief President) of the Rhine Province had ordered in 1835 that no child should be employed regularly until it could be proved by testimony that it had attended regular school for 3 years; children over 12 years should be employed in the morning or afternoon only and for less than 7 hours. The *Oberpräsident* drafted a later regulation in 1839 and provided for its extension to mines and to rolling and stamp mills. The Prussian regulation (which had the force of an Act) was not as differentiated as the British legislation because it covered only one class of young persons from 9 to 16 years and allowed 10 hours' maximum daily work with a possible prolongation of one hour for four weeks at most and included within its scope all kinds of factories. Like the British legislation, it required rest periods, prohibited Sunday and holiday work. Young people had to be registered and the registers had to be submitted to police inspection and to school officers. Violations were to be punished. The obligation to attend school was not changed, and this legally required 5 hours daily, which meant, together with rest periods and working time, a $16\frac{1}{2}$-hour day.

The enforcement of the regulation was not very strict, perhaps because the industrialists were highly influential in the community council which decided upon the salary of the burgomaster, who exercised overall supervision. Reports from the district governments in 1845 did not request new measures, not even for health and morals, although they had expressly been asked about this by a circular from the Ministers of the Interior, of Finance and of Education. This circular also proposed a system of factory inspection by independent honorary men appointed by the government. Another circular from the Minister of Education, also at the beginning of 1845, suggested the establishment of local commissions consisting of the burgomaster, a priest, a doctor, the school director, an employer and 'possibly' a worker. In 1847 the Minister of the Interior (a former *Oberpräsident* of the Rhine Province) asked for control by a commission. Then the revolutionary events of 1848 led to the promulgation of an Ordinance of 1849 which provided for *Gewerberate* (industrial councils) which should supervise the employment in factories. However, this institution, consisting of representatives of industrialists, artisans and merchants, was ineffective. In 1853 a new Act provided for paid factory inspectors, 'where there is a need for them', with the authority of the local police. In the same Act the minimum working age was raised to 10 years, a year later to 11 and two years later to 12 years of age. The maximum daily working time up to the age of 14 was reduced to 7 hours, but the time for instruction was also reduced, to 3 hours. All young workers over 16 had to have a work-book which was to be kept by the employer and presented to the authority at its request. Only three district governments considered the inspectors to be necessary, and one of these retracted at the beginning of the 1860s, while one district government was, according to the judgement of the *Oberpräsident*, 'very inactive'. The reports of the third factory inspector of the Aachen district revealed that the employers ignored the statutory provisions and tried to sabotage the inspections.

In France the Children's Protection Act of 1841 had been a response to the scandals of children's ill-health and even suicide in textile centres which had occupied public opinion since 1827. The British Act of 1833 reinforced the movement for legislation, which was encouraged by Protestant pietism and Catholic sociological studies, as well as an investigation of the situation of factory workers made by order of the French Academy. The Children's Protection Act of 1841, like the legislation in Britain and Prussia, prohibited work by children under 8 years. It also provided for a maximum of 8 hours' work by children between 8 to 12 years and 12 hours for children between 12 to 16 years. Night-work was prohibited for those under 13 years. Decrees were supposed to regulate the time of school instruction for children under 12 years. Rest-periods were left to the discretion of the employer. Supervision was entrusted to special honorary commissions. The Act covered manufacturing industry, which was defined as permanent establishments using mechanical power, and those without such power employing more than twenty workers. Although improvements were made shortly before the outbreak of the February revolution of 1848, effective children's protection was enacted only in 1874 following the British model of inspection. It covered all establishments except domestic ones.

Children's protection before the First World War had generally reached the following stage. Children under 12 years were not permitted to work (Denmark, Belgium, Italy); France connected this with the proof of elementary instruction. Germany and Luxembourg did the same and, like the Netherlands, raised the age to 13 years. There is not the same clear picture as regards the regulation of working time. France, Luxembourg and Germany fixed 10 hours as the maximum for persons under 16, while the Netherlands provided for 10 hours for those under 17, and Denmark also included persons from 16 to 18 years. Italy permitted, for persons under 15 years, 8 hours' work and excluded children under 14 years from dangerous and unhealthy work, and forbade night-work for protected children. Luxembourg gave detailed protection for certain work and prohibited underground work for children under 16 years and work in establishments where explosives were produced or used.

National legislation after the end of the First World War generally followed the international standards as set by the conventions of the International Labour Conference (see Ch. 7, below). These conventions adapted the standards of the previous national legislation regarding the minimum age of employment, night-work in industrial undertakings, children's work at sea and in agriculture. This was achieved between 1919 and 1937 and supplemented and amended after the Second World War. The regulation of non-industrial employment by the ILO occurred in 1932 and 1937, and the question of medical inspections was the subject of a convention in 1946.

Some problems were of a general nature and appeared time and again. One such problem was that of domestic undertakings in which only members of the employer's family worked. These were invariably exempted, but in 1937 ILO Recommendation No. 52 expressed the aspiration of abolishing this exemption in the near future and requested Member States to make efforts to include domestic undertakings in national industrial legislation. Another question was the link between work and attendance at primary schools, apprenticeship or vocational training in undertakings which required continuous work or where work was dangerous or unhealthy. National legal instruments were to distinguish between an absolute minimum age (which the ILO fixed at 14 in 1919 and 15 in 1937) and a protected age in which exceptions could be admitted on the authorisation of the competent authority, either alone or after consultation with the employers' and workers' organisations. Exceptions were to be possible in cases of emergency.

The conventions provided that night-work was to be absolutely forbidden for persons under 16 years. Between 16 and 18 years exceptions could be made. Employment on vessels was prohibited for children under 14 years (1921), later raised to 15 (1936), but between 14 and 15 years the employment was to have the approval of the competent authority after consideration of the health and physical condition of the child and the promotion of his benefit by the work. The employment of persons under 18 years was to require a previous medical fitness certificate (1921). Trimmers and stokers under 18 years were not to be employed, unless in a port where only those were available but then they should be at least 16 years old (1921). The age for admission to agricultural employment was lower than for industry: 14 years 'save outside the hours fixed for school attendance'. The International Labour Office informed the Netherlands government, that it had been the intention to prohibit the employment only of those children who were obliged to attend school.

Conventions of 1932 and 1937 dealt with non-industrial employment filling a remaining gap which the other conventions on children had left. The definition of the line of division between these instruments was left to the competent national authorities who were to consult the principal organisations of employers and workers. The detailed conventions made distinctions in age, obligation to school attendance and the nature of work, which were not to be harmful to health and normal development. Even light work was prohibited at night which was defined for children under 14 years as a period of at least 12 consecutive hours comprising the time between 8 pm and 8 am. For older children the prescription was left to national law. Exceptions could be made in the interest of art, science or education.

Children's protection, as traditionally understood, was completed by the convention of 1946 prescribing an obligatory medical examination for persons under 18 years before the admission to work in industrial undertakings. In occupations with health risks the obligation extended to persons up to 21 years of age. Up to the age of 18 years medical supervision by repeated examinations was required. Similar standards were prescribed for non-industrial occupations.

Women

Women were the second group of workers to be specially protected. This covered, as in Britain, health, the duration of the working day and night-work and, as well, maternity protection. The prohibition of night-work for women was one of the earliest subjects of international agreements (1906; see Ch. 7, below).

In the period before the First World War the view that women should be specially protected was linked to their social and legal position. This was used and understood, as already explained when the British legislation was described, as a strong argument against the demand of women for equal treatment with men. At first the special protection was limited to young women in some Continental European countries. France protected only women under 21 years and treated them like male children between 12 and 16 years (1874). Luxembourg followed in 1876. Belgium confined the protection to the prohibition of underground work for girls under 14 years (for boys under 12 years) in 1884. Denmark only prohibited the work of women in mines and quarries (1881) and refused general protection for women because of the protests of the feminists.

The era of general women's protection began only in the 1890s, later than in Britain. In 1891 Germany prohibited night-work for women (on the same basis as for persons between 14 and 16), but allowed a working day of 11 hours instead of the 10 hours prescribed for young persons between 14 and 16 years. The lunch break could be extended for women who had family duties. The same working day was established in the Netherlands (1889) and France (1893), but the comparable group in those countries was young persons between 16 and 18. Night-work was prohibited in the Netherlands in the same Act and in France in 1892. Italy confined the working day for women above the age of 15 to 12 hours. The impetus for prohibition of night-work for women was given by the international convention of Berne in 1906, which was followed by Luxembourg (1907), Italy (1909), France (1910) and Belgium (1911) but not by Denmark, where women's protection was extremely controversial. The organised women in printing firms voted against special protection for women because they believed this would block the way to better-paid jobs, but the political social-democratic women's organisation favoured protective legislation. The Danish Act on accident prevention (1889) in fact prohibited women from cleaning machines while in motion; France prohibited the carrying of heavy loads (1909) and dangerous work (1914) by women.

Maternity protection began in Germany, as the first step of special legislation concerning working women with the prohibition on work until three weeks' after confinement (1878); this was increased to four weeks, with an additional two weeks if there was no medical certificate to prove fitness (1891). Italy (1907), France (1913) and Denmark (1913) provided for time off for nursing babies.

Women's work was the subject of several ILO conventions after the end of the First World War: on night-work in industrial undertakings which has been twice (1934 and 1948) revised and on maternity protection (1919, revised 1952), but not on the length of the working day. The achievement of the 8-hour working day for all workers solved this problem. The three conventions differ in their definition of the 'night', from 11 hours (1919), to 10 (1934) and finally to 7 hours (1948). An exemption was made for family undertakings, for *force majeure* and in respect of the treatment of raw materials which are subject to rapid deterioration. The period of maternity leave was increased to six weeks after confinement and six weeks before the probable date of confinement (1919), and these twelve weeks could be taken at the discretion of the mother but with a minimum of six weeks' prohibition on work after the date of the confinement (1952). During absence from work the mother was to be paid benefits which were sufficient for the full and healthy maintenance of herself and her child. Nursing time was to be permitted, half-an-hour twice a day during working hours.

During the first half of the twentieth century the emphasis began to shift from protective legislation to the issue of equal rights for women at work, such as equal remuneration and equal admission to jobs in the public sector. This development was interrupted by increasing unemployment after the First World War. The German Nazi government's response to this was to promote a policy of confining women to their traditional role as housewives and mothers. It was considered to be a national duty to have at least four children. At the end of the Second World War the Soviet military government authorised the German authorities of its zone to allow the employment of female workers on building and reconstruction work (1946) but seven months' later the government, on the proposal of the unions, confirmed a list of occupations and workshops in which work by women was prohibited. Thus the legacy of special protection for women persisted into the post-war era.

Disabled Persons

A third group of persons who are protected because of their personal qualities are disabled workers. This ground of protection was at first linked to the origin of the disability. Legislation at the end of the First World War, concerned with the transition from a war-time to peace-time economy, sought to promote the employment of war veterans. Germany had 250,000 demobilised soldiers with a less than 50-per-cent ability to work. Therefore an Order of 1919 on the Employment of Severely Disabled Persons made it compulsory for such persons to be given employment and also made it illegal to dismiss them. By an Act of 1923 it was made obligatory for employers in both the public and private sectors to employ a certain percentage of such workers. In 1924 this was fixed at 2 per cent. The Italian legislation was similar in many ways; a decree of 28 June 1917, which was subsequently modified on several occasions, made it obligatory for anyone employing more than ten persons to take on one war invalid for every twenty workers, as long as the invalid was capable of a minimum amount of work. Similar legislation was enacted in other countries and is an example of the exceptional use of a legal duty to contract to deal with a specific social need of a group of workers.

At the end of the Second World War the problem of reintegration of disabled persons was recognised as a general problem and became part of the ILO Recommendation (No. 71) of the Philadelphia Conference (1944) on transition from war to peace. The Recommendation went beyond the issue of war veterans by declaring that 'Disabled workers, whatever the origin of their disability, should be provided with full opportunities for rehabilitation, specialised vocational training and retraining and employment on useful work'. The development of the new legal idea can be observed best by comparing the zones in post-war Germany. In some, protective legislation continued to cover only disabled war veterans, others (like the states in the American-occupied zone) included the victims of Nazi persecution, but both of these may be considered as a special form of compensation by the state for acts within its responsibility. The new idea which was accepted in the legislation of the states of the British zone and of the Soviet zone was the coverage of all disabled persons, including congenital disability. This is an approach which had already been adopted in Britain in the Disabled Persons (Employment) Act 1944. The Act (s. 1) defined a 'disabled person' as one:

> who on account of injury, disease, or congenital deformity, is substantially handicapped in obtaining or keeping employment, or in undertaking work on his own account of a kind which apart from the injury, disease or deformity would be suited to his age, experience and qualifications.

Provision was made for the vocational training and industrial rehabilitation of such persons. Like the inter-war French, German and Italian legislation on disabled war veterans and the later Dutch law of 1947, the British Act used the technique of requiring employers to take on a quota of disabled persons (from a state-maintained register), and employers were not permitted to dismiss such persons. The quota was fixed at 3 per cent of the workforce of employers with twenty or more employees. This type of provision is more than 'protection'. It signifies the restructuring of labour markets (see Ch. 4, below).

Home-workers

Home-workers are a fourth group who were the subject of special legislation. This group presented the greatest difficulties because it would not be appropriate to include them in industrial legislation if the industrial undertaking was understood simply as the factory in which the work performance was centralised under the command of the employer. Work was done at home, in the rooms of the workers who could decide on their working time. In this sense it was not a contract of employment (see Ch. 1, above) but rather a contract to perform a certain piece of work or to produce a particular product by a self-employed entrepreneur who was given the raw material and produced a finished product which was then sold by the employer. Home-work was a pre-industrial form of production, especially in the textile sector, which utilised the advantages of the division of labour and where home-workers were equipped with machines in the course of time. Supervision by the employer was complicated and was obstructed by family ties because members of the workers' family usually shared the work. Although largely displaced by the factory system, remnants of home-work were one of the most striking forms of exploitation which continued during the period of capitalist industrialisation. It was characterised as an example of the 'sweating system' in Britain. The state in all countries hesitated about giving the necessary protection, although the terrible situation of home-workers was well known. In Prussia, where weavers suffered by their hopeless competition with Britain, the Silesian weavers' riot of 1844/45 was an alarming sign of the desperation of home-workers, later immortalised in the famous naturalistic tragedy *The Weavers* by the Silesian poet Gerhard Hauptmann.

Protection began with the inclusion of home-workers in the anti-truck legislation through an extended definition of the protected workers. But the same was not done with the entrepreneur, who was not considered to be the 'employer' in the technical sense. The German Home-Work Act of 1911 made the home-worker responsible for the proper condition of the workshop. The entrepreneur was obliged to publish the wage scales and to hand out wage books (on payments in kind, the amount of work done and the wage paid) and to maintain a register of home-workers. Home-work could be given only to home-workers so registered. Branch committees (*Fachausschüsse*) could be established in order to give opinions, to make or to consider proposals and to promote 'wage or collective agreements'. These committees were organised on a tripartite basis, with representatives of the entrepreneurs and of the home-workers and with three independent experts as chairmen and assessors. When a demand was made to introduce the British minimum wage system (above) State Secretary von Bethmann-Hollweg rejected this in the German Parliament on the ground that it was a 'first step into the socialist state' (the British Trades Boards legislation had been extended to cover home-workers). Only the Home-Workers' Wage Act of 1929 authorised the committees to declare collective agreements generally binding, to establish minimum wages and give them settlement functions.

In France the decisive step towards minimum wages was achieved by war legislation. An Act of 10 July 1915 provided for the fixing of wages for female home-workers in the clothing industry who produced military kit. The Act essentially aimed at determining the price for piece-work. A notice was to be displayed at the home-workers' place of collection for raw materials, as well as where the finished articles were deposited, showing the net piece-rates. The legislation also provided for several price-fixing institutions to be established (though this legal requirement was not often observed in practice). The *conseils de travail* had to fix the minimum wage for a worker of average skill which was to be the basic piece rate for home-work. The calculation was based on the daily wage of workers of average skill in the same occupation, living in the region in question, and paid by the hour or the day for work executed in workshops, and was to be divided by the number of articles which could be completed per hour or per day. If such a council did not exist in the region, the Prefect had to institute an advisory body for fixing the wages of home-workers. This was to have the same functions as the council, but was to be presided over by a professional magistrate (*Juge de Paix*), aided by two or four representatives of both workers and employers. In case of any disagreement between these councils and committees, a system of arbitration was instituted: this was in the form of a central commission within the Ministry of Labour. This was presided over by a professional magistrate who was an adviser to the Cour de Cassation and comprised two representatives of the workers and two of the employers, members of the commission or council whose decision had been questioned, two *prud'hommes* (one an employer and one a worker) and a permanent investigator from the Labour Office. A civil case could be brought by any appropriate group which had the authorisation of the Ministry, such as a trade union, without having to prove that there was any prejudice to the group itself. Provision was also made for criminal sanctions. These took the form of fines which could be imposed in direct proportion to the number of workers who had been affected. Denmark obliged entrepreneurs to register and provided for the prohibition of unhealthy home-work (1913). In general, home-work was a neglected area in the legislation of Belgium, Italy and Luxembourg, and in the Netherlands an Act of 1933 on home-work remained a dead letter.

The Labour Charter of Berne of September 1919 demanded the prohibition of home-work in dangerous trades and in the food industry and recommended a system of insurance, registration and control by inspection of houses and also minimum-wage regulation. But the recommendation had little success. The ILO could not agree on a convention on this subject, but only on some recommendations.

THE PROTECTION OF ALL WORKERS

Legislation in favour of all workers in the nineteenth century was indirect and partial. It covered some aspects of prohibition of the truck system, in addition to the protection of wages, the regulation of the closing times of shops, the fixing of health and safety standards and the prohibition of Sunday work. There was a prolonged struggle for general regulation of working time, for the 8-hour day, but this was achieved only at the end of the First World War.

Protection of Wages

It is worth examining in some detail the movement towards anti-truck laws in Germany, because this illustrates the complex struggle between bureaucracy, King, 'enlightened' industrialists and workers before protection was achieved. The history of Prussian truck law reveals that this legislation followed pre-liberal traditions. The Prussian *Allgemeines Landrecht* (General Code) of 1794 prohibited the truck system in mines. The Cutlers' Guild of Solingen had earlier done this in its statutes of 1789. But in other trades the truck system flourished. The manufacturers not infrequently paid their workers in products of bad quality. Some control of the manner of payment was achieved by a Cabinet Order of 1828, which regulated payment in foreign currency. But it took a long time before the truck system was prohibited. Negotiations between the three industrial district governors of Aachen, Cologne and Dusseldorf with their chambers of commerce failed in 1831.

The Ministers of the Interior, of Justice and of Finance opposed legislation on the ground that it would violate the freedom of trade. The Minister of Trade answered:

> The freedom of trade seeks and finds its protection in competition in most cases and where this is given, state tutelage is not required. But in the few cases in which competition is impossible by nature and where there is no counterpoint which according to the legislator's aim brings the balance without his activity then it becomes necessary for the legislator to intervene. [Anton, 1892, p. 158]

The Minister of the Interior considered the freedom of contract as the solution. If the worker did not wish to accept payment in goods by contract, he could refuse such a payment. The Minister of Justice added the argument that a prohibition would be fruitless because the employer could get the same effect by wage reductions. Accordingly, nothing was done even when industrialists directly petitioned the King asking for prohibition of the truck system.

The Provincial Parliament of Westphalia applied in 1837 for the prohibition of the truck system and was supported by the *Oberpräsident* of the province. The petition was rejected because of legal difficulties, but there was a promise to reconsider it. In 1843 the Rhine Provincial Parliament took the initiative but did not have the support of the *Oberpräsident* and their proposal was rejected. In the following year the presidents of four factory tribunals[2] proposed the abolition of the truck system in their list of suggestions submitted to the Finance Minister and were supported by the district government of Dusseldorf. A fresh investigation, during which the principles of the English law were communicated by the Prussian government to the Chambers of Commerce, discovered that the factory tribunals were powerless either because the truck system had been contractually agreed upon or in most of the cases in which the payment in goods had been made only the ordinary civil courts were competent. Public opinion failed to move the employers save for the town of Lennep where forty producers had agreed to pay in money. The remaining eight producers refused, but the forty agreed to buy the products from the employees of the eight dissenting employers at the price for which the eight had sold them to the workers and then to sell the goods by public auction at which the names of the dissentients would be exhibited. The fear of public disgrace persuaded the dissentients to change their minds.

Investigations showed that the large majority of abusers were not in the factories but in the home industries. It was stated that the prices of the goods to be bought from the producers were at least 20 per cent higher, and sometimes they were even twice as high as the same goods sold in retail trade. All Chambers of Commerce which reported, the government of Dusseldorf, the *Oberpraŝident* of the Rhine Province and the Chief of the Trade Office voted for the prohibition of truck, and thus worked on the necessary bills. Nevertheless, it was not until January 1848 that commissioners of the Ministries of the Interior and of Finance had an agreed draft. The bill was sent to the National Assembly, which was dissolved some weeks later before a vote had been taken. The draft, however, became part of the Royal Decree of February 1849, and one year later was approved by Parliament. It provided for factory owners and traders to pay wages in money and not in kind. Exemptions were made for housing, fuel requirements, tenancies of land, regular food, medication and medical support and necessary tools and materials. Contracts contrary to these provisions were null and void as well as contracts in which the workers promised to purchase goods from the manufacturers. Claims for payment in respect of credited goods could not be made the subjects of law suits; the proceeds had to be paid to a local sickness, funeral, savings or similar charitable institution. Con-

2. In this area the *conseils de prud'hommes* had been introduced under French rule and had been left after the incorporation of this territory into Prussia.

travention of these prohibitions was subject to penal sanctions. These provisions seem to have been observed. There were no more publicised complaints. They became part of the Reich Trade Act of 1869.

The German development is significant because it reveals the strength of the liberal theory of non-intervention, especially in the higher ranks of bureaucracy. The King (until 1848, still absolute) hesitated to intervene. It required the activities of 'enlightened' industrialists and other reformers, using the British example before truck was prohibited. This represented the first general attack in Germany on the principle of *laissez-faire* because it concerned all workers, but it was able to build on a pre-industrial tradition in the conditions of Germany at the time.

The other Continental countries followed later. Belgium passed Acts in 1887, 1896 and 1901 which prohibited payment of wages in a manner other than in current money and regulated deductions for housing, tools of trade, overalls and so on. The payment of wages in inns or shops was prohibited. The legislation also provided for the time of payment and included payment for piece-work. This Act became the model for Luxembourg's Acts of 1895 and 1906.

In France the workers organised strikes at the end of the nineteenth century and the beginning of the twentieth in protest against the organisation of *economats* ('tommy shops') which forced the workers into a position of almost total dependence on the factory. Such strikes took place, for example, at Decazeville in 1886 and at Longwy in 1905. The strikes of workers in protest against the 'tommy shops' were often supported by local shopkeepers and tradespeople, who considered that these 'tommy shops' caused intolerable competition. On 9 December 1909 a law was passed which was to put an end to these shops. A new clause was added to the *Code du Travail* stating that the wages of all workers must be paid in metal coinage or notes of legal tender, any agreement to the contrary being null and void in law. A further article of the *Code du Travail* made 'tommy shops' illegal. When these regulations were infringed, the penal sanction was a straightforward fine imposed by the police. The prohibition of 'tommy shops' did not, however, make it illegal for payment in kind to be made: the legislator specifically allowed this. Hence the employer could provide the worker with lodgings, clothing, food and so on.

The Dutch Act on the Employment Contract of 1907 (which amended the Dutch Civil Code) dealt with the truck system. It provided for payment in Dutch currency, or in frontier communities in the currency of the neighbouring country if the worker consented. The worker could not be obliged contractually to use his wage in a certain way or to buy at a certain place or from a particular person.

Other types of legal protection concerning the payment of wages were also introduced, usually within the framework of the civil law of obligation. For example in France, the *Code Civil* as well as the *Code de Commerce* were used to establish a general preferential right to wages, and similar norms were introduced in the Dutch Civil Code in 1907. Protection was given to the workers to protect their earnings against distraint (attachment) for debt (e.g. the law of 12 January 1895 in France fixing the proportion of distrainable wages at one-tenth, and bringing such matters within the competence of the *Juge de Paix*). These examples are by no means exhaustive as illustrations of a trend to ensure that all workers' wages were protected.

Safety and Health Standards

The introduction of safety and health standards was at first linked to the protection of children, then women. These standards were readily capable of being applied to men as well. One basis for this was through traditional forms of guild regulation as in the Prussian Trade Act of 1845 which allowed the local police to ensure that guild regulations concerning journeymen and apprentices paid proper attention to health and well-being (*Sittlichkeit*).

Another basis was the concept of 'dangerous undertakings' in respect of which it was illogical to draw any line between children, women and men because of—in the words of the Prussian Trade Act 1845—the 'grave disadvantages, dangers or inconvenience for neighbours and the public'. The justification was not the protection of workers as such but the maintenance of public health and welfare. A Belgian royal decree of 1849, for instance, contained no specific clauses to cover health and safety at work. It merely stated that on every permit for the establishment of a place of work there had to be information concerning the measures taken 'to avoid or to reduce the inconveniences caused by such establishments, as much in the interests of the neighbours as for the workmen' (Art. 2). Further, it said:

> where one is able to prevent the existence of dangers, unhealthy conditions or other discomfort from the work of the planned establishment by imposing certain precautionary measures, a permit will be granted on condition that these measures be observed. [Art. 3]

This procedure for the issuing of permits was amended by the royal decree of 29 January 1863, 'for the greater benefit of industry'. The granting of permits for places of work which were dangerous, unhealthy or caused discomfort to the workers, was left to the discretion of the relevant body. Gradually the terms became more and more precise, and the royal decree of 27 December 1886 finally made it obligatory for any particularly dangerous or unhealthy establishment to list in detail any measures which had been proposed in the interest of the workers and to state clearly and in detail all the conditions imposed—but these measures did not have to be published, and so this information was not available to the workers. It was not until some time later that the royal decree of 21 September 1894 stipulated standards of hygiene in places of work and compensation for workers for any injuries resulting from their conditions of work. Gradually, by means of specific norms applicable to places of work, a body of legislation developed aimed at protecting the workers themselves. For example, regulations were made concerning the fencing of dangerous machinery, ventilation of places of work, dangerous or difficult jobs, the use of certain chemical products, and so on (e.g. the Danish Prevention of Accidents by Machine Work Act of 1889 and the amendments to the German Reich Trade Act in 1891). It must be stressed that the extent of state intervention for the individual protection of workers was linked to the development of the collective organisation of labour relations, both within the place of work and outside. For example, in Belgium the government was authorised to prescribe the necessary measures after hearings at which the industrial councils, the provincial councils, the royal academy, the supreme santitary and labour council and 'also, if necessary' the workers in industry and commerce were heard.

The Length of the Working Day

The most important stage in state intervention in the relationship between employer and employee was the introduction of legislation concerning the length of the working day. The techniques used to bring about such legislation and the reasons for it varied from one country to another, sometimes being treated as a form of individual worker protection and in other cases as part of collective self-regulation of work, in which the protection of the individual worker was only an element. In certain countries, such as Britain, these two objectives co-existed, namely where legislation which generated collective agreements gradually replaced the existing foundations of patchwork individual protection for children and women which had shown itself to be inadequate or ineffectual. The evolution of state intervention on this subject was closely linked with the action of political and trade union movements. The attention given to this subject by the international labour movement, and the action taken, was also important.

Even before the middle of the nineteenth century various movements demanded a reduction in working hours. For example, in Britain a series of demonstrations were held in the 1830s to demand a reduction of the working day, which then averaged from 14 to 16 hours. In his workers' catechism, Robert Owen put forward arguments in favour of the 8-hour day, which he regarded as the longest period of time which the human being can endure at work and remain in good health, intelligent and happy, when one takes into account average stamina and gives both the weak and the strong the right to existence; second, because modern discoveries in the fields of chemistry and mechanical engineering meant that it was no longer necessary to require a longer physical effort than this; third, because 8 hours of work per day coupled with good organisation of work can lead to abundant wealth for all; fourth, because no one has the right to extort from his fellow man more work than is necessary for society, simply in the aim of enriching his own person while making others poor; fifth, because the true interest for any man is that all men be healthy, intelligent, happy and wealthy.

As we have seen, the first examples of state intervention in this field limiting the duration of the working day concerned children and women. The extension of this to cover adult males was demanded in many countries. Sometimes it was a direct result of political change that such limitations on the length of the working day appeared. This was the case in France following the 1848 Revolution. The length of the working day was limited for all workers by the *décret* of 22 March 1848. According to the terms of this law:

> too long a period of manual work not only ruins the health of the worker but also undermines his dignity by preventing him from developing his intelligence; since the exploitation of workers is essentially unjust, vexatious and contrary to the principle of fraternity, the Government of the Republic decrees that the length of the working day is reduced by one hour; hence in Paris where thus far it was fixed at eleven hours it is reduced to ten, and in the provinces where thus far it was fixed at twelve hours it is reduced to eleven hours.

Observance was not very thorough and, as a result of political changes, it was repealed and replaced by a law on 9 September 1848 which reaffirmed the earlier periods of 11 hours in Paris and 12 hours in the provinces. Not until 1919 did a law limit the working day in France to 8 hours.

The economic reasons why it was not possible to achieve this legislation during the nineteenth century are clear. The duration of work was essential to maintain or improve the profitability of the employer's business in competition with other manufacturers. At a time when wages generally covered only the minimum needs of subsistence, these could not be reduced to cover a shorter working day. The legal controversy about the freedom of contract or the freedom of the worker to decide freely how long he chose to work does not sufficiently explain why the conflict was so sharp. Nor does the fear expressed in 1885 by the German Reichs Chancellor Bismarck that a legal maximum working day would induce employers whose workers worked less to increase the working time to the maximum. One of the moral arguments which caused the greatest bitterness among workers was that any limitation on the length of the working day, with its consequent longer periods of rest from work, could lead to the moral deterioration of the working class, a class said to be without culture, which as a result would be left free to indulge its basest passions!

The issue of the 8-hour working day became one of great symbolic importance in the emergence of the international labour movement. The Resolution of the Congress of Geneva of the First International Working Men's Association (1866) declared that the statutory restriction of the working day was a crucial one, without which all other efforts for improvement and emancipation of the working class must fail. International worker solidarity was symbolised by May Day demonstrations from 1 May 1890. In Paris following the May Day demonstration, worker delegates presented the Workers' Charter to the Chamber of Deputies. It proposed, above all, legal enactment of the 8-hour day, a guaranteed minimum wage, regulation of the work of women and children, providing a rest day each week and the abolition of night-work, employment agencies and illegal sub-contracting. This, they argued, would reduce periodic lay-offs due to increasing mechanisation and benefit the small businessman, by increasing the buying power of his working-class customers.

In Germany repeated efforts of deputies of the German Parliament to limit the working day to 12, 11 or 10 hours failed. The amendment of 1891 of the Trade Act, however, gave an indirect solution. It obliged the employer to issue an *Arbeitsordnung* (works regulation) for his establishment which had to contain provisions on the beginning and the end of the regular daily working time including the pauses for adult workers. The workers or the permanent workers' committees had to be heard before the enactment of the works regulation, which then had to be submitted to the competent administrative authority. The amendment of 1891 also contained another provision which was considered as a model in other countries. It provided for Sunday as a day of rest: France, which had abolished a regulation to this effect in 1880, followed the German example in 1906; Italy did so in 1907, Luxembourg in 1913 and Belgium in 1914.

The proclamation of the revolutionary government, the Council of the People's Commissioners in Germany in 1918 immediately changed the scene. This declared that the working day should be limited to 8 hours. At first this applied to manual workers only, but, about four months later, it was extended to cover white-collar workers. Other countries followed: Luxembourg (1918), Denmark (1919), France (1919), the Netherlands (1919—with the 45-hour week), Belgium (1921) and Italy (1923). In Britain as we have seen, apart from the miners who won a legal 8-hour day in 1908 and those trades for which Trades Boards were established after 1909, the achievement of this goal was by collective bargaining on an industrial basis rather than through legislation.

The legislation in some countries was a short-lived triumph because of the employers' strong opposition. Certainly one of the reasons was that they resented the political success of the workers' movement. But they could also refer to the post-war economic crisis and in Germany to the obligation to pay immense war reparations. A decree on working time in 1923 made several exceptions allowing for lengthening the working day by collective agreement or by authorisation by the administration. An Italian decree of 30 June 1926 generally admitted 9 hours' daily work. In the Netherlands the working day was increased to 8½ hours and the working week to 48 hours in 1922. Nevertheless, the 8-hour day had emerged as an international standard. Article 427 of the Treaty of Versailles (1919) had declared, 'the adoption of an 8-hour day and a 48-hour week is the standard to be aimed at where it has not already been attained'. In 1935 an ILO convention (No. 47) provided that working time should be 40 hours weekly and provided that the living standard of the workers should not be reduced in order to achieve this. However, it was twenty-one years before sufficient states ratified the convention for it to come into force.

THE DEVELOPMENT OF STATE INSPECTION

Labour protective legislation was ineffective without an adequate system of enforcement. With hindsight it seems obvious that enforcement requires an independent institution with paid officers. However, factory reforms were at first carried out within the framework of existing institutions. This meant that national legislation trusted at the beginning in local police or local magistrates. The main reasons for their laxity, in all countries, was not simply that these authorities were dependent on the factory owners whom they were supposed to supervise. It was more that they belonged to the same social class, who had feelings of aversion, detestation or even contempt for the uneducated proletarians, and who believed in the liberal ideology of *laissez-faire* and in industrialisation as signs of progress which certainly improved the general economic situation.

This is why the most important development was that of independent state inspectorates to enforce the legislation. Britain started the system of labour inspection, but paradoxically, because of the early growth of collective bargaining, never developed labour inspection as extensively as was later the case on the Continent of Europe. The Health and Morals of Apprentices Act 1802 (see p. 78, above) allowed enforcement by a system of paying 'common informers' a share of the fine in the event of a successful prosecution. This was totally ineffective. A system of factory inspection was not introduced until 1833. The trade unions were suspicious of this because they feared that inspectors would inevitably be drawn from the same social class as the employers and so would be biased. The Act of 1833 provided for the appointment of four inspectors to inspect factories where persons of under 18 years of age were employed. Each of the four persons appointed was a man of experience who had achieved eminence in his own profession. They were of high social origin (barristers, medical practitioners, army officers, etc.). Sub-inspectors were also appointed. In 1876 (despite objections by Redgrave, the first Chief Inspector), a commission recommended the appointment of working-class 'assistants' and in 1887 the first such assistants were appointed, and fifteen were appointed in 1892. The trade unions complained about the inferior status of these assistants, and after 1920 the grade of inspectors' assistants under supervision of a superintendent was allowed to lapse. The features of factory inspection which emerged were as follows: (1) the inspectorate regarded its mission as being advisory rather than compulsory; (2) the inspectorate was recruited from candidates of high educational qualifications; (3) the enforcement of the sanitary provisions in smaller undertakings was devolved to local authorities; and (4) the inspectorate was concerned solely with specific protective legislation (as set out above). It was not a general labour inspectorate concerned with labour legislation as a whole. Its duties were confined to investigation, inspection and enforcement of factories legislation and legislation in certain other industries such as mines, explosives and chemicals. They were not representatives of a government department responsible for labour questions, in particular having nothing to do with labour disputes.

Factory inspectors were introduced in Prussia in 1853, fourteen years after the Act for protection of young persons of 1839, and only 'if there was a need' to supervise the execution of the legal provisions. Only in 1878 was an inspectorate introduced, for all German states, of special public servants (*Beamte*), either exclusively or alongside the ordinary police authorities. These were appointed by the state governments and had the same powers as local police. They had the right to visit the factories at any time and to lay charges in respect of contravention of statutes. They had to report annually to the Federal Council (the assembly of the governments of the states) and to the Reich Parliament.

In France the first plans for a work and factory inspectorate were sketched out only at the end of the nineteenth century; but the work and factory inspectors were administered by the *conseils généraux* (departmental councils); as these councils had to finance the system, they imposed restrictions on the inspectors. An administrative body dependent on the state was created by a law of 2 November 1892; its members had a contract and were recruited by means of a competitive examination. Their duties were general, although gradually various departments dealing with problems of employment and labour developed. The law of 1892 was modified on several occasions, in particular by the laws of 17 July 1937 and of 31 October 1941. There were three bodies within the general organisation governing the work-related problems; the *controleurs* of work and of labour (under the authority of the inspectorate and whose task was to aid the inspectorate), and the administration. The fields subject to this service were progressively extended. The law of 22 March 1941, concerning the work of children, only provided for government control in factories and workshops with mechanical machines or continually burning furnaces, as well as those manufacturing firms employing more than twenty workers all working in the same workshop. In 1928 the competence of the work and labour inspectorate was extended to cover all industrial and commercial places of work and their outbuildings, whatever the nature of the establishment, public or private, lay or religious: even those dealing with state or charitable education were included: co-operatives and craftsmen's establishments as well as public hospitals and lunatic asylums, public administrative offices, the ministry offices, the liberal professions, non-commercial companies, trades' unions and associations of any kind (*décret* of 22 July 1941). Specialised civil servants were made responsible for the inspections, and so on, normally executed by the work and labour inspectorate in sectors such as mining.

With the exception of Denmark, which established two labour

inspectors on an *ad hoc* basis very early (1874), in general the labour inspectorate was introduced in the last decade of the nineteenth and the first decade of the twentieth century in the other European countries. The Netherlands started fifteen years after the first Children's Protection Act (1889) with three special inspectors. The service was reorganised in 1909. The state had ten supervising regions, each with a chief inspector who in most cases had an assessor and a female inspector; a 'working controller' was drawn from the workers and had to report cases to the chief inspector. A general director with experts (in medicine, chemistry and electrical engineering) was the head of the central service at the Hague. Belgium had introduced the labour inspectors and medical inspection by the Acts of 1895, 1896, 1902 and 1905, Luxembourg in 1902 and Italy in 1912.

It is questionable how far the workers were willing to collaborate with the inspectors. In two circulars of 1900 the French Minister of Commerce Millerand regretted that the factory inspectors had only in very few cases contacted the workers. He wrote:

> The worker nearly never goes to the inspector and he rarely writes to him. In the workshop during the inspection the worker nearly never asks the inspector and when he is asked he often shuffles. Often the inspector will not ask him because he fears negative consequences of such a conversation for the workers.

Therefore Millerand recommended contacts with the secretaries of the trade unions. The German attitude was different. The deep distrust of the political working-class movement caused the Prussian Minister of Commerce to warn in 1896 that the social-democratic complaints commissions should neither be officially recognised nor contacted. There was no question of reviving the idea of 'trade councils' (with almost parity representation) of 1849 and to give them supervising authority.

Other countries approached this idea by the appointment of safety delegates in the mines who were elected by the workers (France since 1890, Belgium, 1897 and the Netherlands, 1906). Luxembourg (1902) provided generally that labour inspection was entrusted to two inspectors, a female inspector and a 'workers' delegate' who was taken from a list with three candidates proposed by workers' assemblies.

Usually little consideration was afforded to the problem of the compatibility of the two functions of the inspectorate: the educative function of conciliation and the repressive function of penalising infringements of the law. Nevertheless, it does seem justifiable to state that, at the outset, control of the application of the social laws would appear to be linked to state policies which aimed to allow co-operation between workers and employers to take place. The administration, through extremely varied institutional systems, aimed to allow the application of the legislation by means of encouraging conciliation of the conflicting interests of employers and workers.

GENERAL OBSERVATIONS

Protective labour law began as special legislation with the protection of a particular group (always first children) or in a specific branch of industry. It required much time to recognise the dangers of the use of the new machines and processes and the necessity to protect the health of children in general. Protective legislation was at first confined to manufacturing industry and mines and only later extended to commerce. Agriculture in general remained outside the scope of legislation. It was very rare for a statute to cover all forms of labour, domestic and agricultural ones included. The German Civil Code reached this status with its obligation imposed upon the employer 'to establish and maintain rooms, installations or tools in a way that the servant was protected against dangers to life and as far as the nature of service permitted' (1919). Moreover, protective legislation was generally enforced by the state itself, the participation of elected workers' representatives being an exception.

The factors influencing law-making were similar in all countries, but they had different weight. General political developments played a decisive role. When the franchise was extended to male workers there was the hope for politicians of winning their votes by promising protective legislation. This explains why after the 1880s labour protection became a main aim of policy. But this attitude could also be blocked by political fears, and here the Paris Commune of 1871 provided a serious but only temporary interruption for France and Germany. Also, the fight against the absolute monarchy could, as in Denmark, lead to an interruption in protective legislation. In Germany the monarchy used labour protection as an instrument to keep the middle class quiet and to prevent the workers from becoming too strong by pursuing the aim of such legislation as an independent political force.

The impact of foreign legislation on national developments should not be overlooked. It was the use of the experience, especially of the British legislation, which certainly enabled the other states to accelerate the development to more general provisions. But the importance of the British model should not be overestimated. The statement by Stephan Bauer (1924, p. 401) that the reception of British protective labour law was at least as important for humanity as the reception of the Roman property and obligations law may be doubted. It seems that the legal development of protective labour legislation was a consequence of industrial development (see Introduction, above).

The group of philanthropic advocates was important, especially when it was supported by a strong Conservative Party or Christian social reformers. In Germany the academic socialists, who enjoyed a high reputation, helped to form public opinion in favour of the workers. This was one reason why German labour protective legislation did not meet powerful middle-class opposition. The German example in turn influenced France and Italy. This influence was strongest in the early period of protective legislation. However, independent academic investigations on the situation of factory workers were never accepted by the legislature as sufficient evidence. Even when investigation was made by the likes of Dr Villerme and Benoiton de Chateauneuf by the order of the French Academy (the results of which Villerme published in 1840 in his book *Tableau physique et moral*), a governmental investigation followed before the Children's Protection Act was accepted. It was a general feature of all protective labour Acts to be preceded by official investigations, some of which led to the development of general labour statistics for which special offices of statistics were established: in 1886 in Britain with the Bureau of Labour as part of the Board of Trade; in 1892 in France as Office du Travail; in Belgium in 1895; in Italy in 1902 with the Ufficio del Lavoro; in Germany with a special department at the Reich Office of Statistics in 1904; and in Denmark with a special department for social statistics as part of the Bureau of Statistics in 1913.

Workers, in the early period of protective legislation, were not strong enough to promote legislation. With hindsight this first period of state protection can sometimes be seen as an attempt by the state to compensate for the suppression of collective action by the workers. But it was also the first recognition by the state of the workers as human beings rather than as abstract objects of the principle of equality before the law. The idea of *laissez-faire* was no longer accepted as involving the absolute prohibition of state intervention; it acquired new meaning as a principle of state-controlled social order. Freedom of contract and freedom of competition were allowed subject to limits on extremely bad working conditions. This new conception was later embodied in Article 427 of the Treaty of Versailles: 'labour should not be regarded merely as a commodity or article of commerce'.

With the achievement of universal male suffrage, state intervention changed its nature. For example, in Germany before 1918 the Federal Council objected to many efforts of the Parliament (which was elected according to universal male franchise) to improve protective legislation where social insurance was considered to be sufficient. Universal franchise enabled the workers to use their political power to achieve labour legislation. The struggle for the 8-hour working day symbolised the emerging 'social democracy', for which the framework was laid in most countries by legislation. Labour legislation of this kind was required where the industrial power of the trade unions was too weak to obtain favourable conditions for the workers. Thus in France paid holidays were introduced by law in 1936, while in Britain and Germany they were achieved mainly by collective bargaining before the Nazi period (see Ch. 7, below). While collectively bargained standards were vulnerable to changes in the strength of the unions, changing political fortunes could upset legislation, as shown by the departures from the 8-hour day in the 1920s under the shadow of the unemployment crisis. Other protective legislation developed new ideas. For example, the legislation in favour of disabled workers initiated the concept of equal opportunities in employment to persons who suffered under serious disadvantages regardless of how they had been caused. The protection of working mothers became an aspect of state family and population policy.

Two general lines of development became possible: the first was to treat all protective legislation as relating to individual rights. This was the way which had been proposed by the International Workers' Association in the Labour Charter of Berne (1919) and this was taken up by the 1919 German Constitution. Fundamental social rights like the right to work or the right to safety and health could be established. The second way was for the state to develop its own corporatist policy as the Italian Fascist and the German Nazi state did. Here state intervention was not understood, as it was before, as the complement of the liberal society, but as a step towards a new and universal competence of the state to regulate labour relations. (Use of protective legislation to demonstrate the social prowess of the totalitarian states is considered later in Ch. 7.)

3

Welfare Legislation and Wage-Labour

Bob Hepple

INTRODUCTION

The Industrial Revolution produced a fundamental transformation in the risks to the economic security of individuals. Throughout history livelihood has been threatened by occurrences such as sickness, injury, invalidity, maternity, family changes and old age. In pre-industrial societies these social risks were to some extent absorbed through the hierarchical and paternalistic social structure. The predominantly rural character of these societies meant that the hazards of serious work accidents caused by machinery were relatively small, and income, depending upon an annual crop, was not reduced proportionately by the number of days' illness of individual members of an agricultural community. The family could be expected to protect its own members, guilds and corporations of craftsmen assisted theirs, and the King and Church provided charity for the relief of poverty which was regarded in feudal society as a status and not a social problem.

The age of the machine and the factory meant fatiguing hours of labour, few safety precautions and inadequate medical treatment. A feature of industrialisation was the maiming, disease and early death of the new class of operatives. This new class could derive an income only by working for the owners of capital. In place of the old paternalistic relations in which each member of society could expect to be provided for according to his station in life, there were now relations of exchange, effected through the framework of the contract of employment. When that exchange was disrupted, by illness, injury or other social risks, the worker could no longer turn to the traditional means of support. The family unit was breaking up under the blows of dispossession and migration, the guilds and corporations were in decline, charity was a diminishing activity now mainly entrusted to secular bodies, and the state was preoccupied with maintaining law and order by the penal repression of 'rogues and vagabonds', the propertyless and masterless who wandered through Europe in search of a living.

This convergence, for the first time in history, of the poor in general and a working class wholly dependent on wage-labour, presented early labour law with an insoluble problem, one that could not even be fully comprehended at the time. The market price of wage-labour was generally too low to allow individuals to make savings which could provide them with relief in times of misfortune, and so long as there was an adequate reserve of workers to fill the places of the injured, the ill and the dead, there was no economic incentive to impose any legal obligation on the employer to provide for his sick and needy employees; indeed, as we shall see, the civil obligations of the employer were substantially reduced during the early stages of industrialisation throughout Europe. In any event, the contract of employment was an inappropriate vehicle for dealing with non-vocational risks such as maternity, disability, old age and death. As Dupeyroux (1966, p. 26) has pointed out, the very existence of needy persons outside the market threatened the official optimism of the market that everyone could be provided for according to their merits, so that legal measures were now sought not so much to protect the needy as to protect the market against the needy. This was reflected in the penal nature of the workhouses and the decrease in relief for the poor. 'We deplore the misconception of the poor' said Nassau Senior, the British political economist, 'in thinking that wages are not a matter of contract but of right' (cited in Bowley, 1937, p. 291). The dominant view of the ideologists of the new middle classes during the emergence of industrial capitalism was that the poor had to be kept in fear of starvation in order to remain industrious. Workers accepted the ideology of the market by claiming better wages and conditions within the framework of the contract of employment rather than the abolition of wage-labour itself. The early labour law repressed their combinations, and they turned to other forms of mutual aid against the ravages of industrialism, such as friendly societies and sick clubs, which started clandestinely but gradually achieved official recognition and support.

The mutual aid system provided protection outside the contractual relationship between employer and employee. Protection depended upon the ability of workers to foresee and provide for the risk of misfortune by entering into bilateral and multilateral contracts so as to spread the costs. The poverty of the workers, their lack of education and foresight, and their subjection to frequent changes of economic fortune were severe obstacles to the development of mutual aid of this kind. Moreover, mutual aid was a solution difficult to apply to the problem of family dependants. Those with the lowest incomes, who were usually the most exposed to social risks, were least likely to be able to afford the contributions.

The inability of either the contract of employment or mutual aid to provide security became the focal point of many pressures in the late nineteenth and early twentieth centuries. Broadly speaking, state intervention took two distinct forms. The first was to provide state help for self-help—what is sometimes called 'subsidised freedom'. Workers were left free to choose whether or not to join a mutual benefit society, but the state provided financial assistance and regulation to ensure the solvency of these societies. This solution was most favoured in Italy, Belgium, France and Denmark. It was coupled in these countries, to a greater or lesser extent, with general public relief legislation for those, whether workers or not, who were in need of medical aid and pensions. The second form of state intervention was to render insurance schemes obligatory, sharing the cost between the employer and the insured worker, sometimes with state participation in financing. This was the foundation of national insurance schemes in Germany, Luxembourg, the Netherlands and Britain. Not only were the costs shared but the benefits were 'earned' by the payment of contributions while in work, and those benefits were normally unrelated to the specific needs of the worker. The crucial feature of national insurance was that it was linked to the contract of employment, but grafted on to that contract was a legal obligation to insure against certain social risks. In the words of Dupeyroux, this solution:

> took full account of the specific vulnerability of the wage-earner, thus aimed at specially protecting the wage-earner as wage-earner, and before he became in need of help, not afterwards. In practice this presupposed that these protective measures could be linked to the juridical element, the contract of employment, from which the wage-earner derived his or her legal status. [1966, p. 28]

Some social and legal historians describe these developments, which dominated the history of social security until 1939, as an entirely 'progressive' movement springing mainly from the humanitarian concerns of those who wished to help weaker members of society. Undoubtedly, the new awareness of poverty in the late nineteenth century was a factor. But most modern writers detect extremely complex relationships between economic and political developments and the evolution of social security. One should add (because of the overtones of the words) that 'social security' is itself an anachronism when describing developments before the 1930s because it entered the political and legal vocabulary only with the US Federal Social Security

Act of 1935 and the New Zealand Social Security Act of 1938, and was proclaimed a basic human right by Allied governments in the Atlantic Charter (1941), by the United Nations in the Declaration of Human Rights (1945), by the Council of Europe (1949), and the ILO (1952). The modern concept of social security covers nearly all the measures designed to protect the economic security of individuals, whether or not they are wage-earners. This universalisation took place in Europe only after 1945 and has been marked by the separation of social security law from labour law, although the categories shade into each other like colours of the rainbow. In our period the development of civil liability, mutual aid and national insurance has to be seen as a distinct phase of labour law. The remnants of this development continue to influence modern labour law.

The first aim of this chapter is to explore the roots of the legal techniques for securing the income of workers against a variety of risks. For convenience, these may be classified as (1) the vocational risks of accidents and illness at work, (2) the social risks of sickness, maternity, disability, old age and death, and (3) family dependancy. The distinct social risk of unemployment, rooted in the specific nature of capitalist economic development, is dealt with in Chapter 4, below. We shall attempt to identify a variety of influences: economic developments, political conditions, technological changes, ideologies and social movements. The second aim is to examine the legal techniques themselves. How far were the new laws an adaptation of existing techniques? To what extent did they borrow from other countries? How were these laws integrated into existing legal and social institutions? What, if any, were the consequences of these techniques for the development of social protection?

The chapter begins with a brief historical account of the impact of the Industrial Revolution, then of the Bismarckian reforms in Germany and their influence in other countries, followed by a review of some specific features of the development of protection against vocational and non-vocational risks.

THE IMPACT OF THE INDUSTRIAL REVOLUTION

The Old System of Poor Relief

In medieval times those who fell outside the protection of the family and of the guilds and corporations were cared for by the charity of local parishes and of the Church through the monasteries. In the sixteenth and seventeenth centuries there was a significant increase in the number of beggars and vagrants throughout Europe, creating a crisis for the old system of local administration.

In England the crisis was aggravated by the dissolution of the monasteries (1536–39) and the winding-up of a large number of almshouses and religious guilds (1545–49). This gave the state the spur to assume control of poor relief at an earlier date than elsewhere in Europe. The right of the disabled to assistance had been regulated since the fourteenth century by labour laws which were primarily concerned with stopping the poor from wandering. Major changes were begun by an Act of 1536 which contained the germ of a new locally based system of statutory poor relief. Each parish was made responsible for its own disabled; parish administration was supervised by higher officials;and there were regular collections from all financially-able householders.

The Act of 1601 for the Relief of the Poor, the basis of English Poor Laws until 1834, was—in the words of the Webbs—'within a framework of repression' (1927, I, p. 396). While medieval charity had been indiscriminately concerned 'with the salvation of the giver rather than the behaviour of the recipient' (Rimlinger, 1971, p. 19) the new ideology of mercantilism stressed the aim of forcing the able-bodied poor onto the labour market. One of the key objectives of the English Act of 1601 was, in the words of the statute, 'to set on work all such persons, married or unmarried, who have no means to maintain themselves, and no ordinary and daily trade of life to get their living by'. The Poor Law authorities now supplemented the traditional repression of beggars and vagrants, by flogging, imprisonment and other violent means, with a variety of measures to put the useful poor and their children to work. By the late seventeenth and early eighteenth centuries the more modest aim was favoured of making the poor earn at least the cost of their own keep. Various workhouses, under the control of the parish or 'Guardian of the Poor', were established, but the 'impotent poor', unable to earn a living outside the workhouse, generally failed to earn their keep when forced to work within the workhouse. The story of the English Poor Laws is as much concerned with attempts to create public employment (e.g. the Roundsman and Speenhamland systems and later measures discussed in Ch. 5 below) as with poor relief. The important point to note here is that the Elizabethan Poor Laws gave the sick, disabled and aged poor no individual 'right' to relief or to useful work. These laws imposed an obligation upon the parish to provide relief and work, but how this was carried out was at the discretion of the local justices of the peace and the parish wardens or overseers, with loose central control being exercised by the Court of King's Bench. It was no accident that Sir Matthew Hale, as

Lord Chief Justice head of that Court, was a leading advocate (in his *Discourse Touching Provision for the Poor* published in 1683) of the profitable employment of the poor.

The Protestant states of Germany 'took far greater care [than England] to ensure that church properties were kept for charitable and educational ends' (Beier, 1983, p. 21), but the English model of severe repression of beggars and vagrants was followed. Luther, in his famous essay of 1520, propounded the Protestant work ethic but at the same time insisted that every town should save its own poor from starvation and exposure while expelling foreign beggars. This was reflected in the municipal poor laws (*Armenordnungen*). The dispersed voluntary relief funds were centralised by the treasury statutes (*Kastenordnungen*).

In Denmark, where a centralised system of administration of poor relief was established by the Church Ordinance of 14 June 1539, it was only 150 years later by two decrees of 24 September 1708, one for Copenhagen and one for the rest of the country, that a system for the repression of begging and vagrancy comparable to the English Poor Laws was established. In 1755 the Danish-Norwegian government ordered beggars to be placed in workhouses, of which there was a considerable number.

In those countries such as France, where the Roman Catholic Church retained a dominant role in poor relief, there was no law comparable to the English Act of 1601. However, the objectives were similar to those in England. The more effective police system in France resulted in more vigorous persecution of vagrancy than in England, but this was combined with decrees for the relief of invalids and attempts to set the able-bodied to work. The royal government of the *ancien régime*, like the Tudor and Stuart governments in England, distinguished between the *mendiant*, worthy of assistance, and the *vagabond*, set apart for correction. Under the influence of the physiocrats, charity was increasingly looked upon as an economic rather than a moral activity. In one important respect, however, France did not go as far as England and Germany, because there was no legal obligation on local authorities to provide relief. Following the model of the Hôpital Général of Lyon, other cities and towns followed the policy of 'locking up the poor'. Colbert, moved both by the desire to maintain public order and to provide a disciplined and hardworking supply of labour, went so far in the regulations for Paris in 1680 to provide that children who treated their parents badly or were too lazy to work and girls who were debauched were to come under the parental control of the state in workhouses. This approach continued into the second half of the eighteenth century. A law of 3 August 1764 provided that able-bodied vagrants were to be sent to the galleys, while the aged, the sick and children were to be locked up in the *hôpitaux*. A new institution, the *dêpots de mendicité*, created by administrative order in 1767 and directly under the control of the national government, served as places for the detention of those for whom there were no places on the galleys, as well as many of the sick and aged. The inhabitants of the *dêpots* resembled those of the English workhouse. Similarly, in Italian states, such as Piedmont and Tuscany, the old and sick found themselves compulsorily confined in 'hospitals', alongside the vagrants and beggars.

At the same time, the mercantilists pursued populationist measures in order to provide a supply of labour and of soldiers, such as Colbert's famous decree (1666) creating a form of family allowance. Another traditional form of state intervention was a series of measures to compensate those in specially harmful occupations for services rendered to the King, such as the provision of free medical relief for miners by Henry IV (1604) and the contributory pension for marine officers (1675). Overall however, France and Italy lacked the machinery of poor relief, on a national scale—funded by taxes and administered by state officials—which contributed to England's social stability in comparison with those states.

The Economic and Social Consequences of Industrialisation

The old system of poor relief served the function of disciplining the poor in predominantly rural labour markets. As industrialisation spread westwards from the woollen mills of Yorkshire and the cotton mills of Lancashire across Northern Europe as far as the Rhine, the Poor Laws appeared to become not only unnecessary but also a hindrance to economic growth. They were unnccessary because the dispossessed poor were now subject to the much more effective discipline of the highly competitive market for industrial labour and to the autocratic power of the factory owners. They were denounced as a hindrance to the 'free circulation of labour' by political economists such as Adam Smith, because of the obstacles they placed on the poor to leave their own parishes.

The old system also came under enormous demographic pressures. There was a population explosion with a falling death rate and a continuing high birth rate. After centuries of official measures to increase population, there was now alarm—most vividly expressed in Malthus' *Essay on the Principles of Population* (1798)—at the rapidly increasing (and ageing) population, whose support would lower the standards of living of those who had to provide for them.

The technological changes, to which the new class of industrial workers were exposed, vastly increased the risks of injury, accidental death and disease. The machinery was often rudimentary, safety measures were exceptional, and the long hours of labour increased the dangers of accidents due to fatigue. Medical treatment was sporadic and often elementary, and the possibilities of retraining and re-employment of the disabled were virtually non-existent. It was women and children who suffered the main brunt of disablement and the grinding poverty consequent upon premature death of a male breadwinner.

At this point it must be said that the effects on the new industrial workers were uneven. For example, it is generally believed that the situation of the French workers was more depressed than that of their counterparts in England partly because of the early development of trade unions and the early factory legislation in England.

The Ideology of Liberalism and Individualism

Mercantilist ideas, underlying the old system of poor relief, came under strong attack from the new ideological tendencies associated with French liberalism and British individualism at the time of the Industrial Revolution. In his remarkable article for the *Encyclopédie*, Turgot (1913, I, p. 583) declared both the right to poor relief and the desirability of *laissez-faire*. He advocated public works to employ the poor, but did not want state support or support from private institutions for the poor. The 'autonomy of the will' meant that, in place of traditional support, each individual must rely on his own efforts. Ideologically, Turgot stood between the old paternalism and the new liberalism. He wanted voluntary associations for mutual self-help to meet the risks of old age, sickness and accidents, and at the same time public employment opportunities. Until this could be achieved he advocated non-repressive governmental poor relief.

Ideas such as these reached a critical point during the Revolution. The right of every man to subsistence (*le droit à la subsistance*) was demanded as a fundamental human right in almost every revolutionary declaration of the period, and in the fascinating preliminary studies of a committee for the elimination of begging (*comité pour l'extinction de la mendicité*), set up in January 1790, one can see the germ of modern ideas of social security, based on national legislation and treasury finance (see Ch. 4, below). However, this Comité de Mendicité, in its third report (1790) was anxious to continue the distinction between the aged and infirm and the able-bodied (*pauvres valides*). For the latter the right was to be 'le droit à la subsistance par la travail', or 'through work' (Forrest, 1981, p. 28, citing the words of a deputy).

In Britain it was not this revolutionary political liberalism, which proclaimed liberty as an end in itself, but rather the individualism of the classical political economists which had the major influence. Adam Smith, Malthus, Nassau Senior and others attacked the Poor Laws as being a cause of increasing population and pauperisation as well as a hindrance to labour mobility. Poverty was seen by these economists, as it was by the French Humanists, as a personal and not a social misfortune. The poor were responsible for their own needs and had no claim against the state or the rich. This self-reliance did not preclude public provision for the sick, the orphans and the aged, but in order to discriminate between the 'deserving' and 'undeserving' poor they advocated tight control.

The New Relief Schemes

The new ideology was reflected in dramatic changes in the Poor Laws. These changes resulted in a substantial decrease in the amount of relief in the nineteenth century compared to what there had been under the old régime.

The prime example, which became a model elsewhere in Europe, was the English Poor Law Amendment Act 1834, putting into effect the principles of the famous Report of the Poor Law Commissioners of 1834. The report contained the statement that relief should be concerned only with indigence, or 'the state of a person unable to labour, or unable to obtain in return for his labour, the means of subsistence', and not with poverty, or 'the state of one, who in order to obtain a mere subsistence, is forced to have recourse to labour' (Blomfield, 1834, p. 227). There were two basic principles. First, 'less eligibility', which meant that an individual should be given relief only on condition 'that his situation on the whole shall not be made really or apparently so eligible as the situation of the independent labourer of the lowest class' (p. 228) Second, there was the 'workhouse test' designed to ensure that relief went only to those in need and who were willing to earn it. Relief for the able-bodied otherwise than in 'well-regulated workhouses' was to be unlawful. The aim was to strengthen the free labour market by distinguishing and separating paupers from the poor, although modern historians doubt whether it achieved this purpose. The sick-bays in the workhouses developed into something like general hospitals, catering for the destitute, superintended by local authorities, and the workhouse 'deliberately, publicly carried with it the stigma of pauperism' (Himmelfarb, 1984, p. 176).

In France the revolutionary declarations remained unfulfilled and the legislation was unenforced. The infrastructure for strong central government was absent. Poor relief returned to traditional patterns, despite reorganisation under the Directory and Napoleon. Later the system was strongly influenced by Malthusian ideas, with communal boards distributing relief in workhouses as well as out of doors. In Italy the revolutionary ideas also had little impact upon the condition of the poor. A law of 20 August 1802 required a close check to be kept on the idle and vagrants, voluntary workhouses were to be established in every *dipartimento* and the compulsory workhouse system extended. A few years later the law began to distinguish between the able-bodied and disabled poor, the latter being confined to hospitals. By the 1830s this had emerged as a general pattern in several Italian states, although Catholic ideas of private charity remained influential. The most significant legislative initiatives prior to Italian unification came from Piedmont where the Prime Minister, Cavour, in the law of 20 November 1859, attempted to follow the model of the English Poor Law of 1834 with the aim of depressing the condition of the poor below that of the lowest-paid labourers.

In Germany the laws continued within a traditional paternalistic pattern. The Prussian *Allgemeines Landrecht* of 1794 regarded the obligation of the state to provide poor relief as secondary to other private sources, such as charity and the family. The master was under an obligation to provide medical treatment and food to servants who became ill arising out of or in the course of their service, without deduction from their wages. However, the master could escape this obligation by arranging for the reception of the servant in a public hospital, for which the costs could be deducted from wages. There were special, more favourable, provisions for miners, but nothing was said about factory workers. The *Allgemeines Landrecht* obliged the state to provide only for those who were not covered by the statutory duties or by private charity. This principle, of state relief as a secondary obligation, continued to be influential throughout the nineteenth century, as is shown by the Poor Law of 1854 in the Netherlands, which left to local state organs the residual role of providing relief only to those persons who would be a threat to society if charitable help were refused. Another principle of the Prussian Code was that those who received relief lost the right to vote and to hold public office. This principle was also embodied in the Danish Constitution of 5 June 1849 and in suffrage laws elsewhere.

The new liberal currents were, to some extent, reflected in the Prussian laws of 1842 and 1855, and in an Act of the North German Confederation of 1870, which gradually made it easier for individuals to meet local residence requirements for relief and redefined the duties of regional authorities in respect of transient paupers. But Germany had not yet industrialised, and these concessions to geographical mobility were not the forerunner of liberal reforms; rather they were the prelude to the conservative system of social protection of the Bismarckian period.

The Civil Liability of the Employer for Accidents and Sickness

Both the law and the power relationship between employer and individual worker made any prospect of compensation for accidents or illness illusory. The legal obstacles varied somewhat from one country to another, but they all served the function of protecting the entrepreneur from bearing the cost of work accidents or the illness of the worker. The dominant philosophy of 'no liability without fault' entered into the Romano-Germanic legal systems of the Continent and the common law system of England and Ireland and the hybrid Scots law, albeit by different technical routes. The intellectual sources in the Roman-law-based systems were found in the idea of reparation for damage caused *dolo aut culpa*. The natural lawyers of the seventeenth and eighteenth centuries departed from the strict Roman doctrines and generalised the theory of fault. In the words of Grotius:

> Fault creates the obligation to make good the loss. . . . By a wrong we mean here every fault, whether of commission or of omission, which is in conflict with what men ought to do, either generally or by reason of a special quality. From such a fault, if damage has been caused, an obligation arises naturally, namely that it should be made good. [1919, II, xvii, s. 1]

Some natural lawyers denied any Roman law basis for the action for damages, and claimed that it was based on the customary German law. The work of the natural lawyers culminated in the great codifications: the Prussian *Allgemeines Landrecht* (1794), the French *Code Civil* (1804) and the Austrian *Allgemeines Burgeliches Gesetzbuch* (1811). The Prussian Code (in force until 1900) contained an elaborate system of three grades of negligence with different consequences, and, not surprisingly, it was the simpler French Code, particularly Article 1382, enunciating a general liability for fault, which became the model for almost every civil code ever enacted, except the German Civil Code of 1896.

In practice it was virtually impossible to determine the precise cause of a work accident and prove fault. Statistics indicate that in France fault was proved by employees in only 25 per cent of cases, and in Belgium as late as 1896 that 70 per cent of work accidents were not compensated. There was also Article 1384, Paragraph 1, imposing a quasi-strict liability for dangerous things, which in a celebrated decision of 16 June 1896, the Cour de Cassation invoked in order to give a stoker damages against his employer for personal injuries caused by the explosion of a boiler in his employer's custody, although the stoker could not prove fault on the part of the employer. This happened, however, just before the civil action became irrelevant as a result of the passage of the Workmen's Compensation Law of 1898.

In the course of the nineteenth century there were minor improvements in the employee's right of action in the countries influenced by the French model. In the Netherlands a ruling of the Supreme Court in 1881 laid down that fault was to be defined as 'the omission of those precautions that might prevent or reduce industrial injuries and that reasonably can be required'. But this was limited in effect because the accident had to take place in the course of employment, and the employer was excused if he could prove that he was not in a position to avoid the accident, and contributory fault by the employee, however slight, meant that he lost the action. In Belgium, Sauzet and Sainclette (1883–84) advanced the theory that in the case of industrial injury the worker could sue not from tort but from contract (under Arts. 1135 and 1165 of the Belgian Civil Code). This contractual *obligation de sécurité* (safety obligation) was incorporated into Article 11 of the Belgian law of 1900 and into the Dutch Civil Code (Art. 1638x) in 1907, which will be considered later in relation to workmen's compensation legislation. It was not, however, accepted in France.

In Italy, the Civil Code of 1865 made the employer liable for negligence, but it was generally possible for the employer to escape liability either by proving that there was no fault on his part or that the worker's negligence was the cause of the accident. It was only in the closing years of the nineteenth century that stricter liability was imposed on the employer as a result of *jurisprudence* (case law) which implied in the contract of employment an obligation on the employer to use the utmost care in order to avoid injury to his workers; the employer was presumed to be responsible unless he could disprove fault. Even this solution was of little practical value because of the fortuitous nature of the events causing most accidents. According to Rameri (1904), in 1904, 47 per cent of accidents in Italian industry were caused by events for which no one was responsible, 25 per cent through 'negligence' on the part of the worker, 20 per cent through the employer's negligence and 8 per cent through joint negligence. It was not until 1942 that the new Italian Civil Code (Art. 2087) imposed upon the employer the obligation to take 'all measures which, depending on the particular nature of the work, on experience, and on technical knowledge, are necessary to assure protection of the physical integrity and moral welfare of the employees'. According to Treu (1981, para. 116), this apparently high duty—originally intended to bind employer and employee within the fascist corporative system—did little to alter Italy's bad record of work accidents and industrial diseases, because of the absence of effective enforcement.

In Germany the critical device for resisting claims for compensation by workers was the absence of vicarious liability. The Roman law tradition was that the employer could be liable only for *culpa in eligendo* (fault in selection), and this survived in the *gemeines Recht* of Germany with limited exceptions. Article 831 of the German Civil Code based liability on a presumption of *culpa in eligendo*, and the courts allowed large undertakings to rebut this presumption simply by showing that they had followed the practice of other employers in delegating the task of choosing their subordinates to a responsible head employee. (The French Code, Art. 1384, Para. 2, on the other hand, made the employer strictly liable for all damage done by an employee in the performance of the functions for which he was employed.) There was a protracted controversy in Germany whether the injured worker could sue his employer for breach of a contractual obligation of safety (BGB, Art. 618) and invoke the principle of vicarious liability in the performance of contractual duties (BGB, Art. 278). This idea was, however, never adopted and was finally rejected in 1923.

In English law the ordinary rule of vicarious liability almost exactly corresponded to the French law. However, in the case of *Priestley* v. *Fowler* (1837),[1] the courts contrived to exclude the doctrine of vicarious liability from work accidents caused by the fault of a fellow-employee. According to the 'rule of common employment' developed by the judges, an employer could not be held responsible for an injury caused by the negligence of an employee in the same employment as the injured worker. This was extended by the courts in 1850 to the railway industry and in 1868 it was decided that it applied to managers and supervisors of all kinds. It extended to Scotland, as well as the common law jurisdictions. The result was that although an employer could be held liable to pay damages to a stranger injured through his employee's fault, he had no such obligation when the injury was sustained by one of his own employees. The small employer, in direct contact with the employee might find himself liable for personal negligence, but the larger employer could delegate responsibility to managers and so avert legal liability. By 1868 it had been established that the only duty of the

1. (1837) 1 Meeson & Welsby 1.

employer was to appoint competent managers. Two further obstacles were erected by the courts in the path of workers seeking damages against their employers. These were the doctrines of contributory negligence and *volenti non fit injuria*. Under the first, any fault of the employee contributing to his injury meant that he lost the case. Under the second, a worker who had knowingly consented to run the risk could not complain of the employer's negligence. It was only towards the end of the nineteenth century, when the courts began to display a more protective attitude to workers, that the defence of common employment was avoided in some cases on the ground that the managerial duties of providing competent staff, safe plant and appliances and a safe system of work were 'non-delegable' and so entailed the employer's personal not vicarious liability. But the defence was only finally abolished by statute in 1948. Judicial interpretations from 1891 reduced the scope of the *volenti* defence, but contributory negligence was removed as a complete defence only by a statute of 1945. Another way around the doctrine of common employment (which had been modified by statute in 1880), was found in the case of *Groves* v. *Lord Wimborne* (1898)[2] in which the owner of an ironworks was held liable to an employee who was injured because of the failure of the owner to observe the duty imposed by safety legislation to fence certain machinery. The novelty of this was that factories' and mines' legislation was largely penal in character. Now the 'action for breach of statutory duty' allowed recovery of damages. The statutory duties were often strict, not requiring proof of fault. In contrast, for example, to the German law (BGB, Art. 823) which demanded at least intentional or negligent violation of a safety statute, English and Scots law came to allow recovery of compensation simply on proof that the statutory duty had not been observed. In practice, however, this action provided illusory protection for most workers. The statutory safety duties were haphazard in application, with the result that many groups of workers were excluded and the courts tended to interpret the legislation in ways which limited or excluded the apparently strict duties of the employer.

Surveying the nineteenth-century scene, then, one can safely say that both legal doctrine and the practical difficulties of suing an employer deprived the injured worker of meaningful protection through private law actions. The unfortunate Mr Priestley, who lost his case in England in 1837 for damages against his employer, had to spend some years in the debtor's prison because he could not pay the costs of his action. Another deterrent, besides cost, was the risk of dismissal, which meant that 'a worker was most unlikely to take his master to

2. [1898] 2 Queen's Bench 402.

court, even if he could, unless he had been so badly injured that he had lost his job as a result of his injury' (Bartrip and Burman, 1983, p. 28).

Mutual Aid

The hopeless inadequacy of public and private relief against the social hazards of the Industrial Revolution meant that a substantial part of the burden of spreading the costs of these hazards had to be borne by forms of mutual aid developed by the workers themselves. Since ancient times people in the same occupation and social class have come together in friendly societies to arrange burials, benefits in case of sickness and death, and other financial help. These societies, developed during the early stages of the Industrial Revolution beyond particular callings, had reached their height by the end of the nineteenth century in all the countries with which we are concerned, with the highly significant exception of Germany, where they were of no practical importance. In Britain the societies began to increase rapidly in numbers from 1760 onwards, and it has been estimated that by 1875 there were 4 million members of friendly societies compared to 1 million trade union members. In Italy in the years of industrialisation, aid for the needy was almost exclusively provided by the mutual aid societies. By 1873 there were 1,164 such societies in Italy with about 218,000 members. Twelve years later, in 1885, the number of societies had more than trebled to 4,772 with 781,000 members. In Belgium, where the societies were also extremely important, the number of members trebled in the ten years up to 1895, providing sickness insurance to about 8 per cent of all workers. Similar developments took place about this time in the Netherlands. In Denmark, too, the number of members of 'sick-clubs' increased from 12,000 in 1862 to 120,000 in 1885 and covered the whole country including both self-employed and employed workers. In France, by 1889 there were 8,883 societies with 1.4 million members.

In all these countries friendly societies had a troubled existence until the prohibitions on coalitions of workers were repealed. In many industries friendly mutual insurance is the oldest form of trade union activity. The policy of the state, in the early years of industrialisation, was ambivalent. On the one hand, the societies were capable of reducing the demands on poor relief and making the workers share the cost of their own misery. This encouraged the policy of legitimation, first shown in the British Act of 1793 which conferred rights on the societies to protect their own funds and gave members a privilege against being removed from parishes where they had not acquired a settlement. Indeed, the value of the societies was recognised as early as 1757, when an Act required coal-heavers working on the River Thames to contribute to a friendly society, and in 1792 a similar Act was passed relating to shippers and keelmen in the coal trade. Until 1830 the policy of English law was to place the societies under the supervision of local magistrates so as to relieve demands on the poor rate and to forestall any indulgence by the societies in trade union activity, which was illegal until 1824. It was the trade union aspects of mutual insurance which encouraged the other side of official policy, that of repression. For example, in France the provisions of the Penal Code of 1810 forbidding associations of more than twenty persons compelled the societies to operate in secret until the 1848 Revolution, and then they were placed under strict control (see below). Similarly, in 1810 the Mayor of Ghent forbade the creation of mutual aid societies, and it was only after the abrogation of the *Loi Le Chapelier* in 1866 in Belgium and 1872 in the Netherlands that the clandestine side of mutual aid was fully removed. The absence of any important mutual aid movement in Germany is to be explained precisely by the late start of the German trade union movement and its suppression during the period of the Anti-Socialist Act (1878–1890) while the state was developing a social insurance system.

Piece by piece in the other countries, the employers and public authorities came to recognise and support the friendly societies. The British Act of 1793, mentioned above, was followed by no less than eighteen other regulatory Acts up to 1875. A royal commission (1874) discussed the case for and against state intervention and concluded that the duty of the state was not to provide detailed supervision but instead only to help to societies to remain solvent; for example, by collecting and distributing actuarial data and by protecting members against fraud. After 1830 greater independence was allowed, but at the same time more systematic supervision was encouraged by the transfer from local to central administration. A barrister (who, after 1846, became known as the Registrar of Friendly Societies) had to certify that the rules of each registered society were in conformity with the law. The system of registration was voluntary, and the principal aim of an important Act of 1875 was to make the societies more reliable as insurers by encouraging efficient management. To this end annual accounts had to be submitted to the Registrar, who could also be called upon to resolve disputes with members. The system remained virtually unchanged until 1911. The Shop Clubs Act of 1902, enthusiastically supported by the friendly societies, prevented employers from compelling their workers to join the employer's 'shop club or thrift fund' (a vague expression which included sick clubs). The hostility engendered by employers' attempts in the last decades of the nineteenth century to make compulsory deductions from wages for these clubs may explain the unpopularity among the workers of the idea of compulsory insurance against illness and the relative success of the voluntary societies.

In Italy the state first regulated the societies by a law of 1886, giving them legal status and certain privileges and tax concessions. The regulation was far closer and more restrictive than in Britain. In particular the societies were forbidden from providing disablement and old-age pensions, and there were detailed criteria to which the statutes of the society had to conform. This encouraged strong resistance against state control by the workers' movement. By 1891 the majority of the societies had not asked for and obtained legal recognition; in 1894 only 17.2 per cent of them had been officially recognised, and by 1904 this figure stood at only 27.7 per cent. The mutual aid movement did not grow between 1894 and 1904, and by the turn of the century it was in a state of crisis.

Strict state supervision was also an obstacle to the independent development of the societies in France, where the law of 15 July 1850 and the decree of 26 March 1852 subjected them to close control, which was not substantially relaxed until the Third Republic by laws of 1 April 1898, 15 August 1923 and 28 December 1927. It must be remembered that the *bourses du travail* at this time also played a significant role in protecting workers against accidents and other misfortunes as well as unemployment (see Ch. 5, below).

The political and ideological significance of the societies is best illustrated by the Italian and Belgian experience. In Italy many members were defined as 'honorary' or 'benefactors'. These were managers who gave substantial contributions and played a dominant role in ensuring a moderate role for most of the societies, in opposition to the conflictual working-class policy. There were also many Catholic-based societies. The Catholic position was to oppose state intervention because of the charitable and corporative view of aid for the needy. The socialists began by rejecting state intervention on the grounds that it would strengthen capitalism. Mutual aid had to keep away from bourgeois law. The financial difficulties of the societies and the predominantly reformist tendencies of most societies forced a change of attitude, as reflected in the timid but explicit programmes of social legislation of the *sinistra transformista* (transformist left) in the period following the unification of Italy. This new trend was not put into practice until 1898.

In Belgium, the political influence of the Socialist and Catholic parties was very noticeable. Until the formation of a Belgian Workers'

Party in 1885, the friendly societies' movement was neutral towards the political movements. After that date, socialist leaders actively drew the societies around their party. Following the Encyclical of Leo XIII (1891), the Catholics did the same. The Societies lost their independence but at the same time political affiliation became a source of strength and increased membership. The law of 1894, revising a restrictive law of 1851, encouraged expansion, and the societies began to group in Christian (1906), neutral (1908), and socialist (1913) federations followed by liberal (1914) and professional (1920) ones, reflecting the fragmentation of the labour movement.

The very success of the societies, and their official recognition, also revealed their serious inadequacies as a form of social protection. First, the basic principle of all these societies was the payment of a premium or contribution, so that in general only the higher-paid workers in regular employment could belong. Unskilled and agricultural workers were frequently excluded and, with the notable exception of Denmark, so were the self-employed. The contributions were inadequate to provide sufficient reserve funds. It was at the very moment of greatest need—in the case of epidemics or disasters—and when the rising number of accidents at work created the greatest pressures that the societies were least able to respond. They were forced to turn the screw by raising contributions at just such moments. Even when special funds were established by public donations, to help the victims of major accidents, such as the colliery disaster funds in Britain in the second half of the nineteenth century, they usually proved inadequate to meet the needs of those for whose benefit they were founded. Second, with an ageing population those societies which paid death benefits and old-age pensions came under increasing strain. Third, despite state supervision, not all societies were run on scientific lines and lacked basic actuarial data and efficient financial management. This was an even more acute problem in the case of funds directly managed by trade unions, such as the British coal-miners' accident funds. It was difficult for a trade union, primarily concerned with labour relations and with a fluctuating membership, to base their calculations upon reliable data and to maintain the benefits promised to members.

The solution to this crisis was sought along two distinct lines. The first was to seek state subsidies while retaining the independence of the societies and the voluntary nature of membership. This was favoured in those countries which did not want to break with the liberal tradition and where, as in Belgium and Italy, the friendly societies were an important political force. 'Subsidised freedom' in Dupeyroux's words (1966, p. 40), meant that the state subsidised the free choice of the workers. Dupeyroux points out that there appears to be some correlation between this solution and the political fragmentation of countries which adopted it, such as Italy and Belgium. But the theory does not stand up when one examines the case of Denmark. In that country there was no problem of political or ideological fragmentation, and the explanation for the adoption of state help for self-help may be found in the self-perpetuating tendency of institutions. The sick clubs had spread across most of the country by the late 1880s. In 1887 a commission on the future of sickness insurance proposed that instead of compulsion, the state ought to preserve and support the voluntary system. The first Sick Club Act of 1892 laid down the fundamental principles which were the basis of all future legislation. The state paid a subsidy to the sick clubs, which preserved their voluntary, self-governing character, although they were subject to state inspection. The clubs had to grant members medical assistance, hospital treatment and daily allowances when sick. Those who did not join a sick club had to seek poor relief during their illness and lost the franchise. In 1915 there was a marked increase in government grants to the clubs coupled with an extension of coverage to include chronic invalids.

The earliest examples of state subsidies were the creation of national pension funds in Belgium (1850) and France (1868) to provide retirement pensions on the basis of voluntary contracts. A high point was reached in the Belgian pension scheme of 1900 and the Italian law of 17 July 1898 (No. 350). The former contained the principles of a two-tier pension scheme. The basic pension, providing the minimum needs for survival, was derived from contributions by insured persons and state subsidies. On top of this there could be a contributions-related pension for those who elected to pay more. The Italian law created the National Social Assistance Fund for Disabled and Aged Workers (*Cassa à nazionale di previdenza per l'invalidite vecchiaia degli operai*), which was provided with an initial fund of 10 million lire coming from diverse sources (including residual Church funds, unclaimed loans, etc.). Membership was entirely voluntary, open to manual workers of both sexes, including minors, and old-age pension was awarded at the age of 60 or 65 after at least 25 years' contributions, while a disablement pension was awarded after 5 years' contributions. Given the prevailing low level of wages, only a tiny percentage of the workforce were able to afford the contributions (10,280 members by December 1900).

Surveying the situation towards the end of the nineteenth century in those countries which had opted for state help for self-help, we can see both positive and negative features. On the positive side, the public authorities had now definitely become involved in the protection of wage-earners (and in Denmark of the self-employed as well) with financial help. On the negative side, these schemes presupposed a voluntary effort by those who were often unable to afford the cost of insuring themselves or lacked the foresight to do so.

The second kind of solution to the problems of mutual insurance was to make membership of the societies obligatory for certain categories of people. This, the national insurance principle, had its origins not in a country with a developed mutual insurance movement but significantly in Germany, with its different tradition of a paternalist state coming late to industrialisation and facing the threat of socialism. It is to the legislation initiated by Otto von Bismarck, which came to have a decisive influence on later developments elsewhere in Europe, that we must now turn.

THE BISMARCKIAN REFORMS IN GERMANY

The Economic and Ideological Background

The Industrial Revolution took off in Germany only after 1850, and the results were all the more sudden for that late start in comparison with countries on the West of the Rhine. There were spectacular migrations to the towns, the rapid formation of a propertyless working class and an economic crisis after 1870 following a series of financial adventures. This was accompanied by the simultaneous development of a socialist movement strongly influenced by Marx and Engels, and counting among its leaders Lassalle, Liebknecht and Bebel.

Unlike Britain and France, where basic political questions had been settled before industrialisation took place, Germany was still in the grip of feudal institutions and had to solve the problem of national unification. The German bourgeoisie was weak and the dominant ideology of the landed aristocracy opposed liberalism and supported a hierarchical, patriarchal social order linked to occupation and status. All the main currents of thought in Germany were influenced by the Hegelian concept of the supremacy of the state—the supreme goal to which the individual should aspire. Even the German liberals stressed individualism far less than their French and British counterparts. The German socialists, particularly Lassalle, had strong orientations towards the state. The manifesto of the famous Eisenach socialist conference (1869) declared that 'absolute liberty on the part of individuals who, to an extent, are rivals and unequal in power, does not guarantee the welfare of the community . . . thoughtful state intervention to protect the legitimate interests of all concerned should, at certain opportune moments, be encouraged.' The Gotha programme of the Socialist Workers' Party (1875), scathingly criticised by Marx (1875), reflected the same aim of working 'within the framework of the present-day national state' for a 'just distribution of the proceeds of labour'.

Another important feature in Germany was the ascendancy of governmental bureacracy as the absolutism of the princes declined. The public servants, most notably Otto von Bismarck, were intent upon continuing the tradition of the state as supreme arbiter of the best interests of citizens. As we have seen, there was a tradition of state protection against social risks in Prussia: the *Allgemeines Landrecht* of 1794, in which the state's duty to provide work or sustenance was proclaimed; the obligation on masters to provide medical treatment and food for certain servants; the General Trade Act of 1845, which allowed local administrative units to require all journeymen and assistants to join a sickness fund; a decree of 1849 enabling them to require contributions from independent traders; the law of 1848 which imposed civil liability for accidents at work on railway companies; the obligation on mine-owners to care for miners who became sick or injured in their service; and the *Knappschaftskassen* (compulsory insurance funds) which had existed since the Middle Ages for miners and were reorganised by the Prussian Mines Act 1865. These precedents had been followed in several other German states.

By 1850 the 'welfare monarchy' or 'socialism of the throne' had already been put forward as a solution to the social question. The idea of using a system of social protection for workers for the purpose of securing their loyalty to the state had been tried by Napoleon III but did not lead to any significant development of social rights in France. Bismarck, while Prussian ambassador in France in 1862, had taken a close look at Napoleon III's scheme. He became convinced of the need to win the political support of the emergent working-class movement. Correspondence, discovered in 1927, indicates that he was in systematic contact with Lassalle and this contributed to his understanding of the conditions of the workers and the aims of the socialists. He was also influenced by Wagener, a journalist of the far right, in favour of a state socialist scheme of legislation. From his accession to power in 1863 until his downfall in 1890 Bismarck pursued the twin policies of repression and concession. When he introduced his Anti-Socialist Act, at the same time he proclaimed his desire to implement 'that which seems legitimate in the socialist demands' within the existing social framework. He wanted to attach the workers to the state by making them look to the state rather than self-help and private institutions for social protection. It was inevitable that the dominant Prussian pattern of social legislation should come to form the core of the system of social protection introduced throughout Germany after the promulgation of the Imperial Constitution of 1871.

The Legislation

It was in the 1880s that the decisive shift from the liberal ideas of self-help to that of state protection took place. The 1870s had still been marked by liberal social legislation, such as the Employers' Liability Act of 7 June 1871, which made the employer liable for work accidents due to the fault of a fellow-employee of the injured worker, and laws of 1876 regulating mutual insurance funds. But the international trade depression that began in 1873 and the growth of protectionist trade policies shifted the emphasis to state planning and the promotion of compulsory social insurance. The historic message of Kaiser Wilhelm to the Reichstag on 17 November 1881[3] announced a threefold social insurance system with a corporative administrative structure. After intense debates a law on sickness insurance was enacted in 1883, on accident insurance in 1884 and on old-age and invalidity pensions in 1889. These were followed by seven other Acts, extending their scope *inter alia* to agriculture and to *Beamte* and soldiers (1886). These were then consolidated and improved in the Reich Social Insurance Act 1911, applying to manual workers, followed later the same year by the Social Insurance Act for White-Collar Workers. Together these Acts had 2,204 clauses. A project of the Weimar government to reorganise the law was dropped in 1924.

The basic reform measures were enacted over a nine-year period—according to Bismarck, 'an artichoke cannot be consumed with one bite but only leaf by leaf'. The tactic of disarming his opponents by piecemeal reforms had the consequences that different types of social risk were differently regulated, and the laws were badly arranged and sometimes unintelligible. Administratively this led to a lack of co-operation between the various insurance bodies.

There were, however, certain common principles for all three branches of social insurance. The first was the principle of compulsory insurance. This applied to all workers whose wages were below a certain level. It was these lower-paid workers who were regarded as most in need of protection and most likely to be alienated from the state unless drawn to it in this way. Those whose wages exceeded the minimum level could make a voluntary contribution above the basic requirement and so earn higher benefits. The second principle was that

3. The text of this message will be found in Appendix IV, p. 376, below.

insurance had to be effected with certain self-governing corporations. These corporations were regulated by state insurance offices at three levels: those which formed part of the local administration units; the superior insurance offices which formed part of district offices or were independent; and the Reichs Insurance Office. Two lower instances for white-collar workers existed until 1922 and were then abolished, only the Reichs Insurance Institution for white-collar workers being retained. The insurance offices had a tripartite structure with representatives of employers, workers and the state. Legal decisions were made in special departments of the three-tier structure: decisions-committees, the decisions-chamber and, at Reichs level, the decisions-senate.

In the case of health insurance, Bismarck was willing to draw on the existing guild, factory and mutual insurance associations, partly because he did not regard health insurance as an effective way of tying the worker to the state, given the short-term nature of illness. As a result the insurance corporations were extremely varied: local health insurance established by local administration communities; state health insurance for agricultural and forestry workers, domestic servants and migrant labourers; insurance at plant level in plants with more than 150 workers; guild health insurance; and miners' insurance. The number of members in the different institutions ranged from as low as 50 to as high as 500,000. Initially, two-thirds of the contributions were paid by the employers and one-third by the insured (except in the guilds where contributions were equal), and those who were compulsorily insured could benefit for a maximum of thirteen weeks by receiving free medical care and a daily indemnity equal to half their normal wage.

These benefits were gradually extended by later measures, so as to allow benefits for up to twenty-six weeks, and to provide dependants' allowances and death benefits. If contributions were insufficient to pay regular benefits, the superior insurance office had to intervene and merge the health insurance with other insurance; if this was impossible, the community or regional association (for state insurance), the employer (for plant insurance) or the guild (for guild insurance) had to make up the contributions. Each insurance corporation had to have a statute which was approved by the superior insurance office. A common requirement was that the supervisory board and the committee of management were elected: two-thirds by the workers and one-third by the employers, the board being indirectly elected by the members of that group on the committee. The president of both organs of plant insurance corporations was the employer.

The administration of accident insurance did not fulfil Bismarck's hopes of corporative participation by workers. The workers were represented only on committees that dealt with preventive measures, and for all practical purposes the insurance corporations were under the control of the employers, usually in industrial or regional mutual associations. These corporations in turn were supervised by the state insurance offices. It was the employers who bore the full cost of contributions, assessed according to risk. The worker was entitled to free medical care from the fourteenth week after the injury, and to payments equal to two-thirds of his wage if disabled. Death benefits and dependants' allowances were also added to the scheme.

The insurance scheme for the aged and disabled was administered by regional insurance corporations connected to local administration units and some special corporations for groups such as railwaymen, miners and sailors. These were also under the supervision of the state insurance offices. Contributions were paid in equal shares by employers and workers, and the state paid a direct subsidy. The calculation of contributions was itself a complicated exercise based on risk. The state guaranteed every worker a uniform basic pension, and in addition there were variable supplements based upon the contributions of the employer and worker. The benefits were paid for permanent disablement and temporary disablement; old-age pensions were paid from the age of 70 (reduced in 1916 to 65) and also widows' pensions (for white-collar workers in 1911 but manual workers only in 1952 and generally since 1957).

White-collar workers were preferentially treated from the time their scheme was introduced. The insurance was borne by the Reichs Insurance Institution for white-collar workers. There was parity representation for employers and workers on the board with a chairman for life appointed by the Federal Council.

So we see that the German social insurance scheme as it evolved did not meet all Bismarck's aims, but it was without doubt an important factor in pacifying discontent among workers, and it contributed to the revisionism and collaboration of social democrats with the state. It was this system, nurtured in the paternalist traditions of pre-industrial Prussia and cultivated by Bismarck as a political weapon, that was to have a profound influence on the countries of classical liberalism in the first part of the twentieth century.

The Influence in Other Countries

Important features of the German model were adopted, in varying degrees, into the legal systems of other European countries during the last decade of the nineteenth century and the first decade of the twentieth. How is one to explain this transplantation? At the practical level the German employers publicised their system widely throughout Europe, and many politicians and administrators visited Germany to see for themselves, such as Lloyd George's well-known trip in 1908. The most striking fact is that, unlike Germany (and Austria which copied the Bismarckian model even in technical details), nearly all the later adopters of state-initiated welfare programmes in this period in Western Europe had already passed the stage of industrialisation. As Collier and Messick have shown (1975, pp. 1314–15), the tendency was not for compulsory social insurance to be diffused from the industrially advanced to the less advanced nations but rather the other way around. Those who have studied this phenomenon have suggested several explanations, none of them conclusive.

One group of explanations concentrates on quantitative factors, linking the legislation to features of social and economic development within nations. For example, Pryor (1968, p. 135) has noted that the proportion of the population over 65 increases as per capita income rises, thereby increasing the need for old-age pensions. Pryor (1968, p. 146) also finds that the level of social security expenditure is related to the level of productivity (measured as gross national product per capita), but this applies only if the entire range of economic modernisation is included in the sample of countries. The relationship breaks down if only semi-developed or fully developed economies are considered. Pryor interprets his findings by suggesting that increases in productivity at earlier levels of modernisation produce more spending, but that variations in productivity make no difference once it has reached a certain level. Another argument links the welfare of workers and productivity. This 'human capital' approach suggests that as capital equipment becomes more complex, the pressure on governments increases to introduce schemes which will improve labour productivity by improving the health and efficiency of workers (Rimlinger, 1971, p. 337). It has also been suggested that there is a link between the economic cycle and the first adoption of state-initiated welfare programmes. According to this view, legislation tends to be introduced when there are demands for a redistribution of income so as to develop a home market for increased industrial production. This is illustrated by Woodard (1962, p. 286) with reference to the upsurge of demands for such schemes in Britain during the great depression years of the late nineteenth century.

Whatever the importance of factors such as these, it is clear that none of them in itself constitutes a sufficient condition for the adoption of state-initiated welfare schemes. This leads one to political and sociological explanations. Some writers emphasise the role of great men, such as Bismarck and Lloyd George. Others, such as Rimlinger (1971, pp. 35, 93–8), argue that the principal variable affecting the timing of state-initiated welfare was the extent of resistance by liberal pressure groups who insisted the poor should be self-reliant. In terms of power relationships, one could say that the weaker development of liberal capitalism in Germany meant that there was less resistance to state intervention in welfare, or to the co-optive use of welfare to secure the loyalty of the working-class to the state. George stresses 'the successful attempt of the dominant social groups to buttress the existing social and economic order' (1973, p. 1) in the use of welfare. He argues that the adoption of social security was the result of two primary factors and three secondary ones. The primary ones were the enfranchisement of the working class and the spread of socialist ideas during the late nineteenth and early twentieth centuries. The three secondary factors were the paternalistic humanitarianism of this period; the social surveys which quantified the extent and causes of poverty (see Ch. 4, below); and the realisation that the improvement of health and welfare increased labour productivity.

These views should be examined in the specific political and ideological context of the introduction of social insurance in each country. In Britain, as Halévy argued (1929), the declining rate of economic progress in comparison with the newly industrialising countries such as Germany, had encouraged the growth of the Empire. It was impossible to defend that Empire without a healthy social base at home, and the working class needed to be persuaded that their prosperity depended upon the Empire. It is no surprise that the initiator of the Workmen's Compensation Act 1897 (below) was Joseph Chamberlain, a Tory radical and arch-imperialist. Asquith, later to become Liberal Prime Minister, asked in 1901, at a time when the bad state of health of recruits for the Anglo-Boer War (1899–1902) had been revealed, 'what is the use of talking about Empire if here, at its very centre, there is always to be found a mass of people, stunted in education, a prey of intemperance, huddled and congested beyond the possibility of realising any true sense either in social or domestic life?' (cited in Gilbert, 1966, p. 77). As more became known to the middle classes about poverty (e.g. the Booth & Rowntree surveys in Britain), the explanations changed from moral condemnation to economic and environmental ones.

The changing attitudes of the middle and upper classes were, of course, directly influenced by the rise of working-class movements. The liberal ideology of self-help had been accepted to a high degree by the working classes in countries such as Britain, Belgium and the Netherlands. The trade unions and friendly societies protected the economic and social interests of workers in the new industrial society. The liberal state had come to accept the legitimacy of what Kahn-Freund (1959, p. 224) dubbed collective *laissez-faire*. The regulation of the probity and fair conduct of the friendly societies, and also the various attempts, within the confines of private law, to modify the principles of fault liability for industrial accidents (e.g. Britain in 1880, the Netherlands in 1881, France in 1898 and Belgium in 1900) were not incompatible with this ideology. It is a controversial question, much debated by historians, whether the real impetus for the decisive change to state intervention through compulsory national insurance was provided by the working-class movements. The attitude of the labour movements of Europe seems to have been a varied one.

Pelling (1979, pp. 1–18) suggests that in Britain welfare reforms were not a popular working-class demand because of dislike of the official institutions for relief associated with the Poor Law, and that the trade unions gave support only for limited reforms which would not undermine the 'self-help' solution of collective bargaining. Hobsbawm (1964, Ch. 15), on the other hand, argues that a distinction must be made between the unorganised mass of the poor and the 'aristocracy of labour' within the organised labour movement. The latter did want social welfare. The Marxist-influenced Social-Democratic Federation and the Independent Labour Party put forward specific welfare demands as palliatives pending the eventual socialist transformation based on common ownership of the means of production. The British Labour Party, founded in 1900, put forward an extensive programme for a comprehensive health service, old-age pensions, free education and abolition of the Poor Law, and not a few Labour activists ended their days as administrators of the social service state. The Liberal reforms were, in fact, limited in scope and well within the power of the Liberal Party to grant, without disturbing the social system. The reforms were gradually introduced and gave the Liberals tactical advantages over their opponents. Above all, they shared with Bismarck the desire to undermine the socialist position. In the words of A. J. Balfour, 'Social legislation . . . is not merely to be distinguished from socialist legislation but it is its most direct opposite and its most effective antidote' (cited in Fraser, 1973, p. 129).

By contrast, in France, where the pace of industrialisation was slower than in Britain and neither the agricultural nor industrial sector was dominant, society was deeply split between groups with fundamentally opposed ideologies but which tended to balance one another politically. Amid fierce ideological struggles, the status quo was preserved and social rights developed very slowly. The employers rejected compulsory social insurance altogether, and the CGT strongly resisted the idea of contributions by workers on the grounds that insurance was the responsibility of employers and the state, and denounced the idea of family allowances because it undermined the principle of equal pay for equal work. This may be compared to the situation in Italy, where employers became increasingly favourable to compulsory insurance because of the growing risks of civil liability for accidents and illness, and the moderate socialists, seeking to distinguish themselves from the anarchists and hard-line *operaisti*, declared themselves in support of compulsory insurance. The Catholics, particularly after the Papal Encyclical *Rerum Novarum* (1891) were also moving towards greater public intervention. The Catholic current in Belgium, however, was less amenable to this new approach and the political and ideological fragmentation of the mutual aid societies (above) militated against the national insurance solution. In the Netherlands, right-wing liberals and certain Christian groups advocated state-backed voluntary schemes; left-wing liberals and other Christian politicians favoured compulsory insurance, while a variety of state-financed schemes were wanted by the social democrats and some liberals. The trade unions did not especially support the extension of compulsory insurance, except in the case of industrial injuries. The main impetus for the introduction of social insurance in the Netherlands appears to have been, as in Germany at an earlier date, the reaction of progressive liberal, social-Calvinist and Roman Catholic factions to social upheavals and the rise of the socialist movement after 1880. The big strike movement of 1902–3 was followed by proposals for sickness insurance and health care, and unrest after the First World War prompted the improvement of industrial injuries insurance, old-age and invalidity insurance.

These varied influences help to explain the uneven development of compulsory insurance principles. The extreme example of adherence to a voluntary system is Denmark. Although the German reforms acted as a stimulus, the Danish legislators were able to build directly upon the very strong tradition of private societies, the inborn aversion to compulsion and the widespread acceptance of individual responsibility for protection against social risks. As a result, the voluntary principle of sickness (and unemployment) insurance was preserved even after the state assumed supervision and defrayed part of the cost; in structure the Danish social welfare system established between 1891 and 1933 was an extension of the old voluntary societies. It was only in respect of invalidity insurance, introduced in 1922 without being preceded by private funds, that the German model was closely followed, and workmen's compensation was compulsory from 1898.

In the other countries one finds a tendency, particularly after the

First World War, towards convergence, even where there had earlier been great resistance to compulsory insurance. This convergence was most spectacular and virtually simultaneous in the case of industrial accidents (below). It was slower in the case of non-occupational risks such as sickness, old age and death, but by 1930, when France eventually joined the countries with national insurance schemes, compulsory insurance against social risks had spread to most of Western Europe. We must turn now to examine some of the specific developments up to 1939.

THE DEVELOPMENT OF LEGISLATION ON ACCIDENTS AND ILLNESS AT WORK

The Emergence of Specific Legislation

Legislation to ensure some measure of compensation for accidents at work emerged at the turn of the century in all Western European countries, regardless of their state of industrialisation and their political circumstances. We have seen that in general the civil liability of the employer rested upon the fault principle (above) which conveniently matched the economic interests of the entrepreneur in the early stages of industrialisation. The advocates of reform in all countries were able to use the irresistible argument that work accidents were an inherent part of the organisation and dynamics of production, particularly in certain dangerous trades, and the enterprise causing those accidents should bear the cost irrespective of fault. In the words of an English Judge, Lord Brampton in 1897, the purpose of reforming legislation was to confer:

> upon a large class of workmen, whose necessities compelled them to seek employment in certain specified dangerous occupations, in the course of which accidents, not always possible to be guarded against, are of frequent occurrence, some purely casual, others no doubt attributable to negligence or default of fellow workmen, whom it would be idle to sue, or others whose identity could not be established, a right to claim compensation. [cited in Wilson and Levy, 1939, p. 63]

We have seen that there were precedents in the Prussian law of 1848 which imposed civil liability, regardless of fault, on railway companies, and in the practice of the *Knappschaftskassen* of compulsory insurance for miners reorganised in the Prussian Mines Act of 1865. There were also attempts to modify the classic fault principles by legislation, such as the British Employers' Liability Act of 1880, the Italian law of 1898 on accident compensation and the German Employers' Liability Act of 1871 (above), and by judicial decisions, as in the Netherlands (1881), France (1898) and England (1898). But it was Bismarck's Industrial Accident Insurance Act of 1884 which was the decisive turning point towards compulsory insurance.

The new wave of legislation at the end of the nineteenth century was limited in some countries to an adaptation of the law of civil liability, while in others it went further, following the German model, and established compulsory insurance schemes. In Britain, with the Workmen's Compensation Act in 1897, in France in 1898, Denmark in 1898 and Belgium in 1903, the legislators limited themselves to adapting civil liability. The employer was made responsible for paying a limited amount of compensation to certain categories of workers employed in specific trades which were considered to be particularly at risk in respect of accidents at work. This was not the 'revolutionary' change claimed, both at the time and subsequently, because in several countries (e.g. Netherlands, France, Italy, England) the judiciary was already in the process of modifying civil obligations in the same direction. Where the tort remedy was retained alongside the new workmen's compensation schemes, as in Britain, the judiciary continued this process in the early twentieth century. Workmen's compensation was in fact a compromise solution because where it applied the worker received only limited compensation in return for not having to prove fault on the part of the employer or a fellow-employee.

The legislation was generally based on the following principles. (1) It was not necessary for the injured worker to prove fault, but in most countries there was an exception where the gross negligence (or intentional fault) of the worker himself caused the injury. (2) The first laws applied to certain dangerous trades only, such as railways, mines, quarries, engineering works, certain building operations and factories. (3) The accident had to happen at work; in the classic expression of the British legislation the accident had to be shown to arise 'out of, and in the course of employment'. The meaning of those words was a source of considerable litigation. (4) The employer did not have to pay compensation equal to a full wage. The economic theory that the worker in accepting employment agreed to share the risks was extremely influential and was reflected in the provision that the worker should receive only a proportion of his normal wage (one-half in Britain, but two-thirds in most other European countries). There was also usually a maximum amount which the employer could be called upon to pay, and sometimes there was a principle that the worker could agree to accept a lump sum and forego his rights to a weekly payment. (5) In most countries the tort remedy was abolished for practical purposes, either because (as in Britain) the worker had to elect between his tort and workmen's compensation remedies and would nearly always choose the latter, or because workmen's compensation was made exclusive with regard to certain claims (e.g. Belgium, France) or a tort immunity was granted to employers paying workmen's compensation premiums.

In some countries, in addition to a basic workmen's compensation scheme along these lines, there was also compulsory insurance on the German model (above). This was the case in the Industrial Injuries Insurance Act of 1901 in the Netherlands, in Luxembourg in a law of 1901 and in Italy where the law of 17 March 1898 (No. 80) established a system of compulsory insurance for work accidents through the National Insurance Fund which had existed on a voluntary basis since 1883.

Extensions of the Legislation

Dupeyroux (1966, p. 35) has pointed out that these laws possessed an internal dynamism. Once enacted, there was a universal tendency for them to expand. Dupeyroux shows that there were generally three successive legislative phases: (1) the criteria of what constituted an exceptional hazard, confined to certain trades, was at first broadened and then abandoned altogether; (2) the protection was extended to cover certain occupational illnesses; and (3) the legislation was extended (in a few countries) to cover accidents to and from work. He argues that these extensions can be explained first by the practical reason that rights granted to one section of workers are soon demanded by another section and the protection they seek is less expensive because they are *a priori* less at risk. Second, it can be explained by the theoretical difficulty of justifying discrimination between so-called 'dangerous' activities and others, when by definition the latter are less frequent.

The first phase of these extensions had already occurred before the First World War and gathered momentum after it (e.g. the British law of 1906; French laws of 1906 and 1926; Belgian laws of 1929 and 1930; German laws of 1900, 1911 and 1925; the Dutch law of 1921; and the Danish law of 1916). One change was from the narrow definition (as in the original German law) of 'an accident at the work-place' to an accident 'arising in the course of work' and caused by ('out of') work.

Another was the broadening of the categories of protected persons (e.g. the extension to all those working under contracts of employment earning below a certain wage in Britain in 1906, and the extension to agricultural workers in Italy in 1917, France in 1917 and the Netherlands in 1921).

The second phase of extension, to cover some occupational illnesses, was long resisted because of the practical difficulty of proving that disease was work-related and of the theoretical objection that illness was a risk which the worker should bear. It was mainly after the First World War that an assimilation of occupational accidents and specified diseases was accepted. This process started in the British Act of 1906, and was followed by the Danish law of 1916, the French law of 1919, and by Luxembourg in 1925, Germany in 1925, Belgium in 1927, Netherlands in 1928, Italy in 1929. The ILO Convention No. 18 (1925) on Workmen's Compensation (Occupational Diseases) had a significant influence on this development. Increasing medical knowledge made it possible in the 1930s to relate the cause of some common ailments to occupational circumstances, but the legislators were afraid of opening the floodgates to claims, and benefit was made available only for specified diseases in certain dangerous occupations (e.g. pneumoconiosis of miners).

Very few countries had, by 1939, entered the third phase of extension, to cover accidents to and from work. The pioneer was the Netherlands as a result of interpretations of the law of 1921. Generally this was considered to be too remote from the risks of the production process to be covered by these special laws.

The Spread of Insurance

As might have been expected, even in those countries where insurance was not compulsory, it was the practice of employers to insure themselves against the risk of compensation to their workers. This led to the growth of employers' liability insurance companies, with vast assets, and legislators intervened to regulate the probity and solvency of these companies. The danger remained that the employer would not insure and so there was continuing pressure for compulsory insurance with private companies, or for the state to take over the insurance. One approach to this was the Belgian law of 1903, which allowed the employer to insure himself or to make payments into a guarantee fund which acted only if the employer became insolvent. In Denmark insurance became compulsory in 1916; in Britain it was made compulsory in 1934 but only for colliery owners for accidents and diseases lasting more than six months. By 1939 the advantages to both the victims of accidents and the employers in having systematic insurance on an obligatory basis had become widely recognised, but not extensively implemented.

THE DEVELOPMENT OF PROTECTION AGAINST NON-VOCATIONAL RISKS

Old Age, Disability and Death

Those countries which adopted the compulsory national insurance solution to the social risks of wage-earners expanded and improved the provision for old age, permanent disability and survivorship. In Germany the age at which retirement pensions became payable was lowered in 1916 from 70 to 65, and a number of modest changes in widows' and orphans' pensions were made in the Weimar period. In Britain the Old Age Pensions Act of 1908, providing a state pension as of right to those over 70 years of age, had followed the Bismarckian precedent and also that of the New Zealand Old Age Pensions legislation of 1898. Joseph Chamberlain had proposed, before the Anglo-Boer War, a voluntary contributory scheme leaving a major role to the friendly societies, but the societies opposed this because they feared that a state subsidy might eventually lead to nationalisation of their funds. The compulsory state scheme was a recognition that the friendly societies could not bear the costs of an ageing population often drawing sickness benefits as a kind of disguised pension. The 1908 Act was followed by one in 1925 providing a compulsory old-age pension insurance scheme for all wage-earners over 65 years of age and, after death, to widows and surviving children. Workers in the higher income brackets (above £250 a year in 1925) were excluded. There was a uniform (flat rate) pension, without regard to income for those eligible for compulsory insurance. In Luxembourg as well, those above a certain level of income were excluded until a law of 1931 established private pension plans for the higher income groups. In the Netherlands there were fundamental disagreements which delayed the introduction of a compulsory state insurance scheme for workers until 1913 and it was brought into operation only after the First World War in 1919.

In those countries where the 'subsidised freedom' principle was favoured, there was a tendency to follow in the footsteps of the compulsory state insurance schemes. In Belgium a law of 10 May 1900 had introduced a free pension for workers over 65 who were in need. In

1911 compulsory insurance for old-age pensions for miners, with state subsidies and employers' contributions, was introduced, and after the First World War laws of 1919 and 1920 conferred a free pension on every Belgian within certain limits of age and income. A minimum allowance was established by a law of 1924. A further law, of 29 July 1925, introduced an additional pension scheme for salaried workers under an employment contract. This law embodied the novel principle of an earnings-related pension. Contributions were determined in accordance with the salary level, and the ultimate pension was also related to the worker's salary.

In Italy, where the National Fund for Disabled and Aged Workers had been set up in 1898 linked to the voluntary principle, it was only in 1917, as a result of the demands of war production, that a compulsory insurance scheme was introduced for workers engaged in the auxiliary industries requisitioned by the government for war use (about 2,184 firms with 800,000 workers). This was the thin edge of the wedge, being followed by the decree of 29 April 1919,which provided for earnings-related contributions and a pension for those aged 65 and over proportionate to the contributions paid. An attempt to extend this to some of the self-employed in agriculture was abandoned in 1923 after the Fascists took power. However, from 1926 the fascist movement was converted to the rapid building of a corporative state and, following pension increases in 1928, the régime introduced in 1935 a unified social security system providing compulsory insurance in the case of old age, disablement, tuberculosis, involuntary unemployment and maternity, covering virtually all categories of employed workers. From a formal standpoint there was a substantial growth of social security in the fascist period, but beneath the surface there was a lack of co-ordination and unification and the real level of pensions was not much affected.

In France a law of 5 April 1910 had instituted a system of workers' and agricultural labourers' retirement pensions for those engaged in industry, commerce and agriculture, but this law was never fully applied because the courts were not willing to force employers and workers to pay contributions. There was an unsuccessful bill proposed in 1921 for a system of national insurance. This was indirectly influenced by Bismarck's legislation because Alsace and Lorraine had been incorporated in the German system before they were returned to France. However, it was only in the period 1928–30 that insurance schemes were enacted to protect wage-earners, whose wages were below a certain level, against risks including death, disablement and old age. These schemes were financed by equal contributions by employers and wage-earners.

The debate as to whether old-age pensions should be free or subject to the payment of contributions is most vividly illustrated in Denmark. An Act of 1891 had removed from the Poor Law all those over 60 who were unable to care for themselves. They received 'alms relief' at the discretion of local authorities. In 1922 this was done away with and replaced by a right for those over the age of 65 to receive a pension at fixed rates, varying according to the income of those eligible to receive it. There was a protracted controversy, in commissions and between political parties as to whether old-age pensions should be paid without any contribution by those receiving them. There was no popular support for the surrender of the principle of free pensions, and the social reform Acts of 1933 retained this principle, financing old-age benefits out of taxation.

Sickness and Maternity

The national insurance principle also came to be favoured in most European countries in relation to sickness, but with some important divergences and generally with a much stronger role for the mutual aid societies than in the case of old age, disablement and death. Contractual liability to pay wages during non-vocational illness was generally inadequate. In some countries, such as Britain, various schemes for the employer to continue paying wages for limited periods of illness were established as a result of collective bargaining.

Once again it is necessary to distinguish those countries which followed the national insurance solution from those favouring the idea of state help for self-help. In Germany, during the Weimar period, the national insurance scheme provided free medical treatment and half the basic wage from the fourth day of absence from work for the duration of the illness but not exceeding twenty-six weeks. Benefits could, however, be extended for longer periods of invalidity. Maternity pay was also extended in 1914 and 1923. In Britain the National Insurance Act of 1911 compulsorily insured all those between 16 and 70 in manual employment and all in non-manual employment earning less than a certain amount, and in return any contributor was entitled to enrol on the 'panel' of any doctor who agreed to participate in the scheme and to receive from him free medical treatment. The contributor also received sickness benefit, which like the German scheme lasted for twenty-six weeks and could be extended for disablement. There was a small maternity benefit but apart from this at first only the insured contributor was covered and not his family. An Act of 1919 extended the coverage of health insurance, although still not to dependants of the insured. For those falling outside the scope of the legislation, recourse still had to be had to the Poor Law and the friendly societies. In the Netherlands the attempts to introduce compulsory sickness insurance generated so much conflict that it was not until 1941 that a compulsory health insurance scheme for workers was launched. In France the national insurance scheme introduced in the 1928–30 period limited coverage to workers whose wages were below a certain level, until 1942. As in similar schemes elsewhere, contributions were payable by worker and employer. The complexity of the mixture of public and private administration is striking in the French scheme. There were *caisses* (social security offices), to which the worker could choose to affiliate. These might be private (*caisse primaire*), or the office of the *département* where the worker lived, these in turn being backed by private insurance organisations. The scheme was also complicated by the fact that besides the national scheme, a number of schemes for special groups, established before 1928, continued to exist. The use of private insurance continued to dominate the operation of French national insurance for sickness and maternity, as well as other benefits.

In Belgium the mutual aid societies subsidised by the state reigned supreme in the field of sickness and temporary disability, a situation which changed only under the impact of the Second World War. In Italy a project to have a national sickness insurance scheme was seriously debated but abandoned in the period of Giollitti (before 1921). In the fascist period, the corporatist trade union organisations were given the delegated task of concluding collective agreements covering an entire profession or industry, and a law of 1926 decreed that such agreements must provide for the creation of mutual benefit sickness funds to be financed equally by employers and workers. A move towards compulsory insurance for non-vocational illness was made in 1927 by the obligatory insurance scheme against tuberculosis (which in 1925 caused the death of 60,148 people) and extended in 1939. In practice, however, the major source of insurance against illness continued to be the trade union and corporative mutual aid organisations, co-ordinated in 1938 and united into a single organisation in 1943.

In Denmark the voluntary sick clubs were the basis of health insurance. The Act of 1933 introduced a general obligation of membership in national insurance, but continued to be organised in two kinds of societies, the approved sick clubs, which had as members the entire unpropertied working population including the self-employed, and the sickness insurance societies, which provided an opportunity for the propertied classes to insure themselves against sickness and, should their economic status deteriorate, to transfer to the sick clubs. Active members paid a subscription entitling them to sickness benefits, while those who did not wish to join were compelled only to pay a small contribution as passive members giving them no right to benefits but the right to be accepted for sickness insurance should they later wish to join. Invalidity insurance was organised as a supplement to sickness insurance.

Family Support

In the period after the First World War a new problem emerged, that of providing allowances for family dependants. This is not a specifically vocational problem, because large families effect the economic situation of both wage-earners and the self-employed, but wage-earners as low-income earners are generally more exposed to this problem than other members of the working population, particularly in times of inflation. Before the First World War there were examples of French employers, such as the Klein company at Vizille (Isère) in 1884 and Harmel at Val-des-Bois in 1891, paying family supplements to those workers with children. In France and in Belgium there were pre-war schemes covering some civil servants. During the First World War the allowances to civil servants were increased, and they were generalised to cover most other government employees, railway workers and miners. Immediately after the war in most other countries family allowances were introduced for civil servants. During the war as well, attempts were made in France to generalise the family allowances by setting up employers' equalisation funds (*caisses de compensation patronales*). The employers made contributions (voluntary until 1932) to the fund, which distributed the allowances. Without these funds the spread of the allowance system would have been hindered, and some employers might have refused to employ men with families.

Legal intervention in France, Belgium, Italy, the Netherlands and in Germany took place under a variety of economic, demographic and political influences. The Great Depression, from 1929, made the future of the voluntary compensation funds in Belgium and France insecure. Without compulsion, employers would not have participated. So a Belgian law of 1930 (which had been preceded by one of 1928 applying only to government contractors) and a French law of 1932 made the contributions by employers to equalisation funds obligatory and standardised the allowances, which were extended to all industries and occupations. The allowances were based on the idea of a higher wage for the heads of families. They were strongly opposed by the French CGT (which feared that they would be used as an excuse for depressing wages) as infringing the principle of equal pay for equal work. In 1928 and 1929 the CGT said that the allowances were 'invented by the employers during the fight against the workers' organisations. . . . To counter this false and dangerous philanthropy the Congress demands the application of minimum wages specially determined for the purpose. . . . Family allowances should be completely independent of the work done by the parents.'

On the other hand, the Catholic Church had encouraged the idea of a family wage since the encyclical of Leo XIII *De Rerum Novarum* (1891) and the encyclical of Pius XI *Casti Conubii* (1930) and *Quadragesimo anno* (1931) favoured a differentiation of wages depending upon the family obligations of the worker. This influenced Christian employers and unions, particularly in Italy, where as in most countries state employees were the first to receive allowances. The extension of the scheme to the private sector was begun in 1934 under a collective agreement between the Fascist Confederation of Industry and the Fascist Confederation of Industrial Workers. Industry was changing to a 40-hour week, and the allowances served the function of protecting the earnings of men with children against the reduction in living standards. The scheme was financed by equal contributions from employers and workers. The scheme proved to be unfair to workers in industries where production was continuous or there were regular longer hours, because workers in these industries had to pay the contributions but received no allowances, because these were payable only to those working less than 40 hours. As a result, in 1936, the right to family allowances was dissociated from the number of hours worked in a week. The state also began to contribute to the scheme. In the Netherlands legislation was proposed in 1937 and enacted in 1939, providing family allowances for those wage-earners with at least three children in their care. In Britain, although some private employers had family allowance schemes, there was no legislation.

The demographic impulses behind family allowances can be seen in Nazi Germany, where large families were encouraged by granting financial advantages for the family including state allowances. In France, a *décret-loi* in 1938 sought to encourage the birth rate. Allowances were no longer payable for an only child more than 5 years old, but a new allowance for the *mére au foyer* (mother in the home) was introduced. The allowance was later increased to 10 per cent of the average wage for the *département*. This legislation was reorganised in the important *Code de la famille* in 1939, which extended the right to family allowances to the whole working population.

CONCLUSIONS

This study ends with the Second World War. By that time all the European welfare schemes were in need of fundamental reform. The war had not only disrupted the economic and political structure of Europe but had awakened deep movements for social equality and social security, reflected in the Beveridge Report (1942) in Britain, which in turn had a profound influence on the secretly written programme of the French National Resistance Council[4] on the Belgian *Pacte de Solidarité sociale* clandestinely negotiated between unions, employers and politicians, and on the Van Rhijn scheme worked out by the Dutch government in exile in London. These schemes were implemented at the conclusion of the war. In Germany and Italy, with the collapse of the totalitarian régimes, a new beginning also had to be made. These developments, which constitute the basis of the modern systems of social security, fall beyond the scope of this chapter.

What conclusions may we tentatively draw from the history of legal attempts to deal with social risks from the time of the Industrial Revolution until the Second World War? The general tendency in every country we have considered in this period was towards a system of compulsory social insurance against social risks. The diffusion of these schemes came not from the most industrially advanced liberal capitalist states, but from the socially conservative states where industrialisation was preceded by strong state action to wean the working class from radical socialist ideas. It was adopted in the liberal states when the ideology and practice of self-help was under severe strain.

From the viewpoint of legal development, the coverage and techniques of the laws was dominated by the contract of employment. With the exception of Denmark, where the self-employed were covered at an early date, the preoccupation with wage-earning workers is apparent. The divergences were between those systems which grafted on to the contract an element of compulsory insurance and those which developed state help for self-help, while keeping intact the contract of employment. As Renner said, social insurance in this period was 'not a socialist but an individualistic institution' (1949, p. 233). The problem of work accidents was approached through an adaptation of traditional rules of fault-based liability and was promoted by lawyers 'inspired by *laissez-faire* ideals, seeking to protect the sanctity of contract' (Bartrip and Burman, 1983, p. 220). Insurance was grafted on to the concept of

4. The text will be found in Appendix IV, p. 381, below.

the contract of employment. The first family allowances were linked to the idea of a 'wage'. None of the countries of Western Europe had yet adopted a comprehensive conception of social security. It was only when the problem of protecting the economic security of individuals was severed from the contract of employment, when this protection was recognised as a fundamental human right, that modern solutions were possible. It was from the ashes of labour law, which had failed to provide security, that social security law arose after the Second World War.

4

The Problem of Unemployment

Eliane Vogel-Polsky

INTRODUCTION

Unemployment can be seen as having two dimensions, the individual and the social.

Dismissal is the individual face of unemployment. Legal historians present the development of individual protection against dismissals as a progressive erosion of the primacy of the law of contract. As far as the contract of employment was seen as an appendage of the law of contract and of propery (see Ch. 1, above), the parties concerned were supposed to be theoretically equals and free to make their own law. It was (in de Visscher's famous phrase, 1911) 'equality between a starving stomach and a silver purse'. One could say that the development of the protective function of dismissal law rested upon the guarantee of a 'right to work'. We have seen (Ch. I, above) that the philosophy behind the 'right' to work was that the community has an obligation towards those citizens who are unable to support themselves. For example, in pre-industrial society the rules of the English common law had the incidental function of serving as a form of protection against seasonal unemployment for agricultural labourers. In the eighteenth century, Blackstone (1765, vol. 1, 463) considered it to be contrary to 'natural equity' for masters to have the benefit of their servants' work during the planting and harvesting seasons but to dismiss them so as to avoid supporting them during the unproductive winter. He gave this as the rationalisation for the presumption of yearly hiring of labourers. The effect of this presumption was to protect the local ratepayers who otherwise would have had the responsibility of maintaining agricultural labourers during the winter.

The development of industry gave a new twist to the 'right' to work. The individual worker had to be free to offer his labour-power on the labour market in a relationship that implied that jobs were under the sole control of the employer (see Ch. 1, above). For more than a century the contract of employment was subject, in the Continental countries, only to the general principles of civil law or, in England, of common law. This general framework permitted the employer to terminate the contract unilaterally, often without compensation. Gradually collective bargaining and trade union 'custom and practice' limited this power but then only partially and in certain industries with a very uneven development between different countries. It was only in the twentieth century that the state began to intervene, noticeably in limiting the employer's powers to dismiss in favour of the socially weaker workers. A study of the various techniques used reveals that they were similar in their effects even if they did not appear at the same time or were differently formulated. The 'right' to work then took a new dimension as between employer and worker.

The intervention of the state to provide protection against dismissals was part of a wider recognition of a social responsibility to maintain employment. This reflected changing perceptions of joblessness. At the present time, unemployment is often seen as distinct from the problem of poverty. However, during the nineteenth century care for the unemployed was still synonymous with care for the poor (Ch. 3, above). The idea that unemployment was a special social problem, distinct from the problem of poverty, and which could not be explained in terms of personal inadequacy emerged only in the last decades of the nineteenth century. Unemployment became a burning issue; books, theses and official reports began to be published in large numbers. Chapter 3 (above) describes the ideological, legal and historical context in which state intervention and later on social security developed. Clearly measures against unemployment emerged in the same climate. It is important to stress in this context as well how the linkage between the contract of employment and a system (outside of the contract) aimed to provide security to the jobless was difficult to establish. One may say that the social consequences of termination of the contract by the unilateral action of the employer were not questioned until the end of the nineteenth century.

According to Garraty (1978, p. 130), two approaches to the problem emerged, the first directed towards preventing or at least reducing unemployment, the second seeking to provide support for the unemployed. The preventionists thought in terms of establishing networks of employment offices (labour exchanges), of relocating 'surplus' labour, of devising means of reducing seasonal fluctuations in certain industries or co-ordinating the cycles of activity in different industries so that workers could shift from one trade to another in slack periods, and undertaking government purchases and construction projects so as to increase employment in bad times. The others stressed the idea of providing an income for the unemployed, and ultimately of compulsory unemployment insurance financed by workers, the employers and the state. There is a typical catalogue of the remedies suggested and provided for unemployment in the 1913 study by Lefort (1913, pp. 103ff.): (1) charity; (2) individual savings with a savings bank and a system of subsidiary state assistance; (3) public work policies (locally or nationally organised); (4) work relief; (5) agricultural colonisation (rural work camps); (6) organisation of employment offices and labour exchange agencies; and (7) unemployment insurance (voluntary or compulsory).

One could say that the 'discovery of unemployment' was attributable to the economists. Many of them tried to discover the dynamics of business cycles (like Clément Juglar, Michael Tugan-Baranowski, Eugen von Bergmann, Jean Lescure, Joseph Schumpeter, A. C. Pigou, Albert Aftalion, Ralph G. Hawtrey, Wesley Clair Mitchell). They made efforts to understand the social effects of cycles. For example, Pigou, professor of political economy at Cambridge, argued (1913, pp. 55 ff.) that the prime cause of unemployment was the lack of elasticity of wage rates. But he recognised that adjustment of wages to changes in the price levels could not be achieved without state intervention. He suggested that not only labour exchanges, special educational programmes, subsidised compulsory insurance, but also counter-cyclical public works programmes were needed. Unemployment was 'a problem of industry' as Beveridge (1909, revised 1930) indicated in the title of his famous book.

However, when one looks at the activities of the International Association on Unemployment before the First World War, it is striking that the connection between the individual and the social dimensions of unemployment was not made. The chief question was how to decrease the volume of unemployment. And the answer was to seek economic adjustments while improving the mobility of labour and maintaining complete freedom at the level of the enterprise.

During the First World War, unemployment fell sharply. This demonstrated, according to the Webbs (1927–29, 1963 reprint, vol. 2, p. 668) that there was no 'surplus population for which neither occupation nor wages could possibly be found' and that most of the unemployed could be 'usefully and even profitably' put to work. After the restoration of peace in 1918, state responsibility for helping the unemployed was recognised in most of Europe. 'Public policy towards unemployment was no longer controversial. The methods and the amount of assistance were still debatable but not the principle itself'

(Garraty, 1978, p. 146). Public authorities felt particularly concerned for the welfare of ex-soldiers, prisoners of war and refugees. For example, when in post-war Britain, in 1920, unemployment increased sharply, unemployment insurance became universal (only domestic servants and agricultural workers were excluded). In Italy, a compulsory unemployment insurance system was created during the same period. In Germany, during demobilisation, the revolutionary government obliged the communities to pay unemployment assistance to the jobless and establish a 'productive work relief' programme aimed at employing the jobless on road repair, soil conservation, canal building and similar public works. A network of employment exchanges was taken over by the state in 1919. But, when unemployment rose sharply after 1923, a system of unemployment aid, financed by workers' and employers' contributions, was established. In the boom of 1926, unemployment fell. The Reichstag then passed, in 1927, a very comprehensive Unemployment Insurance Act including agricultural workers and domestic servants. Weigert commented that 'the Germans tried harder than the British to maintain the distinction between insurance payments (*Arbeitlosenhilfe*) and outright public assistance (*öffentliche Fursörge*), classifying aid given to those who had exhausted their benefits without finding work as loans' (1933, p. 169). In France, unemployment was regarded as a less serious problem during this period. Only some skilled workers participated in state subsidised union employment insurance plans. During the War, a central fund to back up departmental and municipal unemployment relief programmes had been set up. After the end of hostilities, the fund was maintained. Employment exchanges were extended and during the early 1920s well over one million vacancies a year were filled through these offices. France in fact suffered from a shortage of manpower and received a vast influx of immigrants, mainly Spanish, Italian, Belgian and Polish workers.

The depression of the 1930s was a dramatic and culminating phase of the problem before the Second World War. Few constructive remedies or responses against unemployment were possible. Millions of workers were on the dole. Trade unions and national governments struggled to deal with their unemployed. But measures aimed to 'reduce' unemployment were primarily protective of those in employment, for example raising the school-leaving age; forcing married women out of the labour market; instituting early retirement schemes; repatriating foreign workers; exporting the jobless overseas and so on. Garraty states that the unions implicitly accepted high unemployment as the price to be paid for maintaining the wage levels of persons with jobs (1978, p. 193). 'They became', wrote Skidelsky, 'more interested in increasing the rate of unemployment benefits than in increasing employment' (1970, p. 23).

By the mid-1930s, most countries in Europe had adopted schemes of extraordinary relief in case of prolonged unemployment. In Germany, three trade union leaders, who were also economists, Wladimir S. Woytinsky, Fritz Tarnow and Fritz Baade (WTB), were urging policies aimed at increasing purchasing power. They saw unemployment insurance as a means to increase consumer demand. When in 1930 the growing rate of unemployment jeopardised the insurance fund, they rejected the proposed small reduction of unemployment benefits and this provoked the fall of the democratic government which became replaced by the dictatorship of the Reich President. After new elections there occurred the reduction of benefits that the unions had hoped to escape. A new WTB plan suggested the stimulation of consumption by inflation. But the chairman of the Social-Democratic Party, Otto Wells, opposed the WTB plan arguing that the Party had first to take care of the employed. It was rearmament by the Nazis which 'solved' the unemployment problem.

By 1938, the British and French governments decided to spend heavily on armaments, in response to German rearmament. This led to a decline in their unemployment. In 1939, with the outbreak of the Second World War unemployment ceased to be a 'problem'. War was the crudest 'solution' of all. The relationship between economic thought and public policy, which has been briefly surveyed here, is summed up by Garraty:

> What made the unemployment of the thirties so disastrous and caused it to last so long was principally a lack of understanding of the dynamics of early twentieth-century capitalism. . . . One of the most curious and indeed dismaying aspects of the Great Depression for those who study it today is the mountain of evidence in the record of governments deliberately doing things in an effort to end the depression that only made it worse. [1978, p. 2]

This chapter examines the record of governmental and legal measures which were applied and transplanted from one country to another in the period up to the Second World War. An understanding why these techniques failed is essential if we are to assess critically the many demands made during the economic depression of the 1980s to break away from the welfare state reforms of the post-war period. Those reforms were themselves a response to the tragedy of unemployment.

SPECIFIC POLICIES RELATED TO UNEMPLOYMENT

Labour Exchanges

The labour exchanges were one of the earliest attempts to regulate the labour market, by matching the stock of vacancies with the flow of jobseekers. At the beginning of the industrial era the theory of the labour market was simple: employers wanted to recruit workers; workers wanted jobs. The labour exchanges brought them together, and through mobility between firms, industries, occupations and localities, the demands of 'buyers' and 'sellers' of labour were met.

In practice, however, the labour market is highly complex, and it took more than a century to develop the possibilities and the strategy of employment services. The first placement bureaux were created as local responses to immediate problems. In the middle of the nineteenth century they existed for particular groups like domestic servants and agricultural labourers. They were frequently set up by charitable societies and complemented their activities for the unemployed poor. At the same time, private profit-making bureaux were in existence and their development led to great abuses. This was especially the case in France, where excessive fees were payable by the jobseekers. Some offices ran boarding houses and forced the workers to lodge in their establishments. Sometimes agreements were concluded between the managers of the bureaux and employers to dismiss people in order to force them to register again with the bureau. In nearly all countries the private profit-making bureaux had a bad reputation and their abolition was demanded by workers' representatives. Nevertheless, in the name of free enterprise their existence was recognised and maintained.

In order to avoid abuses and to give jobseekers and employers better opportunities, new initiatives were taken either by the employers or by trade unions. The employers' concern in creating their own placement offices was to organise and control labour supply; to find skilled or unskilled workers when needed and to replace strikers promptly when industrial conflict arose. The case of Germany illustrates this very well. According to Bueck, the General Secretary of the Central Association of German Industrialists in 1880, the employers wished 'to remain masters in their houses and therefore to take the labour exchanges into their own hands'. In Germany, under the system adopted by the Association of Berlin Metal Industrialists in 1890, the labour exchanges issued certificates to job applicants which qualified them to be hired by employers who were members of the Association. The exchanges checked whether the applicant was known as to be unwilling to work, to like drink, to be disobedient or to support strikes. The employers' exchanges were effectively used in case of strikes. The unions' exchanges did not function as well as those of the employers; they sought to limit access to enterprises which were on strike.

In the course of development of self-help institutions, private trade union agencies appeared. Sometimes they were created for political reasons, as in Germany, where they took care of Social-Democratic workers who had been dismissed because of the Anti-Socialist Act. In France trade union offices existed but they were inefficient, encountering as they did considerable difficulties because of employer hostility. In Denmark the same hostility was shown towards union labour exchanges. In Italy some trade unions organised placements between localities; for example, the National Hatters' Union. Local branches of the union sent a weekly list of vacancies (and wages offered) in their district as well as a list of union men in want of employment. In the glass industry a similar scheme was organised. But despite these efforts, results were meagre, only 100 to 150 men per annum being placed. One of the greatest difficulties to be overcome was the hostility of local workers to non-residents.

The weakness of the trade union labour exchanges derived from the fact that they operated for the benefit of their members only. They tended to protect them against non-unionised workers, they adopted a conservative position towards redundancies and were not fully accepted by the employers. Such criticisms were made, for instance, in the Belgian survey made at the request of the government in 1932 by the Fonds National de Crise. Before state intervention in the field of placement was fully accepted, joint management of labour exchanges, supported by public authorities, appeared to be an attractive formula. This appeared in Germany after the economic crisis of 1890. From that time the principle that placement in employment was essentially a municipal service characterised the German pre-war system. In 1898 the Union of German Labour Exchanges (Verband Deutscher Arbeitsnachweise) was founded. At the beginning of 1910 there were 462 public labour exchanges in the Empire. In 1908–09 the labour exchanges affiliated to the Verband filled 860,901 vacancies. They also took care of the placement of apprentices. In the case of strikes or lockouts, most of them worked as usual, but they informed the applicants of the dispute.

In the Netherlands, in about 1900, municipal authorities began to subsidise private placement agencies run on a non-profit-making basis. Eventually public placement agencies were established when the municipal authorities realised that private organisations—including trade unions—were unable to meet the need. In Denmark those labour exchanges which operated efficiently were based on a tripartite composition and organisation of the managerial board. This was the case of the municipal labour exchange of Copenhagen, which had been created in July 1901 under the control of a committee of eleven persons, of whom one was elected by the magistrates, two by the municipal council, four by the employers' union of Copenhagen and four by the city workers' union. It was also of great importance in Denmark that the activities of the labour exchanges, although organised by local agencies, were co-ordinated within a national network.

In Italy it was not until 1916 that official labour exchanges were added to those already created by private and local initiative. They gave significant support to trade union agencies, partly because a modest financial contribution was made for the organisation of placements and partly because they co-ordinated the vacancies in various local areas and therefore permitted the unions to concentrate on a wider strategy. During the fascist period, placement was totally reorganised under the control of the Ministry of Corporations and through the corporative trade unions. In 1927 the Charter of Labour established labour exchanges under the control of corporative organs of the state. But there was no obligation for employers to apply to them. However, a clause gave precedence in the field of employment to members of the National Fascist Party and of the corporative trade unions. In 1935 an important decision was taken by the Grand Council of Fascism affirming for the first time the principle of numerical requirement and recognising 'the need for restricting to well defined cases the possibility of choice'. The decree of 21 December 1938 (No. 1934) established the principle of numerical requirement while two later decrees specified the categories of skilled workers who could be requested by special nomination (*richiesta nominativa*).

In Belgium the development of placement agencies followed a similar course to the other countries surveyed. The initial development was of private agencies charging fees. These were not numerous and dealt almost exclusively with domestic servants. Special agencies organised by trade unions were established, but they worked for the benefit of their members. Only the more important societies operated efficiently. The first free labour exchange, open to all workers without distinction, was founded in Liège in 1888 by a charitable association. Following this example, exchanges called *bourses du travail* were founded in Brussels, Charleroi, Ghent and Antwerp. They were the result of the initiative of philanthropic societies or municipalities. By 1904 ten were in existence. The government at that time decided to subsidise them under two conditions: they had to be under the joint management of employers and workers, and they had to send annual reports to the Labour Office. Subsidies consisted of an initial grant for opening and an annual sum for working expenses. By 1910 twenty-four had been recognised by the government.

After the First World War state intervention in the field of placement was fully recognised in every country. In most of them they co-existed with the private agencies. In Belgium a royal decree of 19 February 1924 set up the essential rules of the official *bourses du travail*: (1) joint management (public authorities, employers' and workers' representatives); (2) the principal task of these agencies was to organise placement by maintaining the flow of vacancies and submitting unemployed people to employers, working together with the recognised private agencies; (3) the establishment of a link between unemployment insurance and placement, by ensuring that the same agency determined whether the jobseeker was willing to work and ready to take any suitable job offered by the placement bureau (moreover, the jobseeker had to be registered with a local agency under daily control, and unemployment benefits were cut if the jobseeker refused work without a reasonable ground). Claim committees were set up in order to examine the willingness to work of those in receipt of unemployment benefits. Besides the official services, the private *bourses du travail* still remained in action. During the economic crisis of the 1930s the level of unemployment was very high and continued to rise. In order to rationalise the placement services and to reduce registered unemployment, a scheme of reorganisation of the *bourses du travail* was investigated in 1932 by the Fonds National de Crise. In 1934 the Office National du Placement et du Chômage was created. It stimulated the activities of public agencies at local, regional and national levels and controlled the activities of the co-existing private agencies. The number of people unemployed, registered in the official or the private bureaux was surveyed by the employment services. The private agencies had to provide information on their clients and the stock of available vacancies. The weakness of the system was due to the absence of compulsory notification of vacancies.

In Germany the Reich Office of Labour Exchanges was established in 1920 and in 1922 the Labour Exchanges Act was introduced. This Act left the organisation of placement agencies to the local authorities but with self-government and participation by employers and employees. The monopoly of the exchanges was breached by permitting special agencies for white-collar workers and agencies of religious welfare organisations. There was no obligation on employers and workers to use the services of the exchanges. The Labour Exchanges and Unemployment Insurance Act 1927 established the system which still exists.

In Britain W. H. Beveridge, under the influence of the German system, proposed the establishment of public labour exchanges and the Royal Commission on the Poor Laws reported in 1909 that 'the national labour exchange is the foundation of all our proposals. It is, in our view, an indispensable condition of any real reforms'. Beveridge saw the exchanges as fulfilling the dual purpose of reducing the time taken by workers in looking for work, and supplying machinery for compulsory unemployment insurance.

The Labour Exchanges Act 1909 was passed with practically no opposition. The system of labour exchanges established under this Act (sixty-one opened in 1910) was national in both senses of the word: it was intended to extend to all parts of the United Kingdom and it was directly managed and paid for by a national authority, the Board of Trade (forerunner of the Department of Employment). The central office was situated in London. It did not deal with employers or workers directly but served simply for organisation, control and statistics. Under this central office the whole country was divided into eleven principal divisions, each under the charge of a divisional officer who had absolute authority over all the exchanges in his division. Each division was a unit for purposes of control and also for the purpose of 'clearing house' work; that is, the transfer of unemployed people in one place to meet an unsatisfied demand for labour elsewhere. The system was industrial and dealt with skilled and unskilled workers. Every attempt had been made to free the labour exchanges from any form of association with the Poor Law, charity or the relief of distress and to give to them the character of an industrial organisation of which any person might avail himself and 'with as little loss of self-respect as is involved in using the post office or a public road', in Beveridge's words (1911, p. 7). The questions asked of work-people at the exchanges were to relate solely to their industrial qualifications and not to their poverty, family circumstances, thrift or similar matters. The system was free and voluntary. No compulsion was exercisable upon employees or workers to use the labour exchanges against their will. A special fund was established to provide funds for those having to travel to find work. From the start Beveridge insisted, and administrative regulations ensured, that strict 'neutrality' would be observed in trade disputes. Exchanges were closed to employers seeking 'blackleg' labour, and the full co-operation of unions was ensured by providing that a worker was entitled to refuse any job offer which might result in his being paid less than the going union rate.

In the Netherlands a similar pattern is to be found in the Employment Agencies Act (*Arbeidsbemiddelingswet*) of 1930. This Act confirmed the responsibility of municipalities with more than 15,000 inhabitants to establish and maintain municipal employment agencies according to their own needs. Other municipalities could confine themselves to maintaining branches of employment agencies. The Act divided the country into districts; it established the National Employment Office and laid down some fundamental principles for the functioning of the public employment agencies. In 1940, under the German occupation, this decentralised pattern of organisation of employment agencies was replaced by a highly centralised system that was maintained after the Second World War up to the present day. Municipal responsibility was withdrawn. Regional employment agencies were set up and controlled by the National Employment Office. Apart from the period of German occupation between 1940 and 1945, employers' organisations and trade unions participated in the direction of the municipal employment agencies and of the national employment office. The Employment Agencies Act of 1930 required private placement agencies to operate under permits. Private non-profit placement agencies were only tolerated so far as they already existed, but new ones could not apply for a licence. These agencies were of importance for special categories of workers (such as disabled persons and ex-prisoners). Sometimes they were established by collective agreements.

In France, a *décret* of 25 March 1852 created local, municipal and provincial offices (*bourses du travail*) controlled by the Mayor and the Prefect. But the fees were high and they were inefficient. A league for the abolition of the employment bureaux campaigned against them. The law of 14 March 1904 achieved a compromise by increasing the powers of the municipalities and authorising the optional closing of profit-making bureaux. In fact, only 64 were closed out of about 1,400 registry offices in France! The establishment of free municipal exchanges was scarcely undertaken. The Act gave freedom to gratuitous agencies of any kind, and some of these, under the name of trade union or mutual agencies were in reality clandestine fee-paying offices.

Just before the First World War the organisation of neutral agencies became a necessity. It was after 1914 that structured state organisations to deal with employment began to appear. The unemployment resulting from the First World War was evidently the main cause of this development. A central office for the placement of the unemployed and refugees was created. Its task was to help with the rehabilitation of the unemployed and refugees in the north. In 1915 government circulars were sent to all the Prefects, advising the creating of departmental employment councils (*conseils généraux*). These officers were requested to encourage contact with the employers as well as with the workers and their union organisations. Committees composed of workers and employers on an equal footing were instituted associated with these offices. In this way a pyramidal organisation was formed. In 1918 the existing offices were complemented by regional employment exchanges. The system as a whole was placed on a legal basis by the law of 10 February 1925. Subsequent reforms completed this system. A major reform took place on the eve of the Second World War. By a law of 11 July 1938, concerning the organisation of the nation during wartime, and a *décret* of 12 April 1939, services concerning the labour force were placed in their entirety under the jurisdiction of the Minister for Labour. Much closer co-ordination was established between the various employment exchanges and the unemployment fund.

The Vichy régime had the idea of instituting a public employment service (law of 11 October 1940). A network of employment offices dependent on the state was created, composed of regional and departmental offices with local branch offices; the system of consultative committees of workers and employers was maintained. These employment offices had a much broader role. They supervised the private employment bureaux and ensured the execution of the applicable employment policy. They were also associated with the various measures taken to fight against inflation; they dealt with the registration of unemployed workers and investigated and helped those cases where aid had been requested. Besides this they also controlled the work of foreigners; more specifically, they had the task of investigating all requests for work permits. This system was modified by the orders of 3 July 1944 and 24 May 1945 as well as by the *décret* of 20 April 1948. The new system allowed the free employment offices to continue their service. The private fee-paying employment bureaux were at last abolished. The scope of the duties of the state employment service was then extended.

Public Works Programmes

As time passed and high unemployment persisted, some governments expanded public works programmes. Nazi Germany did so on a large scale with the obligatory Reich Labour Service and the *autobahnen* but unemployment was mainly reduced by rearmament. In the Netherlands, public works were used on a modest scale in the 1930s, but Britain, France and Belgium made little use of them.

In Britain, the well-established unemployment insurance system created a political obstacle for those in favour of work relief. The pressure of the 'Treasury view' of public works was a major reason for abstention in this field. In France the same budgetary obsessions were an obstacle for work relief policies; budget-balancing was the major preoccupation. Resettlement of unemployed workers in rural areas again appeared as a remedy. Most of the camps of the 1930s were directed towards young people. The main purpose was not to employ the jobless productively but to prevent youth from disillusionment and from the demoralising effect of unemployment by keeping them occupied. According to Adolf Hitler, the Nazi youth camps were designed to prevent young Germans from 'rotting helplessly in the streets'.

The back-to-the-soil movement reflected the disappointment with industrial society that the prolonged depression had provoked, and symbolised a form of rejection of industrial civilisation, bearing some parallels with the ecological movement of the present day. But another current placed faith in the power of industrial production to eliminate unemployment. Instead of trying to create new jobs, it was argued, society should take advantage of the efficiency of mechanisation to reduce the working time of individuals, and to reduce the age of retirement.

Emigration

The Scope of the Problem

Over the centuries Europe has been a continent of emigration, a reservoir for the colonisation of the Americas and Oceania. But the flow was not constant and depended upon many factors. Kirk (1946, Ch. 5) has compiled statistics which show that the largest spontaneous migrations from Europe were recorded between 1901 and 1905, with an annual average of 1 million; between 1906 and 1910, with an annual average of 1.4 million; and between 1911 and 1915, with an annual average of 1.3 million.[1]

In the early 1920s the population of nearly all the European nations increased considerably, with the exception of France. In the nineteenth century there had been a significant redistribution of population and manpower at the subnational levels in northern and western regions. This brought rural people to the urban and industrial areas. At the turn of the century there was already high industrial concentration in those regions. Examples of high concentration were Britain with over 6 million workers in manufacturing, Germany with nearly 6 million,

1. Additional statistics on emigration will be found in Appendix III, p. 361, below.

France with over 5 million, Belgium with over 1 million. The Netherlands, northern Italy and Denmark had smaller numbers but a not insignificant proportion of industrial labour.

In the early twentieth century, the Americas and Oceania attracted the unemployed and dispossessed poor of Europe. In general there were no governmental measures to prevent emigration from the countries of Europe. This was a *laissez-faire* situation in which migrants took all the risks. But, on the other hand, overseas governments favoured immigration and imposed only limited control of entry. The First World War, however, practically blocked migration. After the war, the USA adopted a restrictive policy with the 1921 Quota Law and the 1924 Immigration Restriction Act. With the exception of the war and post-war periods, both the overseas and the intercontinental migrations affecting Europe were basically determined by economic factors. The prospect of employment opportunities and better living conditions in the receiving countries coincided with poverty and unemployment in the sending countries. However, after the First World War, ethnic, national, political and ideological factors played an important role in international migration. Milos Macura writes:

> Changes in national boundaries, the emergence of new nations, the deliberate policy of the Nazi government in Germany and the revolutionary change affecting political and social structures in the East were the immediate causes of massive population transfers. [1976, pp. 55–6.]

During the Second World War the Third Reich developed a war labour policy for the exploitation of other countries' manpower. By military or political domination over ever larger parts of Europe, Germany for several years acquired mastery over millions of non-German workers. The policy of exploiting military conquests for the forced deportation of foreign labour started with the campaign against Poland in September 1939. Later, every new extension of Nazi domination was followed by a systematic and large-scale utilisation of foreign manpower. The recruitment of foreign workers was in line with the National Socialist doctrine. A systematic use of propaganda in the 'colonised and occupied territories' sought to induce workers to volunteer for work in Germany. It laid great emphasis on the fact that these countries were suffering from large-scale unemployment and that the only efficient way of combating it would be to transfer large numbers of workers to Germany. It is difficult to estimate the numbers involved. According to estimates made by the ILO in 1944, approximately 8,670,000 foreign workers (6,450,000 civilians and 2,000,000 employed war prisoners) were working in the area of greater Germany (ILO, 1944, p. 470). However, an estimate made by the International Federation of Trade Unions (1944, p. 8) in late September 1944 put the number as high as 'up to 15 million'. We have to mention especially the exploitation of Jews. They were used for forced labour either in labour camps, or in the ghettos which were established by the Germans, as well as being sent to concentration camps. About the beginning of 1943, the systematic extermination of the Jews was accelerated, a policy which can be explained by the determination of the Nazis to carry out their geopolitical and racial doctrines. The National Socialist authorities decided that the physical reduction of the European Jews was more important than the utilisation of their labour. After the Second World War, the collapse of Germany gave rise to a large westward migration of Germans and other nationals who supported German occupation of their countries.

Political change in Eastern Europe was another factor in migration. The war-related migration was characterised by an unprecedented number of displaced persons and refugees. Since millions of people were involved, overseas migration from Europe to other Continents again occurred on a large scale. A new aspect of the immediate post-war migration was that most of it was assisted and organised by international efforts. The economic growth of Western countries after the Second World War depended to a large extent on imported labour.

Legal Provisions: Organisations and Methods

By the middle of the nineteenth century, freedom of emigration was generally recognised. It resulted from the general provisions of legislation (e.g. the German law of 9 June 1897, the French law of 18 July 1860, the Belgian law of 14 December 1876, and the British Act of 1825 lifting restrictions on the emigration of artisans). But free movement of population was counter-balanced by the right of the state to protect its territory and population. Under the combined influence of individualist and public-interest theories, most legislation expressly admitted the right of free movement for their citizens only under various legal restrictions. For example, in Italy, the law of 13 November 1919 (Art. 3) provided that 'Emigration is free subject to the limits adopted by the laws'.

The chief limitations on emigration were designed to protect various interests, such as those of creditors, minors and the family, and to ensure fulfilment of military duties, or to satisfy medical or police requirements, or to channel emigration (such as the Dutch Emigration Act of 1936 which prohibited recruitment to work outside Europe without a ministerial licence). There was regulation against exploitation of migrant workers, through public offices or local and specialised private agencies. The lack of knowledge on the part of migrant workers of the legal conditions of work and wages was a frequent source of abuse. Some countries required such information to be given to migrants (e.g. in Germany by the Reichswanderungsamt; in Britain by the Overseas Settlement Committee; in Italy by the Comitati dell'Emigrazione; in the Netherlands by the Landverhuizing Vereeniging, etc.). Special provisions were also adopted concerning the recruitment and the transportation of foreign workers, in particular the terms and conditions of the passage contract. Emigrant 'runners' were severely repressed and the activities of passage brokers and the cost of passage were controlled. Reduced fares were sometimes organised through public subsidies given to migrants whose departure resulted from unemployment.

Great differences are to be found in the various countries of our study. Of special interest is the organisation of the rural exodus in Germany which affected particularly the five eastern provinces of Prussia. The most important cause was the seasonal character of modern agriculture, which was especially marked in the east. An internal migration was organised by public labour exchanges and profit-making private bureaux. The public labour exchanges catered only for German workers. But the Chambers of Agriculture also organised the importation of foreign workmen. In 1905 a German Central Bureau was established which controlled forty-eight frontier offices. The cost of procuring the workers was paid by the employers. But a fee of 2 marks was imposed upon each migrant worker in order to prevent breach of contract. From 1910 these bureaux also procured industrial workers. The emigrants came principally from Austria and Russia, and the large majority of them were unskilled workers. For some seasonal workers a compulsory return at the end of the year was imposed. Seasonal rural workers were badly exploited by profit-making agencies which frequently asked more than 10 per cent of the seasonal wages. In Germany a decree of 21 December 1907 made 'legitimation cards' compulsory for foreign rural workers. These were a kind of work-book (see Ch. 1, above), including the name and address of the employer. Each job change had to be indicated on the card by the police. Breach of contract on the part of the worker gave rise to deportation.

In the Netherlands foreigners formed a substantial part of the labour force during the nineteenth century. It was not until the 1930s that the government enacted protective provisions aimed at giving priority to Dutch workers on the labour market. In 1934 the *Wet tot regeling van het verrichten van arbeid door vreemdelingen* (Foreign Workers' Regulation Act) was passed, which empowered the Crown to stipulate that certain kinds of work should not be done by foreign workers without a written licence from the Minister. The Act did not give any guideline for the exercise of his discretion. An employer who employed foreign workers without licence or in contravention of the terms of the licence could be punished, and the foreigner was liable to expulsion.

Denmark was a country of immigration, recruiting mainly seasonal rural workers from Eastern Europe. The law of 21 August 1908, amended by a law of 1 April 1912, sought to protect foreign workers and regulated their recruitment, contracts, wages and living conditions. The employer was obliged to register the foreign worker and to inform the police of the terms and conditions of employment. A written contract had to be given to each worker. The employer had to insure foreigners under Danish employment injury (accident and disease) insurance in the same way as Danish workers. This legislation was remarkably advanced for its times.

In the nineteenth and early twentieth centuries some 21 million British citizens emigrated to the USA and to the British colonies and dominions overseas. The total numbers (including Scots and Irish) who left averaged 20,000 a year in the 1820s, 50,000 a year in the 1830s, 120,000 a year in the 1840s (the year of the Irish famine), 150,000 a year in the 1880s (the Great Depression) and 110,000 in the 1890s. This was the result of a deliberate policy. A parliamentary committee in 1826 had recommended emigration as a remedy for surplus population, and emigrants were financially assisted. At the beginning of the twentieth century emigration (especially by the Irish) increased considerably from year to year (there were nearly 300,000 emigrants in 1911). The majority of the emigrants no longer went to the USA but to the British Empire (nearly 80 per cent in 1911). This was due in particular to the activities of an official institution (the Emigrants' Information Office) and of private institutions like the East End Emigration Fund, the Salvation Army, the British Dominions Emigration Society, and so on, who contributed towards the cost of passage. At the turn of the century there was also fairly large-scale immigration to Britain, mainly of East European Jews fleeing from pogroms. This immigration gave rise to restrictive measures such as the Aliens Act of 1905.

In Italy mass unemployment was endemic. Emigration acted as a safety valve. There was a large-scale exodus during the 1880s which continued throughout our period. Moreover, regular movements of workers, mainly in agriculture, took place from south to north Italy. Various governments remained completely inactive regarding this phenomenon, so appearing to believe in the principles of economic liberalism in their purest form. There was no intervention on the part of public authorities during the last decades of the nineteenth century. On the contrary, profit-making private agencies exploited migrants and other jobseekers. This abstention coincided with a favourable balance of trade during the same period. It can be said that emigration, especially overseas, made a financial contribution to the industrialisation of Italy. The majority of the emigrant workers sent part of their earnings home to their families or brought back their savings when they returned home. Calculations for the period 1901–13 show that, against a commercial deficit of 10,230 million lire, invisible items showed a credit of 12,291 million lire, over one-third of which came from tourism and over one-half from emigrants' remittances. The majority of those emigrants were poor peasants from the southern regions. Luciano Cafagna comments, 'thus one of the characteristic features of Italian dualism—the extreme poverty of the south—played a part as an organic component of the development process that went on between 1896 and 1913' (1973, p. 325).

During the fascist period in Italy severe restrictions were imposed on emigration, but the régime involved central and southern Italy in the so-called 'battle for corn' and in land reclamation work. The consequence of this policy was a further massive increase in agricultural overpopulation. Between 1921 and 1936 the population of southern Italy increased from 8,900,000 to 10,054,000, while there was a reduction in the working population from 46.6 per cent to 38.8 per cent. This was not even partially absorbed by emigration or colonisation (in April 1936 more than 110,000 southerners were enrolled in the colonial armies). Internal emigrations led to huge numbers of workers from the regions of Apulia, Veneto and Sicily moving to Milan and Turin. During the Second World War the Commissariato per le Migrazioni e la Colonizzazione organised the recruiting of Italians for Germany, and the German labour administration established a special branch office in Rome. It arranged the transportation of workers from Italy to Germany and made all the administrative preparations. A model contract for the employment of Italian industrial workers in Germany was concluded between the German employers and the Italian Fascist Confederation of Industrial Workers, which acted as representative of the workers who were to be sent to Germany. This was the first time, in Italian social history, that specific regulations were adopted to specify and control the type of work, qualifications needed and wage and bonus scales of migrant workers. Unfortunately, these regulations were made by the Fascist Confederation of Industrial Workers in the interests of Nazi Germany. After the Second World War free movement of workers was re-established, and the flow of emigration rose to the numbers of the pre-fascist period. As regards the south, mass emigration was renewed and served as a safety valve against unemployment and as a means of obtaining an inflow of foreign currency.

Remedies Against the Consequences of Unemployment: Unemployment Insurance

By the mid-nineteenth century a number of trade unions had developed benefit funds to sustain unemployed members. But their financial means were limited and unable to deal with major economic crises. Some funds insured only members of trade unions, while others insured any person, even non-unionised, belonging to the same trade or profession.

Belgium pioneered a system of voluntary insurance subsidised with public funds by municipal government. The first experiment was in Liège. From 1898 the provincial council granted subsidies to trade unions with unemployment insurance funds. At that time only two associations were in existence in the province. The 'Ghent system' was the best known. It encouraged any effort made by a worker, either individually or collectively, to protect himself in case of unemployment. It was not relevant to the municipality which financed the benefits whether these efforts consisted of contributions to a savings bank, or membership of a non-profit insurance society or a friendly society or trade union fund. The only requirement was that savings or other individual efforts had been made to secure a minimum livelihood. The basis of the system was partly moral. It was based on the premise that unemployment (like poverty) was the result of the deficiencies of the individual concerned and not of the economic system in which they lived. But in some ways the Ghent system was the beginning of a social reform which regarded unemployment as a social problem. The scheme gave an incentive to people at work to pay contributions which entitled them to a benefit when they were out of work because of unemployment. The municipality contributed to the fund which financed the benefits. Contributors received a supplementary benefit of 50 per cent on top of their contributory benefits. It was a mixture of individualism, self-help and state subsidy. For the first time unemployment insurance was proclaimed to be in the interests of both the individual and of society. It was a compromise solution between individual responsibility and collective action through the municipality.

Indirectly, the Ghent system favoured the trade unions. They were able to organise and recruit members through their unemployment funds. Before the First World War numerous *caisses de chômage* (unemployment funds) were created all over Belgium by the trade unions. Their founders believed that they had a role not as an insurance scheme receiving contributions and giving allowances to unemployed members but rather to prevent the deterioration of the working conditions and of wages. It was said that in periods of industrial crisis the *caisse de chômage* had the same mission to play that the *caisse de résistance* (strike fund) had during strikes. The trade unions regarded unemployment funds as part of their strategy to maintain the level of the wages and to prevent jobseekers from accepting inferior conditions. Since the *caisses de chômage* which were recognised received subsidies from the public authorities, they had to fulfil some conditions related to their statutes and regulations. The Minister of Labour monitored their activities and exercised some control over them.

By 1934 the trade unions had a monopoly of the sytem of unemployment insurance in Belgium. Their funds covered 95 per cent of the insured workers. The number had increased from 126,000 insured in 1914, to 700,000 in 1933. In the latter year a legal reform placed financial control in the hands of official funds which received the contributions and distributed them amongst the various *caisses*. In 1934 the Office du Placement et du Chômage was set up to take charge of the funds and to exercise control over the conditions of entitlement to benefit (e.g. age of admission, duration of unemployment and the means test).

The Ghent system was the model adopted by many cities in the Netherlands, Germany and Italy (in the latter through the active propaganda of the society Umanitaria). In 1905 the French government began contributing to trade unions' insurance plans on a national basis, and few years later, Denmark did likewise. In Denmark, by provisions of the Act of Unemployment Insurance Societies of 9 April 1907, unemployment insurance societies could be recognised and subsidised by the state or the municipalities, the subsidies coming from municipalities being optional and they could not exceed one-third of the total of members' subscriptions. The state subsidy was compulsory and amounted to half the total of members' subscriptions and the municipal subsidy combined.

In those countries the insurance plans were all voluntary. They covered few workers and provided relatively low benefits. Compulsory insurance, financed by workers' and employers' contributions and subsidised by public funds, appeared to be much more efficacious. But the compulsory insurance idea was highly controversial. Liberals maintained that no one should be compelled to contribute and that insurance would undermine incentives to work. It was feared that unemployed people protected by insurance might become loafers and malingerers. This preoccupation explains the care taken to organise adequate tests of unemployment and to implement methods of control over unemployed people.

Private voluntary societies were content to refuse benefits only to insured persons who were flagrantly at fault. But when societies were subsidised by public funds it became a requirement that unemployment should have been entirely involuntary before benefit could be granted. Moreover, the continuance of unemployment was everywhere strictly supervised. This was done by the network of labour exchanges. The unemployed were usually required to register sometimes as often as once or twice daily and were subjected to visits by controllers without warning. A major difficulty was to find out whether or not the unemployed person had left his last situation of his own free will, as was verification of the reason for non-acceptance of a suitable job. The main preoccupation was to ensure that the insured person was making serious efforts to find work. The tests of unemployment were based on inquiries at the labour exchanges, certificates from the last employer and information obtained from the latter. In some systems benefits were refused if dismissal was due to the 'fault' or 'misconduct' of the employee, or if the unemployed person was engaged in 'dishonourable conduct', such as prostitution, concubinage, alcoholism or, in Belgium, the frequenting of cabarets.

This policy was not far removed from the fears of critics in the previous century about indiscriminate relief to the poor. To give benefit to the 'undeserving' unemployed was to encourage idleness and riotous living. This reflected a persistent suspicion that workers were potentially lazy and inefficient. Government subsidies for unemployment insurance appeared to middle-class opinion as a form of public charity and was not readily accepted.

A system of compulsory insurance against unemployment was adopted in Britain in 1911. It is no coincidence that Britain was then the most industrialised country and had experienced severe cyclical unemployment crises. The immediate inspiration for the National Insurance Act 1911 came from Lloyd George's visit to Germany in 1908, where he was much impressed by the Bismarckian model of social insurance, although at the time this did not include a compulsory unemployment benefit scheme. The only model of that kind was a law of the canton of St Gall in Switzerland in 1894, which had been abandoned as a failure after two years. Apart from what Lloyd George believed to be the German inspiration, there were considerable precedents in the 'out of work' benefits provided by trade unions. In 1908 there were 2.3 million trade union members and £1.25 million was paid out in unemployment benefits. Lloyd George's social policy was based, he said, in 'social pity', and it is doubtful whether the conservative and bureaucratic Bismarckian system was based on the same premise. Lloyd George, unlike Bismarck, denied that he had tried to bribe the working classes, and Beveridge, one of the civil servants who planned and built the details, stated bluntly in his memoirs that 'compulsory insurance against unemployment owed nothing to any working model in Germany or elsewhere' (Beveridge, 1911, p. 14). Certainly the compulsory insurance provisions for unemployment were without direct precedent. The National Insurance Act 1911, Part II, applied at first only to those industries such as shipbuilding, mechanical engineering and ironfounding in which severe fluctuations were known to occur and covered one-sixth of the working population ($2\frac{1}{4}$ million workers). The state supplemented the contributions of employers and employed; benefits were limited to one week for five weeks' contributions, with a limit of fifteen weeks in any period of twelve months. It did not cover benefits to dependants. This basic scheme was enlarged in later years. An Act of 1920 covered nearly 12 million workers including non-manual workers earning not more than £250 per year. By 1930, with mass unemployment, benefits were costing £110 million and contributions amounted to only £30 million. For those who exhausted their benefits, 'public assistance' (renamed from 'poor relief') was available. In 1946 the proposals of the Beveridge Report (1942) were implemented in the National Insurance Act, which made little change in the basic structure but extended the scheme to $19\frac{1}{4}$ million workers (all employed earners) and improved the benefits. National assistance was introduced as a replacement for poor relief.

In Germany, as already indicated, the much-admired social welfare legislation of the 1880s had not dealt with unemployment. The primary methods of protection demanded the personal efforts of each individual. These were the ordinary savings banks, co-operative societies (consumers' and building societies) and employers' funds. Mutual insurance was organised by trade unions. Joint unemployment funds supported by employers and employees were insignificant. Subsidised unemployment insurance funds were created in Leipzig and Cologne (*Freiwillige Versicherungskassen*). The proportional indemnity system (*Zuschussystem*) modelled on the Ghent system was adopted in several German towns such as Charlottenburg and Schönberg, near Berlin, Strasburg, Erlangen, Mulhauzen and Freiburg. Later a proportional indemnity system combined with optional funds was adopted by the Bavarian government. The idea of compulsory insurance on a municipal basis was proposed, and in 1906 the government published a memorandum in three volumes on 'The Present Institutions of Assuring against the Consequences of Unemployment in Foreign Countries and in the German Empire'. This included the labour exchanges. But no legislation followed. In 1913 the Reich Chancellor declared that the idea of compulsory insurance was premature. The problem was shelved, but 'demobilisation', the shift from a wartime to peacetime economy, under the pressure of the armistice of 1918, enforced an answer to this question. The decree on relief for persons out of work of November 1918 obliged local communities to care for poor unemployed, and Article 163 of the Weimar Constitution, which took over the formulation of Section 1 of the Socialisation Act of 23 March 1919, declared:

> Every German has without prejudice to his personal freedom the moral duty to exercise his mental and bodily forces as the welfare of the entity demands. Every German shall be enabled to acquire his livelihood by productive work. Where adequate work cannot be provided he will be given necessary support.

An Act on the labour exchanges and unemployment insurance was promulgated in 1927, establishing a new organisation, the Reich Institution for Labour Exchanges and Unemployment Insurance. Placement was combined with unemployment insurance, which completed the German system of compulsory social insurance. Employees and employers had to pay contributions proportional to the wage of the employee. Claim for support could be made only when the unemployed person was willing and able to work and was involuntarily unemployed. There was a waiting period and regular support was limited to a period of six months.

The Weimar Republic developed additional measures against unemployment:

—A decree of 8 November 1920 delayed plant closures by obliging the employers to give advance notice and wait for a certain time before closing a plant. The authorities could then requisition the plant and ultimately expropriate it.

—Work which would not be normally undertaken could be performed as 'productive unemployment protection'. Those 'emergency works' were financed out of the unemployment insurance fund because it was considered to be better to give an opportunity to work rather than support. This competed with the obligatory work (*Pflichtarbeit*) which was demanded from out-of-work persons who were supported by the communities and later on by the Voluntary Reich Labour Service. The motivating force was mainly ethical: to prevent the demoralising consequences of unemployment especially on the youth.

During the Nazi era the idea of the voluntary labour service was continued and combined with premilitary training. Hitler's promise to abolish unemployment was achieved by the new financial credit system of Reich President Dr Schacht, and by encouraging the withdrawal of women from the workforce, rebuilding the German army and organising a powerful armaments industry.

In the Netherlands it was not until the beginning of this century that the government showed an interest in supporting unemployment in ways other than by the Poor Law. In 1906 the first three municipal unemployment funds were established. They subsidised the unemployment benefits provided by private unemployment funds (mostly run by trade unions). After a royal commission in 1914 had advised the introduction of a statutory unemployment insurance scheme and the outbreak of the First World War had caused a sharp rise in the number of unemployed, the government launched a provisional scheme to support the municipal unemployment funds. The financial relationship between the private unemployment funds, municipal support for them and national participation in them was settled by the Unemployment Decree of 1917. The level of unemployment benefits by that time was at most 70 per cent of the average daily wage.

After the First World War two other unemployment benefit funds came into being. First, there was a support scheme to give benefits to workers who were not organised in the voluntary schemes or who had exhausted their benefits under those schemes. Moreover, this support scheme gave a supplementary benefit to those who received a benefit from a voluntary scheme. This support scheme was launched and financed nationally, but administered by the municipalities. Second, there was a benefit scheme for temporary unemployment, run by the employers but receiving a 50-per-cent subsidy from national and local government. These arrangements were revived after the Second World War on the basis of the Extraordinary Decree on Labour Relations 1945. In 1949 the Unemployment Benefit Act (*Werkloosheidswet*) created compulsory unemployment insurance for all workers.

In Italy the city of Bologna was the first to create a savings bank (1837) in order to encourage individual foresight against the risks of unemployment. After 1896 the savings bank of Bologna opened a special account for any workman residing in that town and aged from 21 to 65 years who asked to put aside some money in case of unemployment. By 1910, 795 workmen, nearly all belonging to the building trades, had opened such accounts. By 1881 the Italian Workers' Party (Partito Operario Italiano) had given itself the objective, in its constitution, of setting up an employment department for unemployed workers. However, this kind of initiative only came to fruition with the economic crisis of 1889–90. In that period the first *camere del lavoro* (trade-union-run employment exchanges) came into being with the main purpose of placement. Particularly in the agricultural sector, the activities of these agencies were linked to the fight against unemployment. The *camere del lavoro* often ensured a subsidy for workers who could prove that they were jobless. But they had an insignificant effect. The society Umanitaria of Milan is well known. In 1905 it created an unemployment fund modelled on the Ghent system and satisfactory results were achieved. By the end of June 1910 it had the support of fifty-one trade unions with 13,000 members. After 1906 benefits were accorded not only to workers unemployed through lack of work but also to those locked out in consequence of a wage dispute on a case-by-case basis. After 1908 trade unions wishing to join the fund had to be strictly neutral both in politics and religion and were obliged to dedicate themselves solely to the economic welfare of their members. The subsidies granted by the Umanitaria did not exceed the daily allowance of 50 centimes nor could it be granted to anyone for more than sixty days in one year.

Many Italian trade unions organised self-help schemes for unemployed members. Some cities, like Padua and Brescia granted annual subsidies to trade union unemployment funds. On 17 July 1910 the Italian Chamber of Deputies voted for an annual subsidy to be distributed among the local, regional or national workers' unemployment funds. But the bill was rejected by the Senate (January 1911) amid acute controversy. The bill was criticised for being inclined towards a dangerous form of state intervention favouring only one class of citizens: the workers, and among them the indolent and lazy. In the immediate post-war period a decree of 19 October 1919 provided for the organisation of provincial unemployment funds without distinction by industry and the creation of specific insurance funds linked to one industry or to a specific profession. In 1921 compulsory insurance against unemployment was created for the publishing industry and the paper industry with compulsory participation of employers and workers (*cassa confederale grafica assicurazioni sociali*). During the period of fascism the important Acts relating to unemployment were passed regulating the placement question but no specific regulation was adopted for unemployment insurance.

In France after the First World War the governmental policy did not change and the system remained one of subsidy. In 1914 a Fonds

National de Chômage was set up in order to give financial support to the municipal or regional relief organisations. It was only in 1939 that a decree laid down a new system for the administrative and financial organisation of unemployment benefits. The law of 11 October 1940 was the basis of the post-war national unemployment scheme. It reorganised the placement offices and guaranteed state benefits for unemployed workers. In Belgium it was only in 1945 that a compulsory unemployment insurance scheme was set up.

In conclusion, it may be observed that the remedies against unemployment were of two kinds. First were those seeking to mitigate the consequences of unemployment (e.g. giving financial support to unemployed workers without wages). Second, there were those aiming to affect the causes of unemployment (e.g. providing new job opportunities, rendering the placement of workers easier and increasing their occupational or geographical mobility). These means were complementary. The first one originated in and developed through self-help. The second was mainly administered by the new government system of employment exchanges and placement offices. But the mass unemployment of the 1930s showed up the weakness of the various unemployment insurance schemes and meant that millions of people who could not find jobs had to rely on the old poor relief systems, mainly financed by local authorities. The sheer numbers of unemployed involved in the 1930s highlighted the necessity for radical reform. Central governments were forced to accept responsibility for the unemployed and their financial burdens.

The inter-war period was of vital importance for the emergence of the concept of the welfare state. The idea gained support that it was the duty of the state to organise placement, vocational training or retraining and to provide services to control the extent and consequences of unemployment. Attempts were made to identify and understand the causes of unemployment. Economists made distinctions between various types of unemployment (structural, cyclical, technological, etc.); jurists made distinctions between permanent unemployment and temporary unemployment, short-term and long-term unemployment. The conditions under which benefits for the unemployed were payable became subject to rules, such as those relating to misconduct, which strengthened the disciplinary powers of the employer. At the same time labour legislation moved towards greater protection of employees with long service against the risk of unemployment through arbitrary dismissal. It is to this aspect that we must now turn.

PROTECTION OF WORKERS AGAINST DISMISSAL

The overall picture of the situation of the unemployed would be incomplete if the individual aspects of loss of employment by termination of the contract were not examined. There is a link between unemployment protection schemes and the protection of workers in case of dismissals. The right to work was interpreted as the right of the worker to enjoy some job security. Attempts were made to prevent or to delay the termination of the contract of employment, within a wider context of the policy of promoting a right to assistance and to minimum subsistence. Normally unemployment insurance follows the exhaustion of damages paid by the employer for loss of earnings consequent upon termination of the contract of employment.

The juridical analysis of the contract of employment by the beginning of the twentieth century was that employers and employees were equal partners to a civil contract (see Ch. 1, above). Either party could unilaterally terminate the contract; sometimes this was permitted at will, sometimes after notice and sometimes summarily for good cause. We shall draw distinctions between general and special rules governing the termination of the contract. Then we shall describe the progressive limitation of the unilateral right of dismissal and observe the convergence of the technical means adopted to this end in the various countries surveyed.

General Rules

Frustration, or Force Majeure

As we have already seen, the contract of employment was regarded as essentially personal in nature and so some events lead automatically to its termination; for example, the death of the employer, the winding-up of a company, the internment of the employee. This was based on the broad principle in English law of frustration and, in the civil law systems, of supervening impossibility of performance. Under this principle, if a change of circumstances makes performance of the contract physically impossible (e.g. serious illness or permanent disability of the employee) or its objects incapable of achievement, the contract will be automatically brought to an end without the requirement of dismissal by the employer or resignation by the employee.

By agreement: The Termination of Contracts for a Fixed Period or for a Specific Task

All legal systems recognise that the contract ends when a fixed term expires or a specific task is performed. If the relationship continues after such an event, it is generally regarded as a contract for an indefinite period. If the hiring is ended unilaterally before the expiry of the agreed fixed term, legal systems recognise a right to compensation for the loss of wages.

Both Dutch and English law placed the employee in a less favourable position than the employer. The Dutch Civil Code of 1838 contained a provision (Art. 1639) which allowed the employer to dismiss the worker before the end of the fixed period provided he paid damages amounting to not more than six weeks' wages. But if the worker left the service before the term expired, he forfeited all the wages. This inequality was removed only in 1907. A similar rule existed in the English common law, although it was apparently modified by the Apportionment Act of 1870, which recognised a right to the payment of 'salaries' *pro rata* for the period actually worked.

Ordinary Dismissal in Case of Contracts of Indefinite Duration

In the various countries of our study, contracts of employment of indefinite duration were normally terminable by the giving of notice on either side. 'Notice' has two meanings: (1) it may indicate the unilateral notification that the relationship is at an end. This is a formal legal act and is generally required to be unambiguous (*le congé* in French); (2) it may signify the period of time between the notification and the time when the notice expires (*délai-congé* in France, *délai de préavis* in Belgium). In some countries notice could be given without any formal requirements. It could be verbal or written, so long as the intention to terminate the contract was clearly expressed.

For a very long time the length of notice was implied by custom. In France the period of notice was already provided for in the statutes of the guilds under the *ancien régime*. In England at common law the employer could terminate the contract at any time on giving notice and the employee had no right to be heard in his own defence before being dismissed. The period of notice was determined by custom or, if there was no custom, it was to be 'reasonable'.

In Belgium and the Netherlands, as in England (where there was no other custom), an indication of the length of the notice was derived from the periodicity of payment of wages (daily, weekly, monthly) and upon the nature of the work (manual or intellectual). In Germany, too, factors like age and the level of remuneration were relevant. In Italy a series of decisions of the *probiviri* relying on custom or collective agreements, later became the basis for legislation. The validity of unilateral termination was admitted on condition that notice was given, the length of time depending on the custom prevailing at that time. If notice was not given, then in all the countries surveyed, compensation had to be paid, of a customary nature and usually equal to the sum lost over the period of the notice.

Statutory rules regarding notice were generally only adopted at the beginning of the twentieth century (Table 4.1).

Table 4.1 Statutory rules concerning notice

Country	Law on contract of employment	Specific provision for notice
Belgium	Contract of Employment Act 1900 (for manual workers)	None
	Contract of Employment Act 1922 (for white-collar workers)	Refers to custom
France	27 December 1890, Art. 23 *Code du Travail* 1924	Refers to custom
Netherlands	Contract of Employment Act 1907	Maximum 6 weeks depending on periodicity of wages
Germany	Reich Trade Act 1869; Commercial Act 1897; Civil Code (from 1900)	Maximum 6 weeks depending on periodicity of wages
Britain	Contracts of Employment Act 1963	Minimum 1 week
Denmark	*Tyndeloven* 1854 (rural and domestic workers)	1 month
	Case law for salaried workers	14 days to 3 months
Italy	Royal decree 13 November 1924 (white-collar workers)	15 days to 4 months

The general tendency was to consider notice as a reciprocal and equal obligation of employer and employee. The German courts decided that an agreement for unequal lengths of the period of notice was unlawful as *contra bonos mores*. Moreover, the worker could generally waive his right to notice on any occasion or accept a payment in lieu of notice.

The main beneficiaries of the notice periods appear to have been middle-class employees (white-collar workers) and not manual workers. So far as factory workers were concerned, the length of the notice period depended in many countries not on the law but on collective agreements. In Britain, where manual trade unions were generally strong, employers tended to require longer notice periods by workers so as to protect themselves from lightning strikes. Until 1875 employees who walked out without giving the proper notice risked imprisonment for breach of contract under the Master and Servant Acts (see Ch. 1, above). After the repeal of these Acts, there was no legal reason why trade unions should not seek collective agreements extending periods of notice. Significantly, however, collective provisions of this kind were unusual, and where they did exist the period of notice was as short as two hours to terminate on a Friday in the construction industry. Before 1963 there was no attempt in Britain to regulate the periods of notice by law.

In Denmark rules of notice for salaried employees existed on an equal basis, as a result of case law. Customary notice was from fourteen days to three months.

Protection of Special Groups

Public Servants

Broad similarities are found in the situation of public employees in the various countries. In general, public employees enjoyed considerable security of tenure. In Chapter 1, above, their special legal status was explained. Stability of employment was essential both to the political neutrality and the loyalty of public servants. The question, also discussed in Chapter 1, whether public servants had a contract of employment, was part of the debate whether these servants could be dismissed at any time at the will of the public authorities, with or without notice.

In France the right to defend public servants' actions against disciplinary measures including summary dismissal was accepted in 1903 by the Conseil d'État. In the case in question, an officer was compulsorily retired without being told the grounds for his dismissal or being allowed to give any explanation. No legal text laid down a procedure in respect of this kind of summary punishment. The Conseil d'État decided that the administration had an obligation to follow a special procedure before adopting disciplinary measures or transferring public servants. If this procedure was not respected, the decision taken against the public servants was null and void.

In Germany the *Beamte* (public servant) was also considered as regularly employed on life tenure and could not be dismissed without judicial decision. Under Nazism, the idea of 'personal relations of trust' with the party-state (see Ch. 1, above) led to the removal of those who did not share Nazi ideals. They and non-Aryans were expelled by the law of 1933. In the Netherlands the Contract of Employment Act of 1907 was applicable to all workers except civil servants and railway personnel. This exception was retained in the Extraordinary Decree on Labour Relations of 1945 but civil servants enjoyed stronger protection under special legislation. In Belgium the dismissal of public servants was governed by the principle that public interests took priority over the private interests of each particular servant. In Britain civil servants were in theory dismissable at will, without legal redress, but in practice collective agreements with civil service unions ensured life tenure for the established civil service. In Italy a law of 22 November 1908 unified regulations regarding the status of public employees. A distinction was made between the various grades of officials and employees as regards the termination of the relationship. During the fascist period some of the basic juridical criteria regarding the contract of public employment were questioned: the political climate of 1922–23 influenced the direction taken by the Council of State. In applying the laws on the reduction of staff, the Council undermined the idea of job stability, since exceptional laws were applied allowing for political purges. These were repealed in 1949.

Agricultural Labourers and Domestic Servants

Specific groups, such as agricultural rural workers and domestic servants, were governed by special rules in most countries (the Netherlands being an exception). The rules for agricultural workers were special due to the conditions of work during the planting and harvesting seasons. The custom of yearly hiring had a long tradition in most countries since it reflects the reality of agricultural service. For domestic servants, custom ruled the length of notice to be given by either party. In Britain, for example, this was generally one month. Summary dismissal on the grounds of misconduct of domestic servants was frequently upheld because of the personal nature of the relationship and the high degree of subordination which characterised it.

Women

It was a common practice in many occupations, such as teaching, for women to be dismissed on marriage. In some countries, express terms of the individual contract of employment or provisions of collective agreements mentioned the marriage of a woman as a fair cause of dismissal. During our period there was no specific prohibition of this practice. For a long time no special protection existed for women dismissed on grounds of pregnancy or confinement. France was the pioneer in providing some protection. A law of 27 November 1909 guaranteed that the employment of a woman absent from work for confinement would be kept open. The woman had to be a worker covered by private law. The law provided that:

> the suspension of her contract of employment by a woman who is pregnant during eight consecutive weeks of the period immediately preceding and following the birth of her child cannot be a motive for the employer to break the contract of employment; and the sanction against this is the award of damages to the woman. The woman, for her part, should inform the employer of the reason for her absence.

This protection therefore covered only the immediate period of the birth, not the whole term of the pregnancy. The dismissal of the pregnant woman was not invalid, but such an action could make the employer liable for the payment of damages. In Germany an amendment to the Reich Trade Act in 1927 gave protection to pregnant women against dismissals through the technique of suspension of the contract occurring during maternity leave. In Italy the royal decree of 13 November 1924 on white-collar workers had established the right for female employees to take a total of three months' leave before and after childbirth without losing their jobs. Other countries were much slower in granting this type of right—in Britain it was not conferred by legislation until 1975.

Limitations on the Right to Terminate the Contract

Summary Dismissal for Gross Misconduct

In all the countries of our study, the general rule developed in the late eighteenth and nineteenth centuries was that the employer was entitled to terminate the contract without notice in case of gross misconduct (*motif grave*). In Britain the early decisions on this question commonly arose not out of litigation between masters and servants but out of litigation under the Poor Laws to determine whether a particular community had to provide aid to a destitute person on the ground that he had acquired a settlement by being employed for a certain period.

The object was to do justice between two communities and not between master and servant. For example, it was held that in 1777 a maid-servant could be summarily dismissed for being found pregnant so that she could not acquire a settlement. This does not mean that her employer would necessarily have been justified in regarding this as gross misconduct. Moreover, many of the cases arose out of criminal proceedings, before—in theory at least—master and servant became equal parties to a civil contract. Above all, we find changing social values in the determination of what constituted gross misconduct. For example, in *Turner* v. *Mason*[2] a maid who wanted to see her dying mother left the house against her employer's orders. The court upheld her summary dismissal in judgments 'full of the unattractively robust common lawyer's thinking of the day' (Wedderburn, 1971, p. 74). The evidence, said Baron Alderson, 'does not show that the mother was likely to die that night'. And even if it had done so, this was a 'mere moral duty'; the master always had the right to dismiss the servant for any wilful disobedience.

The criteria of serious misconduct, or the immediate consequences of the continuation of the relationship, or the impossibility of maintaining a normal relationship, were found also in the case law or legislation of other Continental countries. For example, in Belgium, the law did not contain any strict definition of the *motif grave*, for it was stated in the *travaux préparatoires* that the concept has a social dimension and may vary with the aptitudes, qualifications and personal characteristics of the employee. Article 16 of the law of 10 March 1900 (manual workers) stated that the contract comes to an end by the termination at will when a *motif grave* exists. Articles 20 and 21 of the same law gave a list of examples of employee's or employer's misconduct. The same applied under Dutch law (Arts. 1693p and 1639q of the Civil Code). This enumeration was not exhaustive and the courts decided that the main criterion was that the normal maintenance of the relationship was no longer possible. However, even in case of *motif grave* the law did not allow the employer to make a dismissal on the spot when the ground for the dismissal had been known to him for more than two working days. The law of 7 August 1922 (white-collar workers) had very similar provisions, but added formal requirements and imposed a written procedure for summary dismissal. The party had to indicate the motive with great precision and with sufficient certainty for the courts to be able to give it an evaluation. After three days, summary dismissal was no longer possible.

2. (1845) 14 Meeson & Welsby 112.

Giusta causa in Italy

Article 2119 of the Italian Civil Code (1942) governed summary dismissal for gross misconduct. There had to be fault on the part of the worker that rendered the continuance of the contract, even on a temporary basis, impossible. Notice was not required in those circumstances. Before the enactment of the Civil Code, the dismissed worker often appealed to the *probiviri* (under the 1893 Act) in order to ascertain whether the dismissal fell under the heading of *giusta causa* (just cause or justified motive), which made *recesso in tronco* (definitive termination for serious misconduct) legitimate. If the verdict went against the employer, he usually had to pay an indemnity to the worker for failure to give notice. The notion of *giusta causa* constituted an important link with the later development of the requirement of a fair motive for dismissal.

In practice, during the fascist period *giusta causa* was frequently found. This constituted a weapon for employers who wished to avoid the financial burden involved in dismissing workers. It should also be added that apart from Article 5 of the decree of 1924, collective agreements (e.g. the metal-workers' agreement) established the form and requirements for *recesso in tronco* and laid down that in less serious cases lighter penalties, such as fines and temporary suspension from work, could be inflicted. The judges limited themselves to deciding whether *giusta causa* existed or not and on the ensuing penalties to be paid. It could be said that this reveals the highly authoritarian nature of fascism, in which manifestations of dissent and insurbordination were severely penalised by the law and by collective agreements and were the object of widespread repression on the shop floor. However, in cases where dismissals for political reasons took place (e.g. between 1923 and 1935, an ex-socialist worker accused of having organised a strike; and a group of bakers working for a co-operative in Torino accused of having celebrated May Day in a tavern) the judgments were faithful to the values of fascism. At no point in these judgments does one find any dispute that the offences of which the workers were accused were capable of constituting *giusta causa*.

L'abus de Droit in France

The utilisation by the judges of the theory of abuse of rights was the first attempt to control the reasons for dismissal in France. As early as 1858 the judges forbade an employer to use his discretionary power of dismissal 'abusively'. Although the interests of the firm or the 'fault' of the worker often provided a good reason for the employer, employees had the right to claim compensation as soon as it was proved that the employer had terminated the contract without any 'fair motive'. But the Court of Cassation (1872) did not accept this decision and decided that one could not require a legitimate motive for the termination of the contract to be given, nor ask from the employer to prove that it was so. This decision was based on the terms of Article 1780 of the *Code Civil*. The court said that the worker had to prove both that the employer had abused his right *and* had intended to prejudice him at the time he broke the contract.

A law of 27 December 1890 modified the text of Article 1780 of the *Code Civil*; after stating the classic principle of unilateral termination of a work contract of no fixed term, the following was added: 'Nevertheless, the termination of the work contract at the will of only one of the parties to the contract can give rise to a liability to damages'. From this was derived the potential responsibility of the employer. In case law the principle was retained that it was the responsibility of the worker to prove that an offence had been committed by the employer. However, the conditions concerning the responsibility of the employer were somewhat eased. It was no longer necessary to prove that the employer wished to prejudice the interests of the worker. A succession of bills which attempted to shift the onus of the proof concerning the breach of contracts failed (in particular, a bill proposed by the government in 1906). Even the law of 19 July 1928, which stated that 'the court can enquire into the circumstances of the breach of the contract in order to judge better if there has been an abuse of rights' and that 'the sentence should always in every case state the alleged motive given by the party who broke the contract in explicit detail' did nothing to change the position of the Court of Cassation concerning the burden of proof in cases of the breach of a contract of employment. This meant that the protection against abusive dismissals was of little practical value to workers.

Unjust Dismissal in the Weimar Republic

The first attempt to provide a remedy against dismissal without fair reason was made in Germany during the Weimar Republic. This took place against the background of mass unemployment. Individual dismissal was regulated in Article 84 of the Works Councils Act of 1920, which provided that employees who were given notice by the employer could, within five days after the notice, appeal to the (manual or white collar) works council on one of the following grounds: (1) if there were grounds for believing that notice was given on the basis of sex or religion, or because of political, military, confessional or trade union activities or membership; (2) if notice was given without indicating the reasons; (3) if notice was given because the employee refused to perform permanently work other than that which had been agreed upon at the time of recruitment; (4) if the notice was proved to be unfair and not related to the personal conduct of the worker or to the situation of the enterprise. Article 84 also provided an appeal against dismissal without notice on grounds that there was no reason for the dismissal. The appeal to the works council had to include the grounds and the evidence in support of them. If the council found that the appeal was well-founded, it negotiated with the employer, attempting to reach agreement. If this failed, the works council or worker could appeal to the labour court. If the court considered that the dismissal was unfair, the court could recommend that the employer re-engage or reinstate the worker, but the court did not have the power to impose this solution. The remedy of re-engagement or reinstatement was not compulsory. This meant that in practice the degree of protection against dismissal was limited. Financial compensation alone could be awarded. Those who, after the failure of conciliation with the employer, received the legal recognition of their right to work, received in practice compensation amounting to one-twelfth of wages for each year of employment, with a maximum of half the amount of the annual wages (see Ch. 6, below).

Weimar labour law was a pioneer in this field. It was the first statute in Europe which restricted managerial power to terminate the employment relationship for insufficient objective reasons. It was still a very moderate procedure, uneasily attempting to reconcile the interests of the enterprise and of the workers, balancing the right to work (job security) and the rights of property and of free enterprise. Historically, it was a Trojan Horse in the citadel of the employers' discretionary right to dismiss. After the Second World War the protection of workers against unjust or arbitrary dismissal appeared as an important and urgent problem. New legislation was adopted in all the countries of our survey: Germany, 1950; Italy, 1947, 1950, 1966, 1970; the Netherlands, 1945, 1953, 1967, 1976; United Kingdom, 1971, 1974, 1975; Ireland, 1972; France, 1950, 1973; and Belgium, 1955, 1969, 1978. The inspiration belonged to the makers of Weimar labour law.

Conclusions

For the reasons explained in Chapter 1, above, the usual form of the contract of employment became the contract of indefinite duration. It is essential to understand that the right to dismiss was implied by the nature of the contract of indefinite duration. Hence, when the employer did terminate the contract at will, he was exercising a contractual right. He was not seen as breaching a duty or an obligation. Moreover, the co-existence of special rules or statutes governing the ending of the contract of employment with the ordinary principles of the law of contract made possible the avoidance of some protective rules in favour of the worker (e.g. the duty to give a notice) by recourse to general rules applicable to the law of contracts, such as frustration (*force majeure*), mutual agreement, fixed terms of the contract extending the employer's right of summary dismissal on grounds of misconduct, and so on.

The developing industrial society required free movement of labour and freedom to work (see Ch. 1, above). Employers wanted to be completely free to decide whether or not to hire or dismiss workers by reason of their ownership and control of the enterprise. They should not be compelled to suffer restrictions on their managerial freedom. Freedom of contract implies, as its correlative, freedom to terminate the contract. Only gradually were some restrictions over the discretionary power of employers to terminate the contract adopted in the various countries of our comparative survey. To understand this very slow evolution during the period of our study, it is important to classify the dismissals into two categories.

The first category is dismissal as a sanction (punitive dismissal). In this category we find all kinds of summary dismissal used as a sanction against misconduct by the worker, such as breach of an important term of the contract, theft of the employer's property, deliberate damage to the employer's property, refusal to obey reasonable and lawful orders, and so on. All these reasons were known under the concept of *faute grave*, or 'gross misconduct', and they gave rise to a right of summary dismissal. In the same category we may include disciplinary dismissal for participation in a strike (see Ch. 5, below).

The second category is dismissal as release from the contract. In this category we may classify all terminations of the contract of employment of indefinite duration by the requisite notice or, in the case of immediate termination, with financial compensation for the failure to give notice. In this respect the discretionary power of the employer to terminate the contract without giving a reason is quite separate from the right to terminate the contract summarily in case of an important breach by the other side. The right to dismiss was inherent in the contract itself. So long as the minimum period of notice, and in some instances a written procedure, had been respected, the employer was not required to give any reason.

Restrictions on the unlimited authority of the employer to dismiss his employees for whatever reasons he considered fit were quite difficult to introduce into statutes and industrial practices. In the first category it is interesting to observe the evolution towards the modern concept of unfair or unjustified dismissal. In the second category, importance was placed on procedural or formal aspects of the process of termination by notice, including provision for financial compensation in cases of the employer's failure to observe the statutory or contractual rules of notice. So long as the contract of employment was considered merely as a *locatio conductio* (letting and hire), the loss of job could give the employee the right to claim compensation insofar as that loss was attributable to a wrongful action taken by the employer, but reinstatement or re-engagement could not be envisaged.

Control of the employer's motive in the case of summary dismissal was exercised by the courts. They acted *a posteriori*. The employer was not required to give any reason for a dismissal. If the employee felt aggrieved, he could bring an action for wrongful dismissal to which the employer could then plead the reason for dismissal, and if that was shown to be a sufficient reason for a summary dismissal, the employer had a complete defence. From about the beginning of the twentieth century, on the Continent, in cases of summary dismissal the statutes obliged the employer to justify his motive if asked to do so. A second step towards limiting the discretionary power of dismissal was the development of a requirement that the employer should invoke the reason and exercise the right to end the contract within a reasonable period of the alleged misconduct. Otherwise the doctrine of waiver was applied. The employer was considered to have waived his right after a certain period of time (e.g. three days in Belgium). On the Continent the concept of 'waiver' was readily accepted because the main criterion of a *motif grave* was and still is that the normal continuance of the contract was immediately and totally made impossible. If, after the breach of the contract by gross misconduct, the relationship continued for a reasonable term, the alleged misconduct could not be regarded as intolerable.

The discretionary power of the employer to terminate the contract was too strong to allow any *a priori* form of control or the right of self-defence by the employee. No general requirement imposed the right for the employee to be heard before the dismissal. The employer was permitted to terminate the contract unilaterally. The only exception was Article 84 of the Works Councils Act of the Weimar Republic.

As a general rule, termination was unilaterally performed and the innocent party could only sue for his wages or for damages. By the early twentieth century, rules had been developed as regards the amount of compensation to which a wrongfully dismissed employee was entitled. This was normally loss of wages the employee would have earned until the date when the contract would lawfully have ended, on the assumption that the employer would have terminated the contract at the earliest date he could do so. Damages were not recoverable for the manner in which the dismissal took place, for hurt feelings or for the fact that dismissal made it difficult for the employee to obtain alternative employment.

Control of the employer's discretion in the case of dismissal by notice was by the imposition of a requirement that the length of notice should be reasonable. It might be fixed by a custom applicable to the particular industry or occupation, by a term implied in the contract or by minimum periods of notice fixed by legislation. However, it was lawful to waive the statutory right to notice on any occasion or to accept a payment in lieu of notice. One may also note the importance given to continuity of employment. As a general rule, in order to qualify for a longer period of notice, the employee needed a stated period of continuous employment. Job security and seniority were thus interlinked.

Another form of control in some countries was that legislation or the contract itself required the employer to follow a particular procedure in giving notice to an employee. If the procedure was not complied with, this could give rise to a claim for damages. However, the contract was usually effectively terminated. Only in some specific cases, like public employees or disabled persons, was the dismissal in breach of procedure ineffective to terminate the employment relationship.

It was only in 1963 that an ILO Recommendation proclaimed as an international labour standard the concept of 'unfair dismissal'—the basic and important principle that termination of employment must be motivated by a fair reason. In the period of our study this principle had not been generally accepted.

5

Collective Self-Regulation

Antoine Jacobs

INTRODUCTION

Labour law in the form of state regulation, as described in the previous chapters, is the most obvious part of the rules that govern the employment relationship. Of no lesser importance, however, are the rules created by employers and workers' representatives themselves: autonomous regulation as distinct from heteronomous regulation. Autonomous regulation emerged where public authorities, intentionally or unintentionally, abstained from the direct regulation of labour relations. As explained in Chapter 1, this was the case where the regulatory power of the guilds was absent or had disintegrated, and where state regulation of the conditions of employment had declined in importance. In those circumstances employers were able to take advantage of their stronger bargaining position and to impose their conditions on the workforce. The rise of the ideology of freedom of contract in employment relations, as described in Chapter 1, reinforced the social power of the employers. By way of reaction, in view of the unwillingness of the state to intervene, workers increasingly had to rely on combining their own forces in order to build a countervailing power strong enough to extract better working conditions. So, what Kahn-Freund labelled 'collective *laissez-faire*' (1959, p. 224), and is also described as collective liberalism, collective autonomy or collective self-regulation, partially replaced individual *laissez-faire*, individual liberalism, individual autonomy and individual self-regulation in fixing terms and conditions of employment. It still had the hallmarks of *laissez-faire*, since regulation was outside the hands of the state. But it was collective rather than 'individual' because it was joint regulation by employers and trade unions that was the source of the terms of employment, and not individual contracting between employer and worker.

In some countries, such as Britain and Ireland from the mid-nineteenth century and Denmark after 1899, collective self-regulation was much more important than legislation. Kahn-Freund, writing in 1954, epitomised British labour legislation as 'in a sense, a gloss or a footnote to collective bargaining' (1954, p. 66), a state of affairs which continued until as late as 1971. This reflected the ideology of collective self-regulation in the British Isles: trade unionists, employers and politicians alike were agreed that industrial relations needed a minimum of state intervention. In Denmark there were similar shared beliefs. Elsewhere on the European Continent, by contrast, statutory regulation of working life was far more important, but even in those countries collective self-regulation came to play a major role in the improvement of working conditions.

All this did not happen overnight. In several countries it took the whole of the period covered by this study for this recognition of collective self-regulation to be achieved. This chapter aims to give an outline of the various ways in which the law reacted to the rise of trade unions and employers' associations, to collective bargaining and to industrial conflict. We shall analyse the developments in terms of three 'ideal-types' which epitomise the changing legal approaches; namely repression, toleration and recognition.

Repression means that state policy is to suppress the agents of modern industrial relations, notably the trade unions, to prosecute their leaders and to thwart methods of collective regulation such as strikes and collective agreements. The instruments of power the state can utilise are manifold: prohibitions of the criminal law; police measures such as arrest; dissolution of meetings, seizure of pamphlets, and so on. In many cases, the repression may be openly directed towards the trade union movement; in others, repression may come in more subtle guises.

Toleration means that trade unions and employers' associations can operate in full legality. Workers and employers are free to join together; unions may assemble, issue their own newspapers, raise subscriptions, occupy premises, and so on. They have the liberty to negotiate with the employers and to conclude collective agreements. To a certain extent this may even embrace the freedom to take industrial action (strikes, picketing, lockouts, boycotts, etc.). Prohibitions under the criminal law disappear, and the police limit their intervention to cases in which public order is seriously jeopardised. But there is one important characteristic which distinguishes 'toleration' from 'recognition' as described below. The tolerant state takes no positive action to support the rôle of the trade unions. The social climate is still far from advantageous for the unions, for they have to cope with socially superior employers. Civil law is still based on absolute concepts of property and individual contractual freedom, which tends to favour the employers, and the difficulties in organising industrial action almost inevitably lead to infringements of public order, provoking clashes with the police and sometimes the army.

Recognition describes those positive acts by the public authorities or by employers or trade unions towards each other by which the functioning of the system of collective self-regulation is supported. It is more than 'toleration' because it is based on the idea of active encouragement of the system of collective self-regulation, through positive rights, whereas 'toleration' goes no further than to grant immunities against the prohibitions of criminal law or the liabilities of civil law. Recognition may be accomplished by solemn declarations such as the Weimar Constitution in Germany. It may also be achieved by a series of legislative or administrative measures or by judge-made law which reflect the policy of recognition. In all cases it is a first step towards 'recognition' that employers should abandon anti-union behaviour and recognise trade unionism as a countervailing social power. Other symptoms of recognition are the active promotion of arbitration, conciliation and mediation, the recognition of the legal enforceability of collective agreements and (usually) the creation of positive rights to take industrial action. On the other hand, policies which give trade unions and employers representation in public institutions or endow institutions manned by trade unions and employers with public functions may be characterised as *integration*; this is dealt with in Chapter 6, below.

These ideal types are no more than working concepts. Features of repression, toleration and recognition frequently overlap in practice. Broadly speaking, however, one may say that before 1850 labour relations in European countries were characterised by repression. In all these countries trade unions were at first illegal, as were the industrial struggles conducted by workers. As Wedderburn has said:

> the solution offered to that common problem is a central feature of each system of collective labour law. The first stage of the solution was everywhere of the same character. The most repressive, penal restrictions upon organisations of workers were removed as each country proceeded into an era of industrialisation to face the emergence of a proletarian class, troublesome to those in control of social and economic power, but necessary for their new economy. [1980, p. 65]

It was in the period 1850 to 1900 that the characteristic of toleration became dominant, but not without the later sporadic re-emergence of repression in new guises (such as the Anti-Socialist Act in Germany 1878–90). The next stage of development—recognition—ultimately gave rise to various positive *legal* rights for workers and unions in all countries—except Britain and Denmark, where recognition was secured by voluntary agreements. This took place roughly between 1900 and 1950, but with backward leaps such as during the Nazi régime in Germany and the Fascist régime in Italy. The seeds of integration and tripartism were planted in the democratic states in the period from the First World War, as will be shown in Chapter 6 following.

FROM REPRESSION TO TOLERATION

Origins and Nature of the Bans on Combinations

The agents of the system of collective self-regulation (trade unions and employers' associations) and their methods (collective bargaining, strikes, picketing, lockouts, job restrictions, forms of co-operation) were not completely new to the Industrial Revolution. Everywhere in Europe these phenomena can be detected alongside the decline of the guild system, which no longer reflected the medieval ideal of harmonious collaboration of masters, journeymen and apprentices. The masters had usurped all powers within the guilds and sought to restrict access to mastership (see Ch. 1, above). Most journeymen had to abandon the idea of eventually becoming masters themselves, and they had to be satisfied with labour conditions, unilaterally dictated by their masters. In some cases state authorities issued regulations on labour conditions or provided for arbitration, but this did not prevent long working days, child labour, low wages, unemployment and no payment in case of sickness and old age. To secure some relief, journeymen combined in *compagnonnages* (France), *gezellenbroederschappen* (Netherlands), *Gesellenverbände* (Germany) and journeymens' clubs (Britain) for mutual assistance in case of sickness, death, injury, unemployment and for pious, social or cultural aims. Their funds were known by numerous names: *confréries*, *Bruderschaften*, *mutualités*, *pia societa*, *bussen* and friendly societies. Less well established were country-wide clubs of trades such as weaving, wool-combing and other occupations. (In Britain these were called trade clubs or lodges and a federation or union of them was a trade union.) These clubs, in addition to their social and welfare functions, served (particularly in Britain) as a place where masters could recruit skilled workmen. It was only natural that these infantile trade unions should also seek to defend wage rates when cuts were threatened and to increase them when the cost-of-living rose, through negotiations with masters and, sometimes, by inspiring strikes. In fact the first collective agreements were entered into in the eighteenth century between masters and organisations such as these. Sometimes these organisations were also the breeding-place of uprisings of working people against the public authorities.

For many years the law in all parts of Western Europe uncompromisingly repressed these organisations. To mention a few examples: in France *Ordonnances* of King Charles VI, 1382; of Villers-Cotterets, 1539; the *décret* of 2 January 1749; also the famous Edict of Turgot of 1776, which abolished the guilds, contained a ban on coalitions that was maintained even after the abolition of the guilds had been revoked; in Germany the *Reichzunftordnung* (Reich Guild Act) of 1731 outlawed combinations after such combinations had already been suppressed by police orders of the authorities, such as the *Reichspolizeiordnung* (Reich Police Act) of 1530, 1548, 1577 and local and *Land* (state) regulations; in Britain and Ireland there were about forty Acts forbidding combinations in specific trades (some dating from the fourteenth century), and most judges were prepared to declare combinations to raise wages unlawful at common law in the eighteenth century; in Denmark a royal decree of 1734 banned all combinations in Copenhagen, and in the northern and southern Netherlands combinations of workers were outlawed by police regulations.

These examples make it clear that public authorities everywhere were very suspicious of workers' organisations. One reason they had for repressing these combinations was the concern for public order since combinations were often associated with unrest or violence. A second reason for drafting repressive measures was concern for upholding the monopoly of regulation of labour conditions by the guilds or by the state. In Germany the workers could appeal to the Crown if they felt they had been treated unjustly by their masters, and in Britain the statutory bans on combinations complemented state regulation of wages and working conditions in various trades, from the fourteenth to the nineteenth centuries.

At the beginning of the Industrial Revolution fresh bans on combinations were enacted: the *Loi Le Chapelier* of 14–17 June 1791 in France later followed by even more repressive measures especially in Articles 414–16 of the Penal Code (1810);[1] under Napoleonic rule these French measures were extended to the southern Netherlands (Belgium), the northern Netherlands, Italy and parts of Germany (Rhineland); repressive acts were taken against combinations in other

1. Extracts from the texts of these laws will be found in Appendix IV, p. 376, below.

parts of Germany: Saxony (1791 renewed in 1810), Prussia (1794) and Bavaria (1809); the Combination Acts of 1799 and 1800 in Britain and Ireland; and the Order of March 1800 which regulated the guild system and forbade coalitions in Copenhagen, Denmark.

These bans on combinations around the end of the eighteenth century were all enacted at a time of general social and political unrest, when the revolutionary potential of independent working-class organisations alarmed the ruling powers, and the old forms of wage regulation by the state were breaking down. No doubt political fears played a part in their enactment, but apart from France, these new laws simply reiterated and extended existing prohibitions. The French *Loi Le Chapelier* did, however, give rise to a new legal situation. Following the Revolution, combinations of workers initially enjoyed the freedom to associate and to assemble (*décret* of 13–19 November 1790). Because this was not welcomed by those who came to power in the later phases of the Revolution, they retraced their steps in 1791 and enacted a ban on combinations. Obviously such a manoeuvre required public justification. This was done by relying upon the legal thinkers who were hostile to any intermediate structures between the state and the individual. As J. J. Rousseau put it: 'Thus if the general will is to be clearly expressed, it is imperative that there should be no sectional associations in the state, and that every citizen should make up his own mind for himself' (1968, p. 7). This general hostility against intermediate structures had led to the abolition of the guild system (*Décret d'Allarde*, Act of 2–17 March 1791), and it now also served as grounds for the introduction of the ban on combinations, thus restricting the freedom to associate and to assemble. The *Loi Le Chapelier* had an explicit ideological character. This may help to explain why the French ban on combinations resisted change for longer than those in other countries.

It is doubtful whether the bans were successful in suppressing combinations of workers. For example, in Britain the existence of 'combinations of workmen in almost every trade in the Kingdom' was reported in 1804 (four years after the draconian Combination Acts) and 'the alarming extent to which the combinations of workmen in different branches of trades and manufactures have been carried' was mentioned in 1816. In France the repeated enactment of new coalition bans in the years from 1791 proved that combinations of workers were difficult to eradicate. Before and after 1800 combination bans were hardly ever applied to associations of workers which had no economic aims but only social, cultural, religious or educational functions. Such associations were explicitly recognised in Britain under the Friendly Societies Act of 1793. In France, Germany and the Netherlands, such societies were often allowed with the specific consent of the authorities. Moreover, besides the formal anti-combination legislation, other repressive measures were also at the disposal of the authorities. This makes it difficult to judge whether the new anti-combination bans had an instrumental or merely symbolic significance. For instance, in Britain combining workers could also be prosecuted for conspiracy under the common law. Both before and after 1800 more prosecutions took place under the common law than under the statutory combination bans. In France and Germany, police measures are said to have been more effective than bans on combinations in preventing the emergence of trade unions with economic aims.

A particularly repressive sanction against strikes was the legislation on breach of contract, which usually encompassed participation in strikes by individual workers. In Britain the thirteenth clause of the Statute of Artificers of 1563 decreed a month's imprisonment for a person guilty of breaking his contract by leaving his work unfinished. This clause (reintroduced in 1747 and amended in 1766 and 1823) was considered 'ninety-nine times more oppressive' than the Combination Acts of 1799 and 1800. Also in France and in most states of Germany breach of the contract of employment, at least by the worker, was a criminal offence (see Ch. 1, above). Moreover, the law of various German states penalised insubordination and recalcitrance on the part of the worker. Police measures could be used to force the worker to fulfil his duties. It is clear that these provisions seriously curtailed the workers' freedom to strike.

Were the combination bans also applied to combinations of employers, and if so, were they enforced to the same extent? It should be remembered that combinations of employers were rare in the sixteenth to eighteenth centuries, although masters sometimes entered into *ad hoc* agreements, such as not to engage workers who had deserted their former masters. But even if modern employers' associations did not exist at the end of the eighteenth century, this did not mean that the employers were without means of co-operation: they met each other in the boards of the guilds and in other meeting-places such as salons and coffee-houses. And the state sometimes even encouraged masters to organise themselves more effectively, such as the Napoleonic Acts which introduced Chambers of Commerce and Advisory Chambers of manufacturers and tradesmen.

Certainly the combination bans at the end of the eighteenth century purported to include combinations of employers because their restraining effect on trade was recognised in theory. But most of the laws were discriminatory. For instance, in the amending Acts of 1803 and 1810 in France, which tightened up the *Loi Le Chapelier*, workers' associations were penalised in all circumstances while associations of employers were liable to punishment only when they tried to reduce wages. Also, the sanctions against the workers were more severe than those against employers. But what was more important, the repression of combinations of employers was hardly ever put into practice. They were rarely prosecuted and even less often convicted. As Durand and Jaussaud put it: 'Wishing to encourage trade and industry the government feared that any sanction against employers' organisations would cause insubordination among the workers' (1947, p. 69, n. 52). It was also believed that restraint of trade and industrial unrest was more likely to be caused by combinations of workers than by combinations of employers. Additionally, according to the prevailing mercantilist view, which had never rejected employers' associations, associations of masters with the aim of bringing down wages would lead to lower prices. Adam Smith (1776, p. 169) and his followers, on the other hand, considered the combination bans to be an injustice, because combinations of workers could effectively be curbed by the criminal law whereas the combinations of employers could not be. Moreover, they argued that the employer through the concentration of capital is in effect a combination. Combination bans menaced only the weaker party and served to embitter the workers. As a result, many followers of Adam Smith, while not believing that combinations would improve the lot of workers (since the rich employer could sustain a strike for longer than poor workers), pressed for the repeal of the combination bans.

The Repeal of the Combination Bans

In the course of the nineteenth century most of the criminal sanctions against combinations were repealed in all Western European countries: Britain in 1824 (although with some restrictions in 1825), followed by France forty years later (1864, although unions were legalised only in 1884),[2] Germany (1869), the Netherlands (1872), Luxembourg (1879) and Italy (1889). So it took a period of about sixty-five years before direct penal sanctions against combinations had disappeared from the statute books in these European countries. Why did it take so long and what were the reasons behind the repeal of the combination bans?

The story begins in Britain where the soil was so fertile for changes in the social and political field in the first quarter of the nineteenth century. Among the reformers the name of Francis Place, a master who

2. Extracts from the texts of these laws will be found in Appendix IV, p. 378, below.

had once been the secretary of an illegal trade club, deserves to be mentioned because of his perseverance in securing parliamentary support for the repeal of the Combination Acts in 1824. This is not to say that Place and his allies, such as the Radical MP, Joseph Hume and the economist J. R. McCulloch, were warm supporters of combinations of workers. They held the view that combinations could do little to improve the condition of the workers. They believed in the Wages Fund doctrine; namely, that wages had their own natural level dictated by supply and demand which could not be varied over a lengthy period, much above or below the minimum necessary for subsistence. Combinations of workers, they believed, would not be able to change this. Indeed, it was a widespread view in Europe at the time that combinations provoked unrest and violence and damaged economic welfare. Ritscher (1917, p. 159) called this kind of legal thinking *polizeilichen Bevormundung* (police-guardianship). Francis Place, however, believed that penal restrictions were counter-productive. He argued that once the Combinations Acts were repealed, the wider unions of trades, as distinct from journeymen's clubs, would disappear. 'Men have been kept together for long periods only by the oppression of the laws', he wrote, and 'these being repealed, combinations will lose the matter which cements them into masses and they will fall to pieces' (cited in Wallas, 1925, p. 217). Workers would recognise a fundamental harmony between their interests and those of their employers, and the bitter feelings of the working classes towards employers and the state would disappear.

In this line of thought one clearly recognises the inspiration of Jeremy Bentham, who saw the principle of utility as the decisive criterion for legislation. Place and others expected that it would be more beneficial to society to legalise than to repress organisations of workers. The Combination Acts had proved to be ineffective in preventing trade unions from emerging; they had tended to aggravate ill-feeling between masters and workers, prevented the rise of stable, cautiously managed unions and sometimes had even given a violent character to combinations—there were, for instance, acts of destruction and machine-wrecking, during the Luddite outbreaks between 1811 and 1816. Such experiences helped to influence Parliament in 1824 to allow freedom of organisation to wage-earners as a less dangerous policy than that of crude suppression. So it was a marriage of classical economics and utilitarian legal ideas which paved the way for the repeal of the combination ban in Britain. On 21 June 1824 an Act was passed which swept away all existing combination bans in statutory and common law.

This was more than the trade unions had dared to hope for from the unreformed Parliament; but the government was preoccupied with other matters and Place and Hume had succeeded in packing the Parliamentary committee which considered the bill, and then in rushing it through before their opponents were fully aware of what was being done.

The passing of the Act coincided with a period of commercial prosperity, and in this economic climate the newly legalised unions came forward with demands for higher wages accompanied by an outburst of strikes in the winter of 1824–25. This led Sir Robert Peel, then Tory Home Secretary, to set up a new House of Commons select committee, as a result of which an amending Act was passed in 1825. This marked only a small retreat; Peel was willing to meet some trade union claims to lessen support for radicalism. All combinations concerned with wages, prices and hours of work were to be free of criminality under statute and common law, but the Act penalised violence, threats, intimidation, molestation and obstruction. In other words, collective bargaining over wages and hours was legalised, but freedom to strike was severely restricted. This reflected the view, expressed by the classical economist, David Ricardo:

> The true remedy for combinations is perfect liberty on both sides, and adequate protection against violence and outrage. Wages should be the result of free compact and the contracting parties should look to the law to protect them from force being employed on either side. Competition would not, I think, fail to do all the rest. [cited in Hollander, 1979, p. 570]

On the Continent of Western Europe in those days the situation was largely the converse of that in Britain. In France the *Loi Le Chapelier* and the ban on combinations in the Penal Code remained on the statute book after Napoleon's fall in 1813–15. In Germany the situation was confused due to political partition. In some states, like Rhineland, which had been under Napoleonic rule, the combination ban of the French Penal Code was maintained. In others, like Saxony and Bavaria, there were also bans on combinations. In Prussia, however, the legal position was ambiguous. According to one view, the ban on combinations, which formed part and parcel of the old guild system, disappeared when the guilds lost their monopoly about 1810–11; but according to others, the ban on combinations remained unchanged.

In the following decades new prohibitions on combinations appeared in many Western European nations. Thus in Denmark the combination ban of 1800, which applied only in Copenhagen, was extended to cover the whole country in 1823 and was reinforced in

1835. In France the July Monarchy, confronted with an outburst of industrial unrest and upheavals, such as those of the silk weavers in Lyon in 1831, and in Paris in 1834, reacted not only with brute force through the police and army (massacre of Rue Transnonain, 1834) but also by the enactment of a new repressive law against combinations of workers on 10 April 1834. In Germany the spread of combinations of workers and the fear of communism induced the authorities to enact fresh bans on combinations. The German League made a resolution to that effect in 1840. Other bans had been enacted in Württemberg (1836), Saxony (1838), Prussia (1845), Hanover (1847) and Bavaria (1857). Even in Britain new repressive measures re-emerged in the 1830s as a reaction against the spread of trade unionism. The most infamous example was the use of the Unlawful Oaths Act (passed in 1797 to suppress a sailors' mutiny) in the trial in 1834 in which six agricultural labourers from the village of Tolpuddle in Dorset (the 'Tolpuddle martyrs') were sentenced to seven years' transportation to the Australian penal settlement. In the following years the British labour movement turned to political agitation in support of Chartism, the first independent working-class political movement. Only after 1848, when this movement was spent, did unions begin to rise rapidly again.

Belgium had a very liberal constitution after it had broken away from the Netherlands in 1830. In this new constitution the freedom to assemble was unconditionally guaranteed. Nevertheless, the existing combination ban in the penal code was maintained. Blanpain explains that 'the rulers of 1830 did not bother about the freedom of association of the workers. It was only the freedom of the ruling class—and that was notably a political freedom—that was guaranteed' (1960, p. 1518). In this respect the ban on combinations, as an accepted infringement on a constitutionally guaranteed freedom to associate in Belgium in 1830–31 resembled the situation in France in 1790–91 and foreshadowed the repressive aftermath of the 1848 revolutions in France, Germany, Italy and the Netherlands.

The year 1848 was in fact very important for the trade union movement because in Continental Europe, notably in France and in Germany, there were unsuccessful working-class revolutions. In the Netherlands, Belgium, Denmark and the Kingdom of Sardinia, in order to avoid revolution the monarchs made significant democratic concessions. One feature of these changes was the freedom to associate and to assemble, which gradually acquired constitutional status. Numerous trade unions and even national confederations of unions emerged in France, Germany and the Kingdom of Sardinia. There were strong bonds between political and trade union agitation in those days. In France the provisional government of March 1848 promised the workers the right to associate. Freedom of association and the guarantee of equality between workers and employers was promulgated in the 1849 Constitution. In Germany it was at first believed that the trade unions enjoyed the general freedom of association laid down in Article 4 of the Act of 6 April 1848. In Belgium, too, the ban on combinations was seriously questioned for the first time in the revolutionary days of 1848.

But as the counter-revolutionary forces resumed power, all ideas about freedom of workers' associations disappeared. In Germany in the course of 1849 the judges reaffirmed the application of the existing bans on combinations. The Prussian executive followed in 1850 with a regulation on the prevention of the abuse of the right to assemble and to associate, and in 1854 and 1860 it was the turn of the Prussian legislature to extend the 1845 combination ban to domestic servants, agricultural workers and miners. In 1854 the North German Confederation passed a resolution prohibiting associations with political, socialist or communist aims. In Belgium attempts to remove the ban on combinations failed. The story was the same in France with the failure of all attempts to have the combination ban of the penal code repealed. The only change that was made was an amendment to Articles 414–16, so that at least theoretically associations of workers and employers received equal treatment (Act of 27 November 1849). In this respect French law resembled the law in parts of Germany, where the combination bans of Prussia (1845) and Saxony (since 1855) treated combinations of workers and employers alike. This of course does not imply that there was equal treatment in practice. In Italy as well, the combination bans remained on the statute book. In 1859 they were transferred to the new penal code of Sardinia, which after the unification of Italy in 1860 came into force in all Italian regions except Tuscany (Act of 29 May 1864). In the Netherlands at that time, associations of workers hardly existed, yet the combination ban stayed on the statute book without any debate. Only in Denmark was it then the case that the combination ban, although never formally repealed, fell into disuse.

In the 1850s, then, one notices the combination bans still being effectively applied, notably in France and in Belgium. In Germany the combination ban seems to have been applied with moderation. It should, however, not be forgotten that in the 1850s, as in the preceding decades, other methods of repressing industrial organisation and action (such as police intervention) continued to be much more effective than the application of the combination bans through the courts.

It was in the 1860s that the tide started turning in Continental

Europe. In France, Belgium and Germany there was an intensive debate about the repeal of the ban on combinations which did in fact take place in these countries in, respectively, 1864, 1866 and 1869. It is noteworthy that the advocates of repeal legislation used some of the same arguments as those of Francis Place and his allies forty years earlier in Britain: combinations in themselves, they said, are not really useful, but they should be legalised so that the workers themselves may discover this. J. S. Mill, writing in 1848, was often quoted:

> Experience of strikes has been the best teacher of the labouring classes on the subject of the relation between wages and the demand and supply of labour: and it is most important that this course of instruction should not be disturbed. [1965, p. 932]

These people sometimes shared the wishful thinking of Place that combinations would rapidly disappear after having been legalised. As the promoter of the French repeal Act, Ollivier said, 'Avec le temps la liberté des coalitions tuera la grève' (cited in Helmlich, 1977, pp. 144–5). Others, founding themselves on the Wages Fund doctrine, realised that an employer, in fact a combination in himself, could keep wages for too long below their natural level, and they considered combinations useful means of establishing a balance of power between employers and workers. It was often the protagonists of state abstentionism in economic affairs, of *laissez-faire*, who argued along these lines. To them the legalisation of combinations would make it possible for more equitable terms and conditions of employment to be established by way of collective self-regulation. And a well-functioning system of collective *laissez-faire* instead of an unfair individual *laissez-faire* would justify the continued abstention of the state in labour affairs.

To such economic reasoning legal arguments were added, some of them not dissimilar to those used by the English utilitarians some forty years earlier. It was recognised that there was a gulf between law and reality. The spread of trade unionism could no longer be repressed. Moreover, the workers should be taught to respect the law. Why then repress combinations of workers while the combined forces of the employers were largely left untouched? Why deny the worker a right to associate when this right was generally recognised for others? Why deny him the collective exercise of a right (to withdraw his labour) that he was allowed to exercise individually? The arguments against the maintenance on the statute book of the ban on combinations piled up. It was no longer only the liberals who supported the repeal. An increasing number of conservatives agreed, some because they believed that a new kind of economic order might arise, based on organised interest groups (*Berufständische Ordnung*). It is significant that 'the throne' gradually moved to the side of those who wanted combinations legalised. In France this happened during the second decade of the reign of Napoleon III (the liberal Empire), who increasingly pardoned those convicted of combining, allowed workers' representatives to visit the World Exhibition of 1862 in London and to study the position of the English trade unions there, and finally had the partisan deputy Ollivier table the repeal bill. In Germany it was Bismarck who took the side of those who wanted the bans on combinations repealed 'in order to strengthen the confidence of the workers in Kingdom and Government' (cited in Kollmann, 1916, p. 212).

It should not be forgotten that in these years in several Western European states electoral reforms had taken place which secured the vote for increasing numbers of the working classes. Conservatives and liberals, the throne, the nobility, as well as the bourgeoisie, competed for the favour of this new electorate. And they had to recognise the incompatibility of granting the workers political rights while denying them economic rights. In some countries, in particular Belgium, employers pleaded for the repeal of the bans on combinations because they wanted to combine more openly in order to counteract the growing strength of the trade unions.

What of the workers? Did they play an active part in the campaign for the repeal of the ban on combinations? The answer is a complex one. Britain affords an interesting example. Trade unionists were suspicious of the intentions of Francis Place and his allies, because those men were simultaneously supporting the repeal of legislation, such as the apprenticeship clauses of the Elizabethan Statute of Artificers, which craftsmen saw as protecting their interests. Place had dismissed as 'a proof of the ignorance of the journeymen of their real interests' the numerous petitions by workers for the retention or extension of apprenticeship regulation (cited in Thompson, 1963, p. 517). The trade unionists thought that the repeal of the Combination Acts without positive protective machinery would be inadequate, so they gave Place only qualified support. But when it seemed possible that the Combination Acts would be re-enacted in 1825, they organised widespread protests and petitions. Peel responded to the threat of a revolutionary response by the unions by retaining the principle of freedom to associate in his Act of 1825. Contrary to Place's expectations, few of the unions used their new-found freedom to collaborate with the employers. For the next fifteen to twenty years they asserted their independence from the employing classes.

Quite remarkably, at first socialists tended to pay relatively little attention to the issue of trade union legality. Proudhon in France and

Lassalle in Germany initially denied that trade unions could prevent or reduce the exploitation of the working classes. It was not until the 1860s that, under the influence of Marx, the First International spoke out in favour of trade unionism and started to promote the formation of socialist ones in Continental Europe. Unionisation was henceforth considered as a school of class struggle for the workers. By then the movement to remove the combination bans had already succeeded in Britain, where after the defeat of Chartism the unions had turned to economic aims. In Continental Europe, as well, the process of repeal of the bans on combinations was already in full swing. There it was often a few liberal parliamentarians who played a leading role: such as Ollivier in France, Schultze-Delitzsch and others in Germany, Van Houten in the Netherlands.

In some instances the ban on combinations was repealed not by isolated legislation, as was the case in Britain in 1824, France in 1864 and 1884, and in the Netherlands in 1872, but rather as part of more elaborate changes in codes: in Belgium in 1866 on the occasion of the enactment of a new penal code; in Germany in 1869 in connection with the introduction of a new uniform Reich Trade Act; in 1879 in Luxembourg when the Belgian Penal Code was transplanted; and in 1889 in Italy with the enactment of the Zanardelli Penal Code. Although the ban on combinations then became part of legal history, this did not mean that all forms of repression had disappeared or that all restraints on the development of the labour movement had been removed.

Specific Trade Union Legislation

In some Western European countries, like the Netherlands and Denmark, the position of the trade unions in law was clarified at the same time that the ban on combinations was removed from the statute book. Trade unions and employers' associations were put on the same legal basis as all other associations. They enjoyed the advantages of the general law of associations, which was sufficiently liberal in these countries to accommodate their activities. Matters stood differently in Britain, France, Belgium, Luxembourg, Italy and Germany.

In Britain the legal position after the repeal of the Combination Acts in 1824–25 was uncertain. They had no legal capacity, their funds had to be held in private hands, and they could not sue if they were defrauded. This situation seemed to be improved by the enactment of the Friendly Societies Act of 1855, which gave legal protection to societies with benefit functions and therefore it was presumed also to most trade unions. However, in the case of *Hornby* v. *Close* (1867)[3] the judges declared that trade unions were outside the scope of the Friendly Societies Act, being still illegal although not criminal organisations, owing to their tendency to act in restraint of trade. The consequence of this verdict was that the unions had no legal redress against fraudulent officials of the union, their agreements were unenforceable, their members could not enforce benefits and the unions could not hold property. So an Act of Parliament seemed necessary to end this threat by giving legal recognition to trade unions. A royal commission was appointed in February 1867 under the chairmanship of Sir William Erle, which came out in March 1869 with a majority report that recommended the legalisation and supervision of trade unions; a minority report simply urged legalisation without controls. Under the Liberal government of Gladstone the Trade Union Act was passed in 1871, essentially along the lines of the minority report. This Act, for which the newly formed Trades Union Congress (1868) had campaigned, remained the legal basis of trade union freedom for a century. It partially legalised unions by removing the legal consequences of their purposes being in restraint of trade, and set up a system of purely voluntary registration of unions, carrying certain minor advantages. The only concession to state supervision was limited requirements for the auditing and inspection of union funds, in order to deter fraud and negligence. The Act is characteristic of the British approach to labour law before 1971: it had a negative character granting immunity from the judge-made common law doctrines, such as restraint of trade (hostile to trade unionism), but did not confer positive rights with corresponding positive state controls over unions. The Act applied also in Ireland, where it was only from 1941 that various Acts tightened the requirements for enjoying certain rights.

In France the Act of 1864, like the 1825 Act in Britain, had kept the legal status of trade unions uncertain. First, the Act had altered only Articles 414–16 of the Penal Code but had left the *Loi Le Chapelier*, which was still on the statute book, untouched. So while the offence of combination ceased to be known to the law, and some strikes became legal, trade unions remained illegal. Second, the general law on associations in France was very restrictive and required police authorisation for almost every association (Arts. 291–3 Penal Code of 1810). These provisions had been strengthened in 1834, abolished between 1848 and 1850, but reintroduced in decrees of 1850, 1851 and 1853; they were relaxed somewhat in 1868 and 1881 and only finally liberalised in 1901. All this meant that even after 1864 the formation of

3. (1867) Law Reports 2 Queen's Bench 153.

trade unions except for mutual aid purposes (for which specific legalisation existed) was not really freely allowed. The 1864 Act had legalised combinations in the sense of *ad hoc* groups rather than permanent associations of workers. Legislation to that end was not enacted during the period of the Third Empire, but only with the so-called Waldeck-Rousseau Act of 21 March 1884. This Act repealed the *Loi Le Chapelier* and declared the restrictive provisions of the general law on associations in Article 291 of the Penal Code and Article 1 of the 1834 Act inapplicable with regard to trade unions. Members of the same or similar professions were given the right to organise themselves in trade unions (Art. 2), the formation of confederations was allowed (Art. 5) and the trade unions were bestowed with legal personality (Art. 7). The Waldeck-Rousseau Act was, like the British Trade Union Act of 1871, primarily based on liberal concepts, with only small remnants of restrictive measures. It obliged the unions to deposit their rule-books and the names of their officials at the town hall (Art. 4), it stipulated explicitly that combinations could be established only for economic purposes, that confederations could not acquire legal personality, nor could they possess property, and the individual unions could possess property only on a small scale. Although they could offer friendly society benefits, these had to be kept entirely separate and could not be used to subsidise strikes. All these restrictions were thought necessary to avoid political movements gaining power in and through unions. French workers had to wait until 1920 and 1927 for these restrictions to be removed.

What was the effect of the Waldeck-Rousseau Act? The left-republican forces, which were the advocates of the Act, expected it to protect the French trade union movement from radicalisation. In this respect the Act failed to answer its purpose: the moderate wing of the French labour movement (the Barbaret-wing) increasingly lost influence. On the other hand, the initial suspicion which the radical wing of the French labour movement had towards the 1884 Act proved to be unjustified. This wing had objections in particular against Article 4 (the obligation to deposit the rule-book and a list of officials), but gradually the unions abandoned their reservations and about ten years after its promulgation most French unions had registered under this Act. The employers' associations, however, did not register.

French writers differ about the significance of the Act. Louis (1904, p. 133) described it as 'neutral': the Act simply sanctioned a factual situation which could not be undone. The journal *Voix du Peuple* (17 February 1901) was more positive when it commented that the Act forcefully contributed to the rise of numerous unions. Nevertheless, trade unionism remained weak in France. Zeldin (1979, p. 208) points out that it was not the law but more fundamental reasons connected with the nature of French society which inhibited the growth of unions. This was despite the attempts of governments to promote their growth, as seen in the circular of the French Minister Waldeck-Rousseau of 1884 to the *Préfets* in which he pressed them not only to ensure compliance with the provisions of the 1884 Act but also to promote the development of trade unions.

In Belgium there was no legal need for specific trade union legislation. Nevertheless, the government thought it useful to have a special law on trade and professional associations enacted in 1898. The trade unions could see there was no sense whatsoever in creating such a special régime, and only regarded this Act as an attempt to subject them to specific controls, as indeed was the intention. So the trade unions refrained from registration under this Act. Later, an Act of May 1921 guaranteed freedom to join or not to join a union. Nevertheless, Belgian trade unions, until the end of the Second World War, generally had no defined legal status or corporate capacity. This meant that they could not sue or be sued. So they did not enjoy the advantages attached to corporate capacity, but, on the other hand, they did not suffer the possible disadvantages of state regulation of their internal affairs. Luxembourg copied the 1921 Belgian Act in 1936. Earlier, in 1928, the Luxembourg legislature had tried to tempt unions and employers' associations to register under a new Act, but most unions preferred to do without legal status or corporate capacity, as in Belgium.

In Italy, where the ban on combinations was removed in 1889, it was only in 1907 that the Higher Council of Labour decided that professional associations could acquire limited legal status through registration, with consequent civil liability in the event of violation of collective agreements. A decree of 27 October 1918 conferred legal status on industrial associations, one of the conditions being that the object of such an association should be confined to the protection of members from an economic and technical viewpoint, so excluding any attempt to modify the state of the labour market. This appeared to be an attempt to exclude the stipulation of collective labour agreements.

In Germany the situation after the repeal of the ban on combinations (1869) was comparable with that in France after 1864: trade unions could but rarely acquire legal recognition because of the very restrictive general law on associations and on private insurance. But, unlike France, in Germany there was no specific legislation to clarify the legal position of trade unions. Initially the authorities tried to settle this problem in terms of the reform of the general law on associations in the German Civil Code, which provided for administrative control. But the trade unions, holding the new régime to be too restrictive, still refrained from registration under these provisions. The authorities then, in 1906, tabled a bill on *gewerbliche Berufsvereine* (trade professional associations) but this failed. In 1908 the trade unions were deterred even more from registration under the general law on associations when the Reich Act on Associations gave such a broad definition of 'political associations' that it would have subjected the unions to the strict control which this Act imposed on political associations. In 1916, however, the legislature explicitly excepted trade unions from the application of the Act, but even this did not tempt the trade unions to register. After the First World War this extra-legal status of the trade unions remained, but their complete freedom was based on the Weimar Constitution.

It should be emphasised that the repeal of the laws on combination did not always apply to all categories of workers. For example, in Germany the repeal of the ban on combinations applied only to the branches of industry covered by the Reich Trade Order of 1869. So until 1919 combinations in mining, agriculture and for home workers and civil servants were unlawful. In France civil servants were forbidden to join unions and the courts held (1903) that even the sewerage workers of Paris counted as civil servants. Apart from civil servants in general, the police and the army, in particular, frequently faced restrictions on trade union rights. Thus, even in Britain, the Police Act of 1919 forbade the membership of trade unions to police and restricted them to a statutory association under state control. Between 1927 and 1946 (as a reponse to the General Strike of 1926) the Trade Disputes and Trade Unions Act forbade unions of civil servants from affiliating with other unions outside the civil service.

Industrial Disputes and the Criminal Law

Freedom to combine and freedom to strike are distinct but interrelated concepts. We have seen that in Britain the Act of 1825 protected trade unions from statutory and common law restrictions on combinations to raise wages but at the same time curbed the freedom to strike and to picket against blackleg labour by means of vague criminal offences such as 'molestation', 'obstruction' and 'intimidation'. In France, while the Act of 25 May 1864 had in effect legalised strikes, trade unions remained illegal until the Waldeck-Rousseau Act of 1884. But even in France after 1864 the right to strike was severely limited. The use of violence, threats and fraudulent measures in the organisation of a strike were subject to severe criminal sanctions. Moreover, strikers who infringed the 'freedom to work' (*entraves au liberté du travail*) of non-strikers were frequently prosecuted under the provisions of Articles 414–16 of the Penal Code. Similar use was made of the criminal law to permit the employer to continue to recruit blackleg labour during a strike in Belgium (Art. 310 of Penal Code), the Netherlands (Act of 26 April 1872), Luxembourg (Art. 310 Penal Code), Germany (Art. 153 of the Reich Trade Order) and Italy (Arts. 165–6 of the Zanardelli Penal Code).

These measures were consistent with the liberal belief that the freedom to associate and the freedom not to associate were two sides of the same coin. But this took little account of the reality of collective industrial action. To make a strike effective workers naturally wished to prevent the employer from recruiting others to take their places. For liberal reformers, like Emile Ollivier in France, strikes could be transformed into some kind of peaceful discussions between strikers, blacklegs and employers as a prelude to harmonious co-operation between the industrial parties. So the law was expected to draw a line between legitimate peaceful persuasion not to work, on the one hand, and illegitimate acts of intimidation or obstruction. It is a striking feature of the judicial interpretation of the broadly similar laws in all the countries studied that the courts went beyond liberal expectations and severely restricted even the peaceful activities of strikers. In Britain the Criminal Law Amendment Act of 1871 (repealing the Molestation of Workmen Act of 1859, which had legalised some forms of picketing) codified restrictive judicial decisions, revived the vague offences of molestation, obstruction and intimidation, and declared 'persistently following a person' and 'watching and besetting' premises to be crimes. The judges sentenced sixteen farm labourers' wives to hard labour for making the sheeplike noise 'Baa' to blacklegs, holding that this constituted 'intimidation'. 'Black looks' or the presence of strikers in large numbers was also regarded as intimidation; even the mere posting-up of a strike notice was held to be intimidation of employers. In *Bunn*'s case (1872),[4] London gas-stokers were sent to prison for a year merely for threatening to strike unless a colleague dismissed for union activity was reinstated, on the grounds that this amounted to a criminal conspiracy as an 'unjustifiable annoyance and interference with the master in the conduct of their business', even if the acts of the strikers were not independently unlawful, such as molestation and so on.

Parallels can be found in the case law of the other countries. In France it was held to be a crime to put out the lights in order to persuade other workers to go on strike; likewise, it was criminal to say 'C'est bien, nous t'aurons' to blacklegs. In Belgium, minor verbal

4. (1872) 12 Cox Criminal Reports 316.

insults to non-strikers were penalised under Article 310 of the Criminal Code. In Germany a sentence of one month's imprisonment was imposed under Article 153 of the Reich Trade Act on strikers who said 'Pfui' to blacklegs. There were similar interpretations of Articles 165–6 of the Penal Code in Italy. Only in the Netherlands was the use of the criminal law avoided: the 1872 Act was never invoked and its provisions disappeared when a new penal code was introduced in 1886.

Apart from those restrictions, the penal restrictions on labour mobility (discussed earlier in Ch. 1) were also an important sanction against strikes. The obligation to possess a work-book (*livret*) seriously inhibited strikes because the worker who went on strike risked losing his *livret* and so he could not find work. The abolition of the work-book system in the Continental European countries between 1869 and 1890 was an indispensable step towards the decriminalisation of industrial action. In Britain (as discussed in Ch. 1) the criminal sanctions under the Master and Servant Acts against breach of contract were an important weapon against strikes. The repeal of these sanctions in 1875 was also a necessary stage in securing the freedom to strike. Similarly in Germany, when the Reich Trade Act of 1869 repealed the ban on combinations it also removed the criminality of breach of the contract of employment.

Despite the sporadic intervention of legislatures to liberalise the law relating to industrial action, repressive legislation constantly re-emerged. In Britain, as already noted, the Molestation of Workmen Act 1859 had protected certain forms of peaceful picketing, but the Criminal Law Amendment Act 1871 confirmed the criminality of intimidation, molestation and obstruction and added some new offences. The protest campaign against this Act and judicial interpretations (as in *Bunn*'s case, 1872, above) reached its peak during the 1874 general election when newly enfranchised working men supported opposition Conservative candidates who appeared more responsive to trade union pressure than the Liberal government responsible for the 1871 Act. Disraeli's Conservative government (ignoring the recommendations of the Royal Commission on the Labour Laws 1874, which had said no changes were needed) in 1875 introduced the Conspiracy and Protection of Property Act, which repealed the 1871 Act and also reversed the common law as declared in *Bunn*'s case in respect of acts 'in contemplation of furtherance of a trade dispute'. This concept, although not defined until 1906, was, in Wedderburn's words, a 'golden formula which became the bedrock of British workers' rights to organise and to take effective industrial action' for the next century (1971, p. 312). The 1875 Act also replaced the vague offences of 'intimidation', and so on, by narrower and more specific offences. This had the effect of removing from the sphere of criminality most forms of peaceful picketing to persuade others not to work or to communicate information about a strike. These changes did not, however, forestall the use of the civil law against strikers and pickets, to which we shall return later.

In most other European countries, by contrast, the penal laws remained an important restriction on strike action for much longer. In France Articles 414–15 of the Penal Code were not infrequently invoked; in Belgium Article 310 of the Penal Code was strengthened in 1892 in response to the social upheavals of the 1880s and was repealed only in 1921. In Luxembourg the criminal provisions were strengthened in 1898 and repealed in 1936. In the Netherlands, although the specific criminal sanctions were removed in 1886, the general provisions of the Penal Code relating to acts of violence were sharpened in 1904 in response to a railway workers' strike in 1903. In Germany Article 153 of the Reich Trade Act was not repealed until 1918. In Italy the courts punished strikers severely for general offences.

More important than these statutes, however, were the actions of the police. Blacklegs were often introduced under the protection of the police, and on the pretext of preserving public order the police could severely limit the activities of pickets. In France this was promoted by the fact that municipalities according to an Act of 5 April 1886 could be made responsible if they failed to invoke the police or the military to repress a strike. The public authorities frequently arrested and prosecuted trade union leaders for public order offences as a means of curbing strikes. In Germany a similar practice occurred under the famous Strike Order of 11 April 1886 of the Prussian Minister of the Interior, Von Putkammer, and of a Police Order of 1901, prohibiting strikes.

The invocation of the police and the military was explained on the grounds of the general policy of maintenance of public peace, order and security, which demanded that conflicts be resolved exclusively in a peaceful way. Von Putkammer, in his Strike Order, suggested that in these conflicts the police were strictly neutral:

> Every direct or indirect intervention of the police authorities against the freedom of combinations established by statute is excluded and they must abstain from all measures which could appear as an act of partnership with the governmental authority in favour of the employers or vice versa. [cited in Schippel, 1902, p. 741]

This official state neutrality was, however, only a façade. In practice it meant shielding the employers, because the law as it stood was not neutral: it tolerated anti-trade union behaviour on the part of the employers which workers often felt they could not resist except by using violence.

The state for many years showed itself far from tolerant as regards industrial action by its own employees and in the area of essential services. So, for instance, in Britain the 1875 Conspiracy and Protection of Property Act imposed criminal sanctions for breach of contract of service in the gas and water industries (extended to the electricity supply industry in 1919), although this was not used in practice. British practice in the twentieth century has been to take measures to secure supplies by alternative means rather than to impose direct criminal sanctions against strikers in essential services. The Emergency Powers Act of 1920 (invoked on only a few occasions before 1945) enabled the government to use troops to move essential supplies, but industrial conscription was not permitted and the strikes as such were not penalised. Practice elsewhere in Europe was different. In the Netherlands after a major industrial conflict in 1903 railway personnel and civil servants were prohibited under criminal law from taking industrial action. In France similar bills to that end in the early 1900s failed. However, on many occasions strikes in the railways, the postal services and the power stations were broken by requisition measures by the authorities and disciplinary measures against individual strikers. The Requisition Act of 11 July 1938 was used several times between August 1938 and September 1939 to break strikes in essential services. In Italy civil servants and railway personnel were affected by Article 181 of the Penal Code, which provided that abandonment of public office by three or more persons by prior agreement was an offence. In Germany the freedom to strike for workers in the essential services was abolished in 1920–21.

FROM TOLERATION TO RECOGNITION

The Rise of Modern Trade Unions

The trade unions that emerged around the middle of the nineteenth century were markedly different from the former combinations of journeymen and craftsmen. The old associations mostly operated on a local or, at best, regional scale. The new trade unions tended to operate on a national scale with central decision-making bodies. The old trade unions had only weak institutional structures. Sometimes they mushroomed as strike committees only to disappear after a particular struggle. This explains why in the early period the word 'combination' or, in French '*coalition*', embraces both the act of industrial action and the organisation that lay behind it. The new trade unions, however, were permanent organisations usually with a fixed scale of contributions and funds for strikes, sickness, unemployment, superannuation and funeral benefits, a (small) paid staff and their own publications. It is of course impossible within the scope of this chapter to give a complete picture of the development of Western European workers' movements since 1850.[5] The history of trade unions and of industrial relations fills whole libraries. But let us glean some features of this development as a necessary background to the development of collective labour law.

The modern type of workers' organisation was undoubtedly born in Britain about 1850 with the foundation of the Amalgamated Society of Engineers (ASE), the prototype of what Sidney and Beatrice Webb called the 'new model' trade unions, which were large, efficient and concentrated power in the hands of full-time officials. These unions accepted the liberal tenets of self-help and mutual aid and emphasised the desirability of 'conciliation and arbitration' (as collective bargaining was then usually called) with employers; they were disinclined to strike; they used the existing law to the fullest extent possible; and they stressed traditional restrictions on labour supply (e.g. limiting the number of apprentices) to maintain standards. The success of the British new models in achieving acceptability served as an example to the Continent. On the occasion of the Great Exhibition of 1862 delegations of French and German workers went to London and studied British trade unionism. On returning home they reported on the advantages that there were in such organisations for the working class, and this became a major incentive to the spread of reformist-style trade unionism all over Western Europe.

The new model unions, however, were, like the early unions, still mainly organisations of skilled or semi-skilled workers, who continued to emphasise craft exclusiveness and operated mainly in trades where there had been a long tradition of association either as mutual aid societies (Britain, France, Germany, Italy) or as guild organisations (Denmark, where the guilds were abolished as late as 1862). In most countries printers, carpenters and joiners, and tobacco workers were amongst the earliest to organise. In Britain, in addition to the engineers, boiler-makers, iron tradesmen, carpenters and joiners, there was a growth of 'new' unionism among the miners and the cotton-

5. For national summaries, see Appendix I, p. 301, below.

spinners. The last-mentioned groups placed particular emphasis on parliamentary activity to secure the passage of legislation such as the Coal Mines Regulation Act 1860, which provided for improved mines inspection and allowed the miners to appoint their own check-weighmen (many of whom served as union officials) and the improved factories legislation of the second half of the nineteenth century.

In this phase of trade union growth (1850–80) the unions were not yet mass organisations, although by the beginning of the 1870s some of them (notably in Britain) counted already several thousands of members. By 1888 there were 750,000 British trade union members (10 per cent of adult male workers). This period also saw the rise of multi-industrial trade union structures both locally and nationally. In place of the former antagonism between local combinations of workers, local bodies providing co-operation between trade unions in different trades and crafts in the same town now grew up. In Britain in several cities so-called trades councils were founded, starting with Liverpool in 1848, followed by Edinburgh, Sheffield and Glasgow. These councils, open to all organised workers in a town, were a means of facilitating mutual aid and solidarity, especially in times of crisis. In the Netherlands the leaders of the different local trade unions formed so-called *bestuurdersbonden* (local federations of trade union leaders) from the end of the 1860s onwards. In France the *bourses du travail* from 1886, in Italy the *camere del lavoro* from 1891 and in Denmark the local trade councils from 1890 played a similar role. However, there were several important differences between the French *bourses du travail* and the British trades councils. The former were set up by the public authorities rather than by the workers themselves; they were given free buildings and subsidies, and were expected to perform certain public functions, in particular that of labour exchanges (see Ch. 4, above, for details). In these respects the *bourses* had an official character not found in their British counterparts. But the *bourses* were, like the trades councils, local groupings of workers. They were often controlled by radicals who used the subsidies to attack the government, and so they were the scene of frequent struggles between rival unions and the public authorities. While the trade councils played an important part in the function of a national federation of unions, the *bourses*, on the contrary, delayed national unity by setting up their own federation of local *bourses*.

Early attempts at national alliances of unions were short-lived. In Britain Robert Owen's Grand National Consolidated Trade Unions had a brief existence (1829–34); in Germany, in the revolutionary days of 1848, there were three abortive attempts to form federations, and in France the Fédération Nationale (1849) did not survive. It was not until the convocation by Manchester and Salford trades council of a

Trades Union Congress (TUC) in Britain in 1868 that the first permanent federation on a multi-industry basis was formed. This was the outcome of co-operation between unions during the years of threat to their legal status following the decision in *Hornby* v. *Close* (see p. 208, above). In form and purpose the TUC was an extension to the national level of the activities of local trades councils. Individual unions continued to conduct collective bargaining and industrial action; the TUC was an annual meeting of unions to discuss matters of common interest; a TUC 'parliamentary committee' directed union campaigns between annual meetings to influence the political parties to support pro-union legislation.

A distinctive feature of the TUC, in comparison with the national federations later formed in other Western European countries, is that it became the only significant national body to which most unions were affiliated. There were none of the political and confessional splits which divided the labour movement elsewhere. The reasons are twofold. First, the suffrage did not assume the same importance in the formative period of the British unions as it did elsewhere in Europe; minimum labour standards had been secured by industrial struggle before the franchise was extended to the town artisan in 1867 and the country operative and miner in 1885. Second, the unions had given birth to their own independent pragmatic reformist leaders long before the socialist movement became important. In 1900 a number of unions affiliated to the TUC combined with the Marxist Social-Democratic Federation (SDF), the Independent Labour Party (ILP) and the Fabian Society to establish a Labour Representation Committee from which emerged the Labour Party. The Labour Party was thus a product of the trade union movement; the unions, for their part, were not the creation of socialists nor based on a socialist theory of society as in several other European countries. The Irish TUC, formed in 1894, was on similar lines.

Although elsewhere in Western Europe non-ideological confederations saw the light of day—in Germany, Verband Deutsche Gewerkvereine (VDG), 1869; in the Netherlands, Algemeen Nederlandsch Werkliedenverbond (ANW), 1871; in Denmark, the Central Trade Union Committee (1874)—these were in the course of years, eclipsed by major confederations, linked with the socialist political movement. The General German Trade Union Federation—Allgemeiner Deutscher Gewerkschaftsbund (ADGB)—was set up in 1868 primarily as a recruiting ground for the Social Democratic Party (SPD), and was struck down by Bismarck's Anti-Socialist Act. The General Commission of Trade Unions, set up in 1890, was dominated by the SPD, although by 1914 the German unions had developed into an autonomous partner conducting the economic struggle, while the Party concentrated on political issues. In the Netherlands, the National Labour Secretariat—Nationaal Arbeids Secretariat (NAS)—set up in 1893, was at first dominated by syndicalists, but after the defeat of the railways strike in 1903, fifteen socialist-led unions established the Nederlands Verbond van Vakverenigen (NVV) in 1906, on the model of the German ADGB, and collaborated closely with the Social Democratic Workers' Party (SDAP) for universal suffrage and on other issues. In Belgium the Workers' Party (POB), an alliance of working-class and socialist organisations formed twenty years earlier than the British Labour Party, was instrumental in founding the Commission Syndicale of socialist and independent unions. The leaders of the Commission Syndicale and the POB discussed social and political questions in a single assembly. It was only in 1937 that the Commission Syndicale asserted its independence from the POB, calling itself the Confédération Générale du Travail de Belgique (CGTB). In Italy, the Confederazione Generale Italiana del Lavoro (CGIL) was set up in 1906 under the guidance of the Partito Socialista Italiano (PSI).

The French Confédération Générale du Travail (CGT), founded in 1895, was different in both form and inspiration from the trade union federations elsewhere. Before 1914 trade unions were fragmentary and never achieved the mass base they had in Britain, Germany, Italy, Belgium and the Netherlands; most strikes took place without preliminary union organisation. The CGT comprised only a minority of union members; most organised French workers belonged to small provincial unions. The leaders of the CGT adopted a revolutionary anarcho-syndicalist stance, independent of the political parties. They rejected the idea of parliamentary activity and social legislation, and, unlike the British TUC, were not interested in forming a Labour Party. The transformation of the CGT resulted from the sudden abandonment of revolutionary syndicalism by its leaders during the First World War. After the war their *politique de présence* resulted in the negotiation of the 8-hour day (1919) and participation in government bodies—a period of 'integration' discussed later in Chapter 6.

Where the unions were strongly influenced by political ideologies, it was inevitable that they could suffer from the same splits as afflicted the political movements. There was intense rivalry, for example, between the syndicalist federation of *bourses du travail*, formed in 1892, and the National Federation of Unions led by the Guesdist socialists in France. In 1921 the CGT was split when communists and anarchists formed the Confédération Générale du Travail Unitaire (CGTU) of which the Parti Communiste Français (PCF) gained control and expelled most of the anarcho-syndicalists. It was only in 1936 that CGTU rejoined the

CGT. There were important regional differences as well in the ideology and orientation of French unions, reformist demands being more frequently pursued by the well-organised factory-based unions of the north and north-east, and revolutionary aims and political action being more evident in the loosely based unions of the centre, west and south.

The domination of the socialists in the growing trade unions inspired the development of Christian trade unions 'to save the soul of the working man', since socialism was seen as atheist or anti-clerical in character. The Christian social movement opposed the thesis of class struggle and opted for models of class co-operation and peaceful solutions to conflicts. They sometimes propagated associations that embraced both employers and workers, as for example in the Netherlands, the Protestant Confederation 'Patrimonium', founded in 1876. The Christian movement received considerable momentum from the Papal Encyclical *Rerum Novarum* of 1891 (and in the Netherlands also from the Protestant Christian Social Congress of 1891). By the turn of the century Christian trade unionism had become an important factor in Germany, France, Italy and the Benelux countries. During the first quarter of the twentieth century they united in Christian confederations competing with confederations of free trade unions: Gesamtverband der Christliche Gewerkschaften (Germany, founded in 1901); Christeljik Nationaal Vakverbond (Protestant, the Netherlands, founded 1906); Roomsch-Katholiek Werkliedenverbond (Roman Catholic, the Netherlands, established as a merger in 1925 of two older Catholic confederations, founded, respectively, in 1906 and 1909); Algemeen Christelijk Vakverbond (Belgium, founded in 1908); Confederazione Italiana dei Lavoratori (Italy, founded 1918); Confédération Française des Travailleurs Chrétiens (France, founded 1919). In Denmark and Britain where trade unionism was less ideologically based, Christians did not establish their own unions.

This period was also marked by the growth of international co-operation by the trade union movement. The First International set up in 1864 in London has already been mentioned. It was neither a federation of national organisations nor exclusively based on trade unions. It was composed of a mixture of individual members, who joined branches and sections in each country, as well as of affiliated trade unions. It met with fierce government opposition, including statutes in France in 1872 and Denmark in 1873, prohibiting affiliation. In a few cases multinational trade unions were formed such as the International Cigar Workers' Union which, after 1873, united workers in Belgium and the Netherlands. More important were the International Trade Secretariats, which sought to unite in loose associations the national unions of specific trades such as those of boot and shoe workers (1889), miners (1890), printers (1893) and so on. By 1914 there were almost thirty International Trade Secretariats, most of them with headquarters in Germany. Sometimes regional co-operation sprang up, as in 1886, when the first Scandinavian Labour Congress was held in Gothenburg. The socialist-inclined unions decided at a conference held in 1901 in Copenhagen, attended by their representatives from Germany, Belgium, France, Finland and Britain, to hold regular international union conferences in the future. The following year a permanent secretariat of these conferences was assigned to the German Social Democrats. In 1913 the International Federation of Trade Unions (IFTU) was formed out of this International Secretariat of Trade Union Centres, as a confederation of social-democratic (or 'free') trade unions. In 1920 the Christian trade unions established their own international confederation, the International Federation of Christian Trade Unions (usually referred to by its French initials CISC). In 1921 the Red International of Labour Unions (Profintern) was founded, which grouped together the communist-orientated trade unions.

After 1880, in all countries studied, a new phase of trade union growth set in as the unskilled workers became more willing to respond to the call of unionism. (In Britain this development was called the 'new unionism'.) Even more spectacular increases in membership occurred during or immediately after the end of the First World War, and, although most unions sustained losses in the subsequent years of economic depression, by 1939 the level of membership was still higher than in 1913. In Italy after 1923 and Germany after 1933 free trade-unionism was suppressed by the Fascist and Nazi dictatorships (see Ch. 7, below).

A characteristic of this period of trade union growth was the changing composition of the trade union movement, because of the shifts in economic activity. So, whereas in Britain at one time the miners and the textile workers represented the strongest sections of the trade union movement, during this phase there was rapid growth of unionisation among engineering workers, dockers and railwaymen. Another important development in this period was that white-collar workers and civil servants became increasingly unionised, notably in Germany and Britain. In France it was only in 1936, with the electoral victory of the Popular Front, that the *cadres* entered the unions in large numbers. Likewise, in Denmark and the Netherlands it was not until the end of the 1930s that white-collar workers entered the trade union movement to a significant extent. Sometimes white-collar workers joined the existing unions or confederations. More often, however, they formed their own unions and sometimes even their own confederations, such as in Germany the Trade Union Federation of German Workers, Salaried Staff and Civil Services Associations and in France (1937) the Confédération Générale des Cadres.

This stage of trade union growth was also characterised by a rapid growth in female membership of the trade unions. During the earlier stages of trade union development, male trade unionists were often hostile towards female participation in the unions. This situation sometimes caused women to form their own unions (e.g. in Britain in 1919 the Women's Trade Union League, and in Denmark the Women's Labour Union, established in 1901). But the entry of large numbers of women into the labour force during the First World War made it difficult for men to resist female entry into unions, although the percentage of female unionisation and of those holding official positions in the unions remained lower than for males.

Furthermore, this stage of trade union growth was marked by the emergence of trade union presence on the shop floor; notably, the so-called shop stewards' movement in Britain, which grew up in the 1890s and became forceful during the First World War. But the shop stewards' movement developed outside the formal structure of collective bargaining and the trade unions, and when the First World War was over the trade union leadership was concerned with establishing central control over the shop stewards' movement and to replace them by official joint consultative committees.

The Growth of Employers' Associations

During the nineteenth century, apart from some early forerunners of the modern employers' associations like the Comité des Forges (France, 1840), the Mining Association (Britain, 1854) and the Deutsche Buchdruckerverein (Germany, 1869), most combinations of employers were on a local or regional scale, and operated *ad hoc* to cope with lengthy strikes and usually disappeared when the particular industrial conflict was over. It was only during the last fifteen years of the nineteenth century that the employers started to create their own strong permanent organisations. In every one of the countries studied, the years between 1890 and 1914 are the formative period for modern employers' associations. These associations were mostly organised along the lines of trades, but at the turn of the century national multi-industry organisations of employers were formed, such as the Danish Employers' Confederation (DA) in 1896, the Dutch Union of Employers in 1899, the British Employers' Parliamentary Council in 1899, the German Employers' Association and the Union of German

Employers' Associations, both in 1904, the Italian Industrialists League of Turin (1906) and so on. In some cases, such as that of the Danish DA and of the two German confederations that merged in 1913 as the Confederation of German Employers' Associations, the employers' confederations were clearly established to oppose the labour movement. In Britain it was the realisation by employers in industries such as building, engineering and printing that they could be defeated one by one by the craft unions that led them to associate, as in the Engineering Employers' Federation (1897). In other cases, such as the Dutch and Italian confederations, the employers' organisations were established not so much to face the unions but to exert an influence on the legislators. In the Netherlands this provoked the establishment in 1920 of a 'social' confederation alongside the 'economic' confederation of 1899, and this separation of 'social' and 'economic' confederations was to last until the 1960s. Also, in the Netherlands Protestant and Catholic employers established their own employers' associations by trade as well as on a national multi-industry level. On the international level employers began to build federations in certain trades; for example, the International Shipping Federation (1902) and the International Federation of Building and Public Works (1904). At the multi-industry level, the International Organisation of Industrial Employers was formed in 1920. After the First World War employers' associations in most trades and industries were consolidated. In some countries they managed to enforce their authority over their members and to attract a broad membership. But this was not always so. For example, in France employers' associations were generally weak until after the Second World War.

The Movement Towards Recognition

As the state refrained from repressing the trade unions, employers increasingly tended to become more active in counteracting trade unionism. They did so by various means within their managerial power, such as the 'yellow dog' contracts (called 'the document' in Britain),[6] a declaration of renunciation of trade union membership which workmen were required to sign as a condition of employment; the 'yellow union' (so-called from the yellow flower of broom they adopted as their emblem in France), an organisation of workers, friendly to the employer, established or supported by him to counter the influence of independent trade unions; the circulation of blacklists

6. An example will be found in Appendix IV, p. 368, below.

of militant trade unionists in order to prevent them being engaged; and the use of blackleg labour to neutralise the effect of strikes.

But there were also many employers who realised that this warfare could not go on and that it was wiser to recognise trade unions and establish an orderly relationship with them. This occurred in the mid and late nineteenth century everywhere in Western Europe in various trades and enterprises, but for the first time on a national, multi-industry scale in Denmark. In September 1899, after the hardest and longest industrial conflict in Danish industrial history, the central employers' and trade unions' organisations entered into an agreement. In this so-called September Agreement[7] employers and trade unions recognised each others' fundamental rights to exist and function. The employers recognised the rights of trade unions to organise, to strike and to enter into collective agreements. On the other hand, trade unions recognised the right of employers to lockout and their right to direct and distribute work. Both sides of industry bound themelves not to approve or support a strike or a lockout unless certain conditions had been met as to notification and ballots. They agreed to utilise opportunities for mediation and arbitration, and to work together for peaceful, stable and good relations. The September Agreement was immediately recognised by the Danish government. In subsequent years parts of it were backed up by legislation. But the principles of the September Agreement have remained to this day as the basis of the Danish system of industrial relations.

Potentially the September Agreement could have become the Magna Carta of modern Western European industrial relations. But it did not have a direct influence elsewhere in Europe, apart from the Scandinavian countries. This may be attributable to the inaccessibility of the Danish language, or to the special nature of the Danish situation with a marked ideology of 'partnership' in an era in which trade unions elsewhere tended to advocate class struggle. It seems that the September Agreement was entered into because in Denmark the employers believed that a balance of power had been reached on a national scale, which was not the case elsewhere in Western Europe at the time.

One may compare this with the situation before 1914 in Britain. A great number of collective bargaining procedures in particular trades at local level, covering a substantial minority of workers, had been negotiated since the mid-nineteenth century. Many of these were modelled upon the Nottingham Hosiery Board, consisting of equal numbers of employers and workers under the chairmanship of A. J. Mundella, a hosiery employer. But government intervention was at a

7. The text of the Agreement will be found in Appendix IV, p. 383, below.

low level, generally limited to offering advice and conciliation during disputes. The outstanding features of British collective bargaining in this period were its fragmentary character and the absence of any means of legal compulsion. The sharp industrial conflicts of 1889 raised doubts about this *laissez-faire* policy, but the majority of the Royal Commission on Labour, 1891–94, set up in the wake of the unrest, endorsed the long-standing negative policy and the practice of simply 'encouraging' voluntary bargaining through the Board of Trade, the government department responsible for labour matters. The Conciliation Act 1896, which emerged after the Commission's report, did no more than provide machinery to facilitate conciliation and arbitration with the consent of both parties. The Fair Wages Resolutions of the House of Commons of 1891 and 1909 encouraged government departments not to contract with suppliers who failed to observe standards commonly recognised by employers and trade societies in the district. The Trade Boards Act 1909 gave powers to boards consisting of employers and workers and independent persons to determine wages on an *ad hoc* basis in so-called 'sweated trades'. Winston Churchill (1909, cols. 1391–2), as the minister responsible, said:

> The principles on which we are proceeding are to endeavour to foster organisation in trades in which, by reason of the prevalence of exceptionally evil conditions, no organisation has yet taken root, and in which, in consequence, no parity of bargaining power can be said to exist. [1909, cols. 1391–2]

In other words, official policy in the years before the First World War was to 'encourage' voluntary collective bargaining without direct state intervention or legal compulsion. However, there was nothing between unions and employers at national multi-industry level as comprehensive as the Danish September Agreement.

The First World War marked a decisive turning point throughout Western Europe towards state recognition of trade unions. At the outbreak of war the governments and employers in almost every combatant nation perceived the need for co-operation with the trade unions in mobilising the war machine and operating the war economy. The leaders of the trade union movements who had tried internationally to avert war now generally took the side of their governments (Italy was a notable exception; under the slogan *Né aderire—né sabotare*, neither support nor sabotage, the socialist union leaders tried to assert their neutrality). In Germany, Belgium and Britain, trade unionists entered into regular negotiations with their governments. In France and Britain trade unionists entered the government. In all these countries, and even in the Netherlands which had not joined the war, union leaders co-operated with their governments in the many committees set up to administer unemployment relief, rationing of commodities, rent and price controls. During the war, union leaders generally agreed to abandon the right to strike and to permit the direction of labour.

In response to this new mood of collaboration, as well as fears inspired by the Russian Revolution of October 1917, the various governments introduced measures both during and after the war which resulted everywhere in greater state recognition of trade unionism and collective representation. There were, however, significant differences in the methods by which this new policy was advanced. In particular, one may contrast the creation of positive legal rights to recognition and representation in Germany and, later, France with the continued reliance upon encouragement of voluntary collective bargaining in Britain and Denmark.

In Germany in 1916 trade unions had been exempted from the restrictive provisions of the law on associations already described; the union of state railway personnel had been recognised in the same year; and in May 1918, Article 153 of the Reich Trade Act was repealed. The Patriotic Auxiliary Service Act of December 1916 gave trade unions the right to nominate representatives on conciliation and arbitration bodies, and gave employees the right to establish committees at plant level (see Ch. 6, below). When the revolution broke out in November 1918 the employers were ready to make great concessions and the union leaders wanted to protect the economy and their own organisations from the revolutionary situation. Just six days after the outbreak of the revolution, on 15 November 1918, the Stinnes-Legien Agreement (named after the leaders of the employer and union delegations) was signed. In this historic agreement the employers gave formal recognition to independent trade unions, and to collective agreements as a means of regulating labour relations; they agreed to disband the 'yellow' unions and to cease discrimination against union members; they undertook to establish jointly managed employment offices and arbitration bodies, and agreed to recognise workers' committees in plants with more than fifty workers. They also established on 4 December 1918 a Central Joint Labour Committee (see Ch. 6, below). The trade unions also achieved one of their major demands, for the 8-hour working day.

While there are many parallels between the contents of the Danish September 1899 Agreement and the Stinnes-Legien Agreement of 1918, the most striking difference was that in the more legalistic climate of Germany the main principles of the Stinnes-Legien Agreement were soon incorporated into positive statutory rights, and even into constitutional law. The Weimar Constitution of 1919, besides securing the general right of association, expressly recognised the right to form unions and employers' associations for the sake of furthering labour and economic conditions (Art. 159). In addition, the right to bargain collectively was guaranteed (Art. 165). The Weimar Constitution is of historic importance for the development of collective self-regulation because for the first time it invested trade union rights with constitutional status. Before the Second World War, the Irish Republic was the only country to follow the German example: its Constitution of 1937 contained a provision on trade union rights.

The constitutional provisions of the Weimar Republic were supported by the Collective Agreements Decree of December 1918, which gave primacy to the collective agreement over the individual contract, and embodied the principle of 'extension', which enabled the Minister of Labour to extend collective agreements to employments not otherwise covered by collective bargaining. The compulsory effect attached to arbitration awards by the Arbitration Decree of October 1923, and there were several other enactments regulating employment conditions.

In France, too, positive legal rights assumed major importance. The unions had negotiated and obtained an 8-hour law in 1919, enforced by ministerial decrees in individual industries. A law of 1919 regulated collective bargaining, but by 1933 only 7.5 per cent of wage-earners were affected by collective agreements because of the resistance of employers. The victory of the Popular Front at the May 1936 elections brought about dramatic changes. Five days after the election a spontaneous series of strikes and occupations of factories, which surprised even the newly unified CGT (see p. 219, above), led Leon Blum, the socialist Prime Minister, to summon the CGT and the employers' association to a meeting at his official quarters, the Hotel Matignon. In the resulting Matignon Agreement[8] the employers agreed to recognise trade union rights and to stop victimisation of union members. The employers agreed in principle to the 'immediate conclusion' of collective agreements. The Agreement was rapidly forced on the employers by the Popular Front government by laws which established the 40-hour week and guaranteed paid holidays. The legislation also specified in detail the matters to be covered by collective agreements, provided an 'extension' procedure and specified a system of workers' representation at the workplace (see Ch. 6, below). The effects on trade union membership were dramatic, with an increase from 1 million to over 5 million by the end of 1936. (The increase was,

8. The text of the Agreement will be found in Appendix IV, p. 380, below.

however, not uniform, the greatest permanent increase being in the public sector.) A significant aspect of this new legal order was that in the event of unions and employers failing to agree, and in the event of disputes arising about collective agreements, the matter was to be referred to compulsory arbitration.

By way of contrast with this creation of positive legal rights, the route towards recognition was predominantly by voluntary methods in Britain, Belgium, the Netherlands and Denmark. In Britain the 'Whitley councils' were set up from 1916 onwards on a voluntary basis as a result of the recommendations of a Cabinet sub-committee on reconstruction problems under the chairmanship of J. H. Whitley, Speaker of the House of Commons. The councils were collective bargaining bodies. According to a model constitution, each consisted of employers' representatives and trade union representatives covering a particular industry or sector of industry. Some of these, like printing, railways, boot and shoe, building and docks, were industries where there was already established bargaining, but the councils improved the range and scope of bargaining. Others lacked such arrangements and strong government pressure was needed to establish these councils, but it was not found necessary to use legislation. This included local authorities and public utilities. By 1922 seventy-four Whitley councils had been formed. Although the total dropped to sixty-two in 1923, most of these survived until 1939 and many continued in the post-war period. The inter-war years were, however, also marked by occasional bouts of repression, such as the Trade Disputes and Trade Unions Act of 1927, passed in response to the General Strike of 1926. The Act made certain forms of sympathetic industrial action unlawful, and prevented civil servants from joining a union affiliated to the TUC. It was repealed in 1946 by a Labour government.

In Denmark, where the voluntary system had functioned since 1899, sectors of public opinion began to worry about the increasing power of the trade unions. Allegations that the freedom of individuals was no longer respected by the trade union leaders led to the enactment of a Trade Union Act in 1929. Introduced by the Liberal government against the opposition of both the central Employers' Association and the Trade Unions Federation, this Act intended to protect the liberty of the individual against the monopoly power of powerful organisations. The Act made economic and individual victimisation by means of an abuse of collective power, including the use of boycott, punishable. It was, of course, primarily directed against trade unions and led to a number of court cases; in effect the Act was a codification of earlier case law, but with penal sanctions. It never played the decisive role that was intended for it, and in 1937 it was repealed.

The movement towards recognition of independent trade unions and collective bargaining was halted by the rise of fascism in Italy and national socialism in Germany and its spread to the occupied countries. These matters are examined later in Chapter 7.

Conciliation, Mediation and Arbitration

With the growth of trade unionism, the state became increasingly interested in devices to prevent or settle collective industrial conflicts peacefully. There already existed a number of institutions for resolving individual disputes, such as the *conseils de prud'hommes* in France and Belgium and the *collegi di probiviri* in Italy, the latter each with a 'conciliation office' (see Ch. 6, below), and in Britain the machinery for arbitration was first set up under the Combination Act 1800, later under the Arbitration Act 1824. But neither the workers nor the trade unions were involved in these processes, so they were reluctant to use them.

In France, Belgium and Italy this problem was dealt with through the democratisation of the *conseils* and *collegi*. In France, from the 1880s onwards, the trade unions took to organising elections to the *conseils*, demanding an undertaking from their candidates always to decide in favour of the worker, and many unions looked upon the *conseils* as one of the most important means of resolving disputes. Germany took the same road with the establishment by an Act of 1890 of the *Gewerbegerichte* (industrial courts) in which employers and trade unions were equally represented (see Ch. 6, below, for an account of these developments).

In Britain, however, the aversion to individual arbitration remained, and 'conciliation and arbitration' developed in a collective context. From the mid-1850s boards of conciliation and arbitration arose in several industries as a forum for continuous and permanent collective bargaining. By contrast, statutory machineries for arbitration, as envisaged by the Councils of Arbitration Act 1867 and the Arbitration (Master and Workmen) Act 1872, were never effective. Reappraising these machineries, a majority of the Royal Commission on Labour (1891–94) found that relations between employers and unions were best when voluntary agreements were made by procedures the parties themselves had established. The only useful role for government, they believed, was to promote conciliation. This led to the enactment of the Conciliation Act 1896, which simply provided machinery for the parties to use if they wanted it.

By the end of the century the European climate favoured voluntary and statutory conciliation and arbitration. Belgium copied the British Acts of 1867 and 1872 in its Act of 16 April 1887, which created joint boards on a district level to prevent or settle industrial disputes; moreover, many collective agreements with conciliation clauses were concluded. France followed with an Act of 27 December 1892 on voluntary mediation and arbitration, but the resistance of employers meant that this had little effect. In the Netherlands there was an Act of 1897 on *kamers van arbeid* (chambers of labour) but this had little impact. In Italy arbitration was promoted by the *camere del lavoro* and welcomed by the trade union confederation CGL. Between 1909 and 1914 a rich variety of mixed committees and arbitration bodies developed. But the country in which the idea of conciliation and arbitration was to become a striking feature of industrial relations was Denmark. Under the September Agreement of 1899 a permanent arbitration court was established to settle disputes arising from breach of the Agreement. In 1910 this machinery was extended to disputes on all collective agreements and was supplemented by the Official Conciliation Act and a set of standard rules for handling labour disputes, intended to be included in all collective agreements.

After the First World War legislators came forward with new statutory machinery, such as in Germany in the Collective Agreements Decree in 1918; in Britain in the Act of 1919 which established the Industrial Court, a standing body maintained at public expense for voluntary arbitration; in Belgium, Acts of 1918, 1921 and 1926; and in the Netherlands, the Industrial Disputes Act of 1923. All these measures were conceived as a back-up to the system of collective self-regulation. They shared one major characteristic in common, namely that it was left to the parties to decide whether or not to accept the results of conciliation or arbitration. However, there were many differences of detail, such as the degree of priority given to collectively agreed procedures over statutory machinery, whether special institutions were created, the role of independent persons and the extent of the obligations on parties to use the machinery and, in some cases, to postpone strikes or lockouts pending use of the machinery.

Compulsory arbitration in which the result was binding on the parties was the exception. The first example of such a system was the Arbitration Decree of 30 October 1923 in Weimar Germany. The second example was the system of compulsory arbitration introduced in France in 1936. There was a striking difference between the two systems.

The German system of compulsory arbitration was regarded by the trade unions as an inroad on their trade union rights. Although the definition of arbitration (*Schlichtung*) in the Decree was the provision of assistance in the making of 'overall agreements'—that is, the promotion of agreement when voluntary joint regulation failed—the 'order imposing compulsory effect' (*Verbindlicherklärung*) allowed the arbitration authorities to impose a binding award where this was 'deemed to be equitable on a fair balancing of interests and [if its] implementation [is] necessary for economic and social reasons'. In his classic essay on *The Changing Function of Labour Law* in the Weimar Republic, the young Kahn-Freund observed in 1932:

> In the Arbitration Decree and the practice connected with it, the concepts of equity (*Billigkeit*), fairness (*Gerechtigkeit*) and balancing of interests (*Abwägung der Interessen*) are used in order to give the stamp of universal validity to the social policy objectives of the state. In truth, an arbitration system with this kind of compulsory arbitration means that in every case where the parties to collective bargaining cannot reach a voluntary agreement, the conditions of employment cease to represent the outcome of the class struggle and become a reflection of the aims of state social policy. Since, however, state social policy is primarily determined by political power factors, the predominance of arbitration over voluntary negotiation leads to the destruction of the basic idea of collectivism: the regulation of wages and conditions of employment is transferred from the social sphere back into the political sphere. [1981, p. 174]

Kahn-Freund showed that at the end of 1929, while 3.4 million workers were covered by collective wage agreements arrived at by direct negotiations, and 1.1 million by settlements arrived at voluntarily after resort to joint or statutory arbitration procedures, a far greater number, 5.4 million, were covered by arbitration awards. The implications of this were that the state was using the apparatus of arbitration to impose its economic policy—in particular, wage cuts. Moreover, the obligatory nature of the award meant that it became illegal to take industrial action so long as the award was in force.

In France, on the other hand, the unions did not see the compulsory arbitration system of 1936 (several times renewed and amended) as an inroad on their rights but rather as a support for them. In France the employers had generally been unwilling to negotiate with unions, and the unions were too weak to impose their demands by collective action. In that situation, compulsory arbitration could force the employers to negotiate rather than be faced by an obligatory award. Moreover, the right to strike was not restricted by the existence of compulsory arbitration. While in the conditions of the Weimar Republic compulsory arbitration was used to suppress collective self-regulation in the interests of 'order' and 'social peace', in France it made the state (under the Popular Front government) the ally of the unions in reducing the power of the employers. Zeldin reports that 'in the succeeding years all but 4 per cent of disputes were decided by the government', and he comments that 'labour relations and strikes depended increasingly, therefore, on the state, and on public opinion, rather than on the attitudes of the rival parties. The strategy of the social conflict was thus fundamentally altered' (1979, p. 277).

In Britain the majority of unions—unlike those in Australia and New Zealand—disliked the idea of compulsory arbitration, because they were sufficiently strong to succeed by negotiation with employers. Only the pressure of war, in 1915 and 1940, led to the temporary acceptance of forms of compulsory arbitration.

Collective Agreements and the Law

One of the characteristics of the shift from 'toleration' to 'recognition' of collective self-regulation was the support given by the state to the process of collective negotiations between employers and trade unions, and to the results of this process—collective agreements. The earliest examples of such agreements are to be found in most countries in the printing industry (e.g. in London in 1794; Paris, 1843; Berlin, 1848). The willingness of some employers to negotiate despite the legal restrictions against unions is evidenced by the agreement for the silk-weaving industry in Lyon in 1831. But the first major boom in what Beatrice Potter (Mrs Sidney Webb) was later to describe by the term 'collective bargaining' (Potter, 1891, p. 217) occurred in Britain from the mid-nineteenth century onwards, after the main restrictions on combinations had been removed. Continental Europe followed much later. In Denmark this was only after the September 1899 Agreement. In Germany, although the number of collective agreements covering manual workers grew substantially between 1896 and 1913, it has been estimated that only 20 per cent of such workers were covered by 1914 (Kahn-Freund, 1981, p. 22). The turning point came only after the Stinnes-Legien Agreement of 1918 and the subsequent legislation. In France, although collective bargaining had been organised by a law of 1919, Zeldin (1979, p. 276) estimated that by 1933 only 7.5 per cent of wage-earners were affected by it, mainly in mining and shipping. All this changed only after the Popular Front government had imposed the Matignon Agreement on the employers in 1936.

As collective bargaining spread, it underwent an enormous qualitative development. The nucleus remained wages and working hours, but numerous other subjects were added such as holidays with pay, pensions and sick pay, as well as procedural matters such as the exercise of trade union rights and the handling of grievances and disputes. While in origin many collective agreements were designed to end a dispute and recommence work on agreed conditions, the development of joint standing committees and other permanent institutions meant that the collective agreement emerged as a *loi professionel* (industrial code), for an enterprise or for an industry, locally or nationally.

Employers' reactions to these developments were mixed, ranging from, on the one hand, the outright hostility of most German industrialists before 1914 and of the majority of French employers before 1936, to, on the other hand, the encouragement of multi-employer bargaining by British employers in order to defeat plant level militancy, between 1919 and 1939. Trade unions, for their part, tended to view collective agreements differently according to their ideological positions. In France and Italy unions led by the Syndicalists and Communists tended to emphasise the function of collective agreements as an 'armistice' or 'cease-fire' agreement in the continuing class struggle, while those led by Christians and Social-Democrats usually characterised the agreement as *loi professionel*. In Britain the absence of any commitment by trade unions to revolutionary change was reflected in the dual use of collective bargaining as a code of working rules and as a means of control of the labour supply and demarcation of jobs between crafts.

The legal response to the rise of collective agreements took a variety of forms. It must be remembered that initially the law in all the countries not only refused to recognise these agreements but also repressed them. In the period of recognition, when the combination bans were repealed, the legal status of collective agreements was not immediately clarified. The British response was to treat these agreements as lawful but to prevent direct enforcement of them in the courts. This was in part the effect of the Trade Union Act 1871 (s.4), which provided that any agreement between trade unions could not be directly enforced in the courts nor could damages be recovered for breach of such an agreement. The main object was to keep the domestic affairs of trade unions out of the courts, an aim in which the Act had only limited success. But the Act had the side-effect of making collective agreements between trade unions and certain employers' associations unenforceable, because the definition of 'trade union' included many employers' associations. More important than this statutory provision (repealed only in 1971) was the attitude of trade unions and employers who generally did not seek the aid of the courts to enforce their agreements. This state of affairs later led to Kahn-Freund's generalisation that in Britain collective agreements were not legally enforceable because the parties did not 'intend' to create legal relations (Kahn-Freund, 1954, p. 56).

In Continental Europe, where the terms '*contrat collective*', '*Tarifvertrag*', '*collectieve arbeidsovereenkomst*' came into use through academic writings like those of Sauzet and Raynaud in France (Adlercreutz, 1958, p. 30), a different legal view was taken. Legal scholars trained in civil law systems had few doubts that collective agreements fitted into the law of contracts as far as the relationship between the parties to the collective agreement was concerned (the contractual or *obligatory* function). But they found it more difficult to conceptualise a compulsory legally binding effect on the contracts of employment of individual workers (the normative or legislative function). However, Philipp Lotmar in a study first published in 1900, propounded an agency theory, according to which a collective agreement was legally binding because it had been made by representatives of workers and employers and was tacitly accepted by those who worked under the terms of the agreement. Sinzheimer in 1907 developed a more elaborate theory of the collective agreement as a private law contract between two parties, one of whom had to be a workers' organisation. This contract was intended to cover even future contracts of employment. It had three functions: normative or legislative; contractual (*obligatorische*); and social. To attain those effects, however, he judged the intervention of the legislator indispensable. This intervention then came as part and parcel of the founding of a new legal framework for German industrial relations in December 1918.

The German Collective Agreements Decree of 1918 (s.1) gave collective agreements automatic and compulsory effect:

> If the conditions for entering into contracts of employment between associations of employees and individual employers or associations of employers are regulated in a contract which is in writing (*Tarifvertrag*), then the contracts of employment between the parties concerned will be void in so far as they deviate from the regulation of the *Tarifvertrag*.

This compulsory effect given to collective agreements, despite the private-law character of the contract, was a major change from the pre-1918 law which permitted the employer to pay the individual a lower wage than that laid down in the collective agreement. It applied to contracts of employment of which both the employers' and the workers' side were members of a party to the collective agreement. Also embodied in the 1918 legislation, however, was the power given to the Federal Ministry of Labour to declare that a collective agreement should have general effect within its field to employers and employees who were not parties to the agreement.

France got its first statutory regulation on collective agreements in 1919, but this was highly defective. Like the German regulation, the French statute declared the collective agreement binding on contracts of employment of which both the employers' and the workers' sides were members of a party to the collective agreement. The French law went even further than its German counterpart by creating a presumption that the agreement applied also to those contracts of employment of which only one side was a member of a party to the collective agreement, provided the contract of employment did not explicitly stipulate the contrary. But the French statute of 1919 fell short of the German one, first because it did not allow the government the power to give a general effect to a collective agreement, and second because it left easy ways of escape from the binding force of a collective agreeement by withdrawal from membership of a party to an already concluded collective agreement. These defects were corrected only in 1936 when, following the Matignon Agreement, a new statute introduced a second type of collective agreement, intended to operate as an industrial code, created by representative organisations. *Commissions mixtes* (committees of management and labour) were established, and only the most representative organisations could join them. The law of 1936 also introduced an extension procedure similar to that in Weimar Germany. A minister could extend an agreement made by a joint committee to all employers and employees in the trade or region. This system flourished from 1936 to 1939 but was then set aside by war regulations.

In the Netherlands amendments to the Civil Code in 1907 established the binding effect of collective agreements on employment contracts provided the latter did not stipulate to the contrary, and a statute in 1927 provided for the compulsory force of collective agreements (1) on contracts of employment of which both the employers' and workers' sides were members of a party to the collective agreement and (2) on contracts of employment of which only the employer side was a member of a party to the collective agreement (provided the collective agreement did not stipulate to the contrary). An extension procedure similar to that in Weimar Germany was put on the Dutch statute book in 1937. In Belgium there was no statutory regulation of the collective agreement. Several bills to that end failed.

In Italy, before the rise of fascism, the civil law theory of contracts had been applied to collective agreements between the contracting associations. Under the Fascist régime, by an Act of 1926, collective agreements were made by the 'corporative' associations as public agencies and automatically acquired compulsory normative effect.

The position in Britain stands in sharp contrast. As we have seen, the collective agreement was not analysed in contractual terms, partly because of the absence of the civilian traditions of doctrinal development of the law but mainly because of the voluntarist consensus among employers and unions. However, since as early as the mid-nineteenth century, the judges were willing to recognise the normative effect of the collective agreement (at least in respect of substantive matters such as wages) on the individual contract of employment. But this was not done by the means of an agency theory (that the union is empowered to bind its members) nor by a conception of the employers and unions as having quasi-legislative powers. These Continental theories had no direct influence. Instead, English and Scottish lawyers relied on individualistic notions of contractual autonomy, viewing the task of the court as being to ascertain the express or implied intentions of the parties to the individual contract of employment. If the collective agreement was not expressly referred to by individual employer and employee when making their contract (usually they would be silent on this in the typical oral engagement at the factory gate), then the collective agreement could, so far as appropriate, be incorporated by 'custom and practice' or implied term. This meant that potentially the collective agreement could be incorporated into the individual contracts, even of non-union members. However, unlike the compulsory normative effect in Continental countries, the parties to the individual contract were entirely free to contract on terms different from those in the collective agreement (with a few isolated exceptions, such as the cotton industry from 1934 to 1957). This was the case even if the employer was a member of the association which made the agreement, or the employee was a member of a union which was a party to it.

This deficiency in the law in Britain was, however, more apparent than real in the conditions which existed before 1939. Employers who belonged to associations which negotiated agreements were likely to observe them, and since 1891 there had been Fair Wages Resolutions of the House of Commons which in effect obliged government contractors to observe terms and conditions of employment not less favourable than those recognised in collective bargaining by representative unions and employers' associations in the trade or industry. The Resolutions were not 'law' in the strict sense, but merely a direction to the executive. In practice, the possible sanction of withdrawal of government contracts was enough to ensure compliance. Similar techniques were used in the *Décrets Millerand* in France in 1899 (amended in 1937, 1940 and 1955) and in the Netherlands.

Like Britain, Denmark also never saw any general statutory regulation of the collective agreement. In both countries the voluntarist social consensus proved to be adequate so far as both employers and unions were concerned. In Britain this was deeply rooted in the method of collective bargaining, which was largely informal and dynamic rather than formal and static. Moreover, British unions feared that legal enforceability would be used against them to enforce claims for damages for the breach of procedural and 'no strike' obligations. They could point in this respect to experience in Germany, where in 1910 the Reichsgericht (Supreme Court) decided that the conclusion of a collective agreement imposed an implied peace obligation on a trade union. This was followed in the Weimar period but then the legal situation had been changed by the recognition of the compulsory effect of collective agreements. Similarly, in France in 1923 judges held a union liable for supporting a strike in contravention of a collective agreement. Apart from the negative foreign models, British unions could draw on their own experience of the use of the civil law to undermine the freedom to strike, as a reason for opposing the legal enforceability of collective agreements.

Industrial Disputes and the Civil Law

The law on industrial disputes during the transition from 'repression' to 'toleration' was characterised by a certain retreat of the criminal law. During the transition from 'toleration' to 'recognition' the law on industrial disputes was characterised by a certain retreat of the civil law restrictions on the freedom to take industrial action.

As long as the sanctions of the criminal law were available to restrain industrial action, there was little interest in the civil law. But when the criminal law was largely removed from the area of industrial conflict, restraints on the freedom to strike stemming from civil law doctrines emerged. As Hanbury wrote, 'The result of removing so large a part of the law of industrial relations from the orbit of criminal law is that the centre of gravity shifts to the law of torts' (1948, p. 133). Later, in order to allow freedom of collective bargaining, these civil law doctrines were restricted. In Britain this reversal was brought about by the intervention of Parliament. In other countries, notably France and Italy, it was the constitutional recognition of a freedom to strike which was decisive. In yet other countries (such as Belgium and the Netherlands) judge-made law played its part in protecting collective self-regulation. In Britain the main immunities from civil actions were secured in 1906, but in most other countries the threat from the civil law to the freedom to strike was removed only after the Second World War.

In Britain, as we have seen, the Conspiracy and Protection of Property Act 1875 had limited the ambit of the criminal law in 'trade disputes', although it had left this concept undefined. The last decade of the nineteenth century, starting with the dockers' strike of 1889, saw the emergence of the new unions which organised mainly the unskilled general labourers. There was a sharp rise in industrial conflict. Employers had frequent recourse to the courts and the judges developed the common law so as to 'declare' new forms of civil liability. As early as 1853 the courts had decided that a civil action could be brought against a person who knowingly induced a breach of contract between two other persons; indeed, liability for enticing away servants had existed in one form or another since the fourteenth century. In the 1890s this was applied against union leaders who called out workers on strike, thereby inducing them to 'breach' their contracts of employment. Although some moral duties to interfere with a contract could constitute a defence of 'justification' at common law, in 1905 the House of Lords decided that the furtherance of trade union objectives, such as preventing low wages, was not justification for inducing breach of contract. In 1901 the Law Lords extended the tort of civil conspiracy to render unlawful a boycott of an employer organised by a union when he would not dismiss non-union employees. In that same year the House of Lords in the famous *Taff Vale* case[9] (arising from a strike against the victimisation of a trade unionist by the Taff Vale Railway Company) decided that a trade union could be sued for the torts committed by its officials, so laying the union's funds open to attack by the employers when the union engaged in industrial action. Until this decision it had been generally assumed that unions were not to be treated as corporate bodies, liable to be sued in their own name.

The *Taff Vale* case provoked a powerful protest movement; it was one of the reasons for the formation of the Labour Party, and the Liberal government elected in 1905 with Labour support was pledged to reverse the effects of the judicial decisions. The Trade Disputes Act 1906 provided that there could be no actions for damages against trade unions and their officials. It also granted an immunity to 'any person' (not limited to official union action) who 'in contemplation or furtherance of a trade dispute' committed either the new civil tort of conspiracy or who induced some other person to breach a contract of employment or who interfered with the trade, business or employment

9. [1901] Appeal Cases 426.

of another person. These immunities together with the 1875 Act were widely regarded as the basis of the freedom to strike in Britain until the 1960s, when once again the common law was developed by the judges so as to limit this freedom. The only exception was an Act of 1927, after the General Strike, which made certain strikes illegal but it was not invoked and was repealed in 1946. In Denmark effective 'immunity' from civil action emerged from the September Agreement of 1899 under which the freedom to take industrial action, within certain limits, was mutually recognised.

In France, as in Britain, it was for some years assumed that trade unions could not be held liable for damages inflicted in the course of industrial disputes. This view was based on Section 3 of the Waldeck-Rousseau Act of 1884. But from the 1890s judges held unions liable for delicts. They did so by applying the doctrine of abuse of rights and subsequently the provisions of Articles 1382 and 1383 of the Civil Code which create civil responsibility even for negligently causing damage. But the judges often limited the liability of the unions to pay damages to a symbolic franc. French unions did not in this period have the influence possessed by the British trade unions and so no set of immunities comparable to the Trade Disputes Act 1906 was enacted.

In Germany, before the Nazi period, the legal situation was comparable to that in France. Trade unions, even if they were not registered, could be liable both in contract and in delict. In particular, Article 826 (which deals with 'intentional violation of *bonos mores*' causing damage) was effectively applied in various cases. On the other hand, in pre-fascist Italy, and in the Netherlands and Belgium before the Second World War, the civil law was hardly used against trade unions promoting industrial action.

In all the countries, however, the worker remained exposed to disciplinary sanctions by his employer for participating in industrial action. Even after the sanctions of the criminal law had been removed, it was the case in all the countries studied that going on strike, at least without advance notice, exposed the employee to dismissal, except where it was justified by a previous breach committed by the employer (to which the *exceptio non adempleti contractus* could be applied). Sometimes (e.g. in France) it was even held that the employee by deciding to go on strike automatically ended his employment (and might sometimes be ordered to pay damages to the employer).

From the early part of the twentieth century in Italy the *probiviri* were critical of these doctrines and favoured a theory of suspension: in the absence of any express or implied intention on the part of the employees to terminate their employment, the strike should not in itself produce as a consequence the termination of the individual contracts of employment. This theory had been developed by Potthoff (Germany) and Wahl, Rolland and Colin (France), but in none of the countries studied were the ordinary civil courts prepared to accept fully the suspension theory before the Second World War. In France, in the surge of collective bargaining from 1936, it became common to include in collective agreements a clause that no sanctions could be imposed against workers who went on strike. The Court of Cassation took cautious steps towards accepting the suspension theory, but it was in the special Superior Court of Arbitration (set up in 1938 to deal with labour disputes) in a case decided on 19 May 1939 that this theory was fully accepted. It was not until the 1950s that the suspension theory became well established in Italy and Germany. No similar developments took place in Britain and Denmark.

CONCLUSIONS

This chapter has utilised the 'ideal types' of repression, toleration and recognition in order to characterise the development of legal responses to collective self-regulation. Broadly speaking, all the countries studied passed through these phases, though at different times. It would be misleading to regard this as some kind of continuing 'progressive' development. On the contrary, for every step forward from repression to toleration or from toleration to recognition one can find other steps backwards to repression, either limited for a time or for certain groups of workers or as a major attempt to impose a new social order, as in fascist Italy or Nazi Germany. The 'ideal types' simply help us understand some of the similarities in national labour laws; they do not represent an inevitable path of social evolution.

We have seen that a common thread is the emergence of trade unions from illegality. As capitalist markets developed and the old forms of wage regulation by the state broke down, criminal sanctions against combinations were removed, a process which lasted for most of the nineteenth century in Europe. The timing and scope of the removal of penal sanctions depended on a variety of factors. Commercial prosperity and utilitarian ideology in Britain favoured early repeal, while the hostility of French revolutionary ideology to sectional organisations in the state and the political fears of the ruling classes delayed the toleration of trade union activity in Continental countries, and from time to time led to bouts of repression in Britain. The rise of modern economically minded workers' organisations after the defeat of Chartism in England and the unsuccessful revolutions of 1848 on the

Continent, were accompanied by the growth of collective bargaining, sometimes actively encouraged by the employers and their associations. Regular relationships between employers and unions developed throughout Europe, but once again the timing and extent was heavily influenced by national features, such as the ideology of the trade unions and of political parties supported by the workers, the stage at which the franchise was extended to the working class, as well as the class bias of the judges and the different legal traditions of the common law and civil law systems. Decisive changes in the attitudes of the employers occurred as a result of the demands of 'war socialism', and the threat to the established European order posed by the revolutions in Russia and Germany. In the era of recognition the emphasis was on methods of conciliation and arbitration and on the legal enforcement of collective agreements. In this connection we noted the different routes to recognition, through positive legal rights in countries such as Germany (1918–33) and France (1919–39), but by negative immunities and voluntary methods in others such as Britain and Denmark. All of these developments, however, share in common the adherence to pluralism, in marked contrast to the totalitarian systems which emerged in Italy and Germany.

Why did the law have so much trouble in finding the right place for collective self-regulation? Undoubtedly the very concept of collective self-regulation gives the lawyer and the politician numerous problems. Why tolerate associations of workers and employers, which so evidently function 'in restraint of trade' in a capitalist market economy? Why recognise collective negotiation which so evidently contravenes the freedom to contract in a society dominated by individualistic values? Why facilitate industrial action which unmistakeably damages the interests of others? Why accept collective self-regulation as a centre of power, situated between individuals and between individuals and the state? It should not come as a surprise that the answers given by both lawyers and politicians to these questions have necessarily varied according to their respective social and political orientations.

Nor is 'recognition' to be regarded as the end of the 'making' of collective labour law. There is also the phase of 'integration'. This is a subject with which the next chapter is concerned.

6

Workers' Participation, the Representation of Labour and Special Labour Courts

Thilo Ramm

THE PROBLEM

When, in 1898, Sidney and Beatrice Webb's *Industrial Democracy* was translated into German the title was changed into the equivalent of 'The Theory and Practice of the English Trade Unions'. The German title gave a precise understanding of the contents of the book, for the German reader who might otherwise have expected a description of how the ideas of political democracy should be transposed to the plant and to the economy as a whole but without the trade unions. The German translation shows that the participation and representation of workers at plant level or on a regional or national basis could be achieved either through the trade unions or by a separate legal solution produced by legislation, and without or even against trade union wishes. All terms like 'participation', 'representation' or 'co-determination' may be understood in very different senses. They may be used, as in Britain, to characterise the tasks and responsibilities of the trade unions and also of the employers' organisations, or, as in Germany after the November Revolution of 1918, these terms may be used as names for representation of the workers' interest otherwise than by the trade unions.

What these terms have in common is the idea that the workers should participate in decision-making at the level of the plant, and that the representatives of labour should co-operate in some or all aspects of the management of the economy. These concepts of the democratic economy obviously depend upon an acceptance of pluralistic values. They involve the rejection, on the one hand, of the paternal government of the monarch in the state and of the employer in the factory; on the other hand, they also involve the rejection of a revolutionary 'workers' government or workers' control of industries. They further involve the development of special labour courts in which workers are represented in the judicial power of the state. This chapter examines the attempts to establish workers' participation at plant level, and the representation of the interests of labour at regional and national levels, and in special labour courts.

PLANT LEVEL

The starting point was paternalism. During the Middle Ages and at the beginning of the modern period the workshop was the master's house. The 'journeyman', *compagnon* or *Geselle* who was unmarried lived as a member of the master's family and was subject to his paternal authority. This paternal concept, favoured by religion, continued when the workshop was separated from the house, but was still relatively small, and when the employer worked together with the workers. The original sense was maintained in the term 'master in the house', but the authority of the employer gradually came to be based upon property as the new legitimacy. The 'house rule', which during the industrialisation process got the name 'work rule', was established by the employer as the owner of the factory. It could then be legally explained by the concept of 'freedom of contract'. The worker entering the factory concluded an employment contract and thus tacitly accepted the existing works rules. The government of the workshop was centred upon the power of the employer, of his right to organise the division of labour in the factory and of his 'right to command', which characterised the individual employment relationship. But there still remained the legal problem of whether it was to be considered an exchange of services against money between free persons or, as in Germany, a *besonderes Gewaltverhaeltnis* (particular power relationship) of civil law, which was compared with the *allgemeines Gewaltsverhaeltnis* (general power relationship) of public law, which connected the subject and the monarch.

The passive attitude of the workers, who had migrated from the countryside where obedience was traditional, disappeared with the growth of larger-scale production and resentment of the employers' abuse of power. Paternalistic industrial government came into conflict with self-consciousness of the workers, and was no longer accepted as legitimate. The question became: How is the power of the employer to be opposed?

The trade unions were the natural opposition, but they were too weak within the factories. They tended to develop as organisations which had workers from different factories as members. At their inception the trade unions were spontaneous combinations and slowly grew into permanent financially strong and well-organised associations, at least in Britain and Germany. Legal restrictions could deter but not prevent this development. Another reason was even more important. The trade unions were originally organised on a craft basis, and many of those in Britain remained on this basis. The diverging interests of the craftsmen were thus represented by different trade unions and led to many demarcation disputes over 'who does which work'.

Besides this deep gulf between the skilled and the unskilled workers, the distinction between manual and white-collar workers divided the workers. It was not only the nature of their work which separated the 'workers by brain' from the 'workers by hand'. The white-collar workers considered themselves as a separate group which was part of the middle class and not of the proletariat. As the German term '*Privatbeamte*' indicated, they felt a special loyalty to the employer like the *Beamte* to the monarch and therefore required and often received better protection against dismissals (see Chs. 1 and 4, above).

The reasons why the common representation of workers at the plant level through works committees was rare was given by the British Balfour Report in 1929:

> [It] was, no doubt, largely due to the fact that trade union organisation seldom recognises the shop as a unit for trade union purposes, the usual local union being the branch, membership of which is usually determined by place of residence and not by place of employment. This together with the fact that the workers in a shop may be members not only of different branches but also of different unions, tended in normal conditions to prevent work committees, either those of a joint type or those composed of work people only, from forming a definite part of the machinery of negotiations. [p. 302]

Although various forms of work-place union activity existed in Britain before 1914, the real power in the pre-war period was at district or branch level.

The development of 'shop stewards' began in Britain with the Amalgamated Society of Engineers in the machine and shipbuilding industries. The district committees ratified the appointment of delegates in each shop elected by the union members who had to check that all members of the craft belonged to the union, collect subscriptions and see that the craft rules were observed. Sometimes they acted as spokesmen for their members in discussions with works managers and foremen. But Phelps Brown (1965, p. 287), describing the situation in 1906, says that with the exception of mining, workshop representatives usually did not negotiate with management. Shop committees remained on a very small scale, meeting strong opposition from the employers who preferred district negotiations. The introduction of a wage system for piece-work with different payment from shop to shop led to the establishment of 'piece-work committees' during the 1890s, but they had no general competence.

The shop steward system was introduced and retained by collective agreement in Denmark shortly after the September Agreement. It was an agreement of 1900 within the metal trade which constituted the model for later agreements. The Agreement described the function of the shop steward as follows:

> When one or more of his fellow workers, either because they consider themselves aggrieved or for other reasons, desire it, he is obliged to bring their complaints or proposals to the employer if the matter cannot be adjusted satisfactorily with the representative of the latter (the foreman). The shop steward may also raise complaints and direct proposals to the employer with respect to health conditions and measures to prevent accidents and injuries. If no satisfactory adjustment is obtained, the shop steward is free to request his organisation to take the matter up, but work must continue uninterruptedly until a contrary determination is made by the management of the organisation.

The shop steward was bound by the collective agreement and he had no power to interpret it. The election of the shop steward was confined to the members of the trade union concerned. In a plant with several trade unions, several shop stewards had therefore to be elected. The election had to be approved by the trade union and the employers' association. If the association refused to grant approval, the matter had to be negotiated with the trade union and ultimately decided by a court. The shop steward was protected from dismissal and from transfer, unless urgent reasons necessitated such a step. As with the September Agreement, it was a long time before Denmark's example was followed. In the other countries legislative support for workers' pressure was often needed before workers had a representative organ within the plant. This was the case with the mining industry, where the system of payment by weight of coal hewn was a constant source of complaints.

Britain was the forerunner. The Coal Mines Regulation Act 1860 (s.29) made it compulsory for coal-owners to allow a representative of the miners to check the weight of the coal hewn. From 1887 the checkweigher was maintained at the expense of the whole pit, and many of them subsequently became full-time trade union officials. The Checkweighing in Various Industries Act 1919 extended those regulations to other industries in which workers were paid by weight or measure. Prussia introduced the principle of compulsory joint control in 1892 (an amendment to the Mines Act 1865). In Britain after 1887 the miners acquired the right to appoint safety representatives. In France an Act of 1890 provided for the election of an independent safety delegate for a period of three years.

The employers' attitude towards workers' representation at the plant level was not uniform, because fear stood against hope. Many employers feared that workers' committees would become a power centre for the trade unions, which were considered to be the principal enemies when they were under political, especially Marxist, influence treating industrial disputes as 'war schools of the class struggle'. On the other hand, the advantages of the workers' committees were also obvious, because of the enlargement of the factory system and the lack of personal contacts between employer and employees. A plant bureaucracy had been established: conflicts between the different groups of workers with divergent interests could be reconciled by such committees as well as conflict between the employer and the workers. Questions like the time of beginning and ending of rest-periods could more easily be settled. Demands, complaints and suggestions by individual workers could be screened by these committees. And since the committees remained within the sphere of power of the employer, they could be placed in a position of opposition to trade unions. The worker had a choice between collaboration with traditional paternalism or the raising of self-consciousness based on his personal convictions.

Before the First World War there were considerable divergences in the choice made. In Belgium paternalism seems to have been strong and was connected with the successful policy of keeping trade unions out of the plant. In the Netherlands there were very rare cases of *personeelskernen* or *personeelsraaden* (workers' councils). In France several strikes in the large Schneider-Creusot factory were brought to an end in 1899 by an arbitration decision of Prime Minister Waldeck-Rousseau which provided for the nomination of workshop delegates (one delegate for each corporation) who were to hold conferences with the management every two months. But the management of Schneider-Creusot interpreted the decision as allowing them the right to accept individual delegates and prescribed that the delegates must have been members of the corporation for two years. This reluctance was a general one because in France the fear of militant trade unionism was widespread. There was the remembrance of the Jacobin tradition, and the still living shock of the Paris Commune. The threat of revolutionary syndicalism led to the fear that workers' committees could serve as a mode of entry for trade unions into the factory and could facilitate workers' self-administration, taking over of the management of the plants.

Other ways which did not violate the interest of the employers to maintain their 'right to command' like the participation of workers' representatives in plant welfare or profit-sharing institutions found favour and were often discussed but less often realised. By 1894, in Britain only twenty-eight profit-sharing funds existed with workers' participation. In France there were seven cases of profit-sharing funds with workers' participation and a few in the Netherlands. Numerous attempts had been made in France to solve the problems of disputes by establishing *commissions permanentes de conciliation et arbitrage.* Between 1892 and 1907 there were twelve bills, among them the bill of 15 November 1900 which proposed the establishment of permanent workers' delegates at the first stage and a central council at the fifth and last stage. None of these bills, however, was enacted.

The first general step towards *ständige Arbeiterausschuesse* (permanent workers' committees) was made in Germany. The starting point was the *Arbeitsordnungen* (works rules). They could be customary but were mostly written down by the employer and could be compared with statutes promulgated by the absolute monarch. They were even legally recognised to be somewhat like a private statute because the Prussian Mines Act of 1860 had affirmed their promulgation by employers and subjected them to the approval of the mining authorities. This was a temporary regulation, repealed after five years by a new Mines Act, but the question as to the legal nature of the 'works rules' remained. Permanent workers' committees were legally recognised by the amendment of 1891 to the Reich Trade Act which required that before the promulgation of a works rule the employer should hear either all his employees or such a committee. The establishment of the committee, however, still remained voluntary. The amendment to the Prussian Mines Act of 1905 was the first to make the committees compulsory and to transfer to them the jurisdiction relating to checkweighing, working time and method of wage calculation and payment and the administration of a relief fund (into which fines had to be paid by the workers). The Netherlands did not go as far by the decree of 1906 which provided only that the permanent workers' associations (in mines with more than 100 workers) could bring complaints and suggestions on health and safety matters and on employment relations to the attention of the mine management. The Dutch Commercial Code has since 1838 recognised 'ship committees' in the merchant marine.

Recognition of the legal functions of the permanent workers' committees met with violent opposition from both the employers' and the workers' sides. August Bebel, Chairman of the German Social Democratic Party, in a speech on 15 April 1891 spoke of the 'quasi-constitutional fig leaf of capitalism which covers factory feudalism' (cited in Ruckert and Friedrich, 1979, p. 128). Nevertheless, the amendment of 1891 became a turning point because it permitted both the restriction and the affirmation of the power of the employer by the analogy with the political struggles of that time. The political demands of the middle class to share legislative power with the monarch was transferred to the relation between employer and 'his' employees. The 'constitutional factory' corresponded to the 'constitutional monarchy'. For Germany the struggle against the monarchy, which had occurred in Britain in the seventeenth century and in France in 1793 and 1848, coincided with the struggle against the paternalistic government of the factory, against the 'master in the house'. This famous phrase had been used by the German Carl Ferdinand Freiherr von Stumm-Halberg—the owner of mines in the Saar region who employed 3,200 employees—in his speech in the Prussian First Chamber of 28 May 1897. He favoured the military not the parliamentary structure of the plant and feared that the permanent workers' committees would destroy his personal relations with his employees. His opinion was literally the same as that of the Prussian King Friedrich Wilhelm IV when he refused a constitution in 1848.

There were three views in this struggle. Younger 'enlightened' entrepreneurs were conscious of the contradictions in the middle-class policy for political power-sharing, and this explains why in Germany numerous workers' committees were established on a voluntary basis. On the other hand, the political constitutional system was an inducement to the monarch and the conservative powers to support the demands for the 'constitutional factory' as a possible way of diminishing the power of the middle class. Lastly, the application of Montesquieu's doctrine of the separation of powers to the workshop confirmed the employer's right to command because it corresponded with the executive power which was entrusted to the prince.

The amendment of 1891 was a breakthrough. It was implemented by the example of those German states which established the workers' committees for their railways. It was also taken up by some employers. Even the attitude of the trade unions changed, because they saw the possibility of putting up their own candidates at the elections and in particular gaining an organ through which they could control the enforcement of collective agreements within the plant. Therefore the establishment of permanent workers' committees became the subject of collective agreements in breweries, the metal industry and printing establishments. It was accepted by the employers because by that time the trade unions had acquired independence from the Social Democratic Party, and because the workers' interests had already been recognised in social legislation as responsible partners (see Ch. 3, above). The process of co-operation in the area of social security had established mutual trust.

The German example appears to have had an impact upon the development in Italy. Between 1908 and 1914 numerous *commissioni interne* (internal commissions) were established which represented the workers of the entire plant or parts of it; for example, by a collective agreement of 1906 between the motor-car factory Atala at Turino and the Italian Metal Workers (FIOM).

The First World War changed the picture. It began with a phase of collaboration between workers and employers. Common patriotic feelings displaced the attitude of class struggle and established industrial peace. But the situation of the working force was changed by the war: many workers were enlisted into the army and the emphasis shifted from peacetime to war production. In Germany one-third of the workforce was called into the army and another third lost their former jobs. The longer the war lasted, the more skilled workers were replaced by unskilled workers and by women. The necessity for work discipline was regarded as part of the national interest. The workers were compared with the soldiers who risked their lives and their health at the front and received a small payment. Protective labour laws were set aside but the need for production remained. More important, the substitution of the economic system of competition by one of government distribution of raw materials and planning the national interest ('war socialism') required co-operation between employers and employees in order to increase productivity and innovation. In order to achieve this, use was made of the institutions of labour relations established before the war.

In Britain during the war the number of workshop committees grew rapidly. In part this was deliberately encouraged by management as a means of ensuring the observance of shop-floor agreements and wartime regulations. Another more important reason was the growth of an unofficial shop stewards' movement, which was fertilised by the delays in settling matters through the full-time union officials. To some extent the shop stewards' formal role in processing grievances was recognised in collective agreements of 1917–19.

In Germany the solution of the problem was relatively simple: the *Vaterlandische Hilfsdienstgesetz* of 1916 (Patriotic Auxiliary Service Act) established permanent workers' committees as compulsory institutions. There were not mixed commissions as had been proposed by the Whitley Reports in Britain. Thus there was the danger that the ideal of collaboration would not be as well served as in those institutions where the employer and his representatives were permanently present. But at that time the need for collaboration was met simply by the requirements that the permanent workers' committees in the Prussian mines were 'to act in a way that the good terms among the workers and between workers and employer should be maintained or restored' (s. 80f subs. 1).

In France Labour Minister Thomas recommended the establishment of permanent *délégués du personnel* for 'relations of confidence within the plant', but the committees were almost exclusively introduced in plants engaged in war production. There were 347 such firms, but only 57 of these made regular use of mediation. Minister Thomas, together with Renault, warned against these committees being based on a model of trade unions, because this would be too dangerous and would lead to conflict. He preferred mixed committees. Thomas's successor even prohibited workshop committees at the beginning of 1918.

At the end of the First World War the question arose whether the war institutions were just temporary or whether they should be retained. The answer was given under the impact of the Russian October Revolution of 1917. In France, as already said, the workshop committees were prohibited because of the fear of revolutionary syndicalism. In Britain the trade unions were anxious to return to the old situation putting shop stewards under the control of the local union committees and permitting them simply to settle less important questions on the spot. During the war and afterwards there was, however, a growth of industry-wide bargaining; in part this was a deliberate strategy against the revolutionary tendencies which were believed to be connected with the shop stewards' movement. A committee, including representatives of trade unions and employers, under the chairmanship of J. H. Whitley (Speaker of the House of Commons), proposed the establishment of industry-wide negotiating bodies on a voluntary basis in all major industries in 1919. In a supplementary report on works committees (1918) the Whitley Committee conceived industrial relations at works level as being primarily concerned with 'co-operation' rather than negotiation. During the inter-war years the Whitley model of 'joint consultation' at work-place level was mainly applied to the public services, and was embodied in statutory form in the Railways

Act 1921. It was also voluntarily adopted by a number of private firms. It was usual for workers' representatives on these plant-level committees to be elected by the workforce as a whole, including non-unionists. The shop stewards were left outside this structure of joint consultation. Where 'joint consultation' was established at work-place level it was concerned with 'co-operation' rather than 'negotiation'.

The German development was different. The unexpected collapse of state authority when a seamen's mutiny broke out in November 1918 led to the establishment of 'workers' and soldiers' councils' on the Russian model, and there was support for revolutionary syndicalism. The government was handed over by the Reich Chancellor to the Council of People's Commissioners (Rat der Volksbeauftragten) which was based upon a compromise between the Social Democratic majority party and the independent socialists. But the trade unions retained their organisation, and they concluded the famous Stinnes-Legien Agreement of 16 November 1918 (so named after the leader of the employers' organisation and of the trade unions), which saved the structure of the liberal economy and society (see Ch. 5, above). The 'council question' became an important factor in German domestic policy because the councils were soon deprived of their political function by the elections to the Reich Parliament (1919) and the acceptance of the democratic Weimar Constitution. But they retained their social and economic importance.

The Council of People's Commissioners in its proclamation of 12 November 1918, had abolished the Patriotic Auxiliary Service Act of 1916 with the exception of the provisions which concerned the settlement of disputes. This function was given to the permanent workers' committees. But the committees lost their general functions. This regulation lasted for only a very short time. In the decree of 23 December 1918, which recognised collective agreements as legal institutions, the permanent workers' committees were not only reaffirmed but also extended to all plants with more than twenty employees and given the duty 'to look after the economic interests of the manual and of the white-collar workers in the workshop, administration or office in regard to the employer'. In common with the employer, they had to ensure that the competent collective agreements were observed in the enterprise. Where a collective agreement did not exist, the committees or representatives had to participate in the regulation of wages and other labour relations as economic associations of the manual and white-collar workers concerned. It was up to them to promote good relations among manual and white-collar workers and between them and the employer. The other task which was specifically mentioned was safety. The decree made an interesting concession to the trade unions when it mentioned the other representative organs. These organs could be established by a collective agreement provided that it had been declared generally applicable. This provision refers to the Stinnes-Legien Agreement, which had mentioned the establishment of permanent workers' committees for all plants with more than fifty employees to represent them and ensure the observance of collective agreements. An explanation as to why the trade unions had hoped to have the permanent workers' committees as their suborgans is found in the words of Charles Legien the head of the Social Democratic trade unions, in February 1919: 'The works councils are not an effective organisation; they split the unity of the trade . . . All existing laws of solidarity cease to exist for them, everyone is invited to take what he can get' (1919).

Nevertheless, the legal development from the Patriotic Auxiliary Service Act to the decree of 23 December 1918 was continued by the *Betriebsrätegesetz* 1920 (Works Councils Act), which was a concession to the still-existing and still lively revolutionary council movement, which had even been recognised by a collective agreement for the coal industry of 12 March 1919, after a strike. Nevertheless, the word 'council' was only a concession in name, because the councils had nothing to do with self-government of the plant by the workers; not even the word 'co-determination' was used by the Act. The separation of the workers was maintained by the different committees: the manual workers' councils and the white-collar workers' councils. Thus the new institution recognised the diverging interests of the two groups of employees but indicated, as well, that the white-collar workers could now participate in collective labour law. The councils were established in all workshops with more than twenty employees. They were to look after the common economic interests of the employees towards the employer; but they had also to 'support the employer in complying with the goal of the plant' (s.1). Their enumerated tasks were traditional ones like agreement with the employer on works rules for a group of employees (s.78, nr 3) or for all employees (s.66, nr 5) and, as already provided by the Stinnes-Legien Agreement and by the decree of 23 December 1918, the observance of collective agreements or the investigation and decisions of a settlement board on individual complaints of the employees, support in safety matters, mediation in industrial disputes, and, if there was no collective agreement, to co-operate in the regulation of terms and conditions of employment. The support which had to be given to the employer also included the introduction of new working methods, and consultations were to guarantee the standards and productivity. The German version of social self-administration within the plant was realised in the right to co-operate in the administration of pension funds and other welfare institutions of the workshop.

In general, the principle of the 'constitutional factory' prevailed, and there was even provision for the conclusion of a kind of collective agreement with the council as a contracting party on recruiting designed to prevent discrimination because of political, military and trade union activities or membership or on grounds of sex. The manual works council and the white-collar works council were also the first to hear appeals by an employee who had been dismissed by the employer. If the council considered the employee's appeal justified, it had to mediate. If mediation was fruitless, the council or the employee could appeal to the labour court. Another point to note was a change in the structure of companies and corporations which distinguished between the managing board and the supervisory board (which elected and dismissed the managers and controlled their activities). The works council delegated one or two members 'in order to represent the interests and the demands of the employees as well as their views and wishes concerning the organisation of the workshops' onto the supervisory board. The delegated members of the works councils had seats and equal voting rights, but they did not receive payment as did the other members of the supervisory board, merely compensation for their expenses. This was the first attempt to overcome the separation between labour relations and economic affairs.

The problem of dependence on the employer was also the subject of legal regulation. The affairs of the councils and their elections were legally organised and the council members were protected against dismissal. But the necessity of permanent collaboration with the employer and the obligation to consider his views tied the councils to the employer. The difference in the principles of collaboration and of disputes made the relation between councils and trade unions critical. The councils were another type of representation of the workers—as a whole, both on the plant level and on a statutory basis, contrary to the type of voluntary representation of the workers by the trade unions. The competition between the three rival German trade unions was now decided by means of the legal machinery; that is, by the elections to the councils, where also the unorganised workers could nominate and elect their own candidates. The German works councils legislation made it legally impossible to accept 'closed' or 'union shop' regulations. The vote of the workers even strengthened the local unionist council members against central union leadership and bureaucracy.

The legislation brought the revolutionary council movement to an end because it gave the councils moderate functions. It opened the way for trade unions to gain influence in the plants by nominating their candidates. At the end of the Weimar Republic the trade unions had reached this aim in the large enterprises. But in the medium-sized enterprises there was a power struggle between the influence of the trade unions and of the employer; here and in most small workshops the paternal system was often strong enough even to prevent the election of the council.

Very close to the German development was the development in Luxembourg in these years. *Conseils d'usine* (works councils) were introduced by decrees of 1919 and 1920, but when the workshops were occupied by the workers the decrees were withdrawn in 1921 under the pressure of France and Italy. The works councils were reintroduced by a decree of 1925, which was amended in 1929 and 1930. All these decrees referred to an Act of 1915 which authorised the government to look after economic interests during the war and which has remained in force until the present day. Besides this representation of the manual workers, representation of the white-collar workers was established by an Act of 1919, amended in 1938. The councils were confined to industry and did not exist for artisans and in commerce. The members of the councils were legally protected as in Germany, but the competence of the council was more limited: they had the right to be heard only before the promulgation of a works rule. The main committees of the manual works' council had to elect the 'safety men'.

In Belgium an Act of 23 July 1926 introduced in the National Society of Belgian Railways the requirement that workers should be represented on the administration board and that paritarian committees should be established which had to work out the 'statute of the workers'. Italy confirmed the employers' fears on the connection between the works councils and the revolutionary movement. During the First World War the number of voluntarily established *commissioni interne* (internal commissions) was augmented, but at the end of the war the workers also tried to gain control of industry by *consigli di fabbrica* (factory councils). The occupation of the workshops by the workers failed in September 1920. Prime Minister Giolitti's proposal (8 February 1921) to establish control commissions of the workers to ask the employer for information and to meet him in annual consultation sessions was not accepted. Similarly, attempts from 1923 in the Netherlands by the opposition Social-Democrats to introduce works' councils were unsuccessful.

In France the victory of the Popular Front in 1936 brought about a change. The Matignon Agreement provided for the establishment of *délégués du personnel.* The statute of 24 June 1936 said that only when a plant had this institution could it be placed under the régime of collective agreements. A decree of 12 November 1938, which was made under the provisions of an enabling Act, converted the *délégués* into a statutory institution, which, however, was not a permanent basis but was only utilised when a grievance was raised. This statutory measure was one within the framework of government measures which codified the results of the Popular Front. After the outbreak of the Second World War the *délégués du personnel* were confined to plants with 100 (instead of 10) employees. The office of the elected *délégués* was ended and the employer was to appoint the new delegates. Only a few employers did so, however.

The attitude of the totalitarian systems towards works councils was different. In Italy the agreement of Palazzo Vidoni of 2 October 1925, which became the basis for the development of the corporative system, had provided for the abolition of the *commissioni interne* and the transfer of their functions to the local unions. This position was confirmed in 1929 by a resolution of the Central 'Intersyndical Committee' which excluded members of the union committees (*s.c. fiduciari*) from settling disputes at their own plants. In Nazi Germany, after the prohibition of the trade unions and the mixed representation of employees and employers on the German Labour Front, the works councils were also structurally changed by the Act to Order National Labour of 1934. They became mixed bodies. The *Vertrauensräte* (councils of trust) included the *Betriebsführer* (leader of the workshop) who directed the council (Art. 5, s.1). This marked a break with the system of independent workers' representation which, as a rule, had involved separate meetings. The new idea was the representation of the *Gefolgschaft* (retinue), and the leader of the workshop was a copy of the political leader. The council of trust did not represent the interests of the workers against the employer as the works councils had. It was confined to consultation, especially in improving labour efficiency, co-operation and mediation of disputes. 'Works rules' were made by the employer after consultation with the council of trust. It was a return to the 1891 position with the difference that in this case the majority of the council could appeal to the 'trustee of labour', 'if agreement could not be reached on economic or social conditions of the workshops' (Art. 16).

In France the Vichy régime introduced in its Charter of Labour at the plant level the *comités sociaux d'etablissement* (social committees of the plant) as permanent institutions. These were also mixed committees consisting of the 'chief of the enterprise and the representatives of all categories of employees'—manual employees, white-collar workers, lower management (*agents de maîtrise*), engineers and the superior white-collar workers in administrative or commercial functions (*cadres administratifs et commerciaux*). The committee's task was 'social and professional collaboration between management and personnel' (Art. 24, s.1) which excluded 'all interventions in management and administration of the enterprise' and questions beyond this level. Positively, it said that support had to be given to management to solve all questions concerning work and personnel, to initiate an exchange of information and to realise the welfare measures within the workshop (Art. 24, s.2). It was the French version of the German 'councils of trust', but reinforcing an ideology of hierarchy between the different categories of workers.

The explanation for the attitudes of the totalitarian systems is to be seen in their views of trade unions and their experiences with councils. Fascism in Italy had succeeded in developing fascist trade unions but wanted to establish a firm and undisputed power for employers in order to achieve work discipline—which was certainly one of the aims of the Charter of Labour. The Nazis in Germany were full of distrust of trade unions because of their traditional connection with the Social Democrats. But the adaptation of works councils seemed to be possible when the paternalistic tradition was revived, with another meaning and now under the control of the state. The French Vichy régime shared this opinion, and under the influence of the old fear of revolutionary syndicalism considered the trade unions as the real enemies.

The end of the Second World War brought the final breakthrough of workers' representation at the plant level. The common reason was the need to collaborate dictated by the necessity of economic reconstruction with state distribution of goods and state wage and price controls. In Germany the situation was relatively simple. The country was occupied and placed under military government, divided into four occupation zones, but with one common institution: the Allied Control Council. This Council permitted, in a statute of 10 April 1946 (No. 22) the establishment of works councils. The German states which had been established after 1945 promulgated acts on the works councils which described their tasks differently. This made it necessary to reunify the works councils law. This task was achieved after the foundation of the Federal Republic by the Works Constitution Act of 1952. The position of the works councils was very strong during the post-war period because of the political situation. Many works councils were practically governed by communists while the employers had to atone for their affiliation to the Nazi Party. The trade unions had changed their structure shifting from craft to the industrial organisation, and the manual and white-collar organisations had merged in the Deutscher Gewerkschaftsbund (German Trade Union Confederation). They had also unified the different political unions in comprehensive neutral trade unions. The changes justified the question whether the works councils could not become sub-organisations of the trade union, but the traditional dualistic conception of German collective labour relations was retained. On one point, however, the position of the workers was considerably improved. Co-determination in the enterprises which means, according to the German understanding, the plant as an economic institution, was introduced for the mines and the iron and steel-producing industry. The British occupation force had wanted to prevent the restortion of an enterprise structure which could again be used for the preparation of war. They had demanded nationalisation but then accepted a change of the structure of company law for those enterprises. Therefore the supervisory boards (which had to elect and to control the members of the management board) were comprised of representatives of the workers and of the shareholders with an impartial chairman. One member of the managing board, the so-called *Arbeitsdirektor* (labour director) was in charge of employment questions, and it was desirable that he should have the trust of the workers' representatives. This regulation of 1946 was incorporated in a statute (No. 27) of the Allied High Commission of May 1950. The federal statute of May 1951 retained it, following the threat of strike action against political efforts to abolish it.

Development at the plant level took a similar course in France, Belgium and in the Netherlands as far as workers' representation was concerned. All these countries created an institution which encompassed workers and employers (as the French Charter of Labour had done). In France and Belgium, and in the Netherlands, this included safety and health matters. The mixed committees had different names: in France, *comités d'entreprise* (committees of the enterprise); in Belgium, *conseil d'entreprise*, and in the Netherlands, *ondernemingsraad* (both meaning 'council of the enterprise'). In France a decree of 22 February 1945 and a law of 1946 provided that collective agreements could modify the legal requirements. The enterprise was defined as the economic unit which could, but need not, be the same as the same as the technical unit of the workshop. When enterprises consisted of several workshops, provision was made for the establishment of *comités d'établisssement* (plant committees) and the *comité central d'entreprise* (central committee of the enterprise), which consisted of the delegates of the workshop committees. In Belgium this provision was absent. France exempted agriculture and the public service of non-industrial or non-commercial character. In the Netherlands, enterprises which had the status of public corporations were exempted.

The enterprise committees in all three countries were devoted to co-operation between employees and management. They mainly had consultative functions on questions of organisation, administration and business matters. Suggestions were transmitted to general meetings of the shareholders of corporations by two members of the committee and also to the *conseil d'administration* (board of directors). Decisions could be made only for the administration of the welfare institutions of the enterprise, and this function was extended *de facto*, but not *de jure*, to the medical and social services of the plant. The Dutch councils also dealt with general demands, complaints or comments of the employees on the determination of leave, working and rest-times and supervision of safety and sanitary provisions as well as supervision of the observance of the employment conditions. This extension of functions was due to the fact that the Dutch *ondernemingsraad* had to take care of duties which in France and Belgium were the task of other institutions.

Questions had to be answered relating to the election of the workers' representatives on these committees or councils, such as: How were the different categories of workers to be represented, and what was the position of the trade unions? In France a distinction was drawn between manual and white-collar workers as one group and engineers, supervisors and foremen as another. Belgium distinguished between manual and white-collar workers, while in the Netherlands the law just provided that all groups should be considered.

France gave the trade unions which were the 'most representative' in an enterprise the right to propose a list of candidates. At first, election was by a simple majority of those voting, but in 1947 proportional representation was prescribed. In Belgium a similar system was introduced, but proportional voting was already in existence. In the Netherlands it was also the most representative unions that were given the right to propose lists of candidates, although some provisions were made which theoretically opened up the possibility for other unions and groups of independent workers to submit additional lists.

Workers' representation could be organised in two ways: on a statutory basis or by collective agreements. In both cases the question arose of how the trade unions should be accommodated. In France the *délégués du personnel* were revived. As we have seen, they had been introduced in 1936 by collective agreements, but then regulated by a decree of 1938. The composition of the delegations and election procedures were the same as for the enterprise committees. The function of the delegates was to handle individual grievances of workers who had been unsuccessful with the employer and also collective complaints. The trade unions did not oppose this because they had influence on the delegates. In Belgium the *délégations syndicales du personnel* (trade union delegations of the personnel) were established by collective agreements. They had to handle individual grievances and, in general, had to represent the interests of all workers in the workshop, or at least of the organised workers.

This breakthrough in worker representation in three countries, which all had been occupied by Germany during the Second World War, was due to political causes, in particular to the resistance movement and the fight against collaborators with the Germans. It was less than the self-administration of factories and also less than the expropriation of property. In Belgium and the Netherlands it was more an expression of the co-operation between employers and employees which had emerged from the war and which since 1945 has been institutionalised at all levels of industry.

The most complicated situation existed in Italy. After Mussolini's fall and imprisonment and his subsequent liberation by the Germans, Mussolini founded a new Fascist republic in northern Italy, the Republic of Salō, which, echoing back to Mussolini's syndicalist past, became the declared enemy of the middle class. The new structure of the Italian economy was to be based upon the socialisation of the private and public enterprises (January 1944). A new mixed body, the *consiglio di gestione* (managing council) was to institutionalise workers' participation at the management level. In the joint-stock companies the workers were to have an equal number of representatives with the shareholders in the assemblies. The decree of 12 February 1944 was promulgated (30 June 1944) but only sixty-two factories were socialised. After the military collapse the National Liberation Committee for Northern Italy, under the authority of the royal government, declared the Fascist decrees to be invalid but also supported nationalisation and proclaimed elections to other managing councils. By 1946 about 500 managing councils existed, often established by works agreements. There were also regional *comitati coordinatori dei consigli di gestione* (co-ordinating committees of the managing councils), which organised a national congress on 13 October 1947 and demanded the realisation of the constitutional bill. The resulting Article 46 on the Italian Constitution of 1 January 1947, provided that:

> For the purpose of ameliorating the conditions of labour economically and socially and in accordance with the requirements of production, the Republic recognises the right of the workers to participate in the management of enterprises in the forms and limitations determined by statute.[1]

But in practice the managing councils gradually disappeared. The

1. Author's translation.

commissioni interne (internal commissions) were also re-established by the collective agreements of 2 September 1943, 7 August 1947 and 8 May 1953. The commissions were akin to the German works councils because they represented all the workers. There were not only trade union lists of candidates but also independent lists. Up to 1953 manual and white-collar workers had separate commissions, but since then only one commission.

In Britain there was no development along these lines. There had been a revival of work-place trade union organisation during the Second World War. Spontaneous 'joint production committees' or 'joint consultation committees' which had the aim of encouraging war-production emerged and were later supported by the TUC and engineering unions. By 1943 there were 4,169 such committees covering between 2 million and 5 million workers in the engineering and allied industries, and there were similar committees in other industries. Ideologically, these committees had the support of those who saw them as a means of co-operation towards common objectives. The first post-war Labour government (1945–51) encouraged this, and indeed wrote into the statutes nationalising various industries (coal, rail, etc.) the requirement that the boards of the nationalised corporations should create machinery for joint consultation on questions of safety, health, welfare, the organisation and conduct of the industry and other matters of mutual interest. 'Consultation' was a continuous process of informing workers of the facts through their representatives and of conveying the workers' views to management. It was based upon the need for co-operation during the post-war period of recovery. The story of the loss of faith in this philosophy and the rise of the modern powerful shop stewards' movement belongs to the late 1950s and 1960s.

REGIONAL AND NATIONAL REPRESENTATION OF LABOUR

In the period before the First World War, representative bodies were established. Some were called 'chambers' and some 'councils', but this was of no importance because in both cases they were confined to consultative tasks. However, German legal terminology distinguished between the 'workers' chamber', when the chamber merely represented the interests of the workers, and the 'chamber of labour', when the institution encompassed both workers and employers and was to represent their 'common' interests. All forms of national representation were of this mixed type.

Regional and national representation had their roots in a pre-liberal society in which the estates had their specific interests to represent. After the abolition of the estates the form was kept for the representation of the interests of commerce, trade and agriculture. When labour arose as a new interest group it was at first subordinated to common representation with employers as part of one of these older forms. In all those forms there was a problem of how group representation could be reconciled with democratic thought and the concept of laws which represented the *volonté générale* (general will) and excluded particular interests. But before universal and equal suffrage had been accepted, there was a common case at least for hearing the representatives of those who had no deputies in Parliament since the employers enjoyed the privilege of the suffrage based upon income or wealth. These forms of representation were an early legal recognition of the separate interests of workers, and it was believed that they could serve as bridges of understanding between workers and employers.

The first use of this representation in Belgium makes clear the importance of this point. In March 1896 a strike unexpectedly broke out in the coal-mines, and neighbouring plants were seized. Factories were destroyed or burnt down and blood was spilt. All this was accompanied by the enthusiastic support of other workers. The introduction of the *conseils de l'industrie et du travail* (councils of industry and labour) was an attempt to solve the problem. One of the tasks of this new institution was mediation. The 'ideal' type of representative institution was two-tiered. But this was not achieved in Belgium. The councils of industry and labour were to be established as necessary in all communities; by 1908, seventy-seven existed. They were composed of six to twelve sections. A supreme council was provided for the entire country but was never convened. The Netherlands followed in 1897 with the *kamers van arbeid* (chambers of labour) for each community. One branch had to collect labour statistics. But the Chambers of Labour Act did not prove to be a success. By 1915 only 85 out of an original 112 existed. France began in 1891 with the establishment of the Conseil Supérieur du Travail (Supreme Council of Labour) composed of fifty members. At first they were appointed, but from 1899 most had to be elected. The size and composition of the Council was changed several times. A decree of 1900 authorised the Minister of Trade to establish *conseils du travail* for industrial areas, but here the trade unions and the labour courts elected the workers' representatives. In 1904 the establishment of the councils by decree was made subject to an appeal to the Conseil d'Êtât (Council of State) replaced by a statute of 1908 which also changed the name into *conseils consultatifs du travail*. In

Denmark the Work in Factories Act of 1901 provided for the establishment of a labour council by the Minister of Interior. In Britain a tripartite (state, employers, unions) Industrial Council was set up between 1911–1913 to supplement existing methods of consultation and arbitration. This was a direct response to the growth of revolutionary syndicalism and guild socialism during the industrial unrest of this period. In Germany bills of 1906, 1908 and 1910 attempted to establish chambers of labour at regional level. They all failed, however, as Parliament and government could not agree on points such as the scope of their application, the age for election and the eligibility of trade union officials.

All these were state-sponsored institutions. They should be distinguished from the local associations of trade unions, such as the *bourses du travail* in France (from 1886) and the *camere del lavoro* in Italy (from 1891), which received public subsidies (see Ch. 5, above). These associations helped to prevent the dispersal of the trade union movement. But even in Germany, where the trade union movement was centralised in the three different organisations, there was a growing demand for workers' chambers. Evidently a legal institution was needed to overcome the rivalries between the unions and possibly lead to their unification. In Italy Acts of 1902 and 1903 provided for the establishment of the Consiglio Superiore del Lavoro, which had forty-three members and was presided over by the Minister of Agriculture, Industry and Trade. Twenty-two members were delegates from different political and economic corporations, seven were heads of state authorities and the other fourteen were appointed by the King, among them five proprietors and seven workers.

The First World War did not alter this pattern during its initial stages when patriotism was strong and the structure of the labour force was being radically changed by recruitments into the armed forces and a shift to war-based industry. Trade union and labour leaders became members of the War Cabinets as Labour Ministers in Britain and France; in Germany a trade unionist became State Secretary of the Reich Office. The problem of industrial conflicts at plant level during the second period of the war was dealt with in Germany by the Patriotic Auxiliary Service Act 1916 (see p. 250, above), and in Britain one year earlier the Munitions of War Act 1915 made strikes illegal and set up a compulsory arbitration system. The growth of tripartism in this period was reflected in the Munitions of War Tribunals, with a legal chairman and assessors appointed from panels of employers and workers to handle disputes under the Act. But in both countries this kind of collaboration was not entirely effective. In Germany leading Social Democrats were members of strike committees and assisted in achieving settlements. In Britain the prohibition on strikes was successfully defied by South Wales miners.

At the end of the War these controls were abandoned in Britain. In their place the Whitley Committee Reports (1916–19) proposed district and national joint industrial councils of representatives of employers and trade unions in all major industries: the government's role was to be limited to providing in the first instance a chairman and secretary where this was desired and circulating information. They were voluntary and not the result of legislation. By 1921, seventy four such councils had been formed, seven of these in the civil service and government industrial establishments. In the period between 1923 and 1939 about sixty-two of these councils were functioning covering an average of over 2 million workers. They were essentially permanent voluntary negotiating bodies, and they have had a lasting influence on the shape of British industrial relations: by 1965 there were 500 separate industry-wide negotiating agreements covering 18 million of the 23 million British workers. Britain also serves as an example of the use of tripartism to overcome the post-war economic crisis, with the National Industrial Conference (1919–21) and then, after the strike of 1926, the Conference on Industrial Reorganisation and Industrial Relations (1928–29).

In Belgium the Conseil du Travail was reorganised in 1920. The Netherlands established the Hooge Raad van Arbeid (High Council of Labour) in 1919 also on a tripartite basis, the members being appointed by the monarch. Amendments to the constitutions in 1922 and 1937 made it legally possible to attribute law-making power to industrial and professional bodies. In 1933 the Trade Councils Act fell far short of the conceptions of the advocates of the idea of self-determination of interest groups in economic life. This act enabled the monarch to split up economic life in different branches of industry and to establish for the respective branches *bedrijfsraden* (trade councils), consisting of an equal number of employers and workers representatives under an independent chairman. There was no immediate and general grant of such power to all trade councils. The monarch could by separate Acts of Parliament confer law-making power on particular trade councils. But special Acts were never passed, and therefore the twenty-one trade councils which were created served only as a forum for consultation and co-operation. The Act was greeted by apathy from the workers (because of the lack of law-making powers) and opposition from the employers (because they feared every step towards industrial democracy). Like the earlier Chambers of Labour Act 1897, it proved to be unsuccessful. The abolition of these regional chambers of labour in 1923 proved that the economic problems were more concentrated at the national level. Luxembourg by an Act of 1924 established five professional chambers, among them two for white-collar workers and one for manual workers. While these chambers had the right to initiate bills, the French Conseil National Économique (National Economic Council), established by an Act of 1925, had consultative and informative functions only.

The German situation was different because the previously strong state authority had collapsed. The Stinnes-Legien Agreement of 12 November 1918 established, 'in order to carry out the agreement as well as to regulate demobilisation, maintenance of economic life and to secure the livelihood of the working men, especially the severely war disabled', the Zentralarbeitsgemeinschaft (Central Working Community) composed of equal numbers of members of both sides of industry (3 December 1918). Later on in pursuance of the constitutional promise of the Reichswirtschaftsrat (Reich Economic Council) the Provisional Economic Council was established. A decree of 1920 on its composition provided for two departments of the employees and of the employers. A third department had representatives of public corporations, co-operatives, professional classes and of scholars. This third department was a step beyond the central Working Community which consisted only of an employees' and of an employers' side. The Provisional Economic Council disappeared with the Weimar Republic in 1933.

In Britain the Second World War saw a continuation of the development which had begun during the First World War. The institutional structure began with the establishment of a National Joint Advisory Council under the Minister of Labour and National Service on matters of common interest for employers and employees and of a Trade Union Advisory Committee under the Minister of Production and the Air Ministry in the field of production. In May 1940 Ernest Bevin, a leading trade union official became Minister of Labour and National Service and other labour leaders entered the National government. A sub-organisation of production, with a tripartite structure, was developed on a regional basis. This kept contact with the employer-worker advisory committees. In spring 1941 production was more strongly centralised and a Production Executive with a Central Production Advisory Committee on a basis of equal representation was established. The necessities of war production thus brought British industry under a form of government control in which the trade unions participated. This situation lasted after the end of the war and received a boost by the nationalisation of several industries introduced by the Labour Party when it won the 1945 election.

The very last period of the Second World War, after the German retreat from the occupied countries, was similar to that in Germany after 1918. State power collapsed. But outside Germany political authority emanated from resistance movements. The solutions adopted in France, Belgium and the Netherlands are comparable with the German Stinnes-Legien Agreement of 1918. The resistance movement established in France the Conseil National de la Résistance; in Belgium it proclaimed the Pact of National Solidarity (1945), and in the Netherlands the manifesto of the employers and trade unions. The Dutch Stichting van de Arbeid (Foundation of Labour), a private organisation, established on 5 July 1945 was similar in its structure to the German Central Work Community of 1918. It played a major consultative role in the Dutch State Wage Policy until the 1960s, and still exists today. In 1950 the Social Economic Council was established on a tripartite basis (one-third employers, one-third union representatives, one-third independent members) as the chief advisory institution to the government on socio-economic matters and at the same time as the controlling authority of the Dutch system of self-determination of interest groups in economic matters.

The *Wet op Bedrijfsorganisatie* (Organisation of Economic Life Act) provided for the establishment of *bedrijfschappen* (trade authorities) for each branch of industry, consisting of an equal numbers of workers' and employers' representatives and exercising both advisory and law-making powers in economic and social affairs (including terms and conditions of employment by separate statutes). Besides the *bedrijfschappen*, the *productschappen* were also established consisting of those enterprises which produced the same final product. All these councils were public corporations. The results were poor. Only a few trade authorities were established (notably in agriculture, mining and the retail trade) but several in the sectors in which medium-sized and large-scale enterprises prevailed. Only in very rare cases did trade authorities exercise social law-making functions. Like the Chambers of Labour Act 1897 and the Trade Councils Act 1933, the Organisation of Economic Life Act 1950 was also unsuccessful.

In Belgium there were seven National Labour Conferences (between 1944 and 1948) which were made up of representatives from the government, employers and employees. A permanent organisation was the Conseil Paritaire Générale (General Paritarian Council) established by the Labour Minister, who also served as chairman. As a substructure there were the *commissions paritaires* (paritary commissions), established by a decree of 1945 and charged with the conclusion of collective agreements and with the settlement of industrial disputes. A permanent legal organisation at the superior level was developed later and distinguished between economic and labour relations. In

1948 was created the Conseil Central de l'Économie (Central Council of Economy) with a consultative function to Parliament and government and with *conseils professionels* (professional councils) at lower levels. In 1952 the Conseil National du Travail (National Council of Labour) was established which replaced the National Labour Conferences and the General Paritarian Council. It became the legal successor of all preceding special institutions like the General Safety Council, the Superior Council of Labour and Social Welfare and the Councils of Industry and Labour. It was the high point of a labour council system consisting of the paritarian commissions as a substructure. Thus Belgium offered a uniform picture because all economic and labour institutions were of a bipartite nature.

The post-war Italian Constitution promised in Article 99 the establishment of an Economic and Labour Council. This Council, created only in 1957, became the successor of all preceding special institutions like the Industry Council and National Commission on Social Welfare and Labour (founded in 1869).

APPROACHES TOWARDS A COMPREHENSIVE SYSTEM

In Germany and in the Netherlands attempts were made to include different forms of representative bodies of the workers, alone or together with the employers, into a new system of labour relations. Belgium followed after the Second World War.

The debates of the constitutional committee of the German Constitutive Assembly on the draft constitution had already lasted more than a month when the Cabinet presented as an amendment to its bill an article which almost literally became the subsequent Article 165 of the Weimar Constitution.[2] It was not entirely a surprise, because the government had already earlier given constitutional recognition to the workers' councils as the representatives of the workers' economic interests. This declaration also mentioned the formation of work communities for all industrial and trade branches 'for the control and regulation of production and of the distribution of wares'. Article 165 was accepted because it encompassed everything which had previously been discussed or demanded. The chambers of workers were founded under the name of *Bezirksarbeiterräte* (district workers' councils). They had been created by the revolutionary council movement and had even

2. The text will be found in Appendix IV, below, p. 385.

been legally recognised in the mines. The *Reichsarbeiterrat* was the legal form for this collaboration between the different trade unions. It had existed when they had signed the Stinnes-Legien Agreement. This organisation corresponded to the radical council system, but it now became part of the legal system, because all the bodies were given the status of 'statutory representatives'. This radical system was supplemented by a second one, a mixed system of co-operation as it already existed in the collaboration between employers' and employees' committees and with the Central Working Community. The supreme level was now called the Reich Economic Council by the constitution and below at the second level was the *Bezirkswirtschaftsräte* (district economic councils), just a new name for the old chambers of labour. And the lowest primary level was the co-operation between employer and works council.

Changes were made to the district economic councils and the Reich Economic Council. Not only were employers and employees to be represented there but also 'all important professional groups according to their social and economic importance'. The task of these economic councils at the two superior levels was 'to perform all economic tasks and to co-operate with the carrying out of social legislation'. Bills on social and economic policy of principal importance were to be forwarded by the Reich government to the Reich Economic Council for consultation before they were brought before the Reich Parliament. The Reich Economic Council had the right to initiate bills of this kind even against the will of the government. The workers' and economic councils could be given control and administrative competence in their spheres of activity. Between the economic councils and the trade unions and the employers' organisations there was a division of labour because these organisations were also recognised.

Article 165 was thus much less spectacular when seen in retrospect. It marked the extension of the principle of social self-administration as had already been planned on the regional level during the Empire. It could also be considered as the realisation of a project of the 1848 Revolution. In 1848 a bill supported by a minority (which like the majority bill never became law but was the victim of the failure of the Revolution) had provided for mixed representation at several levels. Above the factory committee there was to be a regional *Fabrikrat* (factory council), which was to approve factory rules, determine working time and notice periods, determine the number of apprentices, supervise the sick benefit funds of the factories, draft the statutes of the factory pension funds and represent the interests of the factories at the *Gewerbekammer* (district trade chamber). These trade chambers had the final supervision of all institutions and funds, had to approve the factory pension funds and serve as a means of appealing against decisions of the factory councils. Larger states were to establish central trade chambers. Despite this tradition the realisation of the ideal remained fragmentary. The works councils were introduced and a Provisional Reich Economic Council created. The regional institutions remained on paper, and as the district economic council was never realised, its functions of control over the establishment and activities of the works councils were transferred in 1927 to the labour courts. The Central Working Community collapsed in January 1924, when the Allgemeine Deutsche Gewerkschaftsbund withdrew, as many unions such as the metal-workers and the bricklayers had already done at industry level. The reasons were disappointment with the failure to realise the second (district) level of the councils and the revival of radicalism, especially during the rapid devaluation of the German currency. The Central Working Community was not regarded as achieving the demands of the workers but rather as serving the interests of the employers. Moreover, the Community had developed into a cumbersome institution with 14 branches, 140 sub-committees, a total membership of 300 and a board of 28 members.

The bill on the Reich Economic Council was rejected in 1930 because it abolished the district and the Reich workers' councils and did not gain a sufficient majority to alter the constitutional provision. The Provisional Reich Economic Council disappeared with the Weimar Republic.

Do the reasons for failure lie more deeply than in the few missing votes and in the breakdown of parliamentary government in 1930? There is no simple answer to this question. During the first year of the Republic when the article was a compromise but left room for political development, it might have been realised. But later on the ambiguous nature of Article 165 proved an obstacle. The council system could work within the framework of the existing society. It was conservative, as its roots in the bills of the Empire have shown. But it was also radical because it offered a new system of economic and labour relations after nationalisation. Both political sides could accept the compromise during a revolutionary situation. But afterwards the employers did not wish to promote a possible nationalisation nor did the left radicals want to stabilise the liberal economic system. Furthermore, the trade unions' influence could decrease when not only the employers but other groups were represented in the economic councils—as the example of the Provisional Reich Economic Council showed—and so it attracted the criticism of the unions. No clear answer can be given to the question of whether the realisation of Article 165 could have helped to control the economic crisis at the end of the First German Republic. In Germany the attempts of the Empire to establish a system of co-operation between workers and employers were dictated by political necessity to secure legitimacy for the state against international revolutionary workers' movements.

In the Netherlands the religious parties tried to realise the principle of self-determination by professional groups. They considered that the pre-liberal system of the estates should be applied to modern society as had been proposed by German thinkers like Marlo or the 'hair socialist' Schaeffle or Bishop von Ketteler from Mayence. At first (about 1880) the idea was promoted by the social-Calvinists, then after the Papal Encyclical *Rerum Novarum* (1891) it gained the support of the Roman Catholics (1910 and in their Easter Manifesto of 1919). The Chambers of Labour Act 1897, the Trade Council Act 1933 and the Organisation of Economic Life Act 1950 may all be considered as attempts to realise this concept. None of them, however, established legal co-operation at the plant level as had been done in Germany, and they were thus less complete than Article 165 of the Weimar Constitution. They were not directly dictated by revolutionary pressure, and all were ineffective. The reasons for this failure are similar to those for all the different efforts to introduce representation of the workers at the different levels.

Belgium renewed its system of paritarian representative boards by its Pact of National Solidarity and seems to have profited from the German experiences. The joint committees which were legally organised by a decree of 6 June 1945 were established at branch level by the King at the request of or after consultation with the most representative employers' organisations and trade unions. But they were not restricted to assisting or advisory functions. They also had decision-making powers like the establishment of essential services during industrial disputes, binding decisions on conflicts of work rules in the plant and on whether there were just reasons for dismissing a member of a works council or of a safety committee. The main function of the National Labour Council (with a maximum number of twenty-nine members) was to give advice to the legislature or to the executive. (Its powers were extended in 1968 to conclude collective agreements for the entire country and different branches or for any branch in which a joint committee did not exist or did not work efficiently.) The Belgian experience thus may lead to a revision of the negative judgment on the representative bodies. Certainly one condition for their success is that they be entrusted with decision-making powers. Another is that the trade unions are willing to leave space for their activities.

SPECIAL LABOUR COURTS

We saw in Chapter 2, above, that labour inspection and prosecution developed as means of enforcing protective legislation. Ultimately, the success of legislation and the enforcement of employment contracts depends upon the courts. If the judges are hostile to the spirit of the legislation or if the legal process is inaccessible to the workers, there is little hope for those whose rights are violated. The class bias and lack of industrial experience of the judiciary and the cost, delays and formalities of the ordinary courts are too well known to require repetition here. One of the remarkable developments of labour law in some countries—notably France (1806), Belgium (1809), Italy (1893) and Germany (1890, 1904 and 1926)—was the establishment of special courts or tribunals, with workers' representation, designed to overcome some of these problems.

France was the forerunner. The *conseils de prud'hommes* in France went through two main periods of development. The first was from 1806 to 1880. The institution goes back to the Middle Ages as a special court to settle disputes between merchants and manufacturers. They were abolished in this form in 1791. In 1805, in an address to Napoleon I, the manufacturers of Lyon criticised the fact that the police authorities had legal jurisdiction in cases involving labour conflicts. They said that the police were inept when applying customs of the trade. Napoleon decided to revive the *bureau commun de la grande fabrique* (joint factory office) which had existed in Lyon under the *ancien régime* to serve all the workers in silk works. The *conseil de prud'hommes* of Lyon was created by a law of 18 March 1806, and the law allowed for the extension of the system to other towns. The *conseil de prud'hommes* was made up of manufacturers and foremen. Although the members were elected, the *conseil* did not provide a form of judgment by peers because no workers sat on the *conseil*. Initially they dealt with disputes about the quality of work done and the rate of payment, but this was extended to cover conciliation of other minor disputes, recording of contraventions of work regulations and visits to workshops and factories accompanied by government officials. They were gradually extended to other industries and other towns. Nevertheless, in this period, according to Marcel David, they 'remained closer to disciplinary committees than to an arbitral court of some kind' (1974, p. 12).

It was under the Second Republic that the nature of the *conseils de prud'hommes* was transformed. A decree given on 27 May 1848 stated that all people exercising a profession, including labourers, could vote and stand in the elections. The ideal of parity between manufacturers, foremen, supervisors and all the workers was instituted. The *conseils de prud'hommes* hence represented a 'conquest' for the republicans and the workers, so were therefore threatened by any government whose politics were opposed to this. For this reason the *conseils de prud'hommes* encountered many difficulties from 1848 to 1851.

In the second period from the 1880s onwards the *conseils de prud'hommes* constituted one of the most fundamental elements in the way labour disputes were solved. The workers' movement showed considerable interest in this method of jurisdiction, and made specific demands in order to obtain an improved functioning of the council as well as the extension of the system to cover a wider area, both geographical and professional. For example, at the second *Congrès Ouvriers* (Workers' Congress) in Lyon in 1878, the delegates made the following important claims: they wanted a new method of election, both of the ordinary council members and of the president of the council; a reform of the length of the term of office and of the pay of the council members; and they wished a trade union 'expert' to take over the secretaryship. Besides this, the problem of the removal from office of elected council members was brought up: the electors ought to be able to end the term of office of a council member, a claim which, in David's words, 'shows the sort of precautions the still unstructured movement intended to take against the possible risk of seeing the workers on the council being ignored or "avoided" by the directors and employers' (1974, p. 15).

Numerous private and government bills followed one another through the Chambre des Députés from 1892 on; but the Sénat was systematic in its opposition and none of these bills was passed. One of the fundamental questions was to decide which legal body should be called on to give judgment in cases where a decision made by the *conseil de prud'hommes* was appealed against. On this point, the Sénat finally admitted that it would be advisable to deny the *tribunaux de commerce* the competence they had had until then to deal with such matters. But the claim made by the CGT, for special *conseils de prud'hommes* for appeals only, was rejected, and the Chambre des Députés and the Sénat conciliated, by attributing competence to deal with appeals to the *tribunal civil* (civil court). This development was instituted by two laws. The first law, of 1905, made provisions for judgment by the committee, presided over by a *Juge de Paix* (Justice of the Peace), whose competence would be increased as a last resort when the votes of workers and employers were equally divided; it also provided for the organisation of the referral of appeals to a civil court. But it was the law of 27 March 1907 which aimed finally to unify all the legislation surrounding the *conseils de prud'hommes*. The following are the principal points dealt with by this law: the formation of a *conseil de prud'hommes* could be requested by the local council of the commune in question; the competence of the *conseils* was extended to cover all categories of commerce and industry, as well as mining and businesses concerned with warehousing and transport; women were included in the electorate; there was a reduction in the required period of residence or involvement in a particular profession; and lastly the principle of having alternately an employer and a worker as president of the council was established.

The law of 1907 constituted the basis of the organisation of the *conseils de prud'hommes* and was changed very little by subsequent laws. For example, in 1908 *Juges de Paix* were accorded competence to judge individual labour cases when there was no *conseil de prud'hommes*; also women were given the right to stand for seats on the council. A law of 1919 changed the regulations concerning the elections, increasing the electorate and lowering the requirements for being elegible to stand; it also specified the modes of the competence the *conseils* had *vis-à-vis* the workers; and improved the regulations about the running of arbitration officers. In 1924, legislation concerning the *conseils de prud'hommes* was to constitute the whole of Book 4 of the *Code du Travail*. In 1932 attempts were made by the legislator to extend the jurisdiction of the *conseils* to cover agriculture, but this had no real practical consequences.

In Belgium the French model was followed. It was not until a law of 31 July 1889 that the *conseils de prud'hommes* in that country were put on a democratic basis with an extension of the right to vote to all employers and to all male workers over 25. In 1896 and 1910 there were further extensions to white-collar workers and women and to some categories of domestic servants. A law of 9 July 1926 established new voting rules and provided for assistance to be given to the *conseil* by legal advisers, doctors of law appointed by the Crown. From 1926 the *conseils* had an important influence on solutions to individual industrial conflicts in Belgium.

Italy also provides an interesting example of the creation of 'gownless' courts (*magistratura non togata*) running side by side with the ordinary courts (*magistratura ordinaria*). In 1893 the law on the industrial *probiviri* was passed. The proponents of the new constitution saw it as a means of reducing conflict arising from 'incomprehension and momentary exasperation'. In places where there were factories or industrial establishments *collegi di probiviri* were to be set up in order to resolve individual disputes. In each *collegio* an *ufficio di conciliziano* (conciliation office) and jury were formed. The former was composed of two members, an industrialist and a worker, with an independent chairman. The jury was composed of the chairman and four members, two industrialists and two workers. The functions of the conciliation office and of the jury (the latter having a more limited role) were conciliation and mediation in certain types of individual dispute. The reasons given for this specialised jurisdiction were similar to those in other countries: the lack of expertise of the ordinary magistrates, the formalistic procedure of the civil courts which was incomprehensible to poor or illiterate plaintiffs who lacked representation, as well as the middle-class mentality of the magistrates who were inspired by the belief in the equality of exchange between work and wages at the precise moment when industrialisation was revealing the difference between social classes.

Not everything slipped out of the hands of the ordinary magistrates who continued to deal with problems of wages and work discipline within the scope of the civil law of *locatio*. The *probiviri* were primarily concerned with industrial custom and practice, factory regulations and collective agreements. Norms were generally referred back to the *usi di mercato* (customs of the market) and of the firm. This was supported by Article 1124 of the Civil Code, which allowed the sources of the contractual relationships to be derived from custom, equity and law. In this way the *probiviri* were able to enrich the framework of *locatio*, differing from the legalistic interpretation of the ordinary magistrates in a number of celebrated instances. For example, they held (Milan, 24 June 1903) that illness was no longer a reason to terminate the relationship *de jure*, and (Prato, 27 July 1903) that where motivation was insufficient, damages could be awarded. The *probiviri* disappeared in the corporative period, and only in the 1950s was there a development of a similar institution, and that was not the product of the legislature but an interconfederal agreement (on dismissals) which led to the creation of courts of conciliation.

In Germany separate courts with general jurisdiction over labour disputes (*Arbeitsgerichte*) did not appear until 1926. They replaced earlier trade courts for manual workers (*Gewerbegerichte*) established in 1890 and tribunals for clerical workers (*Kaufmannsgerichte*) established in 1904. While the trade courts had limited jurisdiction and covered only a few trades, the labour courts of 1926 could deal with almost all individual labour disputes and disputes arising out of collective agreements, apart from the conclusion of new collective agreements (i.e. not conflicts of interest). All categories of workers, except civil servants, had access, and unions and works councils could present claims based on their statutory rights. The labour courts consisted of a professional judge as chairman and two lay members, one nominated by the representative employers' associations and one by the trade unions. They operated at three levels: the local labour court (*Arbeitsgerichte*), the regional state labour tribunal (*Landesarbeitsgercht*) and the Reich labour court (*Reichsarbeitsgericht*). The latter was a division of the Reich (Supreme) Court and in this there were three professional judges and two lay members. In his famous critique of the *Social Ideal of the Reich Labour Court*, Kahn-Freund (1981, p. 108) argued, on the basis of his analysis of the case law, that the Court implicitly pursued a socio-political objective (one which he thought was 'in all respects identical' with that of fascism). He regarded the members of the Court as having an aversion to the collectivist assumptions on which Weimar labour law was founded and so had transformed the basic character of that law by their decisions.

In the Third Reich, the jurisdiction of the labour courts over collective disputes vanished with them and their competence in individual disputes became smaller because some of these fell under the newly created 'courts of social honour' (*soziale Ehrengerichte*). After the Second World War the labour courts were given back their pre-Nazi jurisdictions and they steadily increased in importance.

In Britain, despite the traditional aversion of the trade unions to the apparent class bias of the ordinary judiciary, there was no demand for a separate system of labour courts. Apart from the 'munitions tribunals', with a legal chairman and assessors appointed from panels of employers and workers to deal with employment disputes during the First World War, a system of industrial tribunals did not emerge until 1964. This reluctance to create a specialised judiciary is a reflection of the general 'abstention' of the law in labour relations which reached its high point during the very years when trade unions had the greatest political opportunities to seek such courts. When the industrial tribunals did emerge it was mainly as a creation of the civil service rather than in response to a demand by unions or employers. In the Netherlands, as well, specialised labour courts are unknown. Employment disputes are dealt with in the ordinary courts.

GENERAL OBSERVATIONS

All forms of workers' participation, representation of labour and special labour courts raise the question: What was the position of the trade unions?

At regional and national level the representation of labour was the preserve of trade unions. In those countries where suffrage had not yet fully encompassed the working class, national consultations helped to fill a political gap. In times of war or economic crisis governments sought closer co-operation and established institutions of a tripartite structure. The creation of political stability depended, on the one hand, on the willingness of governments to abandon traditional hostility towards unions and to develop powerful new constitutions and, on the other hand, on the willingness of the majority of working-class organisations to work within the parliamentary political sphere, coupled with the success of governments in isolating the revolutionary movement. Where trade unions were strong and real power was denied to representative bodies, these bodies did not develop.

At the plant level no form of workers' participation broke the paternal government of the employer, neither the shop steward system nor the works councils. In plants of small or medium size in which the individual proprietor retained permanent control the employer successfully resisted greater participation. However, institutions of workers' participation were more successful in large plants with a bureaucratic organisation and in which the employer's right to command had been divided among several persons or levels of management.

The statutory creation of institutions such as works councils was the result of political changes. But with willingness on the side of employers and workers' representatives it proved possible to extend the competence of works councils. This was helped by the guarantee by the state of the stability and continuity of co-operation. The type of mixed body in which the employer was also represented depended on mutual trust and the willingness to make compromises. The works councils system had advantages over the shop steward system, when a plurality of trade unions existed, because differences and rivalries between them were then submitted to the judgment of the workers as the electors. In both systems the representatives may by the nature of their representative tasks become increasingly independent of the workers, a tendency which seems more pronounced in a works council than shop stewards system. The problem for all workers' representatives, but especially the problem of the more independent works councils, was that co-operation with the employer at the plant level tended to separate workers' interests at plant level from their wider interests within the employers' corporate multi-plant structure, and from their industry-wide interests against the employers generally. The works councils could therefore be considered to realise the idea of community, a 'work community' between employer and employees and thus a bridge to the national community as a counter to the ideology of class struggle.

The development of special labour courts belongs with the representative boards and the works councils and also with the tripartite system of German social insurance, to a comprehensive system for integrating the workers into liberal society and into the administration of the state. This system, which had an unbroken tradition in Germany (due to the maintenance of a powerful centralised government) and which can also be observed in Napoleon I's establishment of the *conseils de prud'hommes*, was anti-liberal. Liberal thought found its expression in a common judicial power for handling all disputes between citizens. The idea of representation contained hints of feudal society in which the different estates had their representatives. It is significant that even in the middle of the nineteenth century Ferdinand Lassalle, the founder of the German Social Democratic Party, spoke of the 'workers' estate'. When feudal society disappeared and was replaced by competition between individuals, and the workers as disadvantaged individuals demanded and gained freedom of association, a new social system had emerged. The system of collective *laissez-faire* could also provide for settlement of disputes by tripartite boards set up by the parties to collective agreements. Thus the system of representing 'estates' and the system of collective *laissez-faire* came close together in reality.

State protection and the integration of workers into the administration of the state, on the one hand, and self-help, on the other hand, were the two main opposing principles which explain the different developments of the national labour laws. These principles were to come into the sharpest conflict in the period between the two World Wars, to which we must now turn.

7

Epilogue: The New Ordering of Labour Law 1918–45

Thilo Ramm

THE STRUCTURE OF LABOUR LAW BEFORE THE FIRST WORLD WAR

Labour law acquired its structure during the nineteenth century. After the First World War there were further developments, improvements and extensions, but with few new ideas and conceptions. Labour law could be understood and was understood as the realisation of two principles: of self-help and of state-help. Self-help was the basis of the trade union movement and of strikes. This was close to the liberal understanding of economy, of the 'free play of market forces'. But it replaced individual *laissez-faire* with collective *laissez-faire*. Its fullest realisation was achieved in Britain.

State intervention was the opposite idea. It prevailed at a time when self-help was suppressed or weak. It began with the protection of the discriminated groups of children and women who did not occupy an equal legal status with adult men. State intervention also included some protection against the dangers of technology and industrialisation. It was the swan-song of dogmatic liberalism, the principle that the state should not intervene in the economy. But intervention occurred only hesitantly and reluctantly in those areas where the notion of formal legal equality between employer and employees was demonstrably false, as in the case of women and children. State intervention was either the concession made by the middle class, which had control of political power, or it expressed the strength of the monarch who, as in the German states, had maintained power and independence from estates and classes. When the Germans preferred the expression 'state *help*' to 'state *intervention*', they referred to the idea of the state as a person and saw this state help as a means to balance economic liberalism.

State help and state intervention claimed to have the aim of 'protecting' labour. Labour protection law in the wide sense of the word covered all employment protective statutes as well as the law on collective labour organisations and industrial disputes and the law on workers' representation. It was more than labour law because, besides the law on labour relations, it included welfare legislation of the kind discussed earlier in Chapter 3. Until the beginning of the First World War, the latter could even be regarded as the most important and easiest to achieve because the welfare legislation did not violate the freedom of contract, which was the legal expression of the economic free-play of forces. Welfare legislation took the place formerly occupied by the Poor Law and filled it out with new values and matched it to the demands of capitalist industrialisation. This welfare legislation aimed to take over some of the normal risks to the lives of the workers.

The labour law of the nineteenth century was diffuse. It was the answer to political or social challenges. Sometimes it could be compared with the activities of the fire brigade; sometimes it was preventive. A comprehensive legislative plan was never adopted. In Britain, apart from some isolated statutes, the law was sporadically developed by *ad hoc* decisions. Nevertheless, Britain had with 'collective *laissez-faire*' and unemployment insurance legislation a system of industrial relations which proved to be stable for the period from 1906 until the 1960s. The same was true for Denmark from the time of the September Agreement in 1899. Both countries showed a possible solution to the social conflicts between employers and employees on the basis of collective organisation, but this solution was based upon the condition that the trade unions did not work actively to replace liberal society by revolutionary socialism.

Germany was closer than other states to providing a solution by state regulation, especially in the field of social insurance. The compromise between the employers and the works councils on works rules (see Ch. 6, above) under the control of public authority was close to tripartism. But labour chambers were not introduced, nor were the collective agreements legally recognised, nor was the bill on *Berufsvereine* (professional associations) accepted.

Some attempts were made by the legislatures to consider the special nature of individual labour relations (see Ch. 1, above). A modest attempt was made in the German Civil Code of 1896, which gave a few general principles on the *Dienstvertrag* (contract of service). Attempts were also made to elaborate a statute on white-collar workers' pay. Belgium produced its law on Contracts of Employment in 1900. The Netherlands followed in 1907 with a comprehensive Act which even included a provision on the binding force of collective agreements. France, under the promising name of a 'Labour Code', introduced a compilation of her statutes on employment in 1910. But none of these was comprehensive.

THE ESTABLISHMENT OF INTERNATIONAL LABOUR LAW

The end of the First World War saw the beginning of a new era. It brought the recognition of international labour law.

Labour law before the First World War had been national law. This did not prevent one state profiting from the experiences of others, nor did it preclude cautious moves towards international agreements on certain points of labour protection. Britain had been the leading nation with protective statutes and the recognition of self-help. Germany had been the forerunner of social insurance.

The development of national protective legislation was, however, always accompanied by complaints by employers that they would suffer disadvantages in international competition with employers of those countries which had less or no protective labour law. The most striking example was the French decree of 1848 on the 10-hours working day which was promulgated by the provisional government and then abrogated after only five months because of the argument that it would be impossible to conclude an international treaty on this question.

The international unification of protective labour law was, therefore, the natural aim of all who wanted to ameliorate the lot of the working classes. As early as 1818 Robert Owen, the pioneer of British socialism, carried his campaign to end the exploitation of 'human resources', particularly children, into Europe and presented a petition to the Five Powers then meeting at the Congress of Aix-la-Chapelle, appealing to them to regulate working hours throughout the Continent. His petition was dismissed, although the cause was later taken up by Blanqui, Le Grand and Frey. But it was not until the end of the nineteenth century that the movement gained any significance.

In 1889 the Swiss government suggested to the other powers that a diplomatic conference be held at Berne, with the aim of determining a basis for an international agreement on work in factories. But the German Emperor, Wilhelm II, wanting to emphasise his own innovations in social matters, pre-empted the Swiss by calling an international conference for the study of matters affecting the working class in Berlin on 15 March 1890. Fourteen states participated. A problem was that there had been insufficient preparation for such an important conference. Austria, Belgium, Spain, the Netherlands and Portugal were represented by civil servants alone; Germany by civil servants and two employers. France and Britain were the only countries to include worker representatives in their delegations. Nevertheless, the adoption of the following principles on international law was recommended: no women and no children under 14 years of age in southern countries or under 16 elsewhere were to work in mines; children under 14 years of age were to work a maximum of 6 hours a day; children and young persons from 14 to 16 years of age were not to work on Sundays, at night, or in any industry which constituted a danger to the health; the maximum number of hours worked by young persons was to be 10; women were not to work at night and their hours were to be limited to 11 per day; they were also to have a guarantee of one day off per week, if possible Sunday, and post-natal maternity leave for 4 weeks. The Member States attending the conference were to make provision for sufficient inspectors, and they also had to provide for the information of other Member States copies of their new laws on workers protection, the reports of their factory inspectorates and any data resulting from their work.

During the Universal Exhibition in Paris an international congress was organised, on 25 July 1900, to discuss the legal protection of workers, and in 1901 an International Association for Workers' Statutory Protection was formed in Basle. The International Association set out as its aims the encouragement of state intervention and led to the creation of an International Labour Office in Basle, a scientific institute based on the principle of strict political neutrality, which gave information on workers' protection. The Office was at first funded by the Association, but later it increasingly had financial support from the governments of Switzerland, France, the Netherlands, Belgium, the USA, Germany, Austria, Italy and (from 1900) Britain. In 1913 more than three-quarters of the budget came from these governments.

National branches of the Association were formed in the various European countries, with regular congresses held on specific aspects of social protection. At the Cologne Congress in 1902 it was agreed that legislation was necessary, first, to prohibit the employment of women at night in industry and, second, to prohibit the use of white phosphorous in the manufacture of matches and the prohibition of the use of white lead carbonate. It was resolved to request the Swiss Confederacy to call an international conference with the aim of adopting an international convention on these problems. This led to the Berne Conference of 1905–06, which resulted in the signing of two international treaties, one prohibiting the use of white phosphorous in the manufacture of matches (accepted by fourteen nations) and the other prohibiting the employment of women on night work in industry (accepted by seven nations).

The activities of the International Association were supported by the international treaty on workers' protection between France and Italy (1904) and the Swiss resolution on social insurance which made no distinction on nationality, residence or domicile but applied the law of the location of the enterprise. International treaties were concluded by Germany, France, Belgium, the Netherlands and Luxembourg on insurance of workers' accidents. An international conference at Washington (1906) worked out an international convention prohibiting night-work for women. It left the execution to the national governments but obliged them to inform the other countries on whether they had done so and to give periodical reports on the operation of the law. The British government had wanted to set up an international commission which was to be responsible for the organisation of future conferences and for the interpretation of international treaties for workers' protection in the case of disputes, but this proposal was not supported by the other governments at the time.

It took longer for the trade unions to create international organisations, although they were connected with political parties and thus were involved in the activities of the international working-class movement. The Scandinavian unions organised the first international trade union meeting in 1901. At the next meeting at Stuttgart (1902) the German General Commission of the Free Trade Unions was charged with organising an International Central Office of Trade Unions with Karl Legien as International Secretary (from 1903). In 1913 the International Federation of Trade Unions was formally founded at Zurich with an office in Berlin. But this new co-operation ended with the outbreak of the First World War, when workers joined the patriotic front in their own countries and disappointed all who had looked to international socialism as a bulwark against war.

But half way through, attitudes changed. The length of the war, the bitter suffering, the doubts as to the validity and the aims of the war and a revival of international solidarity help to explain why the international activities of the trade unions re-emerged, although separately for the Entente Powers and the Central Powers. The representatives of the trade unions of the Entente met at a conference at Leeds in 1916 and elaborated a resolution which demanded the realisation of fundamental claims of the workers in the World Peace Treaty. The conferences of the representatives of the trade unions of the Central Powers at Berne in October 1917 agreed and improved upon this programme. The charter received its final form in the Manifesto of the International Trade Union Conference at Berne in February 1919.

Germany adopted the ideas of the Berne Conference of 1917 in its draft of international labour law as part of the World Peace Treaty of January 1919, but this was rejected. The Entente Powers established a commission with representatives of their trade unions. Finally, the Versailles Treaty partially accepted in Article 427 the proposals of the international conferences but met severe criticism from the International Trade Union Congress of July 1919, which considered the provisions of the Treaty of Versailles as insufficient.

Article 427 of the Treaty of Versailles declares the following 'methods and principles' to be of special and urgent importance:

> First—The guiding principle above enunciated that labour should not be regarded as a commodity or article of commerce.
>
> Second—The right of association for all lawful purposes by the employed as well as by the employers.
>
> Third—The payment to the employed of a wage adequate to maintain a reasonable standard of life, as this is understood in their time and country.
>
> Fourth—The adoption of an 8-hour day and of a 48-hour week as the standard to be aimed at where it has not already been attained.
>
> Fifth—The adoption of a weekly rest of at least 24-hours, which should include Sunday wherever practicable.
>
> Sixth—The abolition of child labour and the imposition of such limitations on the labour of young persons as shall permit the continuance of their education and ensure their proper physical development.
>
> Seventh—The principle that men and women should receive equal remuneration for work of equal value.
>
> Eighth—The standard set by law in each country with respect to the conditions of labour should have due regard to the equitable economic treatment of all workers lawfully resident therein.
>
> Ninth—Each state should make provisions for a system of inspection in which women should take part, in order to ensure the enforcement of the laws and regulations for the protection of the employed.

Although the Treaty of Versailles declared that this enumeration was neither complete nor final, the International Trade Union Congress of July 1919 complained that it was silent on the following points:

—all demands on school education
—the exemption of women from work on Saturday afternoons
—maternity pay
—the regulation or prohibition of home-work and the inspection of home industry
—the general suppression of restrictions on immigration
—the restriction of the working day in workshops with unhealthy conditions and the prohibition of the use of poisonous substances
—the immediate enactment of the 8-hour working day and of the 48-hour week, and the amendment of the weekly rest of 24 hours to 36 hours
—the acknowledgment of the right to organise by embodying this in statute form and the guarantee of wages which ensured a secure standard of life.

But it was not only the deviation from their substantial demands of which the trade unions complained but also the declaration of their aims to be only 'methods and principles'. The trade unions had wanted to create international law, and this had been also the sense of their organisational demands. In the proclamation 'to all workers of all countries' the Berne Conference of February 1919 demanded the establishment of an International Parliament of Labour, in which delegations from all countries and of all professions should be represented: 'This international parliament should not produce international conventions without legal effect but international statutes which should have the same effect as national statutes on their ratification.' An international legislative power and international sovereignty was sought. The concrete demand was for the establishment of an International Labour Office as a part of the League of Nations with a permanent commission equally composed of representatives of Member States of the League of Nations and of the International Federation of Trade Unions. Annual conferences for the promotion of international labour protection were also called for, half of each conference's members to be representatives of the trade unions of the participating countries. The conference should be able to make decisions of binding force within the area of its competence.

The Treaty of Versailles, however, while establishing an International Labour Organisation and accepting the principle of annual conferences, provided that half the representatives were to be drawn from governments, one quarter from the employers' side and the remaining quarter from the employees' side. The idea of an international parliament and of supranational law-making bodies was rejected. Drafts of conventions required the approval of two-thirds of the delegates and had to be ratified by the Member States in order to be binding. A weak form of control through a complaints procedure which could be initiated by any member to the International Labour Office, was introduced. A control commission could be established, the report of which could be published. When the proposals of the commission were not accepted, there was the possibility of submitting the case to the permanent tribunal of the League of Nations, which could decide according to its discretion and could recommend economic sanctions. While the trade unions had demanded structural changes, the institutions adopted were a compromise between the protection of national sovereignty and the idea of international labour law.

But even in the moderate form of Article 427 of the Treaty of Versailles a fundamental step had been taken. The fundamental rights of the workers became the new foundation of labour law. It was a step towards a new understanding, the beginning of a new era. But all the legal difficulties which are connected with the realisation of the fundamental social rights had already appeared. The resolution of Leeds of 1916 had put forward the principle of the right to work: 'Every workman, no matter to which nationality he may belong, ought to have the right to work where he can find employment'. The 1917 Berne Conference was already more cautious where the freedom of migration was concerned. Prohibitions on emigration and immigration should not be permissible, but there were to be exceptions allowing states to impose temporary restrictions in times of economic depression 'in order to protect native labour as well as alien immigrant labour' and controls and temporary restrictions of immigration in order to protect national health. The German counter-proposal to the Treaty of Versailles added the demand 'of a certain minimum proficiency in reading and writing' in the national language. Article 427 of the Treaty of Versailles then left it to the discretion of individual states whether to place foreign workers under its protective legislation. Workers who legally stayed in the country should, however, be assured of equal economic treatment.

Although the demands of the workers had not been fulfilled, the international activities promoted national legislation and also helped to intensify bilateral arrangements. During the first four years after the ratification of the Treaty of Versailles, the conventions of Washington (1919) on unemployment and on the employment of pregnant women and the convention of Geneva on the right of rural workers to organise stimulated national legislation. The world economic crisis meant a step backwards. Nazi Gemany withdrew from the International Labour Organisation and the League of Nations in 1934.

THE DEMOCRATIC STATES AND LABOUR LAW

When the situation of labour law in the European states, other than Nazi Germany and fascist Italy, between the two World Wars is compared with that of labour law before the First World War, two points may be made. Although there was strong political pressure caused by the successful Russian October Revolution, no revolutionary changes in the social order were made. National labour law remained in the same path of development as before the First World War but approached greater uniformity than had existed before the war.

The First World War posed the question of whether the European nations would return to a liberal economy or whether 'war socialism', as the Germans called their planned economy during the war, would lead to nationalisation or *Sozialisierung* (socialisation).

In Britain the decision was against nationalisation. In 1921 the government gave back full control of the coal-mines to the owners who at once proposed drastic wage reductions. The miners rejected the proposals and were locked out. A general transport strike in sympathy with the miners was threatened. The government declared a state of emergency under an Emergency Powers Act which had been hastily introduced in 1920 during an earlier stage of the miners' dispute. The leaders of the transport unions gave way on what became known as 'Black Friday', 15 April 1921. By June the miners had been starved into submission. In 1926 the story was repeated with major repercussions for labour relations until 1939. After the government withdrew a subsidy from the coal industry and wage cuts were proposed, the miners were locked out. There followed the General Strike of May 1926. The Baldwin (Conservative) government regarded this as an attack on constitutional government and mobilised all the resources of the armed forces, police and volunteers from the middle classes to break the strike. This they succeeded in doing after nine days; but it took another six months before the miners were forced by hunger to return to work. The strike gave the government the excuse to introduce its Trades Disputes and Trade Unions Act 1927, which made illegal general and sympathetic strikes, restricted picketing, prevented civil servants from belonging to unions with outside affiliations and upset the financial basis of trade unionists' support for the Labour Party (see Ch. 5, above). The so-called moderate trade unions and labour leaders were in the ascendant against the more radical, left-wing elements and they entered into a period of collaboration with the employers and governments. In particular, the series of conferences, presided over alternatively by Sir Alfred Mond (the employers' leader) and Ben Turner (president of the Trades Union Congress) were regarded as the beginning of a new period of co-operation by industry, the counterpart of political collaboration by some former labour leaders in the National government from 1931. The ideas of guild socialism and nationalisation receded into the background until a Labour government came to power in 1945.

In Germany the November 1918 Revolution had swept away the monarchies and with them the old state authorities. The revolutionary workers' and soldiers' councils had captured power. The new authority, the Council of the People's Commissioners, assigned to itself the task of realising a socialist programme, but at the conclusion of its proclamation of 12 November 1918 the council said, 'The government will maintain proper production and grant protection against infringements of private property as well as protecting the freedom and security of the individual'. The first parliamentary German Reich government maintained this ambiguous position. It characterised socialisation as one of its legislative intentions on 5 March 1919. A framework Act on socialisation was promulgated on 23 March 1919 which authorised the Reich by legislation, with fair compensation, to transfer economic enterprises ripe for socialisation into the *Gemeinwirtschaft* (common economy). But the practical results were thin. Special Acts on the coal, potash and electricity industries only created compulsory cartels. Socialisation was later abandoned after two years' civil strife, which resulted in the defeat of the Communist Party. In the Netherlands revolutionary plans in November 1918 failed. But the Christian-Democratic Minister of Labour, Aalberse, felt himself 'whipped up to hard work by a forceful monsoon' and within two years an impressive number of labour and social security statutes was passed by Parliament.

The end of the long fight for the 48-hour working week brought another bitter disappointment for the workers. This demand had been a central demand of the international workers' movement for decades. But the expected international victory was not reached. Indeed, different compromises in the various countries were reached which reflected the strength of the workers and their economic situation in the particular countries.

The workers won political rights. Universal suffrage (for males) was achieved in all states. This opened up for workers the possibility of taking advantage of their voting strength. But this increase in political power was off-set by splits in the workers' parties, at first because of their different attitudes towards the First World War (as in Germany) and then, towards the Russian October 1917 Revolution which led to the establishment of communist parties. The German Social Democratic Party participated in many Cabinets of the Weimar Republic. In Britain the Labour Party formed minority governments on two occasions (1924 and 1929). In 1931 MacDonald, Snowden and Thomas deserted the Labour Party to join a National government. The Labour Party gradually revived and entered the War Cabinet in 1940. The party took power on its own in 1945. It is significant that despite its political influence in the period after 1926, the Labour and trade union leadership in Britain did not seek legal measures such as the protection of job security or the legal enforceability of collective agreements, bearing in mind the general weakness of the labour movement.

In the democracies of Continental Europe, on the other hand, there were important measures in relation to unemployment and job security (see Ch. 5, above), the effect of which was to integrate the trade unions into the legal systems of these countries. Other steps in this direction were the growing use of compulsory arbitration (e.g. Germany before 1933 and France after 1936) and the selection of the 'most representative trade unions' (see Ch. 6, above). In general, however, the development of labour law was not different in principle from that in the time before the First World War. It was generally peaceful and gradual in the Netherlands and Luxembourg and also in Belgium. In Britain and in Denmark the system of collective *laissez-faire* proved its stability. But even Weimar Germany and France did not change fundamentally. In Germany during the first fortnight after the November 1918 Revolution the former pre-liberal labour law on domestic and agricultural workers and the restrictions on the right to associate and to assemble were swept away. This and the re-enactment of protective labour law was effected by the proclamation of the People's Commissioners of 12 November 1919. The Stinnes-Legien Agreement of 15 November 1918 laid down the basis for the labour law of the Weimar Republic and the decree of the Council of the People's Commissioners of 23 November 1918 provided that collective agreements were to have immediate and compulsory effect on individual employment contracts. After that the Weimar Constitution gave a number of unfulfilled promises (see Ch. 6, above). Certainly, the Constitution opened the way for a new understanding of labour law by the acceptance of the 'right to organise' (Art. 159), by the protection of the freedom of opinion against all holders of social power, including the employer (Art. 118) and by the development of the type of fundamental social rights which included the 'right to work' in a very restricted form (Art. 163). It advocated general international minimum standards of social rights for the entire working class (Art. 162). There was also new support for the tendency towards state regulation, especially by the labour courts, by the enlargement of social security and by the compulsory arbitration of industrial disputes. But the complete integration of labour law into the state system was not achieved.

The power of the state remained. The defeat of the strike of *Beamte* of the Reich Railways in 1924 marked the failure of the efforts to terminate the special status of the *Beamte* as a group of workers because during the economic crisis the *Beamte* themselves were interested in maintaining their special protection against dismissal. The state with the Technischer Notdienst (Technical Aid Service) which had emerged out of the army, acquired an important weapon which could be used against strikes which threatened the vital interests of the nation, going much further than the Emergency Powers Act of 1920 in Britain. During the years of the world economic crisis, the Reich President by using his emergency powers readjusted wages which had been fixed by collective agreements. At the end of the Weimar Republic the power structure in labour relations had again changed in favour of the state. The authority of the state, which had been destroyed in 1918, was restored and was even less under parliamentary control than before the First World War. In general, Germany had restructured its pre-war industrial system and accomplished it in forms which had been designed before 1914.

France provides further confirmation that the improvement of the workers' situation after 1918 did not substantially alter the former social and economic power structure. The strength of the French employers even survived the alliance between state and trade unions. In 1936 the Socialist and Communist parties had agreed a pact of unified action (the so-called 'Popular Front') which won them the elections of 1936. Numerous strikes and the occupation of factories followed before the new government, under Léon Blum, was formed. The employers asked the government for mediation and agreed with the trade unions the Matignon Agreement, which became the basis of collective agreements and fulfilled the demands of the workers for more wages, paid annual leave and the 40-hour working week. Special demands were the stabilisation of working conditions by collective agreements, recognition of trade unions, the election of workers' representatives and protection against arbitrary dismissals. The social legislation introduced paid annual leave and the 40-hour working week, increased the salaries of the public servants, prolonged obligatory school instruction, changed the organisation of the Bank of France, nationalised the armaments industry and established a plan for public works. A statute of 24 June 1936 on collective agreements provided for obligatory inclusion of provisions on the freedom to organise, the election of workers' representatives in workshops with more than ten persons to supervise safety regulations and to submit demands to the management, regulations on minimum wages, leave and training of apprentices. But this success did not last. After Léon Blum's resignation (1937) the resistance of the employers, the flight of capital and the outbreak of war in 1939 led to the abolition or at least suspension of the new labour Acts.

The government ordered the compulsory evacuation of occupied factories and obliged striking workers to do service, especially during the general strike of July 1938. After the outbreak of the Second World War the government took over the control over the economy, prolonged the working week, reduced wages and replaced the elected workers' representatives by persons who were appointed by the employer. The abolition of most of the important fundamental rights and even the internment of suspected persons without trial took place even before the very same parliament which had a considerable majority of Popular Front deputies authorised Field Marshal Pétain to elaborate a new constitution.

THE TOTALITARIAN STATES AND LABOUR LAW

During the period 1922 to 1945 totalitarian systems were established: the Fascist government in Italy with Mussolini as head and *duce* (leader) from 1922, the Nazi government with Hitler as Reich Chancellor and *Führer* (leader) in Germany from 1933 and the government of Field Marshal Pétain in France from 1940. The war had been the common root of all of them: the political disappointment of the masses and the incapacity to master the shift to a peace economy in Italy, the deep humiliation of the Treaty of Versailles together with inflation and world economic crisis in Germany and the rapid and complete military collapse of France in 1940. All three totalitarian states had a broad negative common basis: they were against both individualism and collectivism, against class struggle, strikes and lockouts, against democracy and equality. Their new common values were social peace, an irrational feeling of community, of the *Volkesgemeinschaft* (national community) as it was said in Germany, and the transfer of the principle of leadership and élitism from politics to economic life and to labour relations. All three systems abolished the traditional separation between the economy and labour relations. There remained considerable distinctions, which did not arise only from the different periods during which the systems were able to develop: Italy had about twenty-three years, Germany twelve years and France four years. It was also the question of the historic conditions they found: Mussolini and Hitler were each the heads of a strong movement with radical members trained in and for civil war, numerous enough to achieve success in the democratic elections before the capture of power. Thus the Fascists and the Nazi Party could be used to take over the state machinery to achieve their aims. Vichy-France, thus called after the residence of President Pétain in the non-German-occupied France, did not have this strong backing of a party. Power was based on the personal authority of Marshal Pétain and on the German support for his use of the state machinery. The common position of the totalitarian system may be described by the words of Mussolini in his speech of 22 April 1930: 'Syndicalism cannot be the aim in itself; either it is developed to political socialism or to the fascist corporation'. Hitler would have added the words 'or it disappears'. All the totalitarian systems shared the belief that it was impossible to have or to keep a system of economic liberalism and social protection. The alternative could therefore only be a new social order. They furthermore agreed that labour relations should be integrated into an economy which was also put under the law of harmony and no longer of competition. But the countries developed in different ways. Italy and France tried to establish a complete new social order in their Charters of Labour, the Italian *Carta del Lavoro* (Charter of Labour) of 21 April 1924 and the French *Loi Relative à l'Organisation Sociale des Professions* (Law Relating to the Social Organisation of Professions) of 4 October 1941. The German *Gesetz zur Ordnung der nationalen Arbeit* (Act to Order National Labour) of 20 January 1934 was basic but not as comprehensive. It was evidently not to be the final form of organisation of the labour relations but was to permit flexibility. Nevertheless, it provided the basic structure of the new system.

A comparison of the three systems may be based upon four main points: the maintenance or non-maintenance of separate organisations of the employees or the employers; the freedom to organise; the structure of the new organisations; the regulation of wages. In Italy Edmondo Rossoni, the creator of the fascist trade unions, originally wanted to establish mixed associations in each branch of the economy. But the only attempt was made in agriculture and this collapsed in particular due to the opposition from the employers. A long fight then ensued between the fascist trade unions and the socialist trade unions, in which the former supported by the government became superior and were recognised by the Confederation of Industrial Employers. In the Vidoni Palace Pact (so-called from the place where the Fascist Party had its headquarters) concluded between Rossoni and the Confederation of Industrial Employers in 1925 the fascist trade unions were recognised to be the exclusive representatives of the workers and the

Confederation of Industrial Employers as exclusive representative of the employers, and the employers promised to make no agreements with their workers except through the fascist unions. The internal commissions, elected by the workers, were to be abolished (as was the right to strike) and their powers were transferred to local syndicates (the term by which the fascist unions were described). This abolition was legalised by a decree-law of 15 November 1925, and the principles of the new 'Syndicalist State' were embodied in the Act of 3 April 1926 and the regulation of 1 July 1926.

According to these legislative measures, only one organisation of employers or employees could be legally recognised by the government for each trade in a city or town. All the employers' associations for a particular trade were to belong to a national federation, with a parallel national federation of employees' unions. These federations in turn belonged to national confederations. The government drew up the *statuti* (charters) to regulate the activities of these organisations and could modify or annul their decisions; their officials, often appointed and removed by the Fascist Party itself from above, had to give an 'undoubted guarantee of national loyalty'; and the government could withdraw recognition as it considered necessary, without any appeal. The Act of 3 April 1926 also provided for the organisation of the professional classes and public officials, authorised by the government and controlled by the Fascist Party.

These authorities were endowed with authority to fix wages and other conditions of labour. They were a preliminary step towards the Corporative State, in which the employers' and employees' organisations were combined with higher units, the corporations which discussed and decided the problems of production. The 'mixed syndicate' (of employers and employees) was only vaguely referred to in the law of 3 April 1926. The regulation of 1 July 1926 gave the name 'corporations' to the central co-ordinating organs with a common upper hierarchy which were to be created to conciliate differences, encourage production, found labour exchanges and regulate apprenticeship. A Ministry of Corporations was established, and on 21 April 1937 the Grand Council of Fascism, the supreme organ of the Fascist Party, promulgated the Charter of Labour or the 'Declaration of the Rights and Duties of the Producer'. The corporations were described as the 'unifying organs of the factors of production and represent the interests of the latter as a whole'. They were recognised by law as 'organs of the state' and could issue rules binding on capital and labour; there could be no recourse to the labour court until the corporative organ had exhausted efforts for conciliation; these organs controlled the labour exchanges and supervised safety laws. The opening words of Article 3 of the Charter stated that 'organisation by trades and professions was free' but immediately went on to give a monopoly of representative functions to those organs which were recognised by the state. In truth, organisations could not be formed or operate without the authority of the Fascist Party. Although Article 3 declared that wages were not to be fixed by general rules but by negotiation, in practice in May and October 1928, in November 1930 and 1934, wages were reduced under general rules.

Article 4 declared that the 'collective labour agreement gives concrete expression to the principle of solidarity by reconciling conflicting interests between employers and employees and subordinating them to the higher interests of production'. In practice the 'negotiation' of agreements concerning wages, hours, disciplinary sanctions, and so on, was carried out by the appointed officials of the organisations at provincial level or in Rome; there was no local negotiation. Agreements had to be approved by the provincial prefect or the Minister of Corporations. As soon as promulgated it was binding on every employer and employee whether or not belonging to the official organisations. It was a completely hierarchical system.

By an Act of 20 March 1930, the National Council of Corporations under Mussolini's direct control was created to perform what were called 'pre-legislative functions'. In 1931 it was divided into several subordinate sections, each covering a different sector, and having the task of giving advisory opinions on economic and social matters, including the recognition of organisations. Unlike the advisory labour councils of various kinds which existed in the democratic countries the representatives were not freely chosen, and the Fascist Council of Corporations could not even make its opinions known to the public against Mussolini's wishes. On occasions when the Council gave advice against the employers' interests, it was ignored. All decisions were in effect in the hands of the Grand Council of Fascism, the National Directorate of the Party, the Council of Ministers and, ultimately, of Mussolini.

Although in a famous speech on 14 November 1933 Mussolini declared that 'the capitalistic method of production is out of date', and that he was 'taking a new and decisive step in the path of revolution', he informed his audience that private enterprise would continue to control production and distribution under the 'supervision of the state'. In 1934 twenty-two corporations were established. Their councils were composed of officials of the national federations together with experts and representatives of the Fascist Party. Each corporation had the task of giving advice to the public administration, conciliating labour disputes, determining wages which became binding only after approval of the National Council and Mussolini and formulating rules regarding 'economic relations and the discipline of production'. While Mussolini had declared that 'the doctrine of *laissez-faire*, the theoretical basis of capitalism' was 'out of date', he had in truth suppressed only the *laissez-faire* of labour by suppressing strikes and autonomous unions and the creation of tame organisations under the direct control of the Fascists.

In Germany the National Socialist Party from the beginning stood in severe opposition to the traditional workers' movement which was organised by the social democrats and the communists. Unlike the Italian Fascists, the Nazis could not succeed in establishing their own powerful trade union. This was one of the reasons why the trade unions and the works' councils were dissolved. They were real or possible power centres of the parties of the Left. Nor was there a place for the employers' organisations. They and the trade unions were, as Rossoni had originally planned in Italy, replaced by a combined organisation of the employees and of the employers, the Deutsche Arbeitsfront (German Labour Front), the federation of the workers of the 'hand and of the brain', as it was called. The German Labour Front was affiliated to the Nazi Party. Membership was voluntary but there was in fact a strong *de facto* pressure to join. The German Labour Front had no legal power to establish employment conditions. This regulation became the task of newly established state officials (from 1933). The *Treuhänder der Arbeit* (trustees of labour) either extended the old collective agreements or made *Tarifordnungen* (collective regulations). The trustees of labour could hear an appeal when a majority of the members of the 'councils of trust' claimed that the decision of the 'leader' of the plant did not comply with the economic or social conditions of the plant. This was not the only supervision of the employers by the state. The employers were integrated into the new economic system which used the former cartels to establish state branches of industry in a planned economy. There was state control of wages. However, enterprises established a system of workshop benefits when unemployment disappeared and there was demand for labour because of the enlargement of the army and the rebuilding of a huge armaments industry. While the workers were controlled by means of the *Arbeitsbücher* (work-books), in which all changes of employment had to be registered, the employers were controlled by the German Labour Front and by the *Ehrengerichte* (courts of social honour), which could pronounce disciplinary sanctions including even the loss of the power to control the plant.

The Nazi system was a method of complete control and integration of all individuals and all groups, and they justified it by the ideology of the *Volkesgemeinschaft* (national community). It included in political and labour relations vigorous racial discrimination against the Jews, and sex discrimination which excluded women from equal work. During the war the system developed into a gigantic exploitation of forced labour performed by inmates of concentration camps—the prisoners of war and the so-called *Fremdarbeiter* (conscripted foreign workers). This was not simply an exceptional development required by the exigencies of the Second World War but the consequence of a system which extended the Nazi ideology of élitism to the Germans as the 'master-race'. The organisation of the economy had not been definitive. In 1935 the skilled workers were reorganised in chambers and regional organisations. At first compulsory cartels were created. The *gewerbliche Wirtschaft* (trade economy) was organised by the Reich Economy Minister and established two organisational forms: the chambers on three levels with the Reich Economy Chamber as the head, and the industrial groups, with Reich groups, economy groups, special groups and special sub-groups. They had a dual function: to represent the interests of the members and to regulate those interests in relation to the state interest. Thus the principle of self-administration was transferred to the planned economy. The employers were doubly represented: in the German Labour Front and, as entrepreneurs, in this organisation of the trade economy. The German Labour Front became occupied with welfare functions such as giving legal aid, taking care of professional training and especially administering leisure-time organisations like Kraft durch Freude (Strength by Joy) or humanisation of labour organisations like Schönheit der Arbeit (Beauty of Labour).

The French Vichy Charter of Labour, with mixed social committees, was closer to Italian corporativism than National Socialism, but the professional syndicates of both sides were less significant than in the Italian model. Their functions were few and mainly consisted of the supervision and representation of members and of the transmission or execution of corporative decisions (Art. 14). In general the French system is reminiscent of the German system of councils as it had been projected by Article 165 of the Weimar Constitution. The institution at the first (workshop) level was the old *conseil d'entreprise* and all the *comités mixtes sociaux* were modelled on those councils, but now within a hierarchical system and with the liquidation of the trade unions. (An underground unified trade union movement became a key part of the Resistance.) The social works committees were supervised by the local social committees. The local, and above them the regional and the national social committees, consisted of the employers, manual and white-collar workers, and the other categories of employees (e.g. the employees with managerial functions and engineers).

It was the reappearance of an old idea which had been already proposed in 1848 in Germany that 'factory councils' should be established consisting of two groups of workers, one member for each separate group of factory workers, one supervisor of each group, both types of representatives to be elected by the workers and the owner of the factory (or his substitute). In Vichy France the composition was equal. The social committees beyond the workshop were organised in professional groups. The committees could establish commissions to which qualified members of the syndicates could also be called. The task of the local social committees consisted of the discussion of questions of salaries and collective agreements, of vocational training, the elaboration of norms on recruitment and of giving notice, of health and safety measures (Art. 31). They could also deal with the security of employment, insurance and pensions, mutual help and support, and family aid. The national social committee served as a means of centralisation and organisation and had to approve the general professional regulations, especially on health matters and job security. The decisions of the lower social committees could be overridden by the higher ones, which also determined their composition. In the national social committees the direct influence of the state was felt by the existence of a State Commissioner appointed by the Secretary of Labour.

In the countries occupied by Germany during the Second World War the trade unions were seen as possible centres of political resistance and were dissolved. The Germans postponed definite solutions to labour organisation until the end of the war, being interested in using the economy for their own purposes during wartime. The Netherlands, which had been put under German civil government, was no exception. In the Netherlands the Germans prohibited the reduction of wages and ordered the four state mediators who had been nominated under the Labour Disputes Act of 1923 to constitute themselves as the National Board of Government Mediators, the College van Rijksbemiddelaars. The Board was authorised to issue binding wage orders whenever collective bargaining and mediation had no results. Between May 1940 and October 1942 when the Board was dissolved by the Germans, the Board developed guidelines of a wage policy such as the socially essential minimum wage needed to maintain an average worker's family, the substitution of collectively bargained wages by compulsory wage orders in a variety of cases and the prohibition on wage incentives in order to recruit employees. The principle was incorporated into post-war legislation when the poor economic situation caused the government to maintain a tough wage policy which was laid down in the Extraordinary Decree on Labour Relations of 1945. This decree was intended as an emergency measure but in fact regulated Dutch wage policy until far into the 1960s.

THE SECOND WORLD WAR AND LABOUR LAW

The Second World War brought similar problems to those of the First World War, but now in a more concentrated form in Britain, the only European country where the labour relations of a free society had not been crushed by the totalitarian régimes. The labour leaders joined Churchill's War Cabinet, and Ernest Bevin, a leading trade unionist, became Minister of Labour. The wartime emergency led to a prohibition on strikes and lockouts (this lasted until 1951) and legislation made it compulsory to submit trade disputes to legally binding arbitration. There were severe penalties against unofficial strikers and limitations on freedom of speech, going much further than the restrictions imposed in 1916–18. The significant fact was that these powers were taken with the active consent of the trade union leaders. In a speech to 2,000 union executive delegates on 25 May 1940, Bevin said, 'I have to ask you to place yourselves virtually at the disposal of the state' and the trade unionists agreed. Despite the harshness of the emergency powers, Bevin used his position to raise the wages of the worst-off workers, such as those in agriculture, forced employers to employ medical and welfare staff and to keep permanent contact with workers' representatives, and made it compulsory to engage labour through trade unions or labour exchanges. Under government auspices, management and unions took advantage of new machinery for joint consultation at all levels of industry. Industrial policy was being determined on an increasingly tripartite basis, with unions achieving parity with the employers. Collective bargaining did not disappear, but on the contrary received an impetus from the atmosphere of collaboration, as witnessed by the creation of forty-six new Whitley councils in large industries during the war.

Keynesian ideas were becoming an accepted part of state 'planning'; the institutions of labour were being informally incorporated into the state's apparatus; and the radical, libertarian, egalitarian, even utopian, ideas engendered by the fight against totalitarianism were raising public expectations that the state would play a major role in transforming society at the successful conclusion of the war. At Bevin's insistence the social welfare aim was inserted in the Atlantic Charter (1941), and in 1942 the Beveridge Report on *Social Insurance and Allied*

Services made its appearance, laying the plans for the post-war 'welfare state'. It rested on the principle of 'comprehensiveness', an expression of 'the solidarity and unity of the nation, which in war have been its bulwark against aggression and in peace will be its guarantee of success in the fight against individual want and mischance'. In place of the piecemeal approach which characterised the approach to welfare before the war (see Ch. 3, above) there was to be adequate protection for the entire population against the whole range of social and economic risks. The Report had a profound influence throughout Europe. Labour law and social security were seen as having an integral part to play in giving workers a sense of social justice. This was achieved by the nationalisation measures (coal mines, railways, etc.) by the post-war Labour government, the implementation of the Beveridge proposals and the strengthening of the traditional system of collective *laissez-faire* in labour relations—for example, by the 'fair wages' policy and the *ad hoc* extension of collectively agreed terms and conditions of employment (see Ch. 5, above). Nearly twenty years passed before Britain's post-imperial economic crisis revealed the limitations of this historic compromise between capital, labour and government.

The economic framework was far worse in the continental European countries because the war damage was greater than in Britain and there was the need for public intervention such as the distribution of food and raw materials and especially the rebuilding of the transport system. It was a continuation of the war situation, but power had been removed from the Nazis and their collaborators. The liberation inevitably also meant a shock to the government structure. It was impossible simply to take over the government. There was need for co-operation and, because of the political similarities, there were repetitions of the German Stinnes-Legien Agreement of 1918.

War and post-war development of industrial relations cannot be exhaustively described simply in terms of nationalisation, improvements of social security, the approach to workers' representation within the enterprise and plant, and representation at the national level, or the extension of the right to vote to women. It was more than this, it was the expectation of a new future based upon freedom and the rule of law. The experience of Hitler's policy of eradicating political enemies and suppressing nations, and his system of forced labour, served as an incentive for the establishment of labour relations based on the principles of a free society and a democratic state. International statements such as the Inter-Allied Declaration of St James's Palace of 12 June 1941 (including Britain, Belgium, Luxembourg, the Netherlands and de Gaulle for France) and the Atlantic Charter of 13 August 1941, despite their relatively vague provisions, were the public responses to the challenge of Nazism, which claimed to have achieved a welfare state. There was a new understanding which is revealed by a comparison of the declaration of the aims and purposes of the ILO at the conference at Philadelphia of 1944 and the Treaty of Versailles. Besides reiterating the statement that labour is not a commodity and the recognition of the freedom to associate, there were added, evidently under the influence of Roosevelt's message of 4 January 1941, promising a post-war world based on four 'essential freedoms', the statement that 'All human beings irrespective of race, creed or sex, have the right to pursue both their material well-being and their spiritual development in conditions of freedom and dignity, of economic security and equal opportunity.' The recognition of traditional fundamental rights was thus combined with the recognition of new social rights. This was achieved by the universal declaration of Human Rights, adopted by the General Assembly of the United Nations, of 1948. The list of social rights included the right to social security (Art. 22), the right to work (Art. 23), the right to rest and leisure (Art. 24), the right to a standard of living adequate for the health and well-being of himself and his family (Art. 25), the right to education (Art. 26) and the free right to participate in the cultural life of the community, to enjoy the arts and to share in scientific advancement and its benefits (Art. 27). The declaration did not create international law; it had no legally binding character and remained a programme, at least for the Western world (the states of the Eastern Bloc abstained). But the concrete formulation of fundamental rights was a positive perspective for the future and laid down the basis of other international declarations, of the Italian Constitution of 1948 and of the constitutions of the newly established German states in the American- and French-occupied zones, which enforced the tradition of the Weimar Republic, and in the rejected draft of the French Constitution of 1946. It was a new beginning in a world which became divided between the two great powers, the USA and the USSR, and in which new states emerged from the status of colonies. The answer to the question of whether or how far the opportunities for a new beginning were seized does not, however, belong to the history of labour law. It belongs to contemporary labour law, which is rooted in the experiences of the past.

APPENDICES

APPENDIX I

The Countries: A Short Guide

BELGIUM

Territory

The northern and north-eastern areas of Flanders, Antwerp and Limburg, populated by the Flemings (whose language is Dutch-based), the south-western areas of Hainaut, Namur and Luxembourg, populated by the French-speaking Walloons, and Brabant (in which lies Brussels), with a mixed population, all formed part of the Austrian provinces in the eighteenth century. Following the French Revolution, there was a short-lived Belgian Republic. In 1795 these territories and the independent principality of Liège were incorporated in France, and in 1815 sovereignty was transferred to the Netherlands. After a revolution and secession from the Netherlands in 1830, the European powers guaranteed independence and 'perpetual neutrality' to Belgium. In 1839 the Grand Duchy of Luxembourg was separated from the Belgian province of that name and ceded back to the Netherlands (see LUXEMBOURG). The province of Limburg was similarly divided. In 1920 Eupen and Malmedy and environs were acquired from Germany, and temporarily returned for the period 1940 to 1944.

Constitutional Development

The Constitution of 1831, the most liberal in Europe at the time, proclaimed popular sovereignty, a constitutional monarch with strictly limited powers, and elections with secret (from 1877) ballot to a bicameral parliament. The lower house was directly elected for a four-year term and the senate for an eight-year term. The King could initiate legislation but his acts had to be signed by his ministers. At first suffrage was confined to men over 25 paying a minimum direct tax (less than 10 per cent of the population).

Legal System

The Napoleonic Codes were imposed on Belgium, replacing the confused mixture of customary and Roman law. The 1831 Constitution stated that it was 'necessary' to revise the Codes 'within the shortest period', but this was done only for the Code of Civil Procedure (1876), the Commercial Code

(1872), Criminal Code (1867) and Code of Criminal Procedure (1878). The Civil Code remained unrevised, apart from some articles amended by the legislature. The 1831 Constitution (Art. 107) prohibited the courts from applying decrees and regulations which conflict with the laws, but the courts cannot pass judgment on the constitutionality of laws made by Parliament, acting together with the King. Court decisions are not binding as precedents, but in practice opinions of the Court of Cassation and courts of appeal are of great persuasive value.

Political Parties

Political conflicts were a complex mixture of class, linguistic and religious struggles. Under Spanish rule the territory of present-day Belgium had been forcibly catholicised. The Revolution of 1830 had been supported by the Catholic hierarchy, with a largely rural base, hostile to the Protestantism of the Netherlands, and by the liberal middle-class, whose main following was in the expanding cities, inspired by the ideas of the French Revolution. There were sharp controversies between these groups over issues such as state control of education. The ruling-class in Flemish and Walloon areas spoke a cultivated French and all official and legal business was conducted in French. There was discrimination in all spheres of life against the Flemings. The rise of Flemish nationalism in the nineteenth and twentieth centuries was thus a reaction to class and linguistic oppression. The Catholics and Liberals alternated in office between 1830 and 1884. The Catholics were divided between a Conservative right wing and more democratic left wing. During this period there was a steady rise in working-class consciousness. This was hampered by the illiteracy and degradation of the Belgian workers as well as the powerful influence of Catholicism. Moreover, workers were in many small units of production. The early strike movements, led by bourgeois militants, such as Ducpétiaux, Quetelet, Dehamme, were severely repressed. In 1864 the First International was set up, and Belgian socialists were prominent in it. Although divided between reformist and revolutionary elements, Belgian branches of the International were responsible for 'putting into the minds of the workers clear ideas on the final goals of socialist democracy' (Bertrand, 1907, pp. 238–9). At the same time there was a growth of co-operative and workers' friendly benefit societies. The Belgian Workers' Party (Parti Ouvrier Belge: POB) was formed in 1885 as an alliance of working-class, co-operative and socialist organisations (similar to the British Labour Party two decades later). The central issue to which the POB directed its efforts was the struggle for universal (male) suffrage. The principal tactic was the general strike. After violent clashes in 1886, there were three major political strikes between 1888 and 1893. In 1893 the franchise was granted to every male over 25 years of age but multiple votes were allowed (under different conditions) to heads of households, landlords, shareholders and some holders of university degrees (*capacitaire*). The number of voters rose from 136,707 in 1892 to over 2 million in 1894. The POB entered Parliament and the Liberals lost ground, but the Catholics gained an absolute majority because of their strength in the countryside. Following further strikes in 1903 and 1913, universal male suffrage was granted with effect from 1919. During the First World War Emile Vandervelde, leader of the POB, served in the government. In the 1919 election the POB gained 70 seats, and the Catholics 73 out of a total of 186. A three-party system (Catholics, Liberals, Socialists) emerged with no party able to govern on its own. The Catholic Party had a multi-class base, including workers and employers; the POB was a party of labour; the Liberals were mainly a party of business. POB support (which remained at about 37 per cent in the inter-war years) was mainly in Brussels and the Walloon provinces, but it also had some strength in Flemish cities. Catholic support (between 40 and 45 per cent in the inter-war years) was mainly in Flanders and in the rural areas of the whole country. There were Catholic–Liberal, Catholic–Socialist and tripartite governments, but the Socialists never had the power to effect major social reforms and moved from socialism to Keynesianism. The tripartite government continued in exile in Britain during the Second World War. Despite the defection of Henri de Man, the POB leader, to the Nazis, the vast majority of the Belgian labour movement refused to collaborate with the occupying power, and discussions between the representatives of employers and workers in the underground resistance movement (in which the Communists also played a significant role) laid the basis for the government of national unity established after the war.

Trade Unions

The unions were from the start appendages of the POB, with little separation of trade union business from the suffrage struggles. In 1898 a Trade Union Commission of the General Council of the Workers' Party (Commission Syndicale Section du Conseil Général du Parti Ouvrier) was set up to co-ordinate union activity, but a number of independent unions were unable to associate. The Commission was reconstituted so as to allow election solely from the ranks of unions and following this in 1907 a number of the independent unions joined the Commission which by 1913 had 129,000 members. Anti-socialist Catholic unions were set up from 1886 onwards, mainly in Flanders, and claimed a membership of 15,000 in 1904, and in 1913, 100,000 members, under the auspices of the General Confederation of Belgian Christian and Free Trade Unions (Confédération Générale des Syndicales Chrétiens et Libres de Belgique). The tripartite coalition government of 1918–21 removed a number of obstacles to trade union organisation, and there was massive recruitment with the membership of the Commission Syndicale rising to 600,000 in 1919 and 700,000 in 1920. Membership remained high in the inter-war depression years, partly because of POB-inspired legislation which brought state subsidies to union unemployment funds. In 1937 the Commission Syndicale became formally independent of the POB under the new name of the Belgian General Confederation of Labour (Confédération Général du Travail de Belgique: CGTB). By 1939 the CGTB claimed 550,000 members and the Christian unions 350,000.

BRITAIN

Territory

'Britannia' was the name applied by the Romans to those parts of the British Isles which they occupied. The term 'Britain' (more properly, 'Great Britain') denotes the whole island containing England, Wales and Scotland. This is the larger of the two principal islands of the British Isles, the smaller being Ireland (q.v.). Wales was annexed by the English Crown in 1284 and after 1536 it was integrated into the English parliamentary and local government system (so much so that from 1746 to 1967 the word 'England' in an Act of Parliament was deemed to include Wales). Scotland was an independent kingdom until 1707. In 1603 there was a union of Crowns when James VI of Scotland succeeded to the English throne as James I of England. By the Act of Union of 1707 Scotland lost its own Parliament (although Scots law was not fused with English Law), and the two countries were united as Great Britain. In 1783 the British Parliament relinquished jurisdiction in Ireland, but from 1 January 1801 the separate Irish Parliament was dissolved and Ireland entered into union with Britain as the United Kingdom. From 1 January 1923 when the twenty-six counties of Southern Ireland became the independent Irish Free State, the United Kingdom included only Britain and Northern Ireland. (In this book, unless the context indicates otherwise, the term 'Britain' is used as interchangeable with 'the United Kingdom'.)

Constitutional Development

The largely unwritten British constitution evolved gradually over the centuries. The foundations of central government in England were laid during the medieval period. The Anglo-Norman kings, especially Henry II (1154–89), created the essential central departments of state, notably the Exchequer and the Chancery (the latter headed by the Lord Chancellor) and a centralised system of law courts to develop the English common law and to supervise the unpaid Justices of the Peace, who until the nineteenth century were the main instruments of local government.

During the Tudor period (1485–1603) the supremacy of the central government over the aristocratic landowners and the Church was finally established, and at the same time the idea developed that the Crown was itself subject to the law. Within the legal system, statute law, enacted by the King *in Parliament*, became supreme. The word 'parliament' in origin meant a parley or conference. At first it was applied to the Great Councils of feudal lords summoned by the king; by the thirteenth century it included the summoning of the Commons (representatives of the knights of the shires, citizens of the cities and burgesses of the boroughs) upon whom the King wished to levy taxes. By the end of the fourteenth century the Commons began regularly to elect their own Speaker to present petitions and convey answers to the King and the Lords. The term 'House of Lords' came into existence in the reign of Henry VIII to describe the meetings of the hereditary peers (created by the King) and the bishops. The decisive revolution took place in the seventeenth century when the Commons in alliance with the common law judges successfully resisted the attempts of the Stuart monarchs to place themselves above the common law and the authority of Parliament. The turbulent events included the beheading of one King and the abdication of another, a civil war and a military dictatorship.

After the restoration of the monarchy (1660) and the Glorious Revolution (1688) a new constitutional settlement was reached. The Bill of Rights (1689) put into statutory form many of the limitations on the royal prerogative won by Parliament (e.g. the Crown was forbidden to maintain a standing army, to suspend the laws or to levy taxes otherwise than by Act of Parliament). With the invitation to William of Orange to succeed to the throne (1689) and the Act of Settlement (1701), Parliamentary supremacy and the independence of the judiciary were assured. Executive responsibility remained with the monarch. In the course of the eighteenth century institutions developed to make the executive responsible to Parliament—political parties, the office of Prime Minister and the Cabinet.

The nineteenth and twentieth centuries witnessed the struggles to make Parliament itself democratic. The Reform Act of 1832 (1) redistributed the seats in the House of Commons so as to allow a transfer to the large towns in the north of England from the 'rotten' boroughs which had been disproportionately represented; (2) widened the franchise by amending the property qualifications (increasing the electorate by 50 per cent so that 5 out of every 100 adults had the vote); and (3) provided for registration of eligible voters so as to reduce corrupt practices. With the decline in the money values of property, the number of voters increased to about 1 million by 1866. The Reform Act 1867 (introduced by the Conservatives under Disraeli) reduced the property qualification in the counties, so increasing the county electorate by 50 per cent, but this still did not include agricultural labourers.

In the boroughs working men were enfranchised by the Act of 1867, which gave the vote to every male householder occupying for one year a separate dwelling and paying the poor rate, and lodgers occupying for a period of one year lodgings to the annual unfurnished value of £10. This doubled the electorate to 2 million. Later nineteenth century reforms introduced the secret ballot (1872) and were aimed at eliminating bribery and corruption. The (third) Reform Act 1884 (introduced by Gladstone) extended to the counties the household and lodger franchise, which had been given to the boroughs in 1867; it also remodelled the occupation qualification so that in counties and boroughs a person occupying any land or tenement of an annual value of £10 could vote, and it gave the vote to any domestic servant, such as a gardener, living separately from his employer, but not to one living in, such as a butler. The main effect was to enfranchise agricultural labourers, increasing the electorate to 5 million.

Women obtained the vote in 1918, although only on equal terms with men in 1928. The Representation of the People Act 1918 (introduced by Lloyd George) made other far-reaching reforms, including the substitution of a six months' residence requirement for all the numerous qualifications which then existed, and the removal of the disqualification on receipt of poor relief. The electorate rose to 21 million, and to 28 million in 1928. The 'one person one vote' principle was only fully established (under a Labour government) in 1948.

While the House of Commons is wholly elected, the House of Lords remained wholly nominated, mainly consisting of hereditary peers and of bishops. Although the approval of both Houses is needed for legislation, the Parliament Act 1911 reduced the powers of the Lords to that of delaying measures passed by the Commons.

Legal Systems

The English common law has developed continuously since the reign of Henry II (1154–89) and the first common law courts (King's Bench and Common Pleas) were operating separately from the administrative organs of government in the early thirteenth century. The common law was never codified but was subject to much reforming legislation. Growing rigidity of common law rights and procedures led to petitions to the monarch, which were dealt with by his Chancellor and, by the fifteenth century, a Court of Chancery. During the next 400 years the rules of common law and of equity were developed independently of each other by separate courts. There was a reformist movement in the nineteenth century which led to the Judicature Acts 1873–75 by which the old courts were abolished and replaced by a Supreme Court of Judicature consisting of the High Court and Court of Appeal. These Acts also brought about a fusion of the administration of common law and equity; in cases of conflict the rules of equity were to prevail over the common law. The alliance between the common lawyers and the House of Commons in the seventeenth century guaranteed the pre-eminence of the common law, and at the same time the judicial acknowledgment of the supremacy of Parliament.

Legislation takes precedence over all other sources of law but it is subject to judicial interpretation in the light of common law. The doctrine of precedent plays an essential part in the practice of the courts. The decisions of the House of Lords' judicial committee, the highest court, are binding on all other courts dealing with similar issues; decisions of the Court of Appeal and High Court bind inferior courts. Legal writing is generally not regarded as a source of law. A system of county courts to deal with minor civil cases was established in 1846, replacing earlier local courts and relieving pressure on the higher courts.

Scots law is very different from English law in form and substance, although since Union the systems have influenced each other. Scots law is based on Roman or civil law and rules of canon, feudal or customary origin. Sheriff courts (similar to the English county courts) deal with minor civil cases, and the Court of Session is a superior court of first instance (the Outer House) and a court of appeal (the principal task of the Inner House). The final appeal court for Scots civil cases is the House of Lords.

Political Parties

After 1660 the restored royalist gentry, closely associated with the Church, came to be called 'Tories' (originally an abusive term applied to Roman Catholic outlaws in Ireland). Those landowners who supported parliamentary sovereignty, together with the non-conformist middle class, merchants and businessmen, who opposed a Catholic King and pressed for the liberties of the subject were called 'Whigs' (also orginally an abusive term applied to Presbyterian zealots). In the eighteenth century the Whigs and Tories, each with their own pamphleteers, took on definite form based largely on family and local bonds. It was not until well past the turn of the eighteenth century that cohesive parties (the Liberal Party formed by an amalgamation of Whigs, Radicals and Reformists; the Conservative Party formed from the old Tory Party), with general policies, emerged in Parliament, but even then 'independents' for long had the majority in the House of Commons.

The Reform Act 1832 forced the Whigs and Tories to organise the registration of voters and the conduct of elections; the Act of 1867 gave a decisive impetus to the growth of local party organisations. These were linked by the formation of the National Union of Conservative and Constitutional Associations in 1867, and the National Liberal Association in 1877. The Labour Party was established in February 1900 as the Labour Representation Committee, by delegates of three socialist organisations, the Social Democratic Federation (1881), the Fabian Society (1883) and the Independent Labour Party (1893) together with sixty-four trade union delegates. It was renamed the Labour Party in 1906. Until 1918 membership of the Labour Party was possible only through an affiliated organisation, but thereafter individual membership was possible. Branch organisations were established in every constituency, but the affiliated trade unions were the

Table AI.1 Electoral strength of the British political parties

	Percentage vote (seats in parentheses)					
Party	1885	1906	1910 (Dec.)	1918	1929	1935
Conservatives	43.6 (249)	43.4 (157)	46.6 (273)	39.6 (382)	38.2 (260)	53.7 (432)
Liberals	47.4 (335)	49.4 (400)	44.2 (271)	25.6[a] (163)	23.4 (59)	6.4 (20)
Labour		4.8 (29)	6.4 (42)	21.4 (62)	37.1 (288)	38.6[b] (158)

Notes:
[a] Split between Lloyd George Liberals and Liberals.
[b] Includes four Independent Labour.

Source: Cook and Paxton (1975 and 1978).

dominant force in the Party contributing about five-sixths of the total membership. (The electoral strength of the parties is shown in Table AI.1.)

Trade Unions

The early unions of the eighteenth century arose among journeymen in the craft trades. They were not direct descendants of the medieval guilds, but they retained guild traditions of attempting to regulate the volume of labour supply, access to jobs and distribution of work. After the repeal of the Combination Acts (1824) trade unions came out into the open and grew rapidly. Between 1829 and 1834 there were strikes at a time of rising trade and a revolt of agricultural workers. New and ambitious unions sprang up, including an attempt to build a general union of all trades (Robert Owen's Grand National Consolidated Trades Union). The penal transportation of six Dorset farm labourers (the Tolpuddle martyrs) in 1834 for administering unlawful union 'oaths' was a prelude to a general decline of these unions, and the rise of Chartism, the first independent working-class political movement. Between 1838 and 1842 this movement (whose Great Charter aimed at democratic parliamentary reform) kept the industrial centres in uproar. Although most of its aims were achieved in the next 100 years, Chartism failed as a political movement. By the end of the 1840s (until the 1870s) Britain was entering a period of economic prosperity and important sections of workers were turning from political to industrial action.

From 1850 to 1870 the 'new model' unions, such as the Amalgamated Society of Engineers (ASE), grew. These unions were characterised by their use of the existing law to the extent it would benefit members, the development of self-education of workers, the use of 'conciliation and arbitration', a disinclination to strike and the extensive development of mutual aid (welfare) functions. Adverse judicial decisions, which threatened freedom of association and freedom to strike, led to political activity on the part of the Trades Union Congress, set up in 1868, and this resulted in the legislation (1871–1906) protecting unions.

Labourers' unions came into existence during the wave of 'new unionism' of the late 1880s and early 1890s, and their new industrial methods were signified by the successful dockers' strike of 1889. These new methods led to hostile judicial decisions, in particular the *Taff Vale* case of 1901, which exposed union funds to civil judgments. The response was political: TUC support for the Labour Representation Committee and the restoration of freedom to strike by the Trade Disputes Act 1906. Once this was achieved, the unions turned again to industrial activity, which reached a high point between 1910 and 1914. Union membership increased fairly steadily from 1909 to 1920 when union density reached 45.2 per cent; this was followed by a substantial slump until 1933 when union density was 22.6 per cent; then there was an upsurge reaching 30.5 per cent in 1938, 38.6 per cent in 1945 and 45.2 per cent in 1948.

From the turn of the nineteenth century until well after 1945 the union movement was dominated by a mixture of general, single-industry and craft unions composed overwhelmingly of male manual workers in the main industries created in the nineteenth century. From the First World War onwards there was also a high level of union membership in the public services, with government encouragement.

DENMARK

Territory

The ancient kingdom of Denmark comprises the northern part of the Jutland Peninsula. The Duchies of Schleswig, Holstein and Lauenberg were ceded to Prussia in 1864. In 1920 the northern part of the old Duchy of Schleswig was returned to Denmark and is known as South Jutland.

Constitutional Development

From 1660 to 1849 Denmark was governed by autocratic kings. Constitutional monarchy was introduced in 1849 and the Constitution was amended in 1855, 1863 and 1866. The upper house (Landsting) consisted of some members nominated by the Crown and some indirectly elected. The lower house (Folketing) was directly elected by all men over 30 except servants, farm workers and paupers, in single-member constituencies. Secret ballot was introduced in 1901 and universal adult suffrage in 1915, when the voting age was reduced to 29. The two chambers shared legislative power; executive power was shared by the king and a council of responsible ministers. The Constitutional Charter of 1915 provided that legislative power should be shared by the King and Rigsdag (Parliament). The Landsting was abolished in 1953.

Legal System

The origins of Danish law are Germanic. In 1683 King Christian V enacted a code for all Denmark, the *Danske Lov*, which abolished all previous legislation. This remained the most important source of law, but it was not exhaustive and was casuistic with few general principles, so giving the legal doctrine of writers an important role. Danish law is closely linked to other Scandinavian legal systems.

Political Parties

In the last part of the nineteenth century three political groupings were formed. The Liberal Party (Venstre) was founded in 1870, with traditional liberal aims of free trade and minimum state control. The Right (Højre) consisted of supporters of the autocratic system, the landlords and property owners. In 1915 the Right was formally established as the Conservative People's Party. The Radical Liberal Party formed in 1905 as a result of a split in the Liberal Party was a smallholders' party encouraging private enterprise and social reform. The Social Democratic Party (SDP), founded in 1871, supported evolutionary socialism and had support mainly from industrial and farm workers. In 1916 the SDP joined the government and a Social Democratic Prime Minister was first appointed in 1924. Thereafter, governments were dominated by the Social Democrats. (The electoral strength of the parties is shown in Table AI.2.)

Table AI.2 Electoral strength of the Danish political parties

	Percentage vote (seats in parentheses)				
Party	1884	1901	1913	1918	1939
Conservatives	38.7 (19)	26.0 (8)	22.5 (7)	18.3 (22)	17.8 (26)
Liberals	56.3 (81)	39.4 (76)	28.6 (44)	29.4 (44)	18.2 (30)
Social Democrats	4.9 (2)	19.3 (14)	29.6 (32)	29.4 (39)	42.9 (64)
Radicals			18.7 (31)	21.0 (33)	9.5 (14)

Source: Cook and Paxton (1975 and 1978).

Trade Unions

The ban on strikes and unions formally imposed in 1800 proved to be unenforceable and fell into desuetude after 1851. The unions, formed on a local basis in single branches of industry, grew from the 1880s, and in 1898 a central organisation, the Danish Workers' Confederation (De Samvirkende Fagforbund:—the LO) was formed. During the 1880s and 1890 the employers made several attempts to unite, and in 1896 the Danish Employers' Confederation (DA) was established. After the serious conflict in spring 1899, the September-Forlig of 5 September 1899 established a framework for labour relations. After a further conflict in 1908, the August-Udvalg, a committee established by the Minister of the Interior, recommended the establishment of a permanent arbitration court, standard rules for handling labour disputes and a general conciliation board. These reforms were implemented in 1910 and, apart from the period from 1929 to 1936, when an Act prohibited certain closed shop agreements, a consensual framework characterised Danish labour relations. At least two-thirds of all workers were covered by collective agreements. By 1939 the DA's members employed some 230,000 employees and the 71 trade unions in the central trade union organisation had 515,800 members (with only 27,300 in non-affiliated unions). At that time the percentage of union members among manual workers and salaried employees was estimated to be about 85 per cent.

FRANCE

Territory

The boundaries of France were enlarged during the Revolution and Napoleonic periods. The Congress of Vienna (1814–15) restored most of the pre-Revolution territory. In 1860 Savoy and Nice were acquired from Piedmont. From 1871 to 1918 Alsace and Lorraine were ceded to Germany; during the period from 1940 to 1944 they were temporarily restored to Germany.

Constitutional Development

1789–1848

Following the collapse of absolute government in 1788, the Estates-General, consisting of nobility, clergy and commons, was convened for the first time since 1614. On 17 June 1789 the Third Estate (Commons) declared itself to be the National Assembly and on 9 July 1789, the National Constituent Assembly, which adopted the Declaration of the Rights of Man and the Citizen (27 August 1789) and the Constitution of 22 December 1789. This conferred the franchise on adult males over 25 years of age on the basis of taxation, excluding domestic servants. They elected local councils and chose delegates to elect departmental councillors and deputies to the Assembly. The first legislative Assembly abolished the monarchy in August 1792 and convened the Convention elected on the basis of manhood suffrage. The Constitution of 1793, which provided for direct elections, was never put into operation. The Constitution of 1795 reintroduced indirect elections, delegates being chosen on a property qualification. In 1799 Napoleon introduced a constitution with manhood suffrage and indirect election by list; the Senate was nominated by Napoleon. Electoral colleges (with electors holding office for life) were introduced in 1802. After the final defeat of Napoleon, the restored Bourbon monarchy (1815–30) was constitutional in form and rested on parliamentary government with two chambers, ministerial responsibility and guarantees for individual rights, but the franchise was restricted to a small and wealthy class. Some of the ministers were *grands seigneurs* of the old order, and the Bourbons, who 'had learned nothing and forgotten nothing', were autocratic, ultra-conservative and repressive. The July Revolution of 1830 resulted in the proclamation of a constitutional monarchy under the Duke of Orléans as Louis-Philippe. The revised constitution reflected the ideas of liberalism, lowering the voting age from 30 to 25 years, and the tax qualification for electors from 300 to 200 francs (100 for some professional classes), but even this doubling of the electorate enfranchised only about 1 in 150 of the population, and the possibilities of rigging elections were manifold.

1848–1940

The February Revolution in 1848 caused Louis-Philippe to abdicate. The Provisional Government of the Second Republic was torn between the moderate liberals, who wanted only constitutional parliamentary government, and the radical democrats and socialists, who wanted universal suffrage and social reforms. The government recognised the 'right to work' and gave the vote to every Frenchman over 21 years of age, so increasing the electorate from 200,000 to 9 million. When they voted, the conservative rural small proprietors inflicted a defeat on the radicals and socialists, who won only 100 out of the 876 seats in the Chamber of Deputies. In May 1848 the Blanquists and other social revolutionaries unsuccessfully attempted a coup and opened the way for conservative reaction.

The Constitution of 4 November 1848 provided for direct elections to the National Constituent Assembly by secret ballot by all men over 21 years of age with 6 months' residence (extended to three years in 1850, so reducing the electorate by one-third). Executive power was vested in the President elected for four years by the whole electorate. In March 1852 the President's powers were extended, making ministers responsible to him and giving him the sole right to initiate legislation. In December 1852 the President, Louis Napoleon Bonaparte, became Emperor as Napoleon III. After 1860 in the phase of 'Liberal Empire' he relaxed his autocratic power; in 1869 the legislative body was given the right to elect its own officials and a cabinet system was reintroduced. In 1870, following the surrender of Napoleon III at Sedan to Prussia, a republic was proclaimed with the Provisional Government of National Defence. The Constitution of the Third Republic was defined only in 1875, but only after the suppression of the short-lived Paris Commune of spring 1871. The Constitution of 1875 provided for a bicameral legislature (Senate and Chamber of Deputies, together known as the National Assembly) with executive power invested in the President, who chose the Prime Minister, who in turn chose the ministers. In practice the President's role in law-making and policy was controlled by the Cabinet. Between 1870 and 1934 the Republic had 88 ministries with an average period in office of 9 months. The Senate had 300 members, 75 chosen by the Assembly and the rest indirectly elected by departments. The Chamber of Deputies was elected by universal male suffrage from single-member constituencies (except from 1885 to 1889, when they were multi-member). Bills could be initiated by the government (*projets de lois*)or by private members (*propositions de lois*). The Council of State (presided over by the Minister of Justice) gave its opinion on any question of administration put to it by the government. The Third Republic retained the 1875 Constitution until 1940, when the National Assembly surrendered power to Pétain as 'head of the French state' and an authoritarian régime was set up with Vichy as the capital and Pierre Laval as its leader. The Constitution of the Fourth Republic was adopted in 1946.

Legal System

Prior to the Napoleonic codification, the 'ancient law' differed from province to province and town to town. The southern provinces were influenced mainly by Roman law, while in the North the customs of Gaul and the Germanic tribes were predominant. In addition, the canon law and commercial usages were also important. Royal ordinances and edicts from the end of the seventeenth century were increasingly used to regulate private law and were later used by the drafters of the Codes.

During the revolutionary period many new principles entered the law, such as freedom of contract and freedom of commerce, equality of persons, the paramount right of private ownership, the suppression of 'intermediate' bodies and the secularisation of the civil law. The codification (1804–10) under the personal supervision of Napoleon unified and modernised French law, synthesising Roman law, customary law, canon law, legislation of the monarchy and the new ideas of individualism and liberty. The Civil Code (*Code Civil des Français*, known as the *Code Napoléon* during the first and second Empires) was for the most part restricted to general principles expressed in simple language, leaving the courts a great deal of discretion on matters of detail. It was introduced in many other countries. The Code of Civil Procedure (*Code de Procédure Civil*) dealt *inter alia* with contentious proceedings before tribunals, whose organisation was regulated by special statutes of 1810 and 1883. These tribunals were (1) the *tribunaux de première instance*, each *arondissement* having such a tribunal; (2) the courts of appeal (*cours d'appel*)—one for each *département*—their judgments being called *arrêts*; (3) the Court of Cassation in Paris, which was not a court of second appeals, but could review the decision of a court of appeal for an error of law (the *pourvoi en cassation* going first to the *chambre de requêtes* and then, if allowed, to the *chambre civil*). Apart from these tribunals there were *Juges de Paix* (Justices of the Peace) deciding minor cases, and also commercial tribunals. The *conseils de prud'hommes*, dealing with disputes between employer and employee are described in Chapter 6. In addition to the Codes already mentioned, there was a Commercial Code (*Code de Commerce*), a Code of Criminal Examination (*Code d'Instruction Criminelle*) and a Criminal Code (*Code Pénal*). Work was begun on a *Code Rural* in 1876, and on a *Code du Travail* (Labour Code) in 1910, but these remained uncompleted.

The sources of law were statutes (*lois*), decrees and ordinances (delegated legislation), customs (*coûtumes*) and customary law (*droit coûtumier*). The main sources of the latter are commercial usages and judicial decisions, in particular those of the Court of Cassation. Article 5 of the Civil Code expressly forbids judges to decide cases 'by way of general regulatory disposition', but it is usual for courts to follow decisions of the Court of Cassation and appeal courts, so developing a large number of principles not to be found in the Codes themselves. Special tribunals are concerned with administrative law, the most important being the Conseil d'Étât created in 1800.

Political Parties

Despite the many factions from the period of the Revolution onwards, it took a long time for clearly defined political parties to emerge. The fragmentation into numerous parties riddled with individualism reflected in part the large number of *petits patrons*, some self-employed and some running small workshops and factories and the relative absence of a homogeneous working class.

The deputies often belonged to more than one group and there was little local constituency organisation. Apart from the Conservative Right parties and the various liberal groupings, there was a variety of socialists, who were weak and divided. The Socialist Workers' Party (Parti des Travailleurs Socialistes de France: PTSF), founded by Jules Guesde in 1880, split after three years. The 'Possibilists' under Paul Brousse, who rejected Marxism, set up the Federation of French Socialist Workers (Fédération des Travailleurs Socialistes de France: FTSF) in 1882. The Guesdists reformed themselves as the French Workers' Party (Fédération des Travailleurs Français: POF). Jean Ademaine's faction split from Brousse in 1890 to form the Revolutionary Socialist Workers' Party (Parti Ouvrier Socialiste Revolutionaire: POSR). There were also a number of independent socialist deputies in the Chamber. It was only in 1905 that a united Parti Socialiste Section Français de l'Internationale Socialiste (SFIO) was created.

After the assassination of Jean Jaures, leader of the SFIO, the Party split. Three socialist leaders entered the wartime Cabinet of 'sacred unity' (*union sacrée*). In 1920 the supporters of the Communist International gained control of the SFIO and changed its name to the Parti Communiste Français (PCF), polling 875,000 votes in 1924 and 796,000 in 1932. The SFIO was re-established under its old name and polled 1,690,000 votes in 1924 and 1,975,000 in 1932. A socialist-communist 'unity of action' pact in July 1934, in face of the fascist threat, lead to a reunification of the trade unions (see below), and at the May 1936 elections, a victory for the Popular Front of socialists, communists and radical socialists. The new government imposed the Matignon Agreement on the employers (see below). The new laws provided that disputes about agreements were to be resolved by state arbitration, and in the next few years all but 4 per cent of disputes were dealt with in this way. Zeldin (1979, p. 277) points out that by making labour relations dependent on the state in this way 'the strategy of social conflict was thus fundamentally altered' and 'in 1944–45 . . . it was the state, not the unions, which emerged as the principal challenge to the employers'. These developments were partly due to the composition of the trade unions.

Trade Unions

The Confédération Générale du Travail (CGT) founded in 1895 comprised only a minority of trade union members (of 860,000 unionists in 1906, the CGT claimed only 300,000), most of whom belonged to small provincial unions, and was extremely weak financially. The CGT adopted a revolutionary anarcho-syndicalist policy, independent of the political parties. The leaders advocated economic struggle, particularly through the tactic of the general strike, as a means to end capitalism. They rejected parliamentarianism, and the idea of forming a Labour Party and were not interested in promoting social legislation. Before 1914, organisation was fragmentary and most strikes were spontaneous. The local *bourses du travail* (BDT), established and subsidised by public authorities, encouraged local trade union growth, and a Federation of BDT, formed in 1892, rivalled national organisations and remained separate even after the formation of the CGT. From 1899 onwards, yellow unions (so-called after the yellow flower of broom they adopted as their emblem) assumed some importance in strike-breaking. There were also independent unions founded by Catholics, particularly in Paris and the north from 1887 onwards.

The CGT was transformed as a result of the First World War. Despite the CGT's declaration that it would call a general strike in the event of war, the leaders suddenly espoused patriotism and abandoned revolutionary syndicalism. During the war CGT officials served on government bodies and after the war negotiated and obtained the 8-hour day (1919); they co-operated in securing the social insurance legislation (1928) and participated in government-sponsored activities (*politique de présence*). The BDT became the state-financed employment exchanges. By virtue of the Matignon Agreement of 1936 employers were forced to recognise and negotiate with unions, and the CGT was normally to be considered the 'most representative union' with which agreements were to be negotiated. In the event of failure to agree or disputes about the interpretation of agreements, there was to be government arbitration: in the next few years, 96 per cent of disputes were decided in this way. Union membership rapidly increased from about 1 million to 5 million in 1936, only to fall again to 800,000 in 1940, the largest permanent increase being in the public sector, with only about 6.3 per cent of workers in private industry belonging to unions in the inter-war years.

There had been a split in the CGT in 1921, when anarchists and communists formed the rival Confédération Générale du Travail Unitaire (CGTU), of which the PCF gained control and expelled most of the anarcho-syndicalists. In 1936 the CGTU rejoined the CGT and by 1938 the communists held a majority in the CGT. By 1946 the CGT had between 5,000 and 6,000 officials. While unions in the north and north-east, based on large factories, were often well organised, the workshop organisations of the centre and west tended to be loosely based with revolutionary aims; in the south political action was in the forefront. Many workers stood outside the union movement and a small section (which later grew larger) organised themselves separately in Christian trade unions.

The Vichy government formally liquidated the CGT and CFTC in November 1940, but an underground unified CGT was re-established, and became a key factor in the Resistance.

GERMANY

Territory

At the beginning of the nineteenth century the lands from the Tyrol to the Baltic, historically associated with the German people, were divided into several hundred sovereign territories, ranging from the Austrian and Prussian monarchies to tiny principalities of imperial knights, within the Holy Roman Empire. The Empire came to an end in 1806, and Napoleon formed the

Confederation of the Rhine in that year. After Napoleon's defeat in 1815 the Bund, or German Confederation, was established with thirty-eight states (thirty-nine from 1817). Fifty-eight per cent of the population were in Austria and Prussia, which did not totally belong to the Confederation. After the Prussians defeated Austria at Sadowa (Königgrätz) in 1866, Germany was divided into three: the North German Confederation in the area north of the Main, dominated by Prussia, which then enlarged its territory; four southern states, which were united with the North in 1870; and Austria which soon became part of the new Austro-Hungarian Empire, and remained severed from Germany even after the collapse of the Empire in 1918, apart from Hitler's annexation (1938–45). The German Empire established in 1871 had 41 million inhabitants and occupied 540,858 square kilometres but lost 70,000 square kilometres in the Treaty of Versailles (1919). At the end of the Second World War Germany lost 114,549 square kilometres to Poland and USSR, and became divided into three parts: the Federal Republic of Germany (FRG: 247, 838 sq. km), the German Democratic Republic (GDR: 107,173 sq. km) and East and West Berlin (884 sq. km).

Constitutional Development

1815–48

The German Confederation had a federal diet which met in Frankfurt, charged with the power to make war and peace, organise a federal army, enact some uniform laws to apply the Constitution and resolve inter-state disputes. There was no executive; Member States enacted the Diet's decisions if they wished to do so, and if they refused the Diet could request another Member State to intervene by force. Austria had the Presidency by permanent right, and Prussia the Vice-Presidency.

In Prussia there was no central representative body. The King ruled through his General Directory and *Kabinett* of secretaries. In 1808 a Council of State became the sole organ of government under the King. A central diet summoned in 1847 was dismissed in the same year by the King.

In Bavaria a constitution was granted in 1818, with an upper house of hereditary, with nominated and *ex officio* members, and a lower house, with members elected on a tax-based franchise; a parliament controlled the budget and taxation, but only the King and his Council of Ministers could initiate legislation.

In Saxony a constitution was granted in 1831, with a lower house directly elected on a tax-based franchise, and the King controlled all legislation.

In Hanover a constitution was granted in 1833 but abrogated in 1837, with a new constitution of 1840 increasing the monarch's powers.

In Württemburg a constitution was granted in 1819 with a lower house indirectly elected on a tax-based franchise and the King retaining the sole right to initiate legislation to raise finance.

In Baden a constitution was granted in 1818 with a lower house indirectly elected on a tax-based franchise; a parliament had powers in respect of finance, but all other matters could be regulated by royal ordinance.

In Hesse-Darmstadt and Hesse-Cassel constitutions were granted in 1820 (amended in 1856) and 1831, respectively, with a lower house indirectly elected on a tax-based franchise, but real legislative and executive power remained with the Grand Duke and Elector respectively (Hesse-Cassel was annexed by Prussia in 1866).

In Brunswick a constitution was granted in 1832 (amended 1851), with a lower house elected on a tax-based franchise, but its parliament had only limited powers, and ministers were responsible to the Crown.

1848–1918

The Federal Diet was dissolved and handed its authority to the new National Assembly on 12 July 1848, but this new central power was not accepted by Austria and it had been dissolved by June 1849. The Federal Diet was reconvened, and after the Olmutz agreement of November 1850 operated until 1866, when the German Confederation ended.

The Parliament of the North German Confederation formed after the Austro-Prussian War, was elected on universal male suffrage and had the right to vote on the budget.

The Imperial German Constitution of 1871 made the Prussian King head of the federation of 22 German princes, under the title of 'German Emperor', provided for a lower house (Reichstag) elected on universal male suffrage by direct and secret election, with power to vote on the budget and to legislate together with the Bundesrat. The electorate grew from 7.9 million in 1871 to 14.4 million in 1912. The Reichstag could be dissolved by the Bundesrat with the Emperor's consent. The twenty-five members of the Bundesrat (with fifty-eight votes of which seventeen belonged to the princes) were representatives of the governments of the Member States. There was no responsible Imperial Ministry, only the Reich Chancellor (who was chairman of the Bundesrat) was answerable to the Reichstag, which could question him and debate Bundesrat policy without a vote.

In Prussia a constitution was granted in 1848 (revised in 1850), with an upper house of aristocrats, large landowners and others appointed by the Crown, and a lower house indirectly elected on a three-tier property qualification. The two houses could but usually did not initiate laws; the ministers could be questioned but were not fully responsible to Parliament. In the other states there were only minor changes in the constitutions (above).

1918–1933

Following the abdication of the Emperor in 1918, and after a brief interlude of soldiers' and workers' councils on the Russian model in 1918, Germany changed from a monarchy to a republic in every state, but it retained its federal unity and its civil service. On 11 August 1919 the National Assembly adopted at Weimar a constitution for the new German Republic. In form it was very democratic, granting the vote to all men and women at the age of 20 and with an elaborate system of proportional representation. Fundamental rights (*Grundrechte*) were guaranteed. An attempt was made to prescribe a system of cabinet government, a popular president as head of state and direct legislation, with provisions for referenda.

The Constitution also aimed at economic democracy by the establishment of workers' and employers' councils and a federal economic council. The Constitution was more unitary and centralised than earlier ones. However, the separate states, now called *Länder*, retained the right to legislate in such vital matters as police, internal administration, education and religion.

What proved to be a subversive of democracy was Article 148, which gave power to the Reich President and Government to rule by decree in cases of 'emergency'. This served as the basis of the 'dictatorship' of the Reich President after 1930, when the parties could not agree on the formation of a cabinet.

1933–45

By July 1932 the National Socialists, with 230 (out of 608) members, became by far the strongest party in the Reichstag and also in most *Länder*. Despite the setback suffered by the National Socialists in the election of November 1932, the President, Hindenburg, appointed Hitler Chancellor to form 'a national government on a constitutional basis' on 30 January 1933.

Within six months the National Socialists had achieved sole power by a reign of terror and intimidation. They proceeded to liquidate the whole parliamentary system including the legislative powers of the Reichstag and of the diets of the *Länder* and of local councils. They suppressed all other political parties, and voluntary associations such as trade unions. Following Hindenburg's death in 1934, Hitler combined in his person the offices of head of state, head of government and Party leader. The 'leader principle' meant the uncontrolled power of appointed leaders in all spheres of life, even in employment relationships. The 'thousand-year National Socialist Reich' lasted just over twelve years.

Legal System

German law, as distinct from Roman or Frankish law, started its life in the ninth century AD. In the Middle Ages territorial law rested largely on custom. However, the *Constitutio Criminalis Carolina*, a criminal code issued by the Reichstag of Regensburg in 1533, was accepted by almost every prince, and in the sphere of private law the reception of Roman law led to a considerable degree of uniformity. Savigny's famous work describing the law of the first half of the nineteenth century was entitled *The System of the Present Roman Law* and Ihering's work on the same subject was called *The Spirit of Roman Law*. The princes issued legislation to adapt territorial customs to the scientific system of Roman law.

During the eighteenth and nineteenth centuries there was a movement towards re-Germanisation under the influence of the natural lawyers and later the historical law school. From the middle of the eighteenth century the princes consciously created new laws, sometimes Romanistic, sometimes Germanic and often a mixture of both. The most famous code, which expressed the legal thinking of 'enlightened absolutism', was the General Law for the Prussian States (*Allgemeines Landrecht*) of 1794. This was a complete civil code and also contained many public law rules which remained valid until 1946. Many other states had their own codes. In the western states of Germany Napoleonic Codes remained in force after Napoleon's fall. After unification, codes were issued which provided Germany with a common law. The most important was the Civil Code of 1896 which came into force on 1 January 1900. A uniform system of law courts was adopted by 1 January 1879, but all courts (apart from the Supreme Court; see below) were appointed by and subject to the state in which they exercised their jurisdiction. The lowest courts of first instance were *Amtsgerichte* (civil and criminal). The *Landgerichte* exercised supervisory jurisdiction over these and also had original jurisdiction. The *Oberlandesgerichte* (of which there were twenty-eight) was an appeal court and also had original jurisdiction in serious criminal cases. The Supreme Court of the Reich was the Reichsgerichte, with appellate jurisdiction over all inferior courts. (The industrial and labour tribunals are described in Ch. 6, above.)

Political Parties

In the German Empire after 1871 there were three main parties, the National Liberals (Nationalliberale), the Centre Party (Deutsche Zentrumspartei) and the Social Democratic party (see below). In 1877 the National Liberals split, with the Liberal Union (Liberale Vereiniging) breaking away on the issue of tariff reform.

Other parties were also formed as the result of splits and mergers. The General German Workers' Association (Allgemeiner Deutscher Arbeiterverein: ADA) was founded in 1863, under the leadership of Ferdinand Lassalle, to promote socialism based on state-subsidised workers' co-operatives. The Union of German Workers' Societies (Verband der Deutschen Arbeiterverein: VDA) was set up in 1864, under the leadership of August Bebel, and joined Marx's First International in 1868. The VDA merged with dissident members of the ADA in 1869 at Eisenach to form the Social Democratic Workers' Party (Sozialdemokratische Arbeiterpartei: SAP), based on Marxist socialism. In 1875 and SAP and ADA merged at Gotha to form the Socialist Workers' Party of Germany, later called the Social Democratic Party of Germany (Sozialdemokratische Partei Deutschlands: SPD). The Party was dissolved by Bismarck's Anti-Socialist Act of 1878, and all meetings and publications attacking the state and private property were outlawed. Despite this, electoral support for Social Democratic candidates steadily increased. In 1890 the legislation was allowed to lapse.

The Erfurt programme of the Party (1891) combined the long-term aim of the dictatorship of the proletariat with immediate demands including the extension of the franchise, the 8-hour day and the extension of social insurance. By 1912 the SPD had captured over one-third of the electoral poll and had more than 1 million individual members. The support of the SPD for the First World War resulted in the incorporation of labour leaders in the organs of state. The Spartacus League (later the Communist Party: KPD) was not powerful enough to lead the November 1918 Revolution to a successful socialist conclusion. After this period, the SPD, more openly reformist than in pre-war days, remained the largest party in the Weimar Republic until 1932, when the National Socialist Workers' Party (Nazionalsozialistische Deutsche Arbeiterpartei: Nazis) came into the ascendant and, after securing power, suppressed all other parties.

Trade Unions

The socialists played a key role in organising trade unions, starting with the cigar-makers in 1865, the printers in 1866 and tailors and wood-workers in 1868. The General German Trade Union Federation (Allgemeiner Deutscher Gewerkschaftsbund: ADGB) was set up in 1868, primarily as a means of gaining support for the SPD. By 1887 there were about 50,000 members. In the period of the anti-socialist laws (1878–90) not only the Party but all individual trade unions were dissolved, including non-socialist ones, but many survived under the guise of friendly societies and workers' clubs.

In 1890 the General Commission of Trade Unions (General Kommission der Gerwerkschaften Deutschlands) was set up, and had over 2 million members by 1914 in relatively few industrial groupings. In addition, there were a number of non-socialist unions. The Christian trade unions (Gesamtverband der Christlichen Gewerkschaften) influenced by Catholic social philosophy, had 283,000 members in 1914. The liberal and anti-socialist Deutsche Gewerkvereine (Hirsch-Duncker) had 78,000 members in 1914, mainly in skilled crafts.

The strength of the unions increased greatly after the First World War. The three principal organisations were the Allgemeiner Deutscher Gewerkschafts-Bund (ADGB) (formed in 1919 as the successor to the General Kommission), Christian unions and Hirsch-Duncker unions. The membership of the ADGB reached a peak of nearly 5 million members in 31 unions in 1929, when the Christian unions had 673,000 members and the Hirsch-Duncker unions 169,000. Between them the unions covered about one-third of the working population, 86 per cent of those being in the ADGB. Although the ADGB included craft unions, there was never a serious conflict between these and the industrial unions. The unions were strongly organised under central control and were more concerned with regulation of wages than regulation of labour supply. The ADGB leadership was closely linked to the SPD.

The Nazis' industrial branch (the National Socialist Factory Cell Organisation) often took part in labour disputes. After coming to power the Nazis occupied all trade union buildings and arrested the leaders and on 13 May 1933 confiscated all trade union property.

IRELAND

Territory

English domination of the whole island of Ireland (Éire, in the Irish language) was finally established when the Gaelic leaders were defeated at the battle of Kinsale (1601). Their lands in the northern province of Ulster were confiscated and settled with Protestant English and Scottish colonists who did not assimilate with the native Roman Catholic population. The Act of Union (1800) dissolved the Irish Parliament and created the United Kingdom of Great Britain and Ireland. Centuries of struggle for independence came to a head in the 1916 Rising, whose supporters established the first Dáil (Parliament) in 1919. In 1921 a treaty with Britain divided the country into the Irish Free State and Northern Ireland; the latter, containing six out of the nine counties in the province of Ulster, remained part of the United Kingdom.

Constitutional Development

The Constitution of the Irish Free State was enacted in 1922, although the armed struggle between pro-treaty and anti-treaty (Republican) factions continued until April 1923. The Constitution provided for internal self-government, with the Executive Council headed by the President, and the legislature (Oireachtas) consisting of the nominated Senate and the House of Commons (Dáil) elected by proportional representation. Initially, men of 21 years of age and over and women of 30 and over had the vote, but from 1923 the age limit for both was fixed at 21. The country remained a British dominion (the King being represented by the Governor-General) and members of the Oireachtas had to take an oath of allegiance to the Crown, but this was removed in 1933.

In 1935 Irish nationality was distinguished from British nationality, and the office of Governor-General, with the Senate, was abolished in 1936. A new constitution was ratified by plebiscite in 1937. This enacted that the 'sovereign, independent democratic state' should be known as Éire and should include the whole island, although *de facto* this was restricted to the twenty-six counties. An elected president (*uachtaran*) was to be head of state, and the head of government was to be known as *taoiseach*. A new senate, partly nominated and partly elected by vocational panels, was established. Following the Republic of Ireland Act 1948, Ireland left the British Commonwealth.

Northern Ireland, under the Government of Ireland Act 1920, obtained its own legislature and government, with limited competence including labour law and industrial relations. As a result there was separate legislation in Northern Ireland from 1922, practically but not quite the same as that in Britain.

Legal System

In ancient times the Brehon laws prevailed but in 1172 Henry II of England proclaimed that the common law of England should replace them. It was only after 1601, however, that Irish law ceased to operate in practice and the judges applied the common law throughout Ireland. Before 1782, the Irish Parliament enacted separate statutes from those in Britain, such as general Acts of 1729, 1743 and 1780 outlawing all combinations of industrial workers. When the Irish Parliament acquired temporary legislative independence from 1782 to 1800, it continued to enact separate legislation. Following the Act of Union, apart from special legislation on combinations among rural workers and tenants in Ireland, British legislation applied throughout the whole of the United Kingdom, including Ireland. Before 1719, the highest court for Ireland was the Irish House of Lords. From 1719 to 1781 the English House of Lords was the final court of appeal from Irish courts. From 1782 to 1800, the highest court was again the Irish House of Lords. From 1801 there was a separate hierarchy of courts in Ireland with a final appeal to the British House of Lords. From 1921 no appeal on labour law matters lay to any court outside the Irish Free State (later Eire). In Northern Ireland from 1922 onwards there was a right of appeal from the Northern Irish Court of Appeal to the British House of Lords. Irish courts were never bound by decisions of the English courts, save the House of Lords in the period when this was the highest court of appeal.

Political Parties

After independence Irish politics were dominated by Fianna Fail, formed in 1926 as the successor to other anti-treaty bodies, and Fine Gael, formed in 1933 by an amalgamation of bodies which were pr-treaty. The Labour Party, with a socialist platform, was formed in 1912 as an organ of the trade unions but separated from them in 1930. Labour representation in the Dáil declined from twenty-three in 1927 to nine in 1938.

Trade Unions

When Southern Ireland was part of the United Kingdom its workers (particularly craft workers) became members of British unions. An Irish Trades Union Congress was founded in 1894. After independence the membership of these unions declined and there was a growth of Irish-based unions. The situation was complex, with some Irish unions organising in both North and South, and some British-based unions, with the majority of members in the North, continuing to organise in the South.

In structural terms the Irish unions continued to resemble those in Britain, with occupational, industrial and general unions and considerable overlap between different sections. The most important were the Irish Transport and General Workers' Union (created in 1909), whose leaders played a prominent part in the Rising of 1916, the Workers' Union of Ireland and the British-based

Amalgamated Transport and General Workers' Union. The ITGWU grew from 5,000 members at the end of the Rising to 100,000 in 1946.

ITALY

Territory

Italy was established as a nation-state in 1860, Venetia being added in 1866 and the Papal States in 1870. In 1919 the South Tirol and the port of Zara in Dalmatia were acquired and Fiume in 1922 (the last two, Istria and part of Venezia-Giulia, being ceded to Yugoslavia in 1945).

Constitutional Developments

1789–1848
There was absolute government in all the Italian states with the following exceptions: (1) the Republic of Venice, governed by a *doge* and Republican Council until the French occupation of 1797, when it was divided between the Austrian Empire and the Napoleonic Cisalpine Republic (it became part of the Kingdom of Italy, under Napoleon, in 1806 and returned to Austria in 1814); (2) the Republic of Genoa, governed by a *doge* and Republican Council until it became part of Napoleonic Ligurian Republic in 1797 (in 1815 it was united with the Kingdom of Sardinia); and (3) the Government of Councillors in Lucca, until the French occupation of 1799 (it became a Bourbon duchy in 1817).

1848–1918
After 1815 there were eight main states: the Kingdom of Sardinia, including Genoa and Piedmont-Savoy; the Kingdom of the Two Sicilies; the Papal States; the Grand-Duchy of Tuscany; the Duchy of Lucca; the Duchy of Parma; the Duchy of Modena; and Lombardy-Venetia (part of the Austrian Empire). There were no permanent parliaments, save for that granted in 1848 in Piedmont-Savoy, the Constitution of which was adopted by the new Kingdom of Italy in 1861.

The Parliament was bicameral. The Senate, whose main function was as a revising body, consisted of royal princes, and Crown appointments for life (in effect made by the ruling ministry). The Chamber of Deputies had 508 members directly elected for 5 years. In 1860 literate male property holders over 25 years of age paying 40 lire in annual taxes (about 5 per cent of the population) could vote; the qualifications were lowered in 1882; universal suffrage for males over 30 years old was granted in 1912; illiterate persons could vote only if they had completed military service. The King selected the Prime Minister, who chose his ministers, who initiated legislation which had to pass both Houses. Laws could also be promulgated by executive decrees and ordinance. The King had power to dissolve Parliament at any time provided he ordered new elections.

1918–45

In 1919 adult male suffrage and proportional representation were introduced. This was replaced in 1923 by a system of election in fifteen constituencies, with two-thirds of the seats being allocated to the party which gained 25 per cent of total votes. In 1925 single-member constituencies were introduced. However, after the Fascists took power in 1922, Parliament ceased to function normally. In 1938 the Chamber of Deputies was replaced by the Chamber of Fasci and Corporations, consisting of the Duce and the members of the Grand Fascist Council. The latter consisted of original members of the Fascist Party when it came to power, ministers and others appointed by the Duce. The Duce was responsible to the King. A republic was established in 1946 and the Republican Constitution came into force on 1 January 1948.

Legal System

Roman law, as developed by the medieval commentators, became the common law of Italy as a subsidiary source of law to local statutes. In the eighteenth century attempts were made to rationalise the various sources of law—for example, Filangieri's (1752–88) *Science of Legislation* and Beccaria's (1735–93) criminal law writings—in Tuscany, Lombardy, Venice and Piedmont. Between 1805 and 1809 the French Codes were introduced, and even after these were abrogated these influenced the Civil Code of Naples and legislation in some other states. Lombardy, including Venice, received the Austrian Civil Code in 1811. Sardinia enacted codes between 1837 and 1854. In 1865 shortly after unification five codes were enacted for the whole of Italy. These were based on the French Codes, and remained in force until gradually replaced during the fascist period. The new codes were the Criminal Code of 1930, the Code of Civil Procedure of 1940, and the Civil Code of 1942. The latter, influenced by German scholarship, abandoned the former division into three books (persons, property, acquisition of property) in favour of six books (persons, succession, property, obligations, labour relations, protection of rights). These codes were later amended, particularly by the expurgation of fascist racial and corporatist concepts.

Political Parties

The Liberal Party was founded by Cavour in 1848 to fight for the unification of Italy. The Republican Party, founded in 1880, dissolved in 1898 and reformed in 1901, followed the doctrines of Mazzini. The Socialist Party (Partito Socialista Italiana: PSI) was formed in 1892, under the influence of the German SPD. The PSI took a neutral attitude to the First World War, but its left-wing (Maximalist wing) preached revolution. The PSI split after the war into three main rivals: a majority PSI, a reformist Partito Socialista Unitario (PSU), and the Communist Party (Partito Communista Italiano: PCI). The Popular Party, an independent Catholic party with social-democratic policies, was formed in 1919. All non-fascist parties were dissolved in 1926. The National Fascist Party, formed in 1919, pursued nationalist, military and imperialist aims and established absolutist dictatorial government under the leadership of Benito Mussolini. (The electoral strength of the parties is shown in Table AI.3.)

Table AI.3 Electoral strength of the Italian political parties

	Percentage votes (seats in parentheses)				
Party	1895	1904	1913	1919	1924
Ministerial and Opposition Liberals	80.2 (438)	64.8 (415)	55.9 (310)		
Radical Party	11.7 (47)	8.4 (37)	11.7 (73)		
Socialist Party	6.8 (15)	21.3 (29)	17.6 (52)	32.3 (156)	
Republican Party		4.9 (24)	3.5 (17)		
Catholic Party			6.0 (29)		
Popular Party				20.5 (100)	9.0 (39)
Centre Coalition				15.9 (96)	
Democrats				10.9 (60)	
Fascist Party					65.3 (325)

(The election of 1924 was not a free election because of Fascist intimidation.)

Source: Cook and Paxton (1975 and 1978).

Trade Unions

Under socialist guidance trade unions grew rapidly after 1901. Organisations of agricultural workers were particularly significant. The socialist unions were grouped together in the General Confederation of Labour (Confederazione Generale del Lavoro: CGdL) in 1906. Its affiliates were organised in large national federations, separately for each branch of agricultural, industrial and commercial activity. These workers were at the same time members of the 'red' chambers of labour where these existed (comprising different branches of economic activity). The member-federations and chambers were based on the express purpose 'to help the working classes in their movement of resistance' (s.3 of the Statute of the CGdL). It was not an organisation of the Socialist

Party as such. In 1908 it had about 258,000 members, 320,000 in 1914 and 2 million in 1920. The rival Catholic Italian Confederation of Workers (Confederazione dei Lavoratori: CIL) was inspired by the Papal Encyclical *Rerum Novarum* (of Leo XIII) and proposed local autonomy and small ownership of means of social advance. It took part in strikes with the object of propagating these ideals: by 1920 it claimed 1 million members. There were also minor Republican reformist unions.

LUXEMBOURG

Territory

A Grand Duchy was created by the Treaty of London in 1837, and became fully independent in 1890.

Constitutional Development

The Constitution of 1868 (modelled on the Belgian Constitution of 1831) introduced a directly elected parliament (the Chamber of Deputies) with franchise restricted to males over 25 years of age paying 30 francs a year tax; in 1902 the tax qualification was reduced to 10 francs. The vote was extended to all adults in 1919. The Grand Duke, a constitutional monarch, shared legislative power with the Chamber and exercised executive power through the Cabinet. There was a Council of State, appointed by the sovereign, to discuss proposed legislation and give opinions.

Legal System

The French codifications remained in force after the fall of Napoleon, and legislation was inspired generally by French and Belgian precedents. German legislation was influential in the spheres of social law and taxation.

Political Parties

From 1868 the Liberals were the dominant party. The Socialist Party (Parti Sociale Démocrate) was formed in 1869 and the right-wing Parti de la Droite in 1914. The Christian Socialist Party became the dominant party in government after its formation in 1914.

Trade Unions

The Confédération Générale du Travail du Luxembourg (CGT) was formed in 1919, the largest affiliate being the Luxembourg Workers' Union (formed 1916).

THE NETHERLANDS (HOLLAND)

Territory

The general territory outlines of the modern Kingdom of the Netherlands were decided by the religious wars of the sixteenth century. This is the sense in which the description is used in this book. Originally the Netherlands denoted the Republic of the United Provinces corresponding to the modern Netherlands (31,000 sq. km), the Southern or Austrian Provinces (28,000 sq. km) and the principality of Liège (5,700 sq. km). In 1795 all these territories were invaded by French armies and, under this pressure, the Batavian Republic was established in the north as a French vassal state, while France annexed the southern provinces in 1797. The Batavian Republic was replaced in1806 by a Kingdom of Holland under a brother of Napoleon, and was annexed in 1810. Following the fall of Napoleon the Kingdom of the Netherlands (Holland and Belgium) was formed under the House of Orange. In 1830 the Southern Provinces seceded and Belgium (q.v.) became a separate kingdom, although this was recognised by Holland only in 1839.

Constitutional Development

1789–1848

There was a Hereditary Stadtholder, and the Parliament, or States-General, was chosen to represent the various social estates. There were semi-independent provincial states until a revolutionary Batavian Republic was proclaimed in 1795. In 1806 Holland became a monarchy; it was annexed to France in 1810; and in 1815 once again became an independent monarchy with the States-General as a two-chamber parliament. The Upper House had representatives of the provinces appointed on the basis of holding high official position or a high level of taxation. The Lower House was elected on a male tax-based suffrage. The King and Council of Ministers had executive power, and they shared legislative power with the States-General.

1848–1918

In 1848 the suffrage was limited to all male citizens over 23 years of age with some wealth or property qualification. The qualifications were lowered in 1887, doubling the electorate. In 1896 the minimum voting age was raised to 25, but the qualifications were reduced. Universal male suffrage and proportional representation were introduced in1917. Women were first granted the vote in 1919.

1918–45

Constitutional amendments in 1922 reduced the period of office of members of the Upper House from nine to six years and restricted executive powers.

Legal System

The French codifications were introduced when the Netherlands became part of the French Empire (1810). They were replaced in 1838 by the Dutch Civil Code, Commercial Code, Code of Civil Procedure and Act on the Organisation of the Judiciary. The Civil and Commercial Codes were modelled on the French Codes, although some Germanic solutions, from the old Dutch law, were adopted. The Civil Code retained its original structure during the nineteenth and early twentieth centuries, although important amendments were made, notably on employment contracts (1907). The sources of law are the Constitution, Acts passed by both Chambers of the States-General (Parliament) and receiving royal assent, regulations in the form of a royal decree, decisions of a minister to whom powers have been delegated by statute or royal decree, regulations of the eleven provinces and of municipalities, and regulations of the subordinate bodies. Court decisions are not binding as precedents, but the lower courts generally treat decisions of the Supreme Court as such. The Act on the Organisation of the Judiciary 1827 established local courts (*kantongerechten*), district courts (*arrondissementsrechtbanken*), courts of appeal (*gerechtshoven*) and the Hoge Raad (Supreme Court). The latter is comparable to the French and Belgian Court of Cassation. No separate labour courts were created.

Political Parties

The Anti-Revolutionary Party (ARP) was formed in 1879 by orthodox neo-Calvinist Protestants, with a policy of opposition to socialism and liberalism, 'based on that traditional national character which the Reformation created and which William the Silent moulded'. The Social Democratic League (SDB) was founded in 1881. It split over the adoption of an extra-parliamentary programme, and was superseded in 1894 by the Social Democratic Workers' Party (SDAP). A left-wing Social Democratic Party (SDP) was set up in 1908 and affiliated to the Communist International in 1919. A Liberal Party was founded in 1885; its left-wing (Radicals) split away in 1901. The Roman Catholic State Party (RKS), whose policy was based on the Papal Encyclicals *Quanta Cura*, *Immortale Dei* and *Rerum Novae*, included conservatives, democrats and some labour leaders among its members, with resultant frequent divisions. The democratic section broke away in 1925 to form the Catholic People's Party. The Christian Historical Union (CHU) was formed in 1908 from a number of former groups of conservative Protestants close to the ARP on political and religious issues but with liberal economic policies. (The electoral strength of the parties is shown in Table AI.4.)

Trade Unions

Unions started in the 1860s among printers, diamond workers, organ-makers, railwaymen and others. The National Labour Secretariat (National Arbeits Secretariaat: NAS) founded by the socialists became exclusively concerned

Table AI.4 Electoral strength of the Dutch political parties

	Percentage vote (seats in parentheses)				
Party	1888	1901	1913	1918	1937
Catholic Party	20.7 (25)	15.7 (25)	14.5 (25)	30.0 (30)	28.8 (31)
ARP	31.4 (27)	27.4 (22)	21.5 (11)	13.4 (13)	16.4 (17)
Liberals	40.7 (46)	27.6 (26)	16.7 (22)	15.1 (15)	12.4 (13)
Social Democrats	0.9 (1)	9.5 (7)	18.5 (15)	22.0 (22)	22.0 (23)

Source: Cook and Paxton (1975 and 1978).

with union affairs after 1896. The movement was at first dominated by syndicalists but after defeat in the 1903 railways dispute (in which the government legislated against strikes on railways and public services) the socialists gained ascendancy. In 1905–06 fifteen socialist-led national unions set up the Nederlands Verbond van Vakverenigen (NVV) on the model of the German ADGB, which fought a united campaign with the SDAP for universal suffrage, and collaborated with the socialist movement generally. Separate Catholic (NKV) and Protestant unions (CNV), all anti-socialist, were also formed, with a combined membership about one-half of the NVV. By 1914 the NVV had about 80,000 members, the NKV 29,000 and the CNV 11,000. By 1920 the NVV had 250,000 members. The basic structure of the unions remained unchanged until 1939.

APPENDIX II

Chronology of Labour Law 1789–1945

Key: *Bel.*, Belgium; *Brit.*, Britain (from 1801–1921 includes Ireland); *Den.*, Denmark; *Fra.*, France; *Ger.*, Germany; *Ire.*, Ireland; *Ita.*, Italy; *Lux.*, Luxembourg; *Neth.*, Netherlands

1789

Fra. Third Estate declares itself a National Assembly and decides to frame Constitution; feudal system abolished; Declaration of the Rights of Man and the Citizen.

1790

Fra. National Assembly sets up a *comité pour l'extinction de la mendicité*; introduction of state supervision of unwholesome industries; Jews granted civil liberties.

1791

Fra. *Loi Le Chapelier* repressing coalitions; abolition of guild regulations; Constitution guarantees constitutional monarchy.

1792

Den. Abolition of slave trade.
Fra. Republic proclaimed; Convention offers to assist all peoples wishing to overthrow governments; French-occupied territories obliged to accept French institutions.

1793

Bel. Liberation from Austrian rule.

Brit. Friendly Societies Act.
Fra. Execution of Louis XVI; Committee of Public Safety with dictatorial powers; Constitution revised; law fixes maximum wages and prices.

1794

Fra. Abolition of slavery in colonies.

1795

Bel. Incorporated in France.
Brit. Speenhamland Act for poor relief.
Fra. Third Constitution giving power to Directory.
Neth. Batavian Republic.

1796

Fra. Publication of Jean Cambaceres' *Projet de Code Civil* (used as basis for *Code Napoléon*, 1801).

1797

Brit. Suppression of naval mutiny and passing of Unlawful Oaths Act (used against Tolpuddle martyrs, 1834).
Ita. Venetian Constitution; Ligurian Republic founded.

1798

Brit. Income tax introduced (10 per cent on incomes over £200).
Ire. Rebellion begins.
Ita. Roman Republic (recaptured by France December 15).

1799

Brit. Combination Act repressing combinations.
Fra. Constitution establishing Consulate with Napoleon as First Consul.
Ita. Parthenopean Republic in Piedmont.

1800

Brit. Further Combination Act; Robert Owen's model factory established in New Lanark, Scotland.
Den. Order forbidding coalitions in Copenhagen.
Ire. Act of Union with Britain (in force 1 January 1801).

1801

Fra. Fifth Constitution establishing Napoleon as ruler.
Ire. Combination (Ireland) Act passed by United Kingdom parliament imposes stricter régime than in British Acts of 1799 and 1800.
Ita. Napoleon annexes Piedmont; law extending system of compulsory workhouses.

1802

Brit. Health and Morals of Apprentices Act.
Fra. Reintroduction of legislation regulating apprenticeship and labour market.

1804

Fra. Napoleon proclaimed Emperor; *Code Napoléon* in force.

1806

Fra. Law establishing *conseil de prud'hommes* in Lyon.
Ger. End of Holy Roman Empire.
Neth. Foundation of Kingdom of Holland under French influence (incorporated in France 1810–13).

1807

Brit. Slave trade by British subjects abolished.
Fra. Introduction of Code of Commercial Law.
Ger. Emancipation of serfs in Prussia.

1809

Fra. Extension of *conseils de prud'hommes*.
Ger. Repression of coalitions in Bavaria.

1810

Bel. Decree on domestic servants.
Fra. Introduction of Penal Code (Arts. 414–16 repress coalitions).
Ger. Renewal of repression of coalitions in Saxony; Prussian Order on domestic servants.

1811

Brit. Luddites destroy machines; Hampden clubs formed to agitate for extension of franchise.
Ger. Prussian edict provides for peasant proprietorship.

1812

Ger. Emancipation of Jews in Prussia.

1813

Bel. Decree on domestic servants.
Brit. Repeal of wage-fixing clauses of Statute of Artificers.
Fra. Prohibition of work by children under 10 years of age in mines.

1814

Brit. Repeal of apprenticeship clauses of Statute of Artificers.
Fra. First Peace of Paris recognising French frontiers of 1792, and independence of Netherlands and former Italian and German states; Louis XVIII issues constitutional charter and claims throne.

1815

Fra. Final defeat of Napoleon; final Act of Congress of Vienna unites Holland, Luxembourg and Belgium in the Netherlands; restores Lombardy and Venetia to Austria; grants Northern Saxony and Rhineland to Prussia; forms German Confederation under Austrian Presidency; recognises Ferdinand IV as King of the Two Sicilies, and restores Pope and minor Italian princes.

1816

Ger. First Constitution granted by Carl-August of Saxe-Weimar.

1817

Brit. Unrest leads to repressive legislation to suspend *habeas corpus* (until 1818) and prevent meetings; treaty with Spain to end slave trade.
Fra. New electoral law with limited franchise.

1818

Robert Owen presents petition for international labour legislation to Conference of Austria, Britain, France, Prussia and Russia at Aix-la-Chapelle.
Ger. Baden and Bavaria granted liberal constitutions.

1819

Brit. Act for the regulation of cotton mills and factories; 'Peterloo massacre' (militia charge on meeting in St Peter's Fields, Manchester, on subject of parliamentary reform and free trade); the 'Six Acts' passed to suppress disorders, limit public meetings, and so on.
Ger. Diet of German Confederation passes Carlsbad Decrees abolishing freedom of press, suppressing political agitation and liberal movements; Württemburg granted liberal constitution.

1820

Fra. New electoral system guarantees strength of Right.
Ger. Hesse-Darmstadt granted liberal constitution.

1821

Brit. First free-trade legislation.

1823

Brit. Master and Servant laws amended and consolidated; death penalty for over 100 crimes abolished; employment of transported convicts allowed in colonies.

Den. Coalitions ban extended to whole country (q.v. 1800).
Ger. Provincial Diets established in Prussia.

1824

Brit. Combination Laws Repeal Act recognises freedom of association.

1825

Brit. Peel's Combination Act limits freedom of association to combinations concerned with wages, prices and hours, and penalises undefined crimes of intimidation, molestation and obstruction; factories legislation amended; restrictions on emigration of artisans lifted.

1827

Brit. Major reforms of English criminal law, reducing number of capital offences, and simplifying offences against property.

1828

Brit. Repeal of Test and Corporation Acts allows Catholics and Protestant dissenters to hold public office.

1829

Brit. Peel's Act established new police force in London and suburbs ('bobbies'); Roman Catholic Relief Act allows Catholics to sit and vote in Parliament.

1830

Bel. Revolution against union with Holland and declaration of independence recognised by Powers.
Fra. July Revolution and election of Louis-Philippe as King with constitutional charter.
Ger. Revolts in Saxony, Hesse and Brunswick followed by granting of constitutions.

1831

Bel. Constitution proclaimed with Leopold of Saxe-Coburg as King.
Brit. Truck Act reforming some abuses of payment of wages.

1832

Brit. Reform bill becomes law after lengthy struggle, allowing redistribution of parliamentary seats, removal of outmoded forms of voting and extension of franchise to wider class of property owners; extended to Scotland and Ireland.
Ger. Metternich's 'Six Articles' passed by German Confederation to suppress opposition.

1833

Brit. Act to regulate labour of children and young persons in textile factories introduces 48-hour week for children and establishes first independent factory inspectors.
Ger. Prussia establishes *Zollverein* (customs union) by treaties.

1834

Brit. Formation of Grand National Consolidated Trades Union led by Robert Owen to organise a general strike for 8-hour day (fails October); farm labourers from Tolpuddle, Dorset, sentenced to transportation for taking unlawful oaths to form trade union; abolition of slavery in British Empire; Poor Law Amendment Act aimed at driving poor onto labour market; reports of commissioners on employment of children in factories; Tory Party (under Peel) accepts policy of liberal conservatism.
Fra. Silk weavers in Lyon revolt, followed by repressive new laws against unions.

1835

Fra. 'September' laws to suppress radical movement.

1836

Brit. Formation of London Working Men's Association (start of Chartist movement).

Fra. Communist League formed in Paris.
Ger. Ban on combinations in Württemburg.

1837

Brit. Case of *Priestley* v. *Fowler* initiates doctrine of common employment barring claims against employer for work injuries due to fault of fellow-employee.
Ger. Constitution of Hanover suppressed (new, less liberal constitution granted 1840).

1838

Brit. Working Men's Association draws up People's Charter demanding manhood suffrage, vote by ballot, annual parliaments and payment of members.
Ger. Removal of ban on combinations in Saxony.
Ire. Poor Law based on English Act of 1834.
Neth. Promulgation of Civil Code and Commercial Code.

1839

Brit. Chartist riots following rejection of petition to Parliament.
Fra. Publication of Louis Blanc's *L'Organisation du travail* advocating national workshops.
Ger. Prussian regulation for reduction of child labour in factories.
Lux. Becomes independent Grand Duchy.

1840

Brit. Chimney-sweeps Act.

1841

Fra. Children's Protection Act regulating hours of work.

1842

Brit. Chartist risings; royal commission reports on condition of labouring population; Mines Act prohibits employment of women and of children under 10 years of age underground in mines.
Ger. Prussian law on poor relief.

1843

Ita. Act on children's hours of work in Austrian provinces.

1844

Brit. Act to amend the laws relating to labour in factories equates women with young persons and protects all workers against unfenced machinery; royal commission on health in towns.
Ger. Silesian weavers' riot.

1845

Brit. Print Works Act.
Ger. Prussian General Trade Act renews ban on combinations and contains health and welfare provisions for workers.

1846

Brit. Repeal of Corn Laws, leading to split in Conservative Party.
Fra. Agricultural and industrial depression.
Ire. Failure of potato crop leading to widespread famine and mass emigration.

1847

Brit. Act to limit the hours of labour of young persons and females in factories (the 'ten hours' Act).
Ger. Ban on combinations in Hanover.

1848

Year of Revolutions and of the *Communist Manifesto*.
Brit. Chartist petition to Parliament fails; Public Health Act passed.
Fra. Revolt in Paris, abdication of Louis-Philippe, proclamation of Republican Provisional Government; national workshops started for relief of poor but suppressed and thousands of Paris workers killed in 'June days'; moderate Republicans win majority in National Assembly; Republican Constitution with single chamber, direct elections and universal suffrage; Louis Napoleon elected President with considerable powers; reduction of working day by one hour by decree of 22 March

repealed by decree of 9 September; decree of 27 May on *conseils de prud'hommes*.

Ger. King agrees to grant constitution in Prussia; Prussian law on work accidents on railways.

Ire. Suspension of *habeas corpus* and insurrection.

Ita. Constitutions proclaimed in Naples, Piedmont-Savoy, Sardinia, Rome and Venice; Sardinia surrenders Lombardy and recognises *status quo* before revolutions, except in Venice.

Neth. Change to constitutional monarchy.

1849

Bel. Decree on public health requires licensing of places of work.

Den. Democratic constitution.

Fra. Communist riots suppressed followed by repressive laws; Constitution of Second Republic adopted; Articles 414–16 of Penal Code amended to treat employers and workers equally in relation to coalitions.

Ger. Attempts at unification fail; German Confederation passes law on payment of wages; agricultural co-operative land banks founded.

1850

Brit. Factories Act attempts to close loopholes in 1847 Act; Act for inspection of coal mines.

Fra. Restrictions on press; abolition of universal suffrage; law regulating mutual aid associations; old-age pensions.

Ger. Liberal constitution granted in Prussia.

1851

Brit. Apprentices and Servants Act protecting domestic servants against ill-treatment.

Fra. Law limiting employer's power to retain work-book, but still under police supervision.

1852

Brit. Poor Law Outdoor Relief Regulation Order allowing relief in some cases in return for work obligations; first congress of co-operative societies; Industrial and Provident Societies Act.

Fra. Napoleon III Emperor; decrees establishing local employment offices, and regulating mutual aid societies.

1853

Brit. Factories Act closes further loopholes.
Ger. Prussian law provides for paid factory inspectors and raises minimum working age to 10 years (12 from 1855).

1854

Brit. End of Chartist movement.
Den. *Tyendeloven* (Act on agricultural workers and domestic servants).
Ger. Extension of ban on coalitions to domestic servants, agricultural workers and miners and ban on associations with socialist or communist aims.
Neth. Poor Law.

1855

Brit. Friendly Societies Act; Merchant Shipping Act.

1857

Den. Trade Law.
Ger. Ban on combinations in Bavaria.

1858

Brit. Property qualification for Members of Parliament removed; Act to remove Jewish disabilities.

1859

Brit. Molestation of Workmen Act modifies criminal law restrictions on picketing and strikes.
Fra. Amnesty and extension of political rights.
Ita. Law on poor relief in Piedmont follows English Act (1834).

1860

Brit. Coal Mines Regulation Act allows miners to appoint their own checkweigher; Lace Works Act.
Fra. Law recognises freedom of emigration.

Ger. Prussian Mines Act affirms legal status of works rules issued by employer.
Ita. First Italian Parliament meets at Turin.

1861

Ger. General Commercial Code adopted.
Ita. Constitution of Kingdom of Italy adopted.

1863

Brit. Act regulating night-work in bakeries; a royal commission (until 1866) on employment of children in trades and manufactures not already regulated by law.
Ger. Lassalle founds General German Workers' Association.

1864

Pius IX issues *Syllabus Errorum* condemning liberalism, socialism and rationalism (*Quanta Cura*); International Working Men's Association (First International) founded in London.
Brit. Factory Acts Extension Act and Workshops Regulation Act extends protection to non-textile factories and lays down sanitary conditions; Chimney-sweeps Act.
Fra. Coalition ceases to be criminal offence and some strikes lawful, but trade unions remain illegal.
Ger. Union of German Workers formed, under leadership of Bebel.

1865

Ger. First modern trade unions formed by socialists; Prussian Mines Act recognises compulsory insurance funds.
Ita. Five legal codes adopted.

1866

Congress of First International demands 8-hour day.
Bel. Coalition ceases to be criminal offence in new penal code.
Ger. Formation of North German Confederation.
Neth. First modern trade unions formed.

1867

Brit. Reform Act extends franchise to most urban skilled workers; Factory Acts and Workshops Regulation Acts extended; Master and Servant Acts modified; Royal Commission on Trade Unions (Chairman, Sir William Erle); Councils of Arbitration Act.
Ger. First socialist elected to North German Reichstag.
Lux. Secession from Netherlands.

1868

Brit. Formation of Trades Union Congress.
Fra. Parliamentary system adopted; freedom of press and assembly granted.
Ger. Establishment of General German Trade Union Federation by social-democrats and of Hirsch-Duncker unions by (liberal) German Progress Party.

1869

Ger. *Gewerbeordnung* (Trade Act) of North German Confederation (from 1871 of Empire) supplants fragmented laws of German states, abolishes penal sanctions against strikes, lockouts and combinations, abolishes work-book system and limits hours of work; German Social Democratic Workers' Party founded; Bebel's social-democrats found International (Marxist) Trade Unions.

1870

Fra. Third Republic established.
Ger. North German Act redefining requirements for poor relief.

1871

Brit. Trade Union Act protects trade unions from illegality; Criminal Law Amendment Act penalises most forms of picketing and strikes.
Den. Foundation of Social Democratic Party.
Fra. Paris Commune (March 18 until May 28).
Ger. Empire established; Employers' Liability Act.
Neth. First trade union confederation.

1872

Brit. Arbitration (Masters and Workmen) Act.
Ger. Vereinigung für Sozialpolitik (Union for Social Politics) founded.
Ita. First modern trade union organisations formed.
Neth. Repeal of ban on coalitions.

1873

Foundation of International Cigar Workers' Union (first international union).
Brit. National Federation of Employers formed.
Den. Law on children's protection.
Ita. Law on children's protection.

1874

Brit. Royal Commission on Labour Laws (Chairman, Chief Justice Cockburn); Act to make better provision for health of women and young persons in manufactures.
Den. Appointment of labour inspectors.
Fra. Children's protection improved; protection of women under 21 years of age; labour inspection introduced.
Ger. Prussia dissolves Social Democratic Party.
Neth. Child Labour Act.

1875

Brit. Conspiracy and Protection of Property Act protects freedom to strike from penal sanctions; removes penal sanctions for breach of employment contract; Employers and Workmen Act provides civil remedies; Artisans Dwelling Act; Friendly Societies Act; reform (1873–75) of system of courts.
Fra. Constitution of Third Republic adopted providing for universal male suffrage, bicameral legislature and *de facto* control of President by Cabinet.
Ger. German Socialist Workers' Party (later called Social Democratic Party) formed by Marxists and Lassalleans.

1876

First International dissolved.
Bel. Law lifts restrictions on emigration.

Brit. Report of royal commission on consolidation, improvement and extension of factories legislation; Industrial and Provident Societies Act.

Ger. Law on registered relief funds.

1877

Ger. Administration and procedure of justice unified.

1878

Bel. Flemish made official language in Flanders.

Brit. Factory and Workshops Consolidation Act.

Fra. Demands by workers' congress at Lyon for democratisation of *conseils de prud'hommes*.

Ger. Anti-Socialist law (to 1890); amendments to Trade Act providing for protection of women and children and paid factory inspectors.

1879

Lux. Removal of penal sanctions on coalitions when Belgian Code transplanted.

1880

Brit. Employers' Liability Act allowing some civil liability for work accidents.

Fra. Foundation of Socialist Workers' Party led by Jules Guesde (reformed as French Workers' Party, 1882); abolition of Sunday-rest regulation.

Ire. Relief of Distress Act; 'boycott' movement by agricultural tenants.

1881

Den. Work by women underground in mines prohibited.

Ger. Kaiser's message to Reichstag on social insurance (17 November).

Neth. Social Democratic League founded.

1882

Brit. Coal Mines Regulation Amendment Act.

Fra. Foundation of Federation of French Socialist Workers led by Paul Brousse.

Ger. First labour colony founded in Westphalia.
Ita. Electoral reform; Commercial Code adopted.

1883

Bel. Work-book system ended.
Ger. Law on sickness insurance.

1884

Bel. Prohibition of work underground in mines of boys under 12 and girls under 14 years of age.
Brit. Reform Act extends franchise to most workmen in countryside; Fabian Society formed.
Fra. Waldeck-Rousseau law legalises trade unions.
Ger. Law on industrial accident insurance.

1885

Bel. Belgian Workers' Party founded.

1886

Brit. First public labour bureaux in England; Bureau of Labour established as part of Board of Trade.
Fra. Municipalities made responsible for failure to invoke military or police aid to repress strikes.
Ger. Prussian Order restricting strikes.
Ita. Law on child labour in workshops, quarries and mines; legal recognition of mutual aid societies.
Neth. New penal code; parliamentary inquiry into conditions of working class.

1887

Bel. Act creating joint boards to prevent and settle industrial disputes; law prohibiting payment in kind (except agriculture).
Brit. Foundation of Independent Labour Party; Coal Mines Regulation Act enables miners to appoint safety representatives. Truck Amendment Act confers powers of enforcement of truck legislation on inspectors of factories and mines.
Ire. Crimes Act dealing with combinations among rural tenants.

1888

Bel. First labour exchanges established.

1889

Second International founded in Paris.

Bel. Law on children's protection; introduction of factory inspectors; democratisation of *conseils de prud'hommes*.

Brit. Dockers' strike and growth of 'new' unionism among unskilled and semi-skilled workers.

Den. Apprentices Act; Prevention of Accidents by Machines Act.

Fra. *Code Rural.*

Ger. Law on old-age and invalidity pensions.

Ita. Zanardelli Penal Code tolerates peaceful strikes and combinations.

Neth. Factory Act on children's and women's employment and establishing labour inspectorate.

1890

First international congress for protection of workers, Berlin; international May Day demonstrations for 8-hour day.

Fra. Law ending work-book system; law establishing workers' representatives in mines.

Ger. Congress of Erfurt of German Social Democrats adopts new programme; establishment of General Commission of Trade Unions; Industrial Courts Act establishing tribunals at local level.

Lux. Grand Duchy becomes fully independent.

1891

Papal Encyclical *Rerum Novarum.*

Brit. First Fair Wages Resolution of House of Commons; Royal Commission on Labour (to 1894) (Chairman, Duke of Devonshire); Act to amend law relating to workshops and factories.

Den. Poor Law.

Fra. Creation of Supreme Council of Labour.

Ger. Amendments to Reich Trade Act include prohibition of night-work by women, consultation with workers on regulation of working day and establishment of permanent workers' committees.

1892

Bel. Penal Code strengthened in respect of strikes.
Den. Sick Clubs Act.
Fra. Establishment of Office du Travail and system of labour inspection; federation of *bourses du travail* formed.
Ger. Prussian Mines Act amended to introduce principle of joint control of checkweighing.
Ita. Foundation of Italian Workers' Party (called Socialist Party from 1893).

1893

Bel. Suffrage reform.
Ita. Law on *probiviri* (industrial courts).
Neth. Establishment of National Labour Secretariat; survey of unemployment by government.

1894

Bel. Decree on health and safety at work and compensation for accidents.
Ire. Irish Trades Union Congress formed.
Ita. Riots of agricultural labourers in Sicily.
Neth. Foundation of Social Democratic Workers' Party.

1895

Bel. Introduction of labour inspectors and foundation of Office du Travail.
Brit. Act to extend law relating to workshops and factories.
Fra. Foundation of Confédération Générale du Travail (CGT).

1896

Bel. Strikes leading to introduction of Councils of Industry and Labour; *conseils de prud'hommes* extended to cover white-collar workers.
Brit. Conciliation Act encourages conciliation and voluntary arbitration; amendments to truck legislation limiting employer's power to fine and deduct wages.
Den. Foundation of Danish Employers' Confederation.
Fra. Report by Office du Travail on public works as means of alleviating unemployment.
Ger. Civil Code adopted (in force 1 January 1900).
Neth. Health and Safety Act.

1897

Bel. Law on appointment of safety delegates by miners.
Brit. Workmen's Compensation Act; formation of Engineering Employers' Federation.
Ger. Commercial Code adopted; amendment to Trade Act on regulation of craftsmen; freedom of emigration recognised.
Neth. Act on Chambers of Labour.

1898

Bel. Formation of Trade Union Commission of the General Council of the Belgian Workers' Party; law on trade and professional associations; Liège provincial government introduces scheme of unemployment insurance subsidised by public funds.
Den. Foundation of Danish Workers' Confederation; law on compulsory workmen's compensation.
Fra. Law on workmen's compensation; law on control of mutual aid societies.
Ger. Foundation of German Union of Labour Exchanges.
Ita. Labourers and peasants riots; law on industrial accident compensation and on pensions.

1899

International Women's Congress in London.
Den. 'September' Agreement between employers and unions.
Fra. Strikes in Schneider-Creusot factory leading to appointment of workers' delegates under Waldeck-Rousseau arbitration decision.

1900

International congress on legal protection of workers, Paris.
Bel. Old Age Pensions Act; law on contracts of employment.
Brit. *Taff Vale* case exposes unions to civil liability for strikes; formation of Labour Representation Committee (renamed Labour Party in 1906).
Fra. Limitation on working day to 10 hours; decree authorising minister to establish *conseils du travail.*
Ger. Publication of the first work of modern labour law, P. Lotmar's essay *Die Tarifverträge zwischen Arbeitgebern und Arbeitehnerm.*
Ita. Giolitti institutes social and financial reforms.

1901

Foundation of International Association for Workers' Statutory Protection, based in Basle; first international congress of trade unions in Copenhagen.

Brit. Factory and Workshops Consolidation Act reduces working week for women to 55½ hours in textile factories and 60 hours in other factories.

Den. Foundation of Women's Labour Union; Work in Factories Act provides for establishment of labour council.

Ger. Prussian police order prohibiting strikes; formation of Federation of Christian Unions.

Ita. Establishment of unions of metal and mechanical workers and of agricultural workers.

Neth. Industrial injuries insurance Act.

1902

Congress of International Association for Workers' Statutory Protection in Cologne.

Brit. Shop Clubs Act preventing compulsory membership of sick clubs and thrift funds; Labour Bureaux (London) Act allowing London to establish bureaux for unemployed.

Ita. Law protecting women and minors; law on rice-field workers; parliamentary bill on contract of employment; Act to establish Superior Council of Labour and Ufficio del Lavoro.

Lux. Introduction of labour inspectorate.

1903

Bel. Law on accident compensation.

Brit. Royal Commission on Labour (Chairman, Lord Dunedin).

Ger. Law on child labour.

Neth. Railways and docks strike leading to ban on strikes by railway personnel and civil servants; first major collective agreements.

1904

International treaty on workers' protection between France and Italy.

Fra. Law increasing powers of local employment offices.

Ger. Foundation of German Employers' Association and Union of German Employers' Associations; law on commercial tribunals for white-collar workers; establishment of special department for labour statistics.

Ita. Law on labour accidents.

1905

Conference of International Association for Workers' Statutory Protection at Berne (to 1906) adopts conventions prohibiting use of white phosphorous in matches and prohibiting employment of women in night-work.

Brit. Unemployed Workmen Act enables local authorities to assist unemployed.

Den. Metal trades agreement recognising shop stewards.

Fra. Creation of unified Socialist Party; law on appeals from *conseils de prud'hommes*.

Ger. Amendment of Prussian Mines Act to introduce compulsory workers' committees.

Ita. The Umanitaria Society in Milan creates unemployment fund.

1906

Conference of International Association for Workers' Statutory Protection in Washington works out details of convention on prohibition of night-work by women.

Brit. Trade Disputes Act grants immunities from civil liability in respect of industrial action; extension of workmen's compensation legislation.

Fra. Miners' strike; introduction of 6-day week; creation of Ministry of Labour; extension of workmen's compensation legislation.

Ita. Foundation of General Confederation of Labour.

Neth. Foundation of Dutch Federation of Trade Unions (socialists); decree recognising permanent workers' association in mines.

1907

Den. Act on unemployment benefits.

Fra. Law unifying and extending *conseils de prud'hommes*.

Ger. Law on associations threatens unions' political objects.

Ita. Law on night-work and Sunday rest.

Neth. Contracts of Employment Act (amending Civil Code).

1908

Bel. Foundation of Christian trade union federation.

Brit. Old Age Pensions Act.

Den. Law on protection of foreign workers (amended 1912).

Fra. Law on work accidents.

Neth. Left-wing Social Democratic Party founded.

1909

Brit. Parliament rejects Lloyd George's Finance Bill; Trade Boards Act (later Wages Councils Act) creates machinery for minimum wages in 'sweated' trades; Labour Exchanges Act.
Fra. Law on reinstatement of women in employment after confinement.
Neth. Protestant and Catholic Trade Union federations founded; labour inspectorate reorganised.

1910

Den. 'August' Committee recommends establishment of permanent arbitration court and general conciliation board.
Fra. Old Age Pensions Act; work begun on Labour Code.
Ita. General Confederation of Industry formed.

1911

Brit. Parliament Act reduces powers of House of Lords; National Insurance Act; Industrial Council (to 1913) set up to supplement other methods of conciliation.
Ger. Social Insurance Act for manual workers codifying and amending earlier legislation; Act on Social Insurance for white-collar employees; Home Work Act.
Neth. Amendments to law on child and female labour.

1912

Ita. Introduction of labour inspectors.

1913

Formation of International Federation of Trade Unions.
Brit. Trade Union Act enables unions to finance political objects, with safeguards for individuals.
Ger. Merger of two employers' bodies into Confederation of German Employers' Associations.
Neth. Old Age Pensions (effective 1919), and Sickness Insurance Act (effective 1930).

1914

First World War (to 1918).
Bel. Old Age, Sickness and Disablement Insurance Law; introduction of Sunday rest day.
Lux. Foundation of Christian Socialist Party.

1915

Brit. Munitions of War Act making strikes illegal and setting up compulsory arbitration system and tribunals.
Den. Universal adult suffrage (age 29).
Ita. Regulations for compulsory arbitration.

1916

Conference of trade unions of Entente powers at Leeds.
Brit. Committee on relations between employers and employed (Chairman, J. H. Whitley MP) (to 1919) leading to voluntary establishment of joint industrial councils in many industries.
Den. Law on industrial accident compensation.
Ger. Patriotic Auxiliary Service Act exempts trade unions from restrictive provisions of law of associations; gives unions right to nominate representatives on conciliation and arbitration bodies; and establishes workers' committees in establishments with more than fifty workers.
Ire. Easter Rising.

1917

Great October Socialist Revolution in Russia; conference of trade unions of central powers at Berne.
Ita. Decree requiring employment of quota of disabled persons.
Neth. Universal male suffrage; decree on unemployment.

1918

End of First World War.
Brit. Suffrage reforms including votes for women; amendments to Trade Boards Act makes absence of collective bargaining primary condition for minimum wage-fixing.
Ger. November Revolution; Government of People's Commissioners (until February 1919); Stinnes-Legien Agreement establishing collectivist

system, followed by Collective Agreements decree giving agreements automatic and compulsory effect, and embodying principle of 'extension'; permanent workers' committees to be set up in all establishments of more than twenty employees; decree of unemployment relief.

Ita. Catholic Trade Union Federation founded.

1919

Labour charter adopted by international trade union conference at Berne placed before Commission on International Labour Legislation, whose final report became Part XIII of the Treaty of Versailles, establishing the International Labour Organisation (ILO); IFTU reconstituted at Amsterdam congress.

Brit. Industrial Courts Act establishing machinery for voluntary arbitration; National Industrial Conference (to 1921) set up; wartime regulations repealed; Police Act bans trade union membership by police; formation of Women's Trade Union League; Coal Mines Act; Checkweighing in Various Industries Act.

Den. Law granting 8-hour day.

Fra. Laws granting 8-hour day and regulating collective bargaining; Federation of Christian Trade Unions formed.

Ger. Weimar Constitution, including recognition of freedom of association and collective bargaining and works councils; ordinances on rural workers, attachment of wages, employment of disabled workers; employment exchanges taken over by state.

Ita. Spread of workers' councils in factories in north; important ideological and political discussions by Ordine Nuovo group led by Gramsci; creation of Catholic Party (later known as Popular Party); first fascist movements; adult male suffrage granted; decree for organisation of provincial unemployment funds; old-age pensions law.

Lux. Works councils on German model introduced (withdrawn 1921); General Confederation of Workers formed.

Neth. Universal suffrage; new Factory Act including 8-hour day and 45-hour week; Apprenticeship Act; Invalidity, Widows and Orphans Pension Act; foundation of High Council of Labour.

1920

Foundation of International Federation of Christian Trade Unions; foundation of International Organisation of Industrial Employers.

Bel. Council of Labour established.

Brit. Unemployment Insurance Act; Unemployed (Relief Works) Act; Emergency Powers Act, enabling government to use troops in strikes.

Fra. Split in French Socialist Party and creation of Communist Party.

Ger. Works Councils Act; Provisional Economic Council established; freedom of workers in essential services to strike removed.
Ita. Occupations of factories by workers fail.

1921

ILO Conventions on children's employment; rights of association of agricultural workers; right of weekly rest. Formation of Red International of Labour Unions.
Bel. 8-hour day, and legal guarantee of right to join and not join unions.
Brit. Railways Act establishes joint consultation machinery.
Fra. Split in CGT and formation of rival CGTU under communist leadership.
Ire. Irish Free State established. Northern Ireland given own legislature within United Kingdom.
Ita. Creation of Communist Party, and Fascist Party.
Neth. Occupational Injuries Insurance Act.

1922

Bel. Law on contracts of employment of white-collar workers.
Den. Compulsory invalidity insurance and Old Age Pensions law.
Ger. Law on representation of works council members on the supervisory board; law on organisation of labour exchanges.
Ita. March on Rome followed by mandate to Mussolini to form government; creation of National Confederation of fascist trade union corporations.
Neth. Working-day increased to 8½ hours and working week to 48 hours.

1923

ILO Convention on unification of protective laws for workmen and labourers.
Ger. Arbitration decree on settlement of industrial disputes; Collective Agreements Order; decree on working time, allowing lengthening of working day.
Ita. Eight-hour day.
Neth. Industrial Disputes (Conciliation and Mediation) Act; abolition of regional chambers of labour.

1924

Bel. Decree of *bourses du travail.*
Fra. Legislation on *conseils de prud'hommes* and on period of notice incorporated in Book IV of *Code du Travail.*

Ita. Decree on periods of notice for white-collar workers; protection of female employees; dissolution of non-fascist trade unions.
Lux. Professional chambers of labour established.

1925

ILO Conventions on workmen's compensation, and on night-work in bakeries.
Fra. National Economic Council with consultative functions established; law on employment exchanges.
Ger. Extension of law on workmen's compensation.
Ita. Palazzo Vidoni agreement between fascist trade unions and employers recognising a single trade union body and abolishing internal commissions.
Neth. Formation of Catholic Peoples' Party.

1926

ILO Conventions on merchant seamen and on slavery.
Bel. Act introducing workers' representation on administration boards of railways and paritarian committees; voting rules and procedures of *conseils de prud'hommes* amended.
Brit. General Strike.
Ger. Labour Courts Act establishes unified labour courts; law on periods of notice for white-collar employees.
Ita. Law regulating labour relationships, including ban on strikes and lockouts; decree allowing 9-hour day (abrogated 1933).

1927

ILO Conventions on sickness insurance.
Brit. Trade Disputes and Trade Unions Act makes general strikes illegal and forbids external affiliation by civil service unions; Acts on labour exchanges and unemployment insurance.
Ger. Act on labour exchanges and on unemployment insurance; protection of pregnant women.
Ita. Charter of Labour outlining social programme of Fascist régime.
Neth. Act providing for compulsory effect of collective agreements.

1928

ILO Convention on the creation of minimum wage-fixing machinery.
Fra. Social insurance legislation; laws on apprenticeship, wages and

accidents of rural workers; extension of competence of labour inspectorate to all industrial and commercial places of work.

1929

ILO Conventions on protection of stevedores.
Den. Trade Union Act preventing victimisation of individuals.
Ger. Home Workers' Wages Act.
Neth. Act on Public Servants.

1930

Papal Encyclical of Pius XI *Casti Conubii*; ILO Conventions on forced or compulsory labour, and regulation of hours of work in commerce and offices.
Bel. Law on compulsory system of family allowances.
Fra. Social insurance scheme comes into force.
Ita. National Council of Corporations formed.
Neth. Employment agencies Act.

1931

Papal Encyclical *Quadregisimo Anno*; ILO Convention on hours of work in coal mines.
Brit. Unemployment Insurance (National Economy) Order providing means test for unemployment insurance.
Ger. Emergency decrees (to 1932) to reduce wages.
Ita. Penal Code including criminal sanctions for strikes and lockouts.

1932

ILO Conventions for protection of stevedores and on admission of children to non-industrial employment.
Fra. Compulsory system of family allowances introduced.

1933

ILO Conventions on old-age, invalidity, widows' and orphans' insurance, and on fee-charging employment agencies.
Den. Act on social insurance and assistance.
Ger. National Socialists liquidate parliamentary system and other political parties; trade unions and employers' associations dissolved and merged

in German Labour Front; replacement of collective agreements by state wages orders; Act on 'trustees' of labour.

Neth. Trade Councils Act establishing trade councils in different industries.

1934

ILO Conventions on night-work by women, workmen's compensation for diseases, hours of work in sheet-glass works and unemployment benefits.

Brit. Unemployment Act severing unemployment insurance from unemployment assistance.

Ger. Act to order national labour.

Ita. Law establishing corporations law on women's labour and family allowances.

Neth. Health and Safety Act; Foreign Workers' Registration Act.

1935

ILO Conventions on employment of women on underground work in mines, limiting hours of work in coal-mines and glass-bottle works, on reduction of working hours to 40 a week and on maintenance of rights under old-age, invalidity, etc., insurance.

Ger. Introduction of workers' passports.

Ita. Introduction of unified corporative social security scheme.

1936

ILO Conventions on recruitment of workers, hours of work on public works, annual holidays with pay, and regarding merchant seamen.

Fra. Victory of Popular Front in elections; reunification of CGT; strikes and occupations involving 3 million to 4 million workers leading to Matignon Agreement and laws on collective bargaining and workers' representatives.

1937

ILO Conventions on minimum age for admission of children to employment, reduction of hours of work in textile industry, safety provisions in building industry, and on labour statistics.

Bel. Belgian Trade Union Commission becomes fully independent of Workers' Party under name of Belgian General Confederation of Labour.

Brit. Factory Act (consolidating earlier legislation).

Ire. Constitution of Ireland adopted.

Ita. General Council of Fascism promulgates Declaration of the Rights and Duties of the Producer.
Neth. Act on extension of collective agreements.

1938

Den. Acts on salaried employees and on public holidays.
Fra. Requisition Act enables government to break strikes in essential services and provides for direction of labour; decree converts workers' representatives into statutory institution with restricted powers.
Ita. Decree establishes principle of numerical requirements in job placements.

1939

Second World War (to 1945); ILO Conventions on migrant workers, indigenous workers, and hours of work in road transport.
Fra. Family Code extending family allowances to whole population.
Ita. Corporations recognised as organs of state.

1940

Belg., *Den.*, *Lux.*, *Neth.* German occupation.
Brit. Conditions of Employment and National Arbitration Order superimposes compulsory arbitration on collective bargaining and bans strikes; National Joint Advisory Council of Ministry of Labour created.
Fra. French National Assembly surrenders power to Petain; Vichy régime established and unions liquidated.

1941

Atlantic Charter.
Fra. Vichy régime adopts Charter of Labour.
Neth. Compulsory health insurance scheme.

1942

Brit. Beveridge Report on Social Insurance and Allied Services.
Ita. Civil Code adopted.

1943

Brit. Voluntary establishment of joint production committees.
Ita. Collective agreements re-establish internal commissions.

1944

ILO Declaration of Philadelphia.
Brit. Disabled Persons (Employment) Act requiring employment of quota of disabled persons.
Fra. Perreux agreement re-establishing unity of CGT in France; declaration of Council of National Resistance.
Ita. Rome agreement on trade union unity.

1945

End of Second World War; UN Declaration of Human Rights.
Bel. Establishment of general paritarian councils and paritarian commissions.
Fra. Decree allowing collective agreements to modify legal requirements.
Ita. Women's suffrage.
Neth. Foundation of Labour established; Extraordinary Decree on Labour Relations.

APPENDIX III

Statistics

Table AIII.1 Population at censuses (000s)

	1800	1850	1900	1939	1945
Belgium	4,166 (1816)	4,530 (1856)	6,694	8,092 (1930)	8,512 (1947)
Britain	10,501 (1801)	20,817 (1851)	37,000 (1901)	44,795 (1931)	48,854 (1951)
Denmark	929 (1801)	1,415	2,450 (1901)	3,844 (1940)	4,045 (1945)
France	27,349 (1801)	35,783 (1851)	38,451 (1901)	41,183 (1936)	39,848 (1946)
Germany	22,377 (1816)	33,413 (1852)	56,367	69,460	[a]
Ireland	6,802[b] (1821)	6,552[b] (1851)	4,459 (1901)	[c]	[d]
Italy	17,237 (circa)	24,351 (1852)	32,475 (1901)	42,919 (1936)	47,159 (1951)
Luxembourg	170 (1839)	193 (1852)	236	297 (1935)	291 (1947)
Netherlands	2,047[e] (1816)	3,057 (1849)	5,104 (1899)	8,923 (1940)	9,625 (1947)

Notes:

[a] *1946*: E. Germany 18,488; W. Germany 46,560.
[b] Civil pop. only.
[c] *1937*: N. Ireland 1,280. *1936*: Rep. of Ireland 2,968.
[d] *1951*: N. Ireland 1,371. *1951*: Rep. of Ireland 2,961.
[e] Excluding the Belgian provinces.

Source: Mitchell. 1978, Table A1.

Table AIII.2 Emigration from Europe by decades (000s)

	1851–60	1861–70	1871–80	1881–90	1891–1900	1901–10	1911–20	1921–30	1931–40	1941–50
Belgium	1	2	2	21	16	30	21	33	20	29
Denmark	—	8	39	82	51	73	52	64	100	38
France	27	36	66	119	51	53	32	4	5	—
Germany[a]	671	779	626	1,342	527	274	91	564	121[b]	618
Italy	5	27	168	992	1,580	3,615	2,194	1,370	235	467
Netherlands	16	20	17	52	24	28	22	32	4[b]	75
United Kingdom and Ireland	1,313[c,d]	1,572[d]	1,849[d]	3,259	2,149	3,150	2,587	2,151	262	755[e]

Notes:
[a] West Germany in 1941–50.
[b] 1932–36.
[c] 1853–60.
[d] Excluding emigration direct from Irish ports.
[e] 1946–50.
Source: Mitchell, 1978, Table A5.

Table AIII.3 Economically active population by major industrial groups (000s)

	Ag., For. & Fishing	Ex. Ind.	Man. Ind.[a]	Const.	Comm., Fin., etc.	Trans. & Comm.	Services[b]	Other Occ.
BELGIUM								
(Males)								
1846	681	44	329	41	45[a]	16[a]	117[a]	—
1900	616	166	738	131	264[b]	72[b]	271[b]	—
1930	505	201	987	238	277	242	304	—
1947	364	188	981	178	307	234	352	5
(Females)								
1846	342	4	310	—	23[a]	1[a]	57[a]	—
1900	249	7	321	1	122[a]	6[a]	225[a]	—
1930	141	6	346	3	166	12	310	—
1947	61	3	307	2	171	16	244	1
BRITAIN								
(Males)								
1851	1,824	383	2,349	496	91	433	482	438
1901	1,390	931	4,062	1,216	597	1,409	1,056	887
1931	1,181	1,272	4,958	1,108	2,314	1,563	2,267	137
1951	1,025	847	6,153	1,390	1,838	1,517	2,806	73
(Females)								
1851	230	11	1,263	1	—	13	1,241	75
1901	86	6	2,123	3	76	27	2,358	75
1931	76	9	2,355	14	1,021	110	2,644	44
1951	117	14	2,654	41	1,322	217	2,560	36

Table AIII.3 (contd.)

	Ag., For. & Fishing	Ex. Ind.	Man. Ind.[a]	Const.	Comm., Fin., etc.	Trans. & Comm.	Services[b]	Other Occ.
DENMARK								
(Males)								
1860[b]	366	—	177	—	—	38	48	119
1901	381	165		43	—	110	64	13
1940	435	4	360	115	155	110	101	10
1950	397	4	402	128	176	117	130	15
(Females)								
1860[b]	361	—	169	—	—	40	53	126
1901	150	67		—	—	21	117	8
1940	127	—	123	1	86	14	330	4
1950	121	—	149	4	103	22	287	8
FRANCE								
(Males)								
1856	5,146	177[c]	2,002[c]	486	510	214	1,174[d]	—
1901[e]	5,581	264	3,083	563	873	603	1,905[d]	—
1936	4,282	350	3,442	679	1,272	904	2,012[d]	—
1946	4,221	369	3,128	1,022	1,169	1,238	1,767[d]	—
(Females)								
1856	2,159	17[c]	1,095[c]	16	228	10	889	—
1901[e]	2,664	6	1,926	2	791	213	1,427	—
1936	2,922	8	1,695	8	859	132	1,698	—
1946	3,263	13	1,630	24	922	275	1,753	—

Table AIII.3 (contd.)

	Ag., For. & Fishing	Ex. Ind.	Man. Ind.[a]	Const.	Comm., Fin., etc.	Trans. & Comm.	Services[b]	Other Occ.
GERMANY								
(Males)								
1895	5,540	789	4,565	1,340	930	598	1,596	150
1939[f]	4,065	723	8,053	2,307	2,115	1,760	2,792	—
(Females)								
1895	2,753	32	1,351	14	300	18	745	51
1939	4,920	11	3,455	68	1,324	137	2,888	—
EAST GERMANY								
1946								
(Males	1,046	228	1,586	411	313	351	529	—
(Females)	1,332	47	1,095	52	303	67	752	—
WEST GERMANY								
1946								
(Males)	2,735	614	4,087	1,125	898	1,035	1,629	—
(Females)	2,852	43	1,467	50	617	124	1,878	—
IRELAND								
(Males)								
1851	1,293	12[g]	257	58[g]	106	—	67	319[g]
1911	716	5	255		53	22	111	164
(Females)								
1851	167	—	430	—	46	—	260	—
1911	59	—	156	—	73	1	182	8

Table AIII.3 (contd.)

	Ag., For. & Fishing	Ex. Ind.	Man. Ind.[a]	Const.	Comm., Fin., etc.	Trans. & Comm.	Services[b]	Other Occ.
S. IRELAND								
(Males)								
1936	542	3	100	62	68	67	98	—
1946	516	3	101	54	62	58	115	55
N. IRELAND								
(Males)								
1926	133	3	107	22	51	21	50	4
1951	93	2	120	40	51	31	54	30
(Females)								
1926	16	—	95	—	19	1	50	1
1951	6	—	87	1	25	3	51	10
ITALY								
(Males)								
1871	5,664	38	1,929	—	167	263	1,176	19
1901	6,466	91	2,528	—	524	416	998	80
1936	6,412	126	2,707	974	1,156	667	865	190
1951	6,228	3,542		1,462	150	731	2,642	—
(Females)								
1871	3,036	—	1,358		33	8	567	4
1901	3,200	1	1,370	—	113	8	592	67
1936	2,431	2	1,342	5	449	35	955	29
1951	2,033	1,365		11	26	54	1,423	—

Table AIII.3 (contd.)

	Ag., For. & Fishing	Ex. Ind.	Man. Ind.[a]	Const.	Comm., Fin., etc.	Trans. & Comm.	Services[b]	Other Occ.
NETHERLANDS								
(Males)								
1849	394	2	191	60	61	55	92	27
1899	512	14	389	130	179	103	129	34
1930	546	48	710	253	360	230	237	33
1947[h]	578	53	918	287	377	239	418	53
(Females)								
1849	158	—	48	—	20	2	134	7
1899	80	2	72	—	40	3	234	—
1930	110	2	145	1	112	10	384	—
1947[h]	169	1	164	2	173	18	413	3

Full titles of headings:
Agriculture, Forestry and Fishing
Extractive Industry
Manufacturing Industry
Construction
Commerce, Finance, etc.
Transport and Communications
Services
Others Occupied

[a] Some transport workers are included with both 'Commerce, Finance, etc.' and 'Services'.
[b] Statistics are of economically active heads of family and their dependents living in. Living-out servants and their dependents and all servants of retired persons and rentiers were included in 'Services'.
[c] Gas, water and electricity workers are included with 'Extractive Industry'.
[d] Includes sanitary services.
[e] Excludes the parts of Alsace and Lorraine ceded to Germany.
[f] 1937 territory.
[g] These statistics cover workers of both sexes, but the number of females in extractive industry and in construction was negligible and was probably very small among 'Others Occupied'.

Source: Mitchell, 1978, Table B1.

APPENDIX IV

Documents

1. A Joiner's Work-Book Issued in Paris by the Prefect of Police (1829)

The present paper has been issued to him on condition that he observes strictly the laws and regulations concerning workers.	Entered my employment on the 15 October and left it on the 15 November 1829.

The Prefect of Police MANGIN	I certify that the person named above worked for me during a period of two months and that his conduct was satisfactory. Paris, the 2 January 1830.
______________________	
Signature of the Worker	

For the Prefect, or on his authorisation,	Seen, going to Pressigny (Sarthe), Paris, the 27 January 1830.
The Secretary-General	
---------------	The Chief Clerk

The Chief Clerk	

Note:

This worker was unable to sign his own name. The first employer kept it from 15 October to 14 November 1829. The second one 'certifies that the person named above worked for me during a period of two months and that his conduct was satisfactory. Paris, 2 January 1830'. Finally the Chief Clerk of the Prefecture, who had signed the paper on the right has inserted a revision on the right: 'Seen, going to Pressigny (Sarthe), Paris the 27 of January 1830.'

Source: Translated from Fohlen and Bedarida, 1962, p. 49.

2. 'Document' Used in the Builders' Lockout in London (1859)

No. 36. Name: HENRY NOBLE, Dated August 18th, 1859, Initials of Foreman or Clerk } G. W. (Geo. Wales)	No. 36. I declare that I AM NOT now, nor will I during the continuance of my engagement with you, become a MEMBER OF OR SUPPORT ANY SOCIETY which directly or indirectly interferes with the arrangements of this or any other Establishment, or THE HOURS OR TERMS OF LABOUR, and that I recognise the right of Employers and Employed individually TO MAKE ANY TRADE ENGAGEMENTS ON WHICH THEY MAY CHOOSE TO AGREE. Dated 18th of August, 1859.

Note:
Frow and Katanka (1968, p. 177) state that this type of undertaking to leave or not to join a union 'first appeared after the numerous strikes which marked the formation of Robert Owen's Consolidated Trade Union of 1834. The employers, in many cases, refused to take on workers who did not give this undertaking. Such an undertaking has ever since been known in trades union history as "the Document" '. The above 'document' was used by a master builder during a lockout of 24,000 builders in London in 1859, after negotiations for the 9-hour day had broken down. Postgate (1923, pp. 167–9) records that although the 9-hour day was not won, the builders' union, with the support of many other unions, succeeded in having the 'document' withdrawn. However, as late as 1968, the Royal Commission on Trade Unions and Employers' Associations (Cmnd. 3623, para. 214) reported instances in which the 'document' was still being used by employers.

Source: Frow and Katanka, 1968, p. 175.

3. Extracts from an Act to Regulate the Labour of Children and Young Persons in the Mills and Factories of the United Kingdom, 29 August 1833

Whereas it is necessary that the hours of labour of children and young persons employed in mills and factories should be regulated, inasmuch as there are great numbers of children and young persons now employed in mills and factories, and their hours of labour are longer than is desirable, due regard being had to their health and means of education: be it therefore enacted by the King's most Excellent Majesty, by and with the advice and consent of the Lords spiritual and temporal, and Commons, in this present Parliament assembled, and by the authority of the same, that from and after the first day of *January* 1834 no person under eighteen years of age shall be allowed to work in the night, that is to say, between the hours of half past eight o'clock in the evening and half past five o'clock in the morning, except as herein-after provided, in or about any cotton, woollen, worsted, hemp, flax, tow, linen, or silk mill or factory, wherein steam or water or any other mechanical power is or shall be used to propel or work the machinery in such mill or factory, either in scutching, carding, roving, spinning, piecing, twisting, winding, throwing, doubling, netting, making thread, dressing or weaving of cotton, wool, worsted, hemp, flax, tow, or silk, either separately or mixed, in any such mill or factory situate in any part of the United Kingdom of *Great Britain* and *Ireland*: provided always, that nothing in this Act shall apply or extend to the working of any steam or other engine, water-wheel, or other power in or belonging to any mill or building or machinery when used in that part of the process or work commonly called fulling, roughing, or boiling of woollens, nor to any apprentices or other persons employed therein, nor to the labour of young persons above the age of thirteen years when employed in packing goods in any warehouse or place attached to any mill, and not used for any manufacturing process: provided also, that nothing in this Act shall apply or extend to any mill or factory used solely for the manufacture of lace.

Persons under 18 years of age not allowed to work at night in the mills or factories herein described.

II. And be it further enacted, that no person under the age of eighteen years shall be employed in any such mill or factory in such description of work as aforesaid more than twelve hours in any one day, nor more than sixty-nine hours in any one week, except as herein-after provided.

Persons under 18 not to work more than 12 hours a day.

III. Provided always, and be it further enacted, that if at any time in any such mill, manufactory, or buildings situated upon any stream of water, time shall be lost in consequence of the want of a due supply or of an excess of water, or by reason of its being impounded in higher reservoirs, then and in every such case and so often as the same shall happen it shall be lawful for the occupier of any such mill, manufactory, or building to extend the time of labour in this Act prescribed at the rate of three hours *per* week until such lost

Extension of hours of working in certain cases.

time shall have been made good, but no longer, such time to be worked between the hours of five of the clock in the morning and nine of the clock in the evening: provided also, that no time shall be recoverable after it has been lost six calendar months.

Providing for unavoidable time lost in cases of accident.

IV. And be it further enacted, that when any extraordinary accident shall happen to the steam engine, water-wheel, weirs, or watercourses, main shafting, main gearing, or gas apparatus of any such mill, manufactory, or buildings, by which not less than three hours labour at any one time shall be lost, then and in every such case such time may be worked up at the rate of one hour a day, in addition to the aforesaid and herein-after restricted hours of labour, for the twelve following working days, but not after.

Loss of time from the want or excess of water in the daytime provided for.

V. And whereas during periods of drought and of floods the power of water-wheels on some streams is wholly interrupted, or so far diminished that the machinery or part or parts of the machinery dependant upon such power cannot be regularly worked at one and the same time, and in consequence thereof a certain portion of the time of such persons as are employed in the working of such machinery may be lost in each day during such period of drought or floods; be it therefore enacted, that it shall be lawful for the occupier of any mill, manufactory, or building, when time is so lost, then and in every such case and so often as the same shall happen, to extend the hours between which persons under eighteen years of age are herein-before allowed to work, (*videlicet*, from five of the clock in the morning till nine in the evening,) as herein-before limited, to such period as may in such case be necessary to prevent the loss of time, and no longer: provided always, that no child or young person within the respective ages prescribed by this Act shall be actually employed a greater number of hours within the twenty-four hours of any one day than this Act declares to be lawful; and provided also, that no child under thirteen years of age shall be employed after the hour of nine of the clock in the evening nor before the hour of five in the morning.

Time for meals.

VI. And be it further enacted, that there shall be allowed in the course of every day not less than one and a half hours for meals to every such person restricted as herein-before provided to the performance of twelve hours work daily.

Employment of children under 9 years prohibited.

VII. And be it enacted, that from and after the first day of *January* 1834 it shall not be lawful for any person whatsoever to employ in any factory or mill as aforesaid, except in mills for the manufacture of silk, any child who shall not have completed his or her ninth year of age.

VIII. And be it further enacted, that from and after the expiration of six months after the passing of this Act it shall not be lawful for any person whatsoever to employ, keep, or allow to remain in any factory or mill as aforesaid for a longer time than forty-eight hours in any one week, nor for a longer time than nine hours in any one day, except as herein provided, any child who shall not have completed his or her eleventh year of age, or after the expiration of eighteen months from the passing of this Act any child who shall not have completed his or her twelfth year of age, or after the expiration of thirty months from the passing of this Act any child who shall not have completed his or her thirteenth year of age: provided nevertheless, that in mills for the manufacture of silk, children under the age of thirteen years shall be allowed to work ten hours in any one day.

The employment of children under 11, 12, and 13 years of age for more than eight hours a day prohibited.

IX. And be it further enacted, that all children and young persons whose hours of work are regulated and limited by this act shall be entitled to the following holydays; *videlicet*, on *Christmas Day* and *Good Friday* the entire day, and not fewer than eight half days besides in every year, such half days to be at such period or periods, together or separately, as may be most desirable and convenient, and as shall be determined on by the Master of such children and young persons; provided nevertheless, that in *Scotland* any other days may be substituted for *Christmas Day* and for *Good Friday*, both or either, as such Master may determine.

Holidays to be allowed.

X. And be it further enacted, that if any child within the age herein-before restricted to nine hours of day labour shall have been employed in any one day for less than nine hours in one factory or mill, it shall be lawful for any person to employ such child in any other factory or mill on the same day for the residue of such nine hours; provided that such employment in such other mill or factory shall not increase the labour of such child to more than nine hours in any one day, or to more than forty-eight hours in any one week.

Children employed in any one mill less than 9 hours not to be employed in any other mill more than the residue of 9 hours.

XI. And be it further enacted, that from and after the expiration of six months after the passing of this Act it shall not be lawful for any person to employ, keep, or allow to remain in any factory or mill any child who shall not have completed his or her eleventh year of age without such certificate as is hereinafter mentioned, certifying such child to be of the ordinary strength and appearance of a child of the age of nine years, nor from and after the expiration of eighteen months after the passing of this Act any child who shall not have completed his or her twelfth year of age, without a certificate of the same form, nor from and after the expiration of thirty months after the passing of this Act any

Children not to be employed without a certificate from a surgeon as to strength and appearance.

child who shall not have completed his or her thirteenth year of age, without a certificate of the same form, which certificate shall be taken to be sufficient evidence of the ages respectively certified therein.

. . .

XVII. And whereas by an Act, intituled *An Act for the Preservation of the Health and Morals of Apprentices and Others Employed in Cotton and other Mills and Cotton and other Factories*, passed in the forty-second year of the reign of His late Majesty *George* III, it was amongst other things provided, that the Justices of the Peace for every county or place in which such mill was situated should appoint yearly two persons not interested in or in any way connected with such mills or factories in such county to be visitors of such mills or factories, which visitors so appointed were empowered and required by the aforesaid Act to enter such factories at any time they might think fit, and examine and report in writing whether the same were conducted according to the laws of the realm, and also to direct the adoption of such sanitory regulations as they might, on advice, think proper: and whereas it appears that the provisions of the said Act with relation to the appointment of Inspectors were not duly carried into execution, and that the laws for the regulation of the labour of children in factories have been evaded, partly in consequence of the want of the appointment of proper visitors or officers whose special duty it was to enforce their execution; be it therefore enacted, that upon the passing of this Act it shall be lawful for His Majesty by warrant under His Sign Manual to appoint during His Majesty's pleasure four persons to be Inspectors of factories and places where the labour of children and young persons under eighteen years of age is employed, and in the case of the death or dismissal of any of them to appoint another in the place of such deceased Inspector, which said several Inspectors shall carry into effect the powers, authorities, and provisions of the present Act; and such Inspectors or any of them are hereby empowered to enter any factory or mill, and any school attached or belonging thereto, at all times and seasons, by day or by night, when such mills or factories are at work, and having so entered to examine therein the children and any other person or persons employed therein, and to make inquiry respecting their condition, employment, and education; and such Inspectors or any of them are hereby empowered to take or call to their aid in such examination and inquiry.

Inspectors to be appointed.

. . .

XXVI. And be it further enacted, that the interior walls, except such parts as are painted, of every mill or factory or building where the process of manufacturing is carried on, shall be limewashed, and the ceilings of all rooms which have rooms or lofts above them, and all ceilings which are plastered, shall be whitewashed once every year, unless permission to the contrary, in writing, be granted by any Inspector.

Interior walls of every mill, etc. to be lime-washed.

XXVII. And be it further enacted, that a copy or copies of such abstract of this Act, and also such copy or copies of any regulation or regulations made in pursuance of this Act, as any Inspector shall direct, shall be hung up and affixed in a conspicuous part or in the several departments of every mill or factory; and such copy or copies of such abstract and of such rules or regulations, so hung up and affixed, shall be signed by the Master or Manager or Overseer of such mill or factory; and such copy or copies shall be renewed by such Master, Manager, or Overseer so often as any Inspector may direct.

An abstract of this Act, and such rules and regulations as any Inspector may determine, shall be hung up in mills.

. . .

XXIX. And be it further enacted, that in case of the employment of any child contrary to the provisions of this Act, or for a longer time than is herein-before limited and allowed, or without a due compliance with the provisions of this Act touching the education of children, or the certificates of surgeons or Magistrates, the parent or parents of such child, or any person having any benefit from the wages of such child, shall be liable to a penalty of twenty shillings, unless it shall appear to the satisfaction of the Justice or Inspector that such unlawful employment has been without the wilful default of such parent or person so benefited as aforesaid.

Parents liable to penalty of 20*s*. for the employment of children beyond the legal hours, etc.

XXX. And be it further enacted, that if any offence shall be committed against this Act, for which the Master of any factory or mill is legally responsible, and it shall appear to the satisfaction of any Justice or Inspector that the same has been committed without the personal consent, concurrence, or knowledge of such Master, by or under the authority of some agent or servant or workman of such Master, it shall be lawful for such Inspector or Justice to summon such agent or servant or workman before him to answer for such offence, and such agent or servant or workman shall be liable to the penalties and punishment for such offence herein provided, and such Inspector or Justice shall convict such agent or servant or workman in lieu of such Master.

Agents and servants of factory owners to be personally liable.

Penalties for offences against this Act.

XXXI. And be it further enacted, that if any employer of children in any factory or mill shall, by himself or by his servants or workmen, offend against any of the provisions of this Act, or any order or regulation of any Inspector made in pursuance hereof, such offender shall for such offence (except in the case of any offence for which some other penalty or punishment is specially provided) forfeit and pay any sum not exceeding twenty pounds, nor less than one pound, at the discretion of the Inspector or Justice before whom such offender shall be convicted: provided nevertheless, that if it shall appear to such Inspector or Justice that such offence was not wilful nor grossly negligent, such Inspector or Justice may mitigate such penalty below the said sum of one pound, or discharge the person charged with such offence.

Penalty for obstructing Inspectors.

XXXII. And be it further enacted, that if any person shall knowingly and wilfully obstruct any Inspector in the execution of any of the powers intrusted to him by this Act, such person shall for every such offence forfeit and pay a sum not exceeding ten pounds.

. . .

. . . Inquiry such persons as they may choose, and to summon and require any person upon the spot or elsewhere to give evidence upon such examinations and Inquiry, and to administer to such person an oath.

Powers and duties of Inspectors for the enforcement of this Act.

XVIII. And be it further enacted, that the said Inspectors or any of them shall have power and are hereby required to make all such rules, regulations, and orders as may be necessary for the due execution of this Act, which rules, regulations, and orders shall be binding on all persons subject to the provisions of this Act; and such Inspectors are also hereby authorised and required to enforce the attendance at school of children employed in factories according to the provisions of this Act, and to order tickets or such other means as they may think fit for vouchers of attendance at such schools; and such Inspectors are also hereby required to regulate the custody of such tickets or vouchers, and such Inspectors may require a register of them to be kept in every school and factory; and such Inspectors are also hereby authorised and required to order a register of the children employed in any factory, and of their sex and hours of attendance, and of their absence on account of sickness, to be kept in such factory; and all registers, books, entries, accounts, and papers kept in pursuance of this Act shall at all times be open to such Inspectors, and such Inspectors may take or cause to be taken for their own use such copy as they may think proper; and such Inspectors shall also make such regulations as may be proper to continue in force any certificates, tickets, or vouchers required by this Act, and such certificates, tickets, or vouchers so continued in force shall have the same operation and effect as new certificates, tickets, or vouchers; and such Inspector shall order and is hereby authorised to order the occupier of any factory or mill to register or cause to be registered any information with relation to the performance of any labour in such mill or factory, if such Inspector deem such information necessary to facilitate the due enforcement of any of the provisions of this Act or of any of the regulations which he may make under the authority of this Act; and such Inspector is hereby authorised to order such occupier of any mill or factory to transmit, in such manner as may be directed in such order, any information with relation to the persons employed or the labour performed in such mill or factory that such Inspector may deem requisite to facilitate the performance of his duties or any inquiry made under the authority of this Act.

. . .

Children in factories to attend a school.

XX. And be it further enacted, that from and after the expiration of six Months from the passing of this Act every child herein-before restricted to the performance of forty-eight hours of labour in any one week shall, so long as such child shall be within the said restricted age, attend some school to be chosen by the parents or guardians of such child, or such school as may be appointed by any Inspector in case the parents or guardians of such child shall omit to appoint any school, or in case such child shall be without parents or guardians; and it shall and may be lawful, in such last-mentioned case, for any Inspector to order the employer of any such child to make a deduction from the weekly wages of such child as the same shall become due, not exceeding the rate of one penny in every shilling, to pay for the schooling of such child; and such employer is hereby required to pay the sum so deducted according to the order and direction of such Inspector.

. . .

Inspectors to make annual reports.

XLV. And be it further enacted, that every Inspector shall keep full minutes of all his visits and proceedings, and shall report the same to one of His Majesty's Principal Secretaries of State twice in every year, and oftener if required, and shall also report the state and condition of the factories or mills and of the children employed therein, and whether such factories or mills are or are not conducted according to the directions of this act and of the laws of the realm. . .

4. An Extract from the highest Imperial Message to the German Reichstag Given on 17 November 1881

'We have already expressed Our belief in February of this year that the cure for social unrest does not lie in the path of repression of social-democratic excesses, but is also to be sought in the provision of positive welfare for the worker. We consider it Our Imperial duty once more to recommend this task most strongly to the Reichstag; and We would look upon all achievements which God might see fit to bless Our reign with even greater satisfaction if We succeeded in carrying with Us in future days the knowledge that We have bequeathed to the Fatherland new and lasting guarantees of internal peace and, for those in need, of help, greater security and an abundance of assistance to which they may lay claim. In the endeavours which We have undertaken in the light of these objectives We are sure of the agreement of all the associated governments and rely upon the support of the Reichstag without distinction between parties. With this in mind the draft law on the insurance of workers against industrial accidents presented by the associated governments in the previous session, having regard to the discussions on the same subject which have taken place in the Reichstag, will first of all be subjected to a process of modification in order to prepare it for the discussions which will be resumed. In addition another bill will be introduced, to support the first one, with the task of providing a similar scheme for industrial health insurance. But even those who through age or invalidity are unable to work, will have a legitimate claim against society as a whole for a higher standard of state welfare than it has been possible to give them up to now. To find the right ways and means to achieve this welfare is a difficult task, but one which is among the most important tasks of every community which is based on the moral foundations of Christian society. A greater movement towards the real strengths of such a national life and the integration of the latest associations, established in corporate form, into the area of state protection and state assistance will, We hope, also make possible the solution of problems for which the use of a similar extent of power alone would not be appropriate.'

Source: Translated from *Drucks des Reichstags des Norddeutschen Bundes* (1868) Nr 60, pp. 520ff.

5. *Loi Le Chapelier* (France), Decree of 14–17 June 1791

Art. 1

The destruction of any form of guild made up of citizens from the same trade or profession being one of the fundamental bases of the French Constitution, it is in actual fact against the law to re-establish them under any pretext and in any form whatsoever.

Art. 2

Citizens from the same trade or profession, businessmen whose shops are open to the public, workers and their colleagues skilled in any trade whatsoever shall not be able, when they join together, to name a president, secretary nor trustees, take any written record, make decisions or hold debates, nor make rules regarding their supposed common interests. . .

Art. 4

If, contrary to the principles of freedom and the Constitution, citizens belonging to the same professions, trades and those practising the same crafts, have been holding debates or reaching agreements among themselves with the aim of agreeing on a specific amount as consideration for their industry and labour, the said debates and agreements, whether or not they be taken under oath, are declared unconstitutional, an infringements of liberty and the Declaration of the Rights of Man, and are thus null and void. . .

Art. 6

If the aforementioned deliberations or agreements . . . contain any threats to businessmen, craftsmen, workmen or foreign day-labourers who would come and work in this locality, or if they are in competition with those who would be content with low wages, all those promoting, instigating and signing the acts or documents shall each be punished with a fine of one thousand [pounds] and three months' imprisonment.

Art. 7

Those who make use of threats of violence in opposition to the workers using the freedom accorded by constitutional, labour and trade laws will be treated as criminals and punished as usurpers of the public peace according to the stringency of the law.

Art. 8

All unlawful combinations composed of craftsmen, workers, their colleagues, day labourers, or those formed by them contrary to the free exercise of industry and trade will be treated as seditious assemblies.

Source: Translated from the French text.

6. Penal Code of 13 March 1810 (France): Articles 414–15

Art. 414

Every combination composed of those who aim unjustly and wrongfully to force down the wages of labourers whom they set to work, followed by an attempt or the commencement of the execution of their plan shall be punished by between six days' and one month's imprisonment and a fine of 200 to 3,000 francs.

Art. 415

Every combination of workers assembled for the purpose of stopping work and at the same time preventing work in a workshop, hindering men from making their way there and remaining there before or after a certain time, and in general attempting to suspend or hinder work, or to put up the price of labour, or commending the execution of any such decision, shall punished by a sentence of between a minimum of one month's and a maximum of three months' imprisonment. The leaders or the instigators shall be punished by a sentence of between two and five years' imprisonment.

Source: Translated from the French text.

7. Law of 25 May 1864 (France)

Art. 1

Articles 414, 415, 416 of the Penal Code are repealed. They are replaced by the following articles:

414 Whosoever, by violent means, taking the law into their own hands, threats or fraudulent means, attempts to bring about and sustain a concerted stoppage of work, with the aim of raising or lowering wages or of infringing upon the free exercise of industry and work, shall be punished by a sentence of between six days' and three years' imprisonment, and a fine of between 16 and 3,000 francs, or either one of these penalties alone.

415 When the acts made punishable by the preceding article are committed as the result of a concerted plan, the guilty parties shall be arrested and sentenced to be put under the surveillance of a senior police officer for a minimum period of two years and a maximum period of five years.

416 Every worker, employer and independent contractor, who has infringed the free exercise of industry and work, by means of fines, bans, proscriptions and express hindrances as the result of a concerted plan, shall be punished by a prison sentence of between six days and three months and a fine of between 16 and 300 francs.

Art. 2

Articles 414, 415 and 416 hereinabove apply to proprietors and farmers, and also to harvesters and farm labourers.

Source: Translated from the French text.

8. *La Loi Waldeck-Rousseau*, 21 March 1884 (France)

Art. 2

Trade unions or professional associations, including those comprising more than twenty people practising the same profession, similar jobs or connected professions contributing to the making of specific products, may combine freely without governmental authorisation.

Art. 3

Professional trade unions are exclusively for the object of the pursuit and the defence of economic, industrial, commercial and agricultural interests.

Art. 4

The founding members of every professional trade union shall lodge the statutes and the names of those who under any title whatsoever, have been entrusted with the administration and direction.

This deposition shall take place at the town hall in the area where the trade union is established, and in Paris at the offices of the Prefect of the Seine.

The Mayor of the Seine Prefect shall impart the contents to the public prosecutor.

Members of each professional trade union charged with the administration and direction of the trade union shall be French and shall be in possession of their civil rights.

Art. 5

Professional trade unions duly established according to the limitations of the present law may freely combine with each other in pursuit and in defence of their economic, industrial, commercial and agricultural interests.

These associations (*Unions*) shall disclose the names of the trade unions constituting them in compliance with Paragraph 2 of Article 4.

Source: Translated from the French text.

9. The Matignon Agreement, 7 June 1936 (France)

During the widespread strikes of June 1936 the Prime Minister Léon Blum assembled some representatives of the Confédération Générale de la Production Française (CGPF) and the Confédération Générale du Travail (CGT). An agreement was reached on the evening of 7 June. Draft bills will be presented on the 40-hour week, paid holidays and the collective agreements.

The representatives of the CGPF and the CGT meeting with the Prime Minister as chairman and arbitrator, have reached the agreement below:

Art. 1

The representatives of employers concede the immediate establishment of collective bargaining agreements.

Art. 2

These contracts shall include in particular Articles 3–5 hereof.

Art. 3

The observance of the laws binds all citizens; the employers recognise freedom of expression, and hence the rights of workers to freely associate and to belong to a professional trade union constituted in accordance with Book 3 of the Labour Code.

The employers agree not to take into consideration the fact that they belong or do not belong to a trade union when making decisions concerning recruitment, the conduct and distribution of work and measures for discipline and measures for dismissal.

If one of the contracting parties contests the motive for the dismissal of a worker as having been carried out in violation of a trade union right mentioned above, the two parties shall exert themselves to discover the facts and to find an equitable solution to the disputed case. This mediation does not bar the parties' rights to obtain damages in a court of law for the wrong occasioned.

Art. 4

The wages paid in real terms to all workers from 25 May 1936 will be readjusted, on their return to work, on a decreasing scale starting at 15.6 per cent for the lowest earners up to 7 per cent for the highest earners. The total wages for each establishment must not, in any case, be increased by more than 12 per cent. The agreed increases in wages from the aforesaid date will be set off against the readjustment of the wage structure. However, these increases will remain secured for their part, excluding the aforementioned readjustments.

Negotiations for the fixing by collective agreement of minimum wages by region and category, which will take immediate effect, shall especially include the necessary readjustment of abnormally low wages.

The representatives of employers intend to initiate the necessary readjustments to maintain the normal relationship between the grading of employees and wages paid.

Art. 5

Besides the specific cases already regulated by law, in each establishment comprising more than ten workers, two or several delegates of the workers (whether they be nominees or deputies) shall be appointed depending upon the importance of the establishment, in accordance with an agreement between the trade union organisations or, in their absence, among the interested parties. These delegates are authorised to put to the management individual complaints which have not been satisfied directly, relating to the application of the laws, decrees and regulations of the Labour Code, the scale of wages and the measures for health and safety.

All male and female workers aged 18 years and over will constitute the electorate, on condition that they have spent at least three months in the establishment at the time of election and have not been deprived of their civil rights.

Electors of French nationality defined above will be eligible for election from the age of 25, if they have worked in the establishment without interruption for a year, subject to the proviso that the length of their working period will have to be reduced if it means that there are less than five people eligible.

Art. 6

The representatives of the employers undertake that there will be no sanctions for taking strike action.

Art. 7

The confederal delegation of workers instructs its striking members to return to work as soon as the directorate of the company has accepted the general agreement that has been reached and as soon as the spokesman concerned with its effect has had talks with the company directors.

Source: Translated from *Bullétin du Ministère du Travail*, 1936, p. 222.

10. The Programme of The Conseil National de la Résistance (CNR) Resolved at the Plenary Session on 13 March 1944 and Called '*Le Programme d'Action de la Résistance*' (France)

With the aim of reaching, and with the means to put into effect, the aim of the rapid liberation of territory, representatives of the movements, groups, parties and political tendencies, groups at the heart of the CNR, proclaiming that they have made up their minds to remain united after the liberation . . .

In order to advance essential reforms:

(a) *The Economic Plan*

—the setting up of a genuine democracy and social economy involving the removal of the widespread, traditional economic and financial powers from the management of the economy;
—a sensible organisation of the economy ensuring that individual interests are subordinate to the public interest and are freed from the professional dictatorship adopted in the shadow of fascist régimes;
—the stepping up of national production along the lines of a plan decided by the government after consultation with representatives of all who are part of this production;
—the return to the nation of all the means of monopolised production, the fruits of common labour, some sources of energy, some of the riches of the subsoil, some insurance companies and some of the large banks;
—the development and support of production co-operatives, purchasing and selling co-operatives, and agricultural and craft co-operatives;
—within the framework of the business enterprise, the right of access to management and administrative positions for workers of the requisite qualifications, and worker participation in the running of the economy.

(b) *The Social Plan*

—the right to work and the right to rest, notably by the re-establishment and improvement of the contractual organisation of labour;
—a considerable readjustment of wages and the guarantee of a level of wages and treatment ensuring security, dignity and the possibility of a totally decent life for each worker and his family;
—the guarantee of national purchasing power by means of a policy tending towards the stabilisation of currency;
—the restoration of an independent trade union movement, with its traditional freedoms, endowed with far-reaching powers in the management of economic and social life;
—a complete scheme of social security, aiming at ensuring that all people have the means of existence in every case where they are incapable of finding work, with control given to the representatives of the government's interests;
—security of tenure, the regulation of the conditions of recruitment and dismissal, the re-establishment of delegates from some industrial units;
—the raising and safeguarding of the standard of living for farm labourers by means of a policy of remunerative agricultural prices improving on and spreading the experience of the Office du Blé by means of social legislation giving wage-earning agricultural workers the same rights as wage-earning industrial workers, by a system of insuring against agricultural disasters, by the setting up of a reasonable rate of wages for farming and sharecropping, by

means of making home ownership easier for young farming families and by the realisation of a scheme for rural equipment;
—a pension allowing old workers to end their days in a dignified manner;
—compensation for the victims of disasters and allowances and pensions for the victims of fascist terror;
—an extension of the political, social and economic rights of the indigenous and colonial peoples;
—the real possibility, for French children, to benefit from education and to have access to the most advanced education whatever their parents' financial status might be, so that the most prestigious jobs may in fact be open to all those with the requisite abilities to perform them, and if a genuine élite results, it will not be a social élite but an intellectual élite, and that élite will be continually replaced by the upwardly mobile population.

Source: Translated from a publication of the CNR entitled *Les Jours Heureux*, edited by *Libération-Sud.*

11. The September Agreement between the Danish Employers' Association and the Danish Federation of Labour, 5 September 1899

1. All agreements concerning hours of work, wage conditions, price lists and rules of arbitration which were in force when the stoppage of work began continue in force, subject to modifications contained in the following conditions.

2. The Danish Employers' Association and the Danish Federation of Labour hereby acknowledge each other's right to decree and approve stoppages of work, but no lockout or strike of any kind may be decreed or approved by either side before it has been approved by at least three-quarters of the votes cast at a competent meeting. The intention to bring a proposal of stoppage of work before such a meeting shall be notified to the Executive Committee of the other side in writing and by registered post at least fourteen days before the proposed stoppage is to take effect, and the decision of the meeting shall be made known to the other side at least seven days before the stoppage takes effect. Both sides bind themselves not to approve or support a strike or lockout which conflicts with this condition. A strike or lockout is considered to exist if the factory or workshop is systematically evacuated or is gradually closed down through the action of the central organisation of either side (or of one of its affiliated organisations) or with its express or tacit approval after due notification from the other side. It is hereby agreed that it shall be regarded as a breach of this agreement if either of the central organisations supports an unaffiliated workers' or employers' organisation in a dispute with either of the central organisations or their affiliated organisations.

3. The central organisations shall be responsible for ensuring that the agreements concluded between them are respected and carried out by all affiliated organisations.

4. The employer's right to direct and distribute the work and to use what

labour may in his judgment be suitable at any time is acknowledged by and, if necessary, must be supported by the workers' central organisation. As regards a worker or workers to whom a definite job has been allotted with an agreed piece-work rate without any reservations, and who is carrying out the job properly, the employer is not justified in altering the conditions to the detriment of the worker without making good any economic loss sustained by the worker in consequence. A dispute arising in this particular respect is to be decided by mediation, or if necessary by arbitration, to which all complaints by employers and workers of a breach of this agreement or abuse of it shall be referred.

5. Salaried foremen, as such, shall have full liberty not to become members of a trade union. By salaried foremen is understood persons who are the employers' chosen representatives in relation to the workers, who do not undertake piece-work and who are not interested in piece-work earnings.

6. Agreements concerning price lists and other working conditions can be denounced only after at least three months' notice, while the *terminus ad quem* (term of expiration) must be stated in every agreement. Existing agreements remain unaffected by this condition until they run out.

7. After a dispute is settled, there must be no boycotting of any kind by either side.

8. After the termination of the dispute all workers shall return to the jobs on which they were employed when the dispute began. It is taken for granted that all workshops will be opened at the same time and as far as possible to the same extent as when the stoppage began. Similarly, all the workers shall as far as conditions permit resume work in the same workshops where they were employed before the lockout.

9. It is taken for granted that the Federation of Labour will be willing to work together with the Danish Employers' Association for peaceful, stable and good relations, and first and foremost that under no circumstances will any organisation try to prevent any worker from exercising his natural right to do as good work and as much work as his abilities and training permit. It is also considered important that the central organisations shall co-operate in discouraging overindulgence in alcohol wherever it may occur. A term of notice between employers and workers in various professions is regarded as being in the interest of both parties. Of equal importance are arrangements for payment of overtime, rates of apprentices on piece-work and the establishment of fairly uniform rules for arbitration for the settlement of industrial disputes in all trades. The central organisations therefore agree to work together for a satisfactory solution of these problems.

10. In the case of a breach of agreement by an affiliated organisation or by an industrial worker or employer, the question shall first be dealt with by the Executive Committee of the central organisations, unless existing agreements provide other arrangements for dealing with the matter or if such arrangements have been tried without success. If this does not bring about a solution, either of the central organisations, through its Executive Committee, can institute proceedings in the Copenhagen courts.

11. If either of the central organisations is thought to have violated this

agreement, the Executive Committee of the other may bring the question before the same courts.

12. The foregoing agreement is signed by the Executive Committee of the Danish Federation of Labour on behalf of all its affiliated organisations and certain unaffiliated workers' organisations and is binding on all these; and by the Executive Committee of the Danish Employers' Association on behalf of all its affiliated organisations and is binding on all these.

13. Trade unions or employers cannot, by resigning from the central organisation, escape the obligations entered into by this agreement. They continue to apply until the central organisation concerned terminates the agreement in regard to that particular employer or union.

Source: Danish Employers' Association.

12. The Weimar Constitution, 11 August 1919

Art. 157

Labour stands under the special protection of the Reich. The Reich will create a unified labour law.

Art. 159

Freedom of association to maintain and improve economic and working conditions is guaranteed for everyone and for all occupations. All agreements and measures which seek to limit or impede this freedom are unlawful.

Art. 165

Manual workers and salaried employees are called upon to participate, on equal terms and together with the employers, in the regulation of wages and working conditions as well as in the general economic development of the productive forces. Organisations on both sides and the agreements between them shall be recognised.

In order to protect their social and economic interests, manual workers and salaried employees shall be legally represented in establishment workers' councils (*Betriebsarbeiterräte*) as well as in district workers' councils (organised for each economic area) and in a Reich Workers' Council.

In order to achieve the overall tasks of the economy and to participate in the implementation of the socialisation laws, the district workers' councils and the Reich Workers' Council shall come together with representatives of the employers and other interested groups of the population in district economic councils and a Reich Economic Council (*Reichswirtschaftsrat*). The district economic councils and the Reich Economic Council shall be so constituted that all important occupational groups are represented according to their economic and social significance.

Draft legislation on social and economic policy matters of basic importance must be submitted by the Reich government to the Reich Economic Council for its expert opinion before it is introduced in Parliament. The Reich Economic Council itself has the right to propose such draft legislation. Even if the Reich government does not agree with a particular draft statute, it must still bring it before the Reichstag stating its point of view. The Reich Economic Council has the right to nominate one of its own members to introduce draft legislation in the Reichstag.

Powers of supervision and administration can be transferred to the workers' councils and the economic councils in the areas assigned to them. The regulation of the structure and tasks of the workers' councils and the economic councils, as well as their relationship to other social self-governing bodies, is exclusively a function of the Reich.

Source: Translated from the German Text.

BIBLIOGRAPHY

Anon (1868a), *Enquête de l'académie de médecine sur l'emploi des femmes dans les travaux souterrains des mines*, Bulletin de l'Académie, 3rd series, vol. III (Brussels)

Anon (1868b), *L'enquête du département des travaux publics en 1869 sur la situation des ouvriers dans les mines et les usines métallurgiques de la Belgique* (Brussels)

Anon (1960), *Geschidenis van de Socialistische Arbeidersbeweging in België* (Antwerp)

Anon (1953), 'The development of labour legislation on young workers in the United Kingdom', *International Labour Review*, vol. 67, pp. 64–91.

Anon (1968), 'Sur les notions de contrat', *Archives de Philosophie du Droit*, vol. XII (Paris)

Aaron, B. (ed.) (1971), *Labour courts and grievance settlement in Western Europe* (Berkeley and London)

Aaron, B. & Wedderburn, K. W. (eds.) (1972), *Industrial conflict: a comparative legal survey* (London)

Abello, L. (1910), *Della locazione di opere* (Naples and Turin)

Abrams, P. (1982), *Historical sociology* (nr Shepton Mallet, Somerset)

Acquarone, A. (1965), *La organizzazione dello stato totalitario* (Turin)

Adan, M. (1898), 'La notion de chômage peut-elle faire l'objet d'une assurance?', *Bulletin de l'Association des Actuaries belges*, no. 4 (15 September)

Adlercreutz, A. (1958), 'The rise and development of the collective agreement', *Scandinavian Legal Studies*, vol. 2, pp. 11–53

Agosti, A. & Bravo, G. M. (eds.) (1979), *Storia del movimento operaio del socialismo e delle lotte sociali in Piemonte* (Bari), vol. I

Alexander, E., Cornil, M., Ernst-Henrion, M. & Marcelis, F. (1963), *Genèse du droit social au cours du XIXe siècle, Travaux et conférences* (Brussels)

Amulree, Lord (1929), *Industrial arbitration in Great Britain* (London)

Anderson, A. (1971), 'The political symbolism of the labour laws', *Bulletin of the Society of Labour History*, no. 23, pp. 13–15

Andreani, E. (1968), *Grèves et flutuations: la France de 1890 à 1914* (Paris)

Anton, G. K. (1953), *Geschichte der preussischen Fabrikgesetzgebung bis zu ihrer Aufnahme durch die Reich gewerbeordung* (Leipzig, reprinted Berlin, 1953)

Arnaud, A. J. (1969), *Les origines doctrinales du Code Civil français* (Paris)

Arrivabene, C. J. (1843), *Situation économique de la Belgique exposée d'après les documents officiels* (Brussels)

Arrivabene, C. J. (1845), *Sur la condition des laboureurs et des ouvriers belges et sur quelques mesures pour l'améliorer* (Brussels)

Aspinall, A. (ed.) (1949), *The early English trade unions: documents from the Home Office papers in the Public Record Office* (London)

Atiyah, P. S. (1979), *The rise and fall of the freedom of contract* (Oxford)

Auge-Laribe, M. (1932), 'Labour conditions in French agriculture', *International Labour Review*, vol. 25, p. 51ff.

Bagwell, P. S. (1974), *Industrial relations in 19th century Britain* (Dublin)

Bakels, H. L. & Opheikens, L. (1982), *Schets van het Nederlandse Arbeidsrecht*, 6th edn (Deventer)

Balella, G. (1927), *Lezioni di legislazione del lavoro* (Rome)

Balella, G. (1951), *Cento anni di legislatione sociale 1848–1950* (Milan)

Balfour, A. J. (Chairman) (1929), Final Report of the Committee on Trade and Industry (Parliamentary papers, vol. VII (Cmnd 3282), session 1928–29) (London)
Barassi, L. (1901), *Il contratto di lavoro nel diritto positivo Italiano* (Milan)
Barjonnet, A. (1968), *La CGT*, Collection Politique, no 25 (Paris)
Bartrip, P. W. J. & Burman, S. (1983), *The wounded soldiers of industry: industrial compensation policy 1833–97* (Oxford)
—— & Fenn, P. T. (1980), 'The conventionalisation of factory crime', *International Journal of the Sociology of Law*, vol. 8, pp. 175–86
Baudry-Lacantinerie, G. & Wahl, A. (no date), *Del contratto di locazione*, 2 vols. (Milan)
Bauer, S. (1912), *An international labour policy* (London)
—— (1919), *International labor legislation and the society of nations* (Washington)
—— (1924), 'Arbeiterschutzgesetzgebung', *Handwörterbuch der Staatswissenschaften*, ed. L. Elster, A. Weber & F. Wieser, 4th edn, vol. 1 (Jena)
Bayliss, F. J. (1962), *British wages councils* (Oxford)
Beier, A. L. (1983), *The problem of the poor in Tudor and early Stuart England* (London and New York)
Bellet, M. D. (1894), 'Le chômage et son remède', *Le Monde Économìque*, 11 August
Benson, J. (1974), 'Colliery disaster funds 1860–97', *International Review of Social History*, vol. XIX, pp. 73–85
—— (1975), 'English coal miners' trade union accident funds 1850–1900', *Economic History Review*, 2nd series, vol. xxviii, pp. 401–12
Bercusson, B. (1978), *Fair wages resolutions* (London)
Bernert, G. (1972), *Arbeitsverhältnisse im 19. Jahrhundert Eine kritische dokmatische Analyse der rechtswissenschaftlichen Lehren über die allgemeinen Inhalte der Arbeitsverträge und Arbeitsverhältnisse im 19. Jahrhundert in Deutschland* (Marburg)
Bertrand, L. (1907), *Histoire de la démocratie et du socialisme en Belgique depuis 1830*, 2 vols. (Brussels)
Betocchi, C. (1897), *Il contratto di lavoro nell'economia e nel diritto* (Naples)
Beveridge, W. H. (1911), 'Labour exchanges in the United Kingdom', Report no. 26, *Conférence Internationale sur le chômage*, 18–21 September 1910, vol. 3 (Paris)
—— (1930), *Unemployment: a problem of industry* (London; first published 1909)
BIT (ILO) (1927), Études et documents, series A (no. 29), *La liberté syndicale*, vol. II (Geneva)
—— (1933), Études et documents, series A (no. 39), *La conciliation et l'arbitrage des conflits du travail* (Geneva)
Blackstone, W. (1765), *Commentaries on the laws of England*, 4 vols. (Oxford; reprinted with errata and annotations, London, 1966)
Bland, A. E. *et al.* (1950), *English economic history: selected documents* (London)
Blanke, T. (1975), *Kollektives Arbeitsrecht* (Reinbek bei Hamburg)
Blanpain, R. (1960) 'De verovering der syndicale vrijheid in België', *Arbeidsblad*, p. 1518ff
—— (ed.) (1979), *International encyclopedia for labour law and industrial relations*, 10 vols. (Deventer)
Blelloch, D. (1938), 'A historical survey of factory inspection in Great Britain', *International Labour Review*, vol. 38, pp. 614–19
Blomfield, C. [Bishop of London] (Chairman) (1834), 'Administration and operation of the laws for the relief of the poor', Reports of Commissioners, Session 4 February to 15 August 1834, vol. xxvii (London)
Bonenfant, P. (1934), *Le problème du paupérisme en Belgique à la fin de l'ancien régime* (Brussels)
Bornhak, C. (1892), *Das deutsche Arbeiterrecht systematisch dargestellt* (Münich and Leipzig)

Bouchet, – (1908), *Assistance publique en France pendant la Révolution* (Paris)
Bouvier-Ajam, M. (1957, 1969), *Histoire du travail en France* (Paris)
Bowley, M. (1937), *Nassau senior and the classical economists* (London)
Braudel, F. & Labrousse, E. (1977), *Histoire économique et sociale de la France* (Paris)
Brentano, L. (1870), *On the history and development of guilds, and the origin of trade unions* (London)
—— (1872), *Die Arbeitsgilden der Gegenwart* (Leipzig)
—— (1877), *Das Arbeitsverhältnis gemäss dem heutigen Recht* (Leipzig)
Briggs, A. (1961), 'The welfare state in historical perspective', *European Journal of Sociology*, vol. 2, pp. 221–58
Brown, K. D. (1982), 'Trade unions and the law' in *A history of British industrial relations 1875–1914*, ed. K. D. Brown (Brighton)
Brugmans, I. J. (1973), *De arbeidende klasse in Nederland in 19e eeuw*, 9th edn (Utrecht)
Bruhat, J. & Piolot, M. (1966), *Esquisse d'une histoire de la CGT (1895–1965)* (Paris)
Bugni, E. (1907), *Massimario della giurisprudenza dei Probiviri, di tribunali e di corti* (Milan)
Bulow, K. (1942), *Laerlingeloven i Praksis* (Copenhagen)
Cafagna, L. (1973), 'The industrial revolution in Italy 1830–1914' in The Fontana Economic History of Europe, vol, 4, *The Emergence of Industrial Societies* Part One, ed. C. M. Cipolla (Glasgow), pp. 279–328
Caire, G. (1971), *Les syndicats ouvriers* (Paris)
Camerlynck, G. H. (ed.) (1968), *Traité de droit du travail* (Paris)
Carlsen, H. G. (1960) *Traek af Funktionaerrettens udvikling* (Copenhagen)
Carpenter, L. P. (1976), 'Corporatism in Britain 1930–45', *Journal of Contemporary History*, vol. 11, pp. 3–25
Carson, W. G. (1974), 'Symbolic and instrumental dimensions of early factory legislation' in *Crime, criminology and public policy*, ed. R. G. Hood (London)
Charles, R. (1973), *The development of industrial relations in Britain 1911–1939* (London)
Chatelet, F. *et al.* (1978), *Histoire des idéologies* (Paris)
Cherubini, A. (1977), *Storia della previdenza sociale in Italia* (Rome)
Chevaleer, M. L. (1958), *Classes laborieuses, class dangereuses à Paris pendant la première moité du XIXe siècle* (Paris)
Chlepner, B. S. (1956), *Cent ans d'histoire sociale en Belgique* (Brussels)
Churchill, W. S. (1909), Speech on Trade Boards Bill, House of Commons Debates, 5th series, vol. 2 (24 March), cols. 1391–92
Cipolla, C. M. (ed.) (1972–76), *The Fontana economic history of Europe*, 6 vols. (Glasgow)
Citrine, N. A. (1950), *Trade union law* (London; 3rd edn by M. A. Hickling, 1967)
Clarkson, J. D. (1925, reprint 1970), *Labour and nationalism in Ireland* (New York)
Clegg, H. A. (1985), *A history of British trade unions*, vol. 2, 1910–1933 (Oxford)
—— & Chester, T. E. (1954), 'Joint consultation' in *The system of industrial relations in Great Britain*, eds. A. Flanders and H. A. Clegg (Oxford)
—— Fox, A. & Thompson, A. F. (1964), *A history of British trade unions since 1889*, vol. 1, 1889–1910 (Oxford)
Cocito, F. (1918), *Commento alla legge degli infortuni sul lavoro*, 3rd edn (Turin)
Cole, G. D. H. (1925–27), *A short history of the British working-class movement 1789–1925*, 3 vols. (London; new edn continued to 1947, published in 1948)
—— (1938), 'A study in legal repression' in his *Persons and periods: studies* (London); Also in W. M. Citrine (ed.) (1934) *The Martyrs of Tolpuddle* (London)
Collier, D. & Messick, R. E. (1975), 'Prerequisites versus diffusion: testing alternative explanations of social security adoption', *American Political Science Review* vol. 69, pp. 1299–315
Conseil Supérieur du Travail (1896), *Rapport sur la question du chômage* (Paris)
Cook, C. & Paxton, J. (1975), *European political facts 1918–73* (London)

—— & —— (1978), *European political facts 1848–1918* (London)
—— & —— (1981), *European political facts 1789–1848* (London)
Cooper, W. M. & Wood, J. C. (1947) *Outlines of industrial law* (London; 6th edn, 1972)
Cordie, C. (ed.) (1964), *Benjamin Constant* (Milan)
Cordova, R. (1974), *Le origini dei sindacati fascisti* (Bari)
Cordy, A. (1967), 'Les grandes étapes de développement de la législation sociale 1866–1966', *Revue Belge de Sécurite Sociale* pp. 902–22
Creighton, W. B. (1979), *Working women and the law* (London)
Dal Pane, L. (1958), *Storia del lavoro in Italia dagli inizi del sec XVIII al 1815* (Milan)
Daly, M. E. (1981), *Social and economic history of Ireland since 1800* (Dublin)
Dankwardt, H. (1874), 'Der Arbeitervertrag', *Jherings Jahrbuecher*, vol. 14, p. 228
David, M. (1974), 'L'évolution historique des conseils de prud'hommes en France', *Droit social*, special edn, ed. G. Lyon-Caen, p. 10ff
Dechesne, L. (1932), *Histoire économique et sociale de la Belgique* (Paris)
de Cluveaux, M. (1894), 'L'assurance contre le chômage', *Le Monde Économique*, 11 August
de Felice, R. (1968), *Mussolini il fascista: L'organizzazione dello stato fascista* (Turin)
Delsinne, L. (1936), *Le mouvement syndical en Belgique* (Brussels)
Deppe, E., Fülberth, G., Harrer, H.-J. *et al.* (1977), *Gesichte der deutschen Gewerkschafts bewegung* (Cologne)
de Rosa, A. & di Vittorio, A. (1975), *Il capitale e la rivoluzione industriale* (Messina-Florence)
Derry, T. K. (1933), 'The repeal of the apprenticeship clauses of the statute of apprentices', *Economic History Review*, 1st series, vol. IV, pp. 67–87
de Schwenitz, K. (1943), *England's road to social security* (New York)
de Visscher, C. (1911), *Le contrat collectif de travail* (Ghent)
de Vries, C. W. & J. (eds.) (1949), *Texts concerning early labour legislation*, vol. 1, 1791–1848 (Leiden)
Dicey, A. V. (1914), *Lectures on the relation between law and public opinion in England during the nineteenth century*, 2nd edn (London)
Dobb, M. (1946), *Studies in the development of capitalism* (London; 2nd rev. edn, 1963)
Dobson, C. R. (1980), *Masters and journeymen: a prehistory of industrial relations 1717–1800* (London)
Dolleans, E. & Dehove, G. (1953), *Histoire du travail en France* (Paris)
Dreyer, E. (1957), *Lov om almindelig Arbejderbeskyttelse* (Copenhagen)
Dübeck, I. (1979), *Arbejdsretten i Støbeskeen* (Aarhus)
Duboff, R. B. (1966), 'Economic thought in revolutionary France', *French Historical Studies*, vol. 4, p. 437ff
Ducpetiaux, E. (ed.) (1832), *Des moyens de soulager et de prévenir l'indigence et d'éteindre la mendicité* (Brussels)
—— (ed.) (1855), *Budgets économiques des classes ouvrières en Belgique* (Hayez)
—— & Visschers, A. (1870), *L'enquête de 1870 sur le travail des enfants*, 3 vols. (Brussels)
Duguit, L. (1950), *Il diritto sociale, il diritto individuale e la transformazione dello Stato* (Florence)
Dunlop, O. J. & Denman, R. D. (1912), *English apprenticeship and child labour: a history* (London)
Dupeyroux, J. J. (1966), *Évolution et tendances des systèmes de sécurité sociale des Pays Membres des Communautés Européennes et de la Grand-Bretagne* (Luxembourg) [Study for EEC]
Durand, P. & Jaussaud, R. (1947), *Traité de droit du travail* (Paris)
Dutton, M. (1723), *The laws of masters and servants in Ireland* (Dublin)
Ebel, W. (1964), *Quellen zur Geschichte des deutschen Arbeits rechts (bis 1849)* (Göttingen, Berlin, Frankfurt am Main)

Eden, F. M. (1797), *The state of the poor: or an history of the labouring classes in England* (London)

Einaudi, L. (1972), *Le lotte del lavoro* (Turin)

Elmquist, H. J. V. (1918), *Den kollektive arbejdsoverenkomst som retligt problem* (Copenhagen)

Elster, L. & Landmann, V. (1898), 'Arbeiterschutzgesetzgebung (in Deutschland)', *Handwörterbuch der deutschen Staatswissenschaften*, vol. 1, 2nd edn (Jena)

Emden, C. S. (1923), *The civil servant in the law and constitution* (London)

Engels, F. (1892), *The condition of the working-class in England in 1844* (London; first published in German in 1845, and in English in New York in 1886)

Eörsi, G. (1979), *Comparative civil (private) law: law types, law groups, the roads of legal development* (Budapest)

Equal Opportunities Commission (1979), *Health and safety legislation—should we distinguish between men and women?* (London and Manchester)

Erdmann, G. (1966), *Die deutschen Arbeitgeberverbände im sozialgeschichtlichen Wandel der Zeit* (Neuwied and Berlin)

European Coal and Steel Community (1965), *Le contrat de travail dans le droit des Pays Membres de la CECA* (Luxembourg)

Eusebio, L. (1909), *Dizionario di giurisprudenza probivirale sul contratto di lavoro* (Turin)

Feig, J. (1911), *Compte rendu de la Conférence Internationale du chômage*, Rapport présenté à la conférence, 3 vols., 18–21 September 1910 (Paris)

Ferenczi, I. (1912), 'Le Chômage et les migrations ouvrières internationales', Rapport présenté au Comité International de l'Association Internationale de la lutte contre le chômage (Ghent)

Finer, H. (1937), *The British civil service* (London)

Fischer, W. (1963), 'Government activity and industrialisation in Germany (1815–70)' in *The economics of take-off into sustained growth*, ed. W. W. Rostow, pp. 83–94 (London)

Flinn, M. W. (1961–62), 'The Poor Employment Act 1817', *Economic History Review*, 2nd series, vol. 14, p. 82ff

Fohlen, C. & Bedarida, F. (1962), 'L'éré des révolutions (1765–1914)' in *Histoire générale du travail*, ed. L-H Parias (Paris)

Follows, J. W. (1951), *Antecedents of the ILO* (Oxford)

Foot, S. (1980), *The effect of the Elizabethan Statute of Artificers on wages in England* (Exeter)

Forrest, A. (1981), *The French Revolution and the poor* (Oxford)

Fox, A. (1974), *Beyond contract: work, power and trust relations* (London)

—— (1984), *History and heritage: the social origins of the British industrial relations system* (London)

Francois, L. (1974), *Introduction au droit social* (Liège)

Fraser, D. (1973), *The evolution of the British welfare state* (London)

Fraser, W. H. (1974), *Trade unions and society: the struggle for acceptance 1850–1880* (London)

Freedland, M. (1976), *The contract of employment* (Oxford)

Friis, H. (1950), *Scandinavia between East and West* (New York)

Frow, E. and Katanka, M. (1968), *1868: year of the unions: a documentary survey* (London)

Fulbrook, J. (1978), *Administrative justice and the unemployed* (London)

Gagel, A. & Jülicher, F. (1979), *Arbeitsförderungsgesetz (Kommentar)* (Munich)

Galenson, W. (1952), *The Danish system of labor relations* (Cambridge, Mass.)

Galgano, F. (1976), *Storia del diritto commerciale* (Bologna)

Garraty, J. A. (1979), *Unemployment in history: economic thought and public policy* (New York)

George, M. D. (1927), 'The Combination Laws reconsidered' *Economic History*, vol. 1 (supplement to *Economic Journal*), pp. 214–28

—— (1935–36), 'The Combination Laws', *Economic History Review*, 1st series, vol. VI, pp. 172–8
George, V. (1973), *Social security and society* (London)
Gerin, P. (1959), *Catholiques liégeois et question sociale, 1844–1914* (Brussels)
Ghera, E. (1979), *Diritto del lavoro* (Bari)
Giannini, M. S. (1970), 'Impiego pubblico (teoria e storia)', in *Enciclopedia del diritto*, vol. XX (Milan), pp. 2931ff
Gibbon, I. G. (1911), *Unemployment Insurance* (London)
Gilbert, B. B. (1966), *The evolution of national insurance in Great Britain* (London)
Giugni, G. (1956), *Ideologia e pratica della azione sindacale, La Nuova Italia* (Florence)
Goetz-Girey, R. (1965), *Le mouvement des grèves en France, 1918–1962*, Collection l'économie, no. 3 (Paris)
Gosden, P. H. J. H. (1961), *The Friendly Societies in England 1815–1875* (Manchester)
Grotius, H. (1919), *De jure belli ac pacis*, ed. P. C. Molhuysen (Leiden; first published 1625)
Gurvitch, G. (1947), *Sociology of law* (London)
Habbakuk, H. J. & Postan, M. (1965), *The industrial revolutions and after: incomes, population and technological change*, The Cambridge Economic History of Europe, vol. 6 (Cambridge)
Halévy, E. (1929), *Imperialism and the rise of labour 1895–1905* (London; first published in French 1926)
—— (1934), *The rule of democracy 1905–14* (London; first published in French 1932)
Hammond, J. L. & B. (1919), *The town labourer 1760–1832* (London)
—— (1923), *Lord Shaftesbury* (London)
Hanbury, H. G. (1948), 'Industrial relations in Crime and Tort', vol. 1 *Current Legal Problems*, pp. 126–39
Harris, J. F. (1972), *Unemployment and politics 1886–1914* (Oxford)
Hasselbalch, O. (1979), *Arbejdsretlige Funktioner* (Copenhagen)
Hattenhauer, H. (1980), *Geschichte des Beamtentums* (Cologne)
Hatzfeld, H. (1971), *Du paupérisme à la Sécurité sociale 1850–1940* (Paris)
Hay, D. (1977), 'Employers and social policy in Britain: the evolution of welfare legislation 1905–14', *Social History*, vol. 1, no. 4, pp. 435–55
Hay, D., Linebaugh, P., Rule, J. G., Thompson, E. P. & Winslow, D. (1977), *Albion's fatal tree: crime and society in 18th century England* (Harmondsworth)
Hay, J. R. (1975), *The origins of the Liberal Welfare Reforms 1906–1914* (London)
Hedges, R. Y. & Winterbottom, A. (1930), *The legal history of trade unionism* (London)
Helmich, U. (1977), *Arbeitskampfe in Frankreich: ein Beitrag zur Sozial- und Rechtsgeschichte 1789–1939* (Maisenheim am Glan)
Henderson, W. O. (1958), *The state and the industrial revolution in Prussia 1740–1870* (Liverpool)
Henriques, U. R. Q. (1971), *The early Factory Acts and their enforcement* (London)
Hepple, B. A. (1981), 'A right to work', *Industrial Law Journal*, vol. 10, pp. 65–83
—— & O'Higgins, P. (1971), *Public employee trade unionism in the United Kingdom: the legal framework* (Ann Arbor)
——, —— & Neeson, J. (1975), *A bibliography of the literature on British and Irish labour law* (London)
—— & —— (1981), *Employment Law*, 4th edn (London)
——, ——, Hepple, J. & Stirling, P. (1981), *Labour law in Great Britain and Ireland to 1978: a companion volume to 'A bibliography of the literature on British and Irish labour law'* (London)
Herkner, H. (1921), *Die Arbeiterfrage*, 7th edn (Berlin and Leipzig)
Hetherington, H. J. W. (1920), *International labour legislation* (London)

Hill, C. (1969), *Reformation to industrial revolution* (Harmondsworth)
Hilton, G. W. (1960), *The truck system: including a history of the British Truck Acts, 1465–1960* (Cambridge)
Himmelfarb, G. (1984), *The idea of poverty: England in the early industrial age* (London)
Hobsbawm, E. J. (1962), *The age of revolution—Europe 1789–1848* (London)
—— (1964), *Labouring men: studies in the history of labour* (London)
—— (1969), *Industry and empire* (Harmondsworth)
—— (1977), *The age of capital 1848–1875* (London)
—— & Rude, G. (1969), *Captain Swing* (London)
Hollander, S. (1979), *The economics of David Ricardo* (Toronto)
Horion, P. (1937), *La durée du travail industriel et commercial et les congés annuels payés* (Brussels)
—— (1965), *Nouveaux précis de droit social belge* (La Naye)
Horn, P. (1975), *The rise and fall of the Victorian servant* (London)
Horowitz, D. (1963), *The Italian labour movement* (Cambridge, Mass.)
Hovde, B. J. (1943), *The Scandinavian countries, 1720–1865*, 2 vols. (Boston)
Hromadka, W. (1979), *Die Arbeitsordnung im Wandel der Zeit* (Cologne)
Hueck, A. & Nipperdey, H. C. (1963), *Lehrbuch der Arbeitsrechts*, 7th edn (Berlin and Frankfurt am Main)
Hunt, E. H. (1981), *British labour history 1815–1914* (London)
Hutchins, B. L. & Harrison, A. (1926), *A history of factory legislation*, 3rd edn (London; first published in 1903)
Illum, K. (1938), *Den kollektive arbedjsret* (Copenhagen; 3rd edn 1964)
International Federation of Trade Unions (1944), *Bulletin*, p. 8ff
International Labour Office (ILO) (1938), *Labour courts. An international survey of judicial systems for the settlement of disputes* (Geneva)
—— (1944), 'The mobilisation of foreign labour by Germany', *International Labour Review*, vol. 50, p. 470
Jaccard, P. (1960), *Histoire sociale du travail de l'antiquité à nos jours* (Paris)
Jacobi, E. (1927), *Grundlehren des Arbeitsrechts* (Leipzig)
Jacquemyns, G. (1929), *Histoire de la crise économique des Flandres (1845–1850)* (Brussels)
Jannaccone, P. (1894), 'Il contratto di lavoro', *Archivo giuridico*, vol. 53, p. 131ff.
Jenks, C. W. (1970), *Social justice in the law of nations: the ILO impact after fifty years* (London)
Jevons, W. S. (1882), *The state in relation to labour* (London; 4th edn published in 1910; Dutch translation published in Haarlem, 1888)
Jocteau, G. C. (1978), *La magistratura e i conflitti di lavoro durante il fascismo 1926–1934* (Milan)
Julliard, J. (1971), *Fernand Pellouriter et les origines du syndicalisme d'action directe* (Paris)
Kahn-Freund, O. (1954), 'Legal framework' in *The system of industrial relations in Great Britain*, eds. A. Flanders & H. A. Clegg (Oxford), pp. 42–127
—— (1959), 'Labour law' in *Law and opinion in England in the twentieth century*, ed. M. Ginsberg (London), pp. 215–63; reprinted in *Selected Writings*, pp. 1–40
—— (ed.) (1965), *Labour relations and the law* (London)
—— (1966), 'The personal scope of English labour law: "servant", "employee", "workman" ' in *Studi in memoria di Ludovico Barassi* (Milan), p. 211ff
—— (1967), 'A note on status and contract in British labour law', *Modern Law Review*, vol. 30, pp. 635–44; reprinted in *Selected Writings*, pp. 78–86
—— (1974), 'On uses and misuses of comparative law', *Modern Law Review*, vol. 37, pp. 1–27; reprinted in *Selected Writings*, pp. 294–319
—— (1977a), *Labour and the law*, 2nd edn (London; 3rd edn edited and with an introduction by P. Davies and M. R. Freedland, 1983)

—— (1977b), 'Blackstone's neglected child: the contract of employment', *Law Quarterly Review*, vol. 93, pp. 508–28
—— (1978a), 'Common law and civil law—imaginary and real obstacles to assimilation' in *New perspectives for a Common Law of Europe*, ed. M. Cappelletti (Leyden), p. 137ff
—— (1978b), *Selected Writings* (London)
—— (1979), *Labour relations: heritage and adjustment* (Oxford)
—— (1981), *Labour law and politics in the Weimar Republic*, ed. and with an introduction and appendices by R. Lewis and J. Clark (Oxford)
Kaskel, W. (1928), *Arbeitsrecht*, 3rd edn (Berlin)
—— & Dersch, H. (1957), *Arbeitsrecht*, 5th edn (Berlin, Göttingen and Heidelberg)
—— & Sitzler, F. (1912), *Grundriss des sozialen Versicherungsrechts* (Berlin)
Keeling, F. (1914), *Child labour in the United Kingdom: a study in the development and administration of the law relating to the employment of children* (London)
Kendall, W. (1975), *The Labour Movement in Europe* (London)
Kerr, C., Dunlop T., Harbison, F. & Myers, C. (1960), *Industrialism and industrial man* (Cambridge, Mass.)
Kirk, D. (1946), *Europe's population in the interwar years* (Princeton, NJ)
Koch, H. H. (1936), *The Danish Public Assistance Act* (Copenhagen)
Kofod, L. (1976), *Ferieloven* (Copenhagen)
Köhler, P. A., Zacher, H. F. & Partington, M. (eds.) (1982), *The evolution of social insurance 1881–1981: Studies of Germany, France, Great Britain, Austria and Switzerland* (London and New York)
Kollmann, H. (1916), *Die Entstehungsgeschichte der deutschen Koalitionsgesetzgebung* (Heidelberg/Breslau)
Kosellek, R. (1967), *Preussen zwischen Reform und Revolution* (Stuttgart)
Kruse, F. V. (1920), *Den Kollektive Arbejdsaftale* (Stockholm)
Kuborn, H. (1868), *Aperçu historique sur l'hygiène publique en Belgique depuis 1830*, Rapport Académie (Brussels)
Kuczynski, J. (1937), *Labour conditions in Western Europe 1820 to 1935* (London)
—— (1958), *Geschichte der Kinderarbeit in Deutschland 1750 bis 1939*, vol. 1 (Berlin)
Kuhnic, S. (1978), 'The beginnings of the Nordic welfare states', *Acta Sociologica*, vol. 21 (Supplement)
Lambert, E. (1933), 'Comparative Law' in *Encyclopedia of the Social Sciences* (New York), pp. 126ff
Landes, D. S. (1969), *The unbound Prometheus: technological change and industrial development in Western Europe from 1750 to the present* (Cambridge)
La Palombara, J. C. (1957), *The Italian labour movement: problems and prospects* (New York)
Laroque, P. (1938), *Les rapports entre patrons et ouvriers* (Paris)
Lassen, J. (1897), *Håndbog: obligationsretten, speciel del* (Copenhagen)
Lefort, J. (1913), *L'assurance contre le chômage à l'étranter et en France* (Paris)
Lefranc, G. (1963), *Le mouvement socialiste sous la Troisième République (1875–1940)* (Paris)
—— (1967), *Le mouvement syndical sous la Troisième République* (Paris)
—— (1970), *Grèves d'hier et d'aujourd'hui* (Paris)
—— (1975), *Histoire du travail et des travailleurs* (Paris)
—— (1976), *Les organisations patronales en France. Du passé au présent* (Paris)
Leger, L. & Crokaert, P. (1923), *Le contrat d'emploi—Travaux préparatoires et commentaire théorique et pratique de la loi du 7 août 1922* (Brussels)
Legien, C. (1919), Speech on Works Councils published in *Social Praxis*, 3 April 1919
Leroy, M. (1913), *La coutume ouvrière* (Paris)
Levasseur, E. (1903), *Histoire des classes ouvrières et de l'industrie en France de 1789 à 1870*, 2nd edn (Paris)

Levenbach, M. G. (1964) 'Arbeid' in *Nederlands Bestuursrecht*, Part III (Alphen aan den Rijn)
—— (1965) 'Il contratto di lavoro nel diritto olandese' in *Il contratto di lavoro nel diritto dei paesi membre della CECA* (Brussels and Milan) [Study for EEC]
Liebman, M. (1979), *Les socialistes belges 1885–1914* (Brussels)
Logan, D. W. (1945), 'A civil servant and his pay', *Law Quarterly Review*, vol. 61, pp. 240–67
Lorwin, V. R. (1954), *The French labour movement* (Cambridge, Mass.)
Lotmar, P. (1900), 'Die Tarifverträge zwischen Arbeitgebern und Arbeitehmern', *Archiv für soziale Gesetzgebung und Statistik*, vol. 15, p. 1ff
—— (1907; 1908), *Der Arbeitsvertrag nach dem Privatrecht der Deutschen Reiches*, 2 vols. (Leipzig)
Louis, P. (1904), *L'ouvrier devant l'État* (Paris)
Lyons, F. S. L. (1971), *Ireland since the famine* (London)
Macura, M. (1976), 'Population in Europe (1920–70)' in *The Fontana economic history of Europe*, vol. 5, *The Twentieth Century*, Part One, ed. C. M. Cipolla, pp. 1–87.
Magrez-Song, G. (1961), 'Les organismes précurseurs du Conseil national du travail, *Revue du Travail*, pp. 1103–1156
Maine, H. S. (1861), *Ancient law* (London)
Malthus, T. R. (1960), *On population*, ed. G. Himmelfarb (New York; first published 1798)
Mantoux, P. (1928), *The industrial revolution in the 18th century: an outline of the beginnings of the modern factory system in England* (London)
Marchetti, L. (1910), 'L'organisation du placement en Italie', Rapport no. 33 presented to the Conférence Internationale du Chômage (Paris), pp. 18–21
Marquand, H. A. *et al.* (1939), *Organised labour in four continents* (London)
Marx, K. (1954), *Capital*, vol. 1 (London; first published in German in 1867; in English 1887)
—— (1850) 'The Class Struggles in France: 1848 to 1850' [reprinted in *Surveys from Exile*, ed. D. Fernbach], (Harmondsworth, 1973)
—— (1875), *Critique of the Gotha Programme*, in German in *Marx-Engels-Werke*, vol. 19, Berlin, 1956–64; in English in *The First International and after*, ed. D. Fernbach, (Harmondsworth, 1974)
—— & Engels, F. (1848), 'Manifesto of the Communist Party'; English translation by Samuel Moore, 1888, reprinted in *The revolutions of 1848*, ed. D. Fernbach (Harmondsworth, 1973)
—— & —— (1953), *On Britain* (London and Moscow)
Mason, T. W. (1978), *Sozialpolitik im Dritten Reich*, 2nd edn (Opladen)
McCarthy, C. (1977), *Trade Unions in Ireland 1894–1960* (Dublin)
McGregor, O. R. (1957), 'Social research and social policy in the nineteenth century', *British Journal of Sociology*, vol. 8, pp. 146–57
McLennan, G., Held, D., Hall, S. (1984), *The idea of the modern state* (Milton Keynes and Philadelphia)
Melis, G. (1980), *Burocrazia e socialismo nell'Italia liberale* (Bologna)
Menger, A. (1894), *Il diritto civile e il proletariato* (Turin)
Mengoni, L. (1965), 'Contratto e rapporto di lavoro nella recente dottrina italiana', *Rivista della Società*, p. 674ff
—— (1971), *Lezioni sul contratto di lavoro* (Milan)
Merli, S. (1973), *Proletariato di fabbrica e capitalismo industriale, La Nuova Italia* (Florence)
Middlemas, K. (1979), *Politics in industrial society: the experience of the British system since 1911* (London)

Mill, J. S. (1965), *Principles of political economy, with some of their applications to social philosophy* (Toronto—text of 7th edn, 1871; first published in 1848)
Millerand, A. (1903), 'Les traités du travail', *La réunion de Bale: revue politique et parlementaire*, vol. XXXVIII (Paris)
Milne-Bailey, W. (1929), *Trade union documents* (London)
Minchinton, W. E. (ed.) (1972), *Wage regulation in pre-industrial England* (London)
Mitchell, B. R. (1978), *European historical statistics 1750–1970*, abridged edn (London)
Molenaar, A. M. (1953–58), *Arbeidsrecht* (Zwolle)
Mommsen, W. J. (ed.) (1981), *The emergence of the welfare state in Britain and Germany 1850–1950* (London)
Moses, J. A. (1982), *Trade unionism in Germany from Bismarck to Hitler 1869–1933*, 2 vols. (London)
Moster, H. & Bernhardt, R. (ed.) (1980), *Beiträge zum ausländischen öffentlichen Recht und Volkenrecht* (Heidelberg)
Mozzarelli, C. (1972), *Per una storia del pubblico impiego nello stato moderno: il caso della Lombardia austriaca* (Milan)
Naphtali, F. (ed.) (1928), *Wirtschaftsdemocratie Ihr Wesen, Wes und Ziel* (Berlin)
Napier, B. (1975), 'The contract of service: the concept and its application' (unpublished PhD thesis, Cambridge)
Neufeld, M. F. (1961), *Italy: school for awakening countries* (Ithaca)
Neumann, F. (1942), *The structure and practice of Naional Socialism* (New York)
Neuville, J. (1976), *La condition ouvrière au XIXème siècle*, vol. 1 (Brussels)
Nikische, A. (1961), *Arbeitsrecht*, 3rd edn (Tübingen)
Oberschall, A. (1965), *Empirical social research in Germany: 1866–1914* (The Hague)
Peliing, H. (1963), *A history of British trade unionism* (Harmondsworth)
—— (1979), 'The working-class and the origins of the welfare state' in *Popular politics and society in Victorian Britain*, 2nd edn (London), pp. 1–18
Pera, G. (1969), *Serrata e diritto di sciopero* (Milan)
Perna, C. (1978), *Breve storia del sindacato* (Bari)
Perreau, C. (1912), *La notion du contrat de travail* (Paris)
Perrot, M. (1974), *Les ouvriers en grève 1871–1890* (Paris-Haye)
Peters, H. (1978), *Die Gesichte der sozialen Versicherung*, 3rd edn (Sankt Augustin)
Phelps Brown, E. H. (1965), *The growth of British industrial relations* (London)
—— (1983), *The origins of trade union power* (Oxford)
Philip, J. R. (1934), 'Early labour law in Scotland', *Juridical Review*, vol. 46, p. 121ff
Pic, P. (1903), *Les lois ouvrières—traité élémentaire de législation industrielle* (Paris)
Picard, R. (1926), 'Labour legislation in France during and after the war', *International Labour Review*, vol. 13, p. 889ff
Pigou, A. C. (1913), *Unemployment* (London)
Pilotti, R. (ed.) (1914), *Legislazione operaia in Italia* (Citta di Castello)
Pirenne, H. (1920), *Histoire de Belgique*, vol. V (Brussels)
Planiol, M. (1907), *Traité élémentaire de droit civil* (Paris)
Poggi, G. (1978), *The development of the modern state: a sociological introduction* (London)
Polanyi, K. (1944), *The great transformation* (New York)
Pollard, S. (1981), *Peaceful conquest: the industrialisation of Europe 1760–1970* (Oxford)
Postgate, R. W. (1923), *The builders' history* (London)
Pothier, R. J. (1818–23), *Pandectae Justinianeae, in novum ordinem digestae*, 24 vols. (Paris)
Potter, B. (1891), *The cooperative movement in Great Britain* (London)
Poynter, J. R. (1969), *Society and pauperism* (London)
Preller, L. (1978), *Sozialpolitik in der Weimarer Republik* (Düsseldorf)
Pryor, F. (1968), *Public expenditures in communist and capitalist nations* (Homewood, Ill.)

Putnam, B. W. (1908), *The enforcement of the statutes of labourers during the first decade after the Black Death 1349–1359* (New York)
Rameri, S. (1904), *Legge e regolamento per gli infortuni degli operai sul lavoro* (Turin)
Ramm, T. (1968), 'Nationalsozialismus und Arbeitsrecht' in *Kritische Justiz*, p. 108ff
—— (1979), 'Die Arbeitsverfassung des Kaiserreichs' in *Festschrift für Walter Mallmann* (Baden-Baden), pp. 191–211
—— (1980), 'Die Arbeitsverfassung der Weimarer Republik' in *In Memoriam Sir Otto Kahn-Freund* (Munich), pp. 225–46
Redenti, E. (1906), *Massimario della giurisprudenza dei probiviri* (Rome)
Redgrave, A. (1878), *The Factory and Workshop Acts 1878* (London); 21st edn by I. Fife and A. E. Machin, 1966
Renner, K. (1949), *The institutions of private law and their social functions*, English translation, ed. and with an introduction and notes by O. Kahn-Freund (London). First published 1904 as 'Die Sociale Funktion des Rechtsinstitute' in Marx-Studien, *Blätter zur Theorie und Politik des Wissenschaftlichen Sozialismus*, vol. 1 (Vienna), and revised and republished in 1929 as *Die Rechtsinstitute des Privatrechts und ihre Sozial Funktion* (Vienna)
Reynaud, J. D. (1975), *Les syndicats en France* (Paris)
Ricardo, D. (1817), *The principles of political economy and taxation* (London)
Rich, E. E. & Wilson, C. H. (eds.) (1967), *The economy of expanding Europe in the sixteenth and seventeenth centuries*, The Cambridge Economic History of Europe, vol. 4 (Cambridge)
Richards, P. (1979), 'The state and early industrial capitalism', *Past and Present*, no. 83, pp. 91–115
Rigola, R. (1946), *Storia del movimento operario italiano* (Milan)
Rimlinger, G. V. (1971), *Welfare policy and industrialisation in Europe, America and Russia* (New York)
Ritscher, W. (1917), *Koalitionen und Koalitionsrecht in Deutschland* (Stuttgart and Berlin)
Riva Sanseverino, L. (1950), *Il movimento sindacale cristiano dal 1850* (Rome)
Robson, W. A. (1935), 'Industrial law', *Law Quarterly Review*, vol. 51, pp. 194–210
—— (1938), 'La législation industrielle en Angleterre au cours des 50 dernières années' in his *Introduction à l'état du droit comparatif*, vol. 3 (Paris), pp. 455–68
Rodota, S. (1981), *Il terribile diritto* (Bologna)
Romagnoli, U. (1974), *Lavoratori e sindacati fra vecchio e nuovo diritto* (Bologna)
Romano, R. & Vivanti, C. (ed.) (1976), *Storia di Italia* (Turin)
Roppo, E. (1977), *Il contratto* (Bologna)
Rosenstock Franck, L. (1934), *L'économie corporative fasciste en doctrine et en fait: ses origine historiques et son évolution* (Paris)
Rostow, W. W. (1956), 'The take-off into sustained growth', *The Economic Journal*, vol. LXVI, no. 261, p. 32ff
—— (ed.) (1963), *The economics of take-off into sustained growth* (London)
Rousseau, J. J. (1762), *Du contrat social* (Amsterdam, reprinted with an essay by B. de Jouvenel, Paris, 1978)
Rubin, G. R. (1977), 'The origins of industrial tribunals: munitions tribunals during the First World War' *Industrial Law Journal*, vol. 6, pp. 149–64
—— (forthcoming), *War, law and labour, 1915–21* (Oxford)
Rückert, J. & Freidrich, W. (1979), *Betriebliche Arbeiterausschusse in Deutschland, Grossbritannien und Frankreich im spaten 19, und fruhen 20 Jahrhundert* (Frankfurt am Main)
Rusciano, M. (1978), *L'impiego pubblico in Italia* (Bologna)
Ryan, W. P. (1919), *The Irish labour movement from the twenties [1820s] to our own day* (Dublin)

Saitta, A. (1975), *Constituenti e constituzioni della Francia rivoluzionaria e liberale (1789–1875)* (Milan)
Salvemini, G. (1936), *Under the axe of fascism* (London)
Scelle, G. (1929), *Le droit ouvrier* (Paris)
Schaeffle, A. (1893), *The theory and policy of labour protection* (London)
Schippel, A. (1902), *Sozialdemokratische Reichstags-Handbuch* (Berlin)
Schloss, D. F. (1904), *Unemployment in foreign countries: Report to the Board of Trade on agencies and methods for dealing with unemployment in certain countries* (London)
Schmoller, G. (1918), *Die soziale Frage Klassenbildung, Arbeiterfrage, Klassenkampf* (Munich and Leipzig)
Semmel, B. (1960), *Imperialism and social reform* (London)
Shorter, E. & Tilly, C. (1974), *Strikes in France 1830–1968* (London and New York)
Shotwell, J. T. (1934), *The origins of the International Labour Organisation*, 2 vols. (New York)
Simitis, S. (1984), 'Zur Verrechtlichung der Arbeitsbezeihungen' in *Verrechtlichung von Wirtschaft, Arbeit und Sozialer Solidarität—Vergleichende Analysen*, eds. Zacher, Simitis, Kübler, Hopt & Teubner (Baden-Baden)
Simon, D. (1954), 'Master and servant' in *Democracy and the Labour Movement*, ed. J. Saville (London)
Sinay, H. (1965), *La grève: Traité Dalloz de droit du travail*, vol. VI (Paris)
Sinzheimer, H. (1907), *Der korporative Arbeitsnormenvertrag. Eine privatrechtliche Untersuchung*, vol. 1, vol. 2 (1908) (Leipzig)
—— (1910–11), 'Die Fortentwicklung des Arbeitsrechts und die Aufgabe der Rechtslehre', *Soziale Praxis*, vol. 20, p. 1237ff
—— (1916), *Ein Arbeitstarifgesetz Die Idee der sozialen Selbsbestimmung im Recht* (Munich and Leipzig)
—— (1927), *Grundzüge des Arbeitsrechts*, 2nd edn (Jena, first edn, 1921)
—— (1928), 'Die Demokratisierung des Arbeitsverhältnisses: Vom Sachenrecht über das Schuldrecht zum Arbeitsrecht' in F. Naphtali (ed.) *Wirtschaftsdemokratie. Ihr Wesen, Weg und Ziel* (Berlin), ch. 3
—— (1933), 'Die Krisis des Arbeitsrechts' *Arbeitsrecht*, 20, cols. 1–10
Skidelsky, R. (1970), *Politicians and the slump: the Labour Government of 1929–1931* (London)
Smith, A. (1776), *An inquiry into the nature and causes of the wealth of nations* (London; text of 3rd edn, 1784; reprinted Oxford, 1976)
Solari, G. (1980), *Sozialismo e diritto privato influenza delle oderne dottrine socialiste nel diritto privato* (Milan)
Spaguolo Vigorita, L. (1967), *Subordinazione e diritto del lavoro (problemi storico-critici)* (Naples)
Spitaels, G. (1969), *Le mouvement syndical en Belgique* (Brussels)
Stevns, J. P. J. (1906), *Tyendretten efter dansk Lovgivning* (Copenhagen)
Stolfi, N. (1934), *Diritto Civile, I contratti speciali* (Turin)
Stolleis, M. (1976), *Quellen zur Geschichte des Sozialrechts* (Göttingen, Frankfurt am Main and Zurich)
Sugarman, D. (ed.) (1983), *Legality, ideology and the state* (London and New York)
—— & Rubin, G. R. (1984), 'Towards a new history of law and material society in England, 1750–1914' in *Law, economy and society 1750–1950: essays in the history of English law*, eds. G. R. Rubin and D. Sugarman (Abingdon), pp. 1–123
Supple, B. (1973), 'The state and the industrial revolution 1700–1914' in *The Fontana economic history of Europe* vol. 3 *The Industrial Revolution*,ed. C. M. Cipolla (Glasgow)
Tarello, G. (1973), *La ideologia della codificazione nel secolo XVIII* (Genoa)
Taylor, A. J. (1972), *Laissez-faire and state intervention in nineteenth-century Britain* (London)

Teuteberg, H. J. (1961), *Geschichte der industriellen Mitbestimmung in Deutschland, Ursprung und Entwicklung ihrer Vorläufer im Denken und in der Wirklichkeit des 19 Jahrhunderts* (Tübingen)

Thomas, M. W. (1948), *The early factory legislation: a study in legislative and administrative evolution* (Leigh-on-Sea)

Thompson, E. P. (1963), *The making of the English working class* (London)

—— (1977), *Whigs and hunters: the origin of the Black Act* (Harmondsworth)

Thomson, D. (1966), *Europe since Napoleon* (Harmondsworth, revised edn; first published 1957)

Tillyard, F. & Robson, W. A. (1938), 'The enforcement of the collective bargain in the United Kingdom', *Economic Journal*, vol. 38, pp. 15–25

Tissier, A. (1904), *Le code civil et les classes ouvrières* in *Law Code civil Livre du Centenaire*, ed. Rousseau, vol. 1 (Paris)

Tournerie, J. A. (1971), *Le ministère du travail (Origines et premiers développements)* (Paris)

Treu, T. (1981), 'Italy' in *International Encyclopedia for Labour Law and Industrial Relations*, ed. R. Blanpain (Deventer)

—— & Romagnoli, U. (1977), *I sindacati in Italia: Storia di una strategia (1945–1976)* (Bologna)

Troplong, R. (1841), *Della permuta e della locazione* (Naples)

Turgot, A. R. J. (1913–23), *Oeuvres de Turgot et documents le concernant* with biography and notes by G. Schelle 5 vols. (Paris)

Ullmann, P. (1977), *Tarifverträge und Tarifpolitik in Deutschland bis 1914. Entstehung und Entwicklung, interessenpolitische Bedingungen und Bedeutung des Tarifvertragswesens für die sozialistischen Gewerkschaften* (Frankfurt am Main and Bern)

Ungari, P. (1970), 'In memoria del socialismo giuridico—Le scuole di diritti privato sociale', *Politica del diritto*, vol. 2, p. 241ff

van der Borght, R. & Honigmann, –. (1898), 'Der Arbeiterversicherung (in Deutschland)', *Handwörterbuch der Staatswissenschaften*, vol. 1, 2nd edn (Jena)

Vandervelde, E. (1906), *La Belgique ouvrière* (Paris)

van Esveld, N. E. H. & van Aerde, A. J. O. M. (1978), *Introduction to Dutch law for foreign lawyers* (Deventer)

Van Houtte, H. (1920), *Histoire économique de la Belgique à la fin de l'ancien régime* (Ghent)

Vardaro, G. (1981), 'Il diritto del lavoro nel Laboratorio di Weimar', vol. 2–3, *Politica del diritto*, p. 293ff

Veermersch, A. (1904), *La législation et les oeuvres en Belgique* (Paris)

Veneto, G. (1974), *Contrattazione e prassi nei rapporti di lavoro* (Bologna)

Veneziani, B. (1972a), 'La composizione dei conflitti collettivi nel periodo precorporativo', *Rivista di diritto del lavoro*, vol. 24, pp. 209–300

—— (1972b), *La mediazione dei pubblici poteri nei conflitti collettivi di lavoro* (Bologna)

Verband Deutscher Arbeitsnachweise (1911), 'Public labour exchanges in Germany', Report no. 3, *Conférence Internationale sur le Chômage*, 18–21 September 1910, vol. 2 (Paris)

Verdier, J. M. (1966), *Les syndicats: Traité Dalloz de droit du travail*, vol. V (Paris; revised edns 1976 and 1979)

Verhaegen, B. (1916), *Contribution à l'histoire économique des Flandres* (Louvain)

Villemerme, Dr. (1971), *Tableau de l'état physique et moral des ouvriers employés dans les manufactures de coton, de laine et de soie*, Union Générale d'Editions Collection 10/18 no. 582 (Paris)

Vita Levi, M. (1876), *Della locazione di opere e degli appalti* (Turin)

von Humboldt, W. (1792), *Ideen zu einem Versuch, die Grenzen der Wirksamkeit des Staates zu bestimmen* (Berlin; partially published 1792, completed 1851)

Wallas, G. (1925), *The life of Francis Place 1771–1854*, 4th edn (London; first published 1918)

Wallin, M. (1969), 'Labour administration: origins and development' *International Labour Review*, vol. 100, pp. 51–110

Ward, J. T. (1970), 'The factory movement' in *Popular movements c.1830–1850*, ed. J. T. Ward (London)

—— (1971), *The factory system*: vol. 1; 'Birth and growth'; vol. 2; 'The factory system and society (Newton Abbott) [Collection of documents]

Watson, A. (1974), *Legal transplants: an approach to comparative law* (Edinburgh)

Webb, S. & Webb, B. (1898), *Industrial democracy* (London)

—— & —— (1920), *The history of trade unionism 1666–1920*, revised edn (London; original edn published in 1894)

—— & —— (1927–29), *English local government*, being volumes 7–9 of *English Poor Law history* (London; reprinted in 2 vols. with a new introduction by W. A. Robson, 1963)

Weber, M. (1954), *Law in economy and society*, ed. and with an introduction and annotations by M. Rheinstein (Cambridge, Mass.) [Mainly ch. 7 '*Rechtssoziologie*' of *Wirtschaft und Gesellschaft* (1925) (Tübingen)]

Wechselmann, S. (1936), *The Danish National Insurance Act* (Copenhagen)

—— (1945), *Social Denmark* (Copenhagen)

—— (1948), *Social services in Denmark* (Copenhagen)

Wedderburn, K. W. (1971), *The worker and the law*, 2nd edn (Harmondsworth)

Wedderburn of Charlton, Lord (1980), 'Industrial relations and the courts', *Industrial Law Journal*, vol. 9, pp. 65–94

—— (1983), 'Otto Kahn-Freund and British labour law' in *Labour law and industrial relations: building on Kahn-Freund*, eds. Lord Wedderburn, R. Lewis and J. Clark (Oxford), pp. 29–80

Weigert, O. (1933), 'The development of unemployment relief in Germany', *International Labour Review*, vol. 8, p. 169ff

Whiteside, N. (1979), 'Welfare insurance and casual labour: a study of administrative intervention in industrial employment 1906–26', *Economic History Review*, vol. XXXII, p. 507ff

Wiesser, H. (1915), *British working-class movements and Europe 1815–48* (Manchester)

Wilson, A. & Levy, H. (1939), *Workmen's compensation*, 2 vols. (London)

Windmuller, J. P. (1969), *Labour relations in the Netherlands* (New York)

Wissell, R. (1971), *Des Alten Handwerks Recht und Gewohnheit*, 2nd edn (Berlin; further edns 1974 and 1981)

Wittert van Hoogland, E. B. F. F. (1940), *De parlementaire geschiedenis der sociale verzekering 1890–1940* (Haarlem)

Wolf, M. (1981), 'Allgemeine Grundsätze des Kündingungsrechts und des Kündigungsschutzrechts' in *Gemeinschaftskommentar zum Kündigungsschutzgesetz und sonstigen kündigungsschutzrechtlichen Vorschriften, marginal data 1 till 42*, ed. Becker, Friedrich *et al.* (Neuwid and Darmstadt)

Wood, J. (1832), *Right of labour to legislative protection demonstrated* (London)

Woodard, C. (1962), 'Reality and social reform: the transition from *laissez-faire* to the welfare state', *Yale Law Journal*, vol. 72, pp. 286–328

Wrigley, C. (1982), *A history of British industrial relations 1875–1914* (Brighton)

Zachariae, C. S. (1868), *Corso di diritto civile francese* (Naples)

Zeldin, T. (1973–77), *France, 1848–1945*, vol. 1: 'Ambition and love' (Oxford) [Paperback ed. 1979]

Zucchini, C. (1908), 'Note sur la caisse d'Épargne de Bologne', *Actes du Congrès des Assurances sociales de Rome*, vol. III, pp. 667–72

Zumbrunn, W. (1974), *Die Anfänge des englischen Gewerkschaftsrechts* (Basle and Stuttgart)

Zweigert, K. & Kötz, H. (1977), *An introduction to comparative law*, vol. 1: 'The framework', translated by T. Weir; originally published in German under the title *Ein Führung in die Rechtsvergleichung auf dem Gebeite des Privatrechts. Band I: Grundlagen* (Tübingen)

INDEX